KILKENNY

Eoin Swithin Walsh has a Master's degree in Modern Irish History from UCD. He has written extensively on various aspects of Irish history, with articles appearing in local newspapers and periodicals. He has worked with the 1916 Rebellion and Michael Collins walking tours of Dublin, and currently works in the civil service in a governmental role.

KILKENNY

In Times of Revolution
1900–1923

Eoin Swithin Walsh

Foreword by Diarmaid Ferriter

MERRION
PRESS

For my grandmothers; Nanny Alice Walsh (1911–2003), Clogga, Mooncoin and Granny Kitty Long (1923–2003), Tobernabrone, Piltown, County Kilkenny.

Never forgotten.

First published in 2018 by
Merrion Press
An imprint of Irish Academic Press
10 George's Street
Newbridge
Co. Kildare
Ireland
www.merrionpress.ie

9781785371974 (Paper)
9781785371981 (Kindle)
9781785371998 (Epub)
9781785372001 (PDF)

British Library Cataloguing in Publication Data
An entry can be found on request

Library of Congress Cataloging in Publication Data
An entry can be found on request

Interior design by www.jminfotechindia.com
Typeset in Minion Pro 11/14 pt

Cover design by www.phoenix-graphicdesign.com
Cover front: Kilkenny Castle under siege, 2/3 May 1922 (Getty Images).
Cover back: Anti-Treaty prisoners shake hands with their Free State jailers, just
prior to their release after the Battle of Kilkenny, 6 May 1922
(courtesy of Kilmainham Gaol Museum, 20PC-1A45-11).

Contents

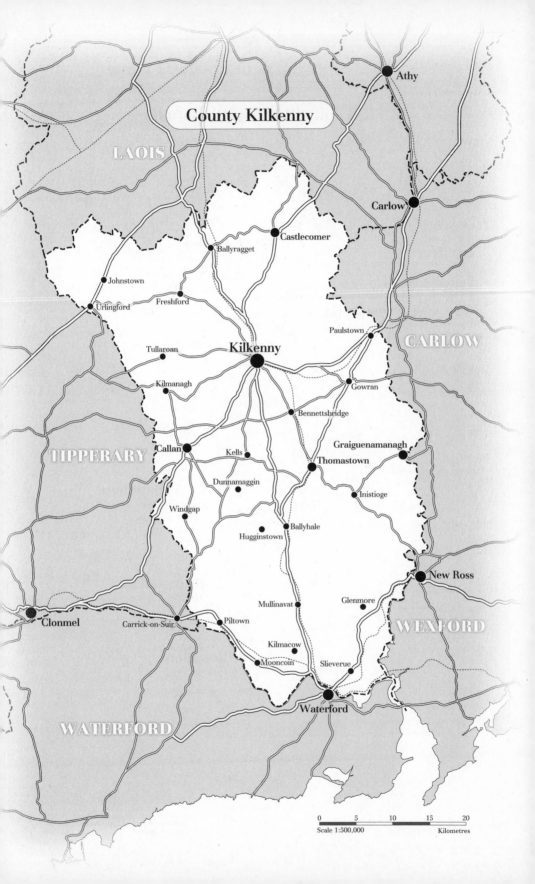

County Kilkenny

LAOIS

CARLOW

TIPPERARY

WATERFORD

WEXFORD

Athy

Carlow

Castlecomer

Ballyragget

Johnstown

Urlingford

Freshford

Paulstown

Tullaroan

Kilkenny

Kilmanagh

Gowran

Bennettsbridge

Callan

Kells

Graiguenamanagh

Thomastown

Dunnamaggin

Inistioge

Windgap

Hugginstown

Ballyhale

New Ross

Mullinavat

Glenmore

Clonmel

Carrick-on-Suir

Piltown

Kilmacow

Mooncoin

Slieverue

Waterford

| 0 | 5 | 10 | 15 | 20 |

Scale 1:500,000

Kilometres

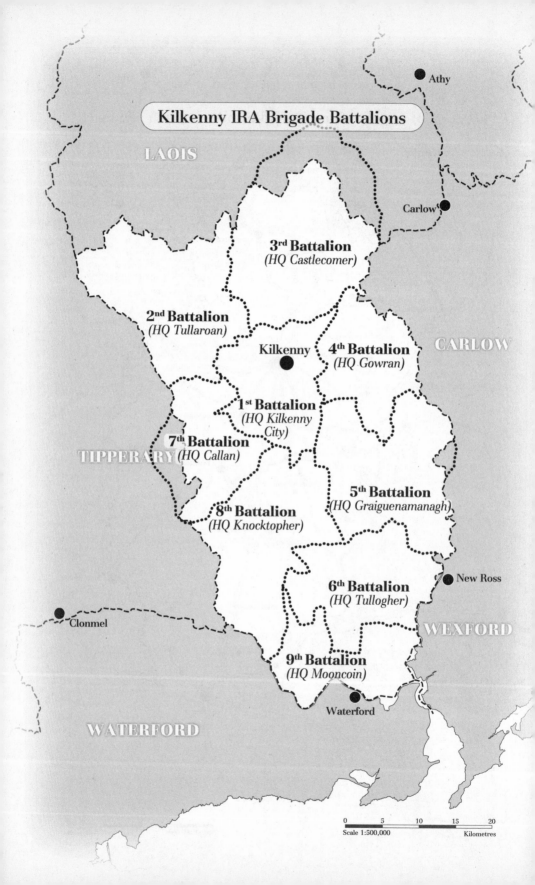

Kilkenny IRA Brigade Battalions

LAOIS

CARLOW

TIPPERARY

WEXFORD

WATERFORD

Athy

Carlow

3rd Battalion
(HQ Castlecomer)

2nd Battalion
(HQ Tullaroan)

Kilkenny

4th Battalion
(HQ Gowran)

1st Battalion
(HQ Kilkenny City)

7th Battalion
(HQ Callan)

5th Battalion
(HQ Graiguenamanagh)

8th Battalion
(HQ Knocktopher)

New Ross

Clonmel

6th Battalion
(HQ Tullogher)

WEXFORD

9th Battalion
(HQ Mooncoin)

Waterford

```
0      5      10     15     20
Scale 1:500,000              Kilometres
```

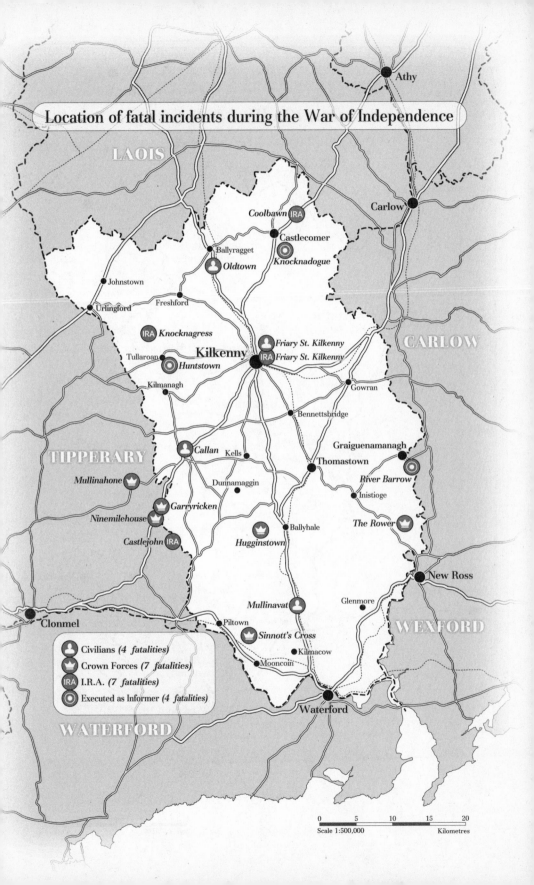

Location of fatal incidents during the War of Independence

LAOIS

CARLOW

Athy

Carlow

Coolbawn IRA
Castlecomer
Ballyragget
Knocknadogue
Oldtown

Johnstown

Freshford

Urlingford

IRA Knocknagress

Kilkenny

Friary St. Kilkenny
IRA Friary St. Kilkenny

Tullaroan
Huntstown

Kilmanagh

Gowran

Bennettsbridge

Callan
Kells

Graiguenamanagh
Thomastown
River Barrow

TIPPERARY

Mullinahone

Dunnamaggin

Inistioge

Garryricken

Ninemilehouse

Ballyhale
The Rower

Castlejohn IRA

Hugginstown

New Ross

Mullinavat

Glenmore

WEXFORD

Clonmel

Piltown
Sinnott's Cross

Kilmacow

Mooncoin

Waterford

👤	Civilians *(4 fatalities)*
👑	Crown Forces *(7 fatalities)*
IRA	I.R.A. *(7 fatalities)*
◉	Executed as Informer *(4 fatalities)*

WATERFORD

0   5   10   15   20
Scale 1:500,000   Kilometres

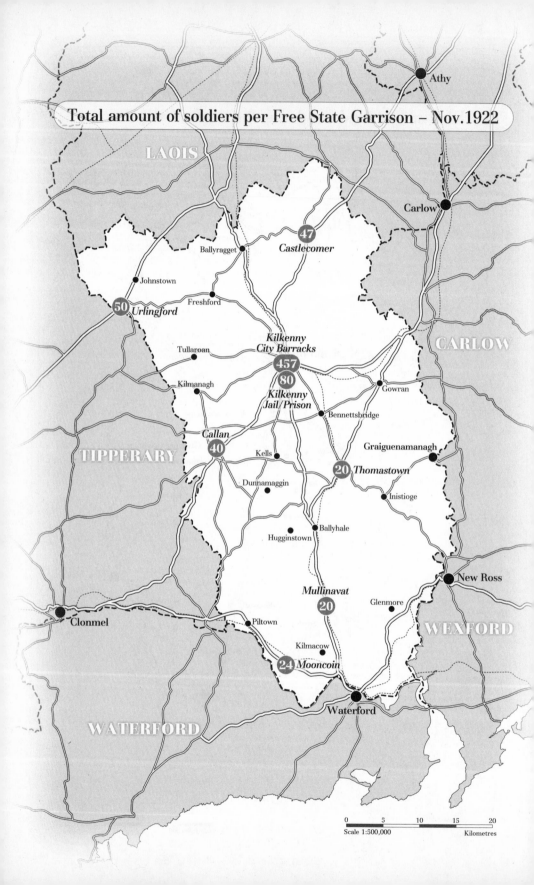

Total amount of soldiers per Free State Garrison – Nov.1922

LAOIS

Athy

Carlow

Castlecomer 47

Ballyragget

Johnstown

Freshford

Urlingford 50

Kilkenny
City Barracks
457
80
Kilkenny
Jail/Prison

CARLOW

Tullaroan

Gowran

Kilmanagh

Bennettsbridge

Callan
40

Kells

Graiguenamanagh

TIPPERARY

Dunnamaggin

Thomastown 20

Inistioge

Ballyhale

Hugginstown

New Ross

Mullinavat
20

Glenmore

Clonmel

Piltown

WEXFORD

Kilmacow

Mooncoin 24

Waterford

WATERFORD

0   5   10   15   20
Scale 1:500,000   Kilometres

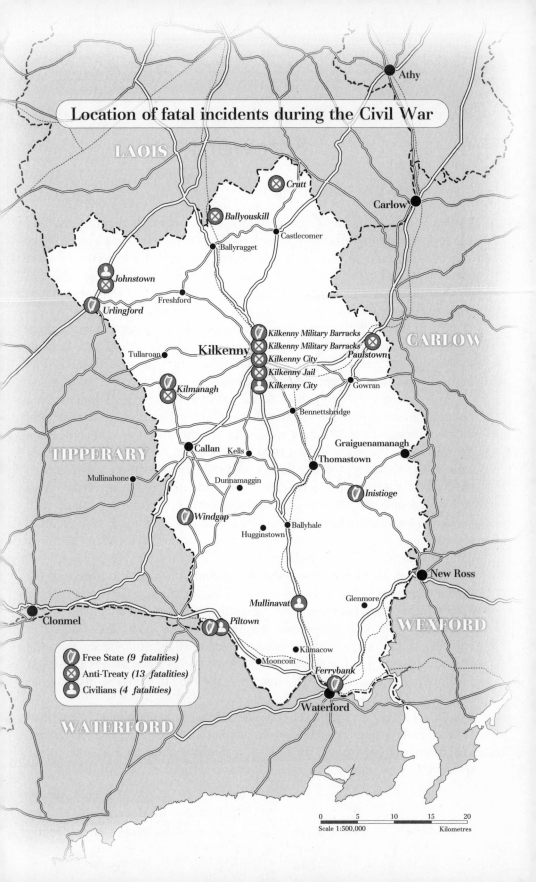

Location of fatal incidents during the Civil War

LAOIS

⊗ *Crutt*

⊗ *Ballyouskill*

● Ballyragget

● Castlecomer

Carlow

● Athy

CARLOW

👤
⊗ *Johnstown*

🎗 *Urlingford*

● Freshford

🎗
⊗ *Kilmanagh*

● Tullaroan

Kilkenny

🎗 *Kilkenny Military Barracks*
⊗ *Kilkenny Military Barracks*
⊗ *Kilkenny City*
⊗ *Kilkenny Jail*
👤 *Kilkenny City*

⊗ *Paulstown*

● Gowran

● Bennettsbridge

TIPPERARY

● Mullinahone

● Callan ● Kells

● Dunnamaggin

🎗 *Windgap*

● Hugginstown ● Ballyhale

Graiguenamanagh ●

● *Thomastown*

🎗 *Inistioge*

● New Ross

🎗
👤 *Piltown*

👤 *Mullinavat*

● Glenmore

WEXFORD

● Clonmel

● Kilmacow

● Mooncoin

Ferrybank

🎗

● Waterford

WATERFORD

🎗 Free State (*9 fatalities*)
⊗ Anti-Treaty (*13 fatalities*)
👤 Civilians (*4 fatalities*)

0   5   10   15   20
Scale 1:500,000   Kilometres

Foreword

This is a valuable and original county study, approached with verve and insight. County Kilkenny has been relatively overlooked in accounts of the War of Independence to date, largely because the violence experienced there was low-intensity. This book rectifies the neglect by making very good use of archival material, including the Bureau of Military History statements taken from veterans of the War of Independence in the 1940s and 1950s, collections relating to the revolutionary period in the National Archives, especially those relating to the administration of local government, and Dublin Castle Records in the National Archives in Kew, London. The author has also researched an impressive array of contemporary newspapers.

Due attention is given here to administrative as well as military and political questions and the social and economic origins and consequences of different forms of revolutionary endeavour or reluctance to engage. The book does justice to the multiple local factors that affected the level of revolutionary activity in Kilkenny – the influence of neighbouring counties in Munster, the historic strength of attachment to constitutional politics in certain areas and a particular reliance on agriculture and fishing. It is thus a reminder that economic imperatives have to be factored in to any assessment of the level of revolutionary activity in Leinster; there was a relationship between prosperity and the scale of republican violence.

The book also underlines some of the contradictions and ironies of the period. Ernie O'Malley, who was sent to Kilkenny by IRA GHQ to engender greater republican activity, complained that the county was 'slack', with inadequate leadership and communications, but his own carelessness was apparent in his carrying of documents containing information on the local IRA which came into the possession of Crown Forces when he was arrested at Inistioge in December 1920. This documentation led to the arrest of a number of leaders of the West Kilkenny Brigade.

This is a well-written book of considerable depth, underpinned by excellent research and, during this period of commemorative reflection and scholarship, will contribute handsomely to deepening understanding of Kilkenny in the revolutionary era and local manifestations and versions of national themes.

Diarmaid Ferriter
Professor of Modern Irish History
University College Dublin

Introduction

There is perhaps an assumption that the study of the Irish Revolutionary period in the first decades of the twentieth century has been exhausted. That there is no more that can be written or that no new opinions can be formed on the events of that period. However, the local aspect of the 'revolutionary decade' – with its parochial dimensions, politics and rivalries – has yet to be fully explored and understood. This publication attempts to remedy that, specifically with regard to the county of Kilkenny.

'County Kilkenny was slack. It was difficult to meet officers; dispatches took a long time to travel ... Poor material I thought. No direction from above and no drive.'[1] These unambiguous words are taken from War of Independence veteran Ernie O'Malley's celebrated publication *On Another Man's Wound*. Upon reading these words some years ago, this author was curious to ascertain if this was indeed an accurate reflection of County Kilkenny's contribution to this pivotal period in Irish history. Either way, surely a county's experience of the War of Independence could not be surmised in a few brief sentences?

Upon attempting to discover the answer to this question, it quickly became clear that focusing on just the military aspect of the War of Independence was not going to tell the full story. Therefore, the net has been cast wider, to encompass the years before the fight for independence and the Civil War which followed it. In addition, a two-pronged approach is used for examining this era of Kilkenny's history; that is to say, the important military elements will be investigated in tandem with life for the ordinary people. Thus, the spectrum of study includes social and political microhistories of the period.

This publication has been written with the aim of being accessible to all readers – for history buffs, or for those who have never read Irish history previously. Therefore, concise descriptions will be utilised throughout to explain the different organisations and personalities of the era. In a similar way, events that were happening on the national stage will be intertwined with the story of what was unfolding in County Kilkenny. In this way, it will (hopefully) be easier for the reader to contrast where Kilkenny fits into the bigger picture.

To put the military aspect of the revolution into context; County Kilkenny had a population of approximately 75,000 during the second decade of the twentieth century. At a maximum point, around 3,500 men and women were members of 'illegal organisations'. A much smaller subset of the 3,500 actually took an active part in the revolution.

So what about the lives of the estimated 70,000 people who were also living in Kilkenny but not directly involved? What was their experience of this period? As burnings and attacks accumulated during the violent periods of the revolution, families, friends, neighbours and cousins were brought to the coalface whether they liked it or not, in what must have been an incredibly anxious time. A war had come to their front door.

On the other hand, if a person had a lot to lose materially or otherwise, they may have been content for the status quo to be maintained. Farming prices went through a boom and bust during this period, so many Kilkenny farmers would have been more concerned with that story than anything to do with politics. In addition, some Kilkenny inhabitants had different agendas (socialism, feminism, agrarian unrest etc.) other than national freedom. Thus, many competing views existed in Irish society, and just like most histories it was never black and white, but instead, there were many different shades of grey in between.

The Military Aspect

The aforementioned quote from Ernie O'Malley's book is extracted from the chapter that deals with his infamous arrest by Auxiliaries in County Kilkenny in December 1920. This arrest is often the only occasion Kilkenny features in general histories of this period. But is O'Malley's story about Kilkenny accurate; or could his arrest have tainted his entire image of Kilkenny during the period?

When O'Malley's book was originally published in 1936 it caused enormous offence to the leading Kilkenny participants of revolutionary-era Kilkenny, as can be adjudged by their numerous letters to local and national media in which they accused O'Malley of seeking a 'brighter halo on other men's wounds'.[2] In contrast, historian Michael Hopkinson was more generous with his analysis of the county's contribution, stating that 'the reputations of the brigades and columns of the IRA in Kilkenny have suffered by comparison with nearby Tipperary'.[3]

It was not the intention of this author to mention every single personality and altercation of the era, but by applying a broad scope, many forgotten stories and personalities will hopefully come to the fore. Therefore, a more nuanced view of Kilkenny's contribution to the revolutionary period will present a much clearer picture.

Why Now?

Another question that can be asked is; why study this period now? The obvious motivation is that many centenary anniversaries have come or are on the horizon. There are, however, three other reasons why now is an advantageous time to re-examine this period of Kilkenny's history. Firstly, the historical sources that have become available in the past two decades offer a wider range of viewpoints that were not previously available to historians. Chief among these is the Bureau of Military History Witness Statements (BMHWS), which are a collection of accounts taken during the 1940s and 1950s that detailed specific individuals' involvement in the revolutionary period, usually up to the period of 1921. These statements were only opened in 2003 (after the last 'IRA pension' recipient had died) and were digitised some years afterwards. Kilkenny participants in the revolutionary era have left eighteen statements, although there are many more references to County Kilkenny in other accounts.[4] Like all sources, caution is advised, as these are wholly one person's perspective of events.

In addition, the Military Service Pensions Collection (MSPC), which is arguably more important as a local source, has only been digitally accessible since 2014 (the vast collection is being released in stages). This collection contains applications and supporting material for military pensions which were offered to veterans of the conflict in the years and decades after the establishment of the Free State. This collection includes a much wider range of people than the BMHWS and the files contain minute detail on events that occurred throughout County Kilkenny during the era. Most importantly, the collection includes information on the Truce and Civil War periods, something that was mostly absent from the BMHWS. It was in the best interests of the applicants to state all activities they partook in, which has now become an unintended benefit for historians.

From a British perspective, many of their files relating to this period have also been digitised and released to the public. Some of these have been released 'early' as they were intended to remain private for 100 years. Most importantly are the martial law era records in relation to Kilkenny (January–July 1921) which contain records of arrests, house raids, court-martials and inquiries into deaths amongst other topics.

What has been termed the 'democratisation of history' is another reason why now is an opportune time to reassess this era. Many sources have been digitised and made available online. From the perspective of studying local history, this is incomparable to what went before. The digitisation of newspapers is a prime example. In the past, a researcher could literally spend months trawling through newspapers in a local library looking for small snippets of information about a topic, or else just ignore that source altogether as it was excessively time-consuming. Nowadays, hundreds of newspaper titles from this period can be examined for information relating to a specific subject or event. The same can be said for censuses, civil registration records, and other archival data which were not digitised as recently as five years ago. Therefore, new technologies let us compare, contrast and validate information to form a more complex narrative of the history.

Thirdly – and possibly most importantly – the simple passage of time can be seen as beneficial. None of the people who had a direct involvement in the fighting or politics of the time are still living. The hurt and anguish that people suffered made it difficult for many to discuss their involvement. While some of this pain may have been passed to second and third generations of a family, time has allowed the raw feelings to dilute and dissipate, as the principal players are no longer with us.

Those who may have been forgotten from general accounts of this era because of class, gender, or falling on the 'wrong side' of history, can now emerge from the shadows. Most importantly, it is not the aim of this author to judge anyone's choices, beliefs or reasoning for taking a particular course of action a century ago.

One thing has become very clear through researching this period; no matter if an individual was a politician, was for or against the Treaty, was an IRA flying column member, a British soldier, an RIC police officer, an informer, or a mother looking after her children – most people believed they were doing the *right* thing at the time. This is something we must not forget when analysing the motivations of these tumultuous years of Irish history.

County Kilkenny: An Overview

And what of County Kilkenny? For those who are unfamiliar with the county, it is situated in the southeast of the country. In terms of land area, Kilkenny comes in exactly half way of Ireland's thirty-two counties, being the sixteenth biggest – or smallest – depending on your perspective. What is now Kilkenny

City was one of the first places settled by the Normans in the 1170s. Prior to this, the area was dominated by the Osraige tribe. Notably, the Roman Catholic and Anglican diocese of the area are still called 'Ossory'. The county was one of the first to be 'shired' (turned into a county) by the new Anglo-Norman settlers in 1225. The name of the county itself comes from the Gaelic 'Cill Chainnigh', which means 'Church of Canice'. Saint Canice founded a monastery in the sixth century near the present-day Canice's Cathedral in the city. In the 1340s, Friar John Clyn, who was a Kilkenny-based Franciscan monk, wrote a diary of his first-hand experiences of the Black Death in Kilkenny. His record is believed to be the only surviving eyewitness account in either Ireland or Britain of the doomsday-type disease.

The City of Kilkenny – which received its royal charter in 1609 – was the headquarters of a Confederation (a parliament in all but name) in the 1640s which eventually ruled over most of the country. It came to an abrupt end with the arrival of Oliver Cromwell in 1650. The Ormonde dynasty, whose family name was Butler, lived at Kilkenny Castle until 1936.

The designer of the original White House in Washington DC, James Hoban, was born in Callan, along with the founder of the Christian Brothers, Edmond Ignatius Rice. The famous philosopher George Berkeley after whom a town and university in California are named, was also born in the county, near Thomastown. Another family that emigrated from the area in the nineteenth century was the d'Isignys, who came from an area near Gowran. One of their offspring would eventually become famous in Hollywood. That person was Walter d'Isigny, but as the family name altered, he became known as Walt Disney.[5]

The black-coloured Kilkenny marble was much sought after through the centuries and was quarried near the present-day city in an area now aptly known as Blackquarry. The marble used to grace the footpaths of the main thoroughfares in Kilkenny City, hence the informal title; 'The Marble City'. The various mines in the north of the county have continued that tradition in more recent times with the mining of coal and limestone. In later years, the county is perhaps most famous nationally for its hurling escapades, but ironically the first ever game of Gaelic football was played in the county – in Callan – in 1885.[6] During the same era, a Kilkenny woman became the first non-American to win the US Open Tennis Championships. Mabel Cahill was born in 1863 in the Ballyragget area and emigrated to America in 1889. In 1891 she defeated Ellen Roosevelt (first cousin of Franklin D. Roosevelt) to win her first US Open title. She died in 1905 and was inducted into the International Tennis Hall of Fame in 1976.[7]

As the scope of this publication is purposefully broad, it is the hope of the author that each reader will at least find one story, personality, or event that interests them; and perhaps some forgotten element of Kilkenny's history will be brought back to life in the minds of the reader.

CHAPTER 1

Calm Before the Storm
(1900–1915)

*'Farmers as a result of good prices for their products were well off. The
battlefields seemed a long distance away. No one in particular was
fretting about a German invasion of Ireland.'*

County Kilkenny in the first two decades of the twentieth century was,
relatively speaking, a prosperous area with a mainly rural and agricultural
based populace. Kilkenny, much like Ireland generally, was not a hotbed of
revolution at the turn of the new century. Indeed, there was little evidence to
suggest the turn of events which would occur in a few short years. The population
of the county in 1911 stood at 74,962, which was a reduction of over 60 per
cent from pre-Famine levels. Kilkenny City was the largest urban area in the
county with a population of 10,514 in 1911, followed by the smaller towns of
Callan (1,987), Thomastown (959), Castlecomer (872) and Graiguenamanagh
(844), respectively. If the populations of the surrounding areas are included,
Castlecomer District had the largest population outside of Kilkenny City, with
a total population of 5,423. In their religious denominations, the population
was 95 per cent Roman Catholic, 4.5 per cent Church of Ireland, while the
remainder was made up mostly of Presbyterians and Methodists.[1] As is the case
today, the city was dominated by a large Norman castle, which was at the time
still inhabited by the Marquess of Ormonde and his family. The main industry
aside from agriculture was brewing, specifically the Smithwick and O'Sullivan
breweries based in the city. In addition, one of Ireland's few coalfields was the
main industry in the north of the county, centred around Castlecomer.

Land

Farming, along with the ownership of land, was a recurrent theme in the
history of County Kilkenny. The exceptional quality of the land meant local

people were reasonably prosperous compared to other counties, which, in turn, contributed to very low unemployment in Kilkenny City and County at the beginning of the twentieth century.[2] Even during the Famine years, the quality of the land helped Kilkenny to the 'enviable position' of being ranked twenty-second out of the thirty-two Irish counties with regard to the annual average rate of 'excess mortality'.[3] That is to say, County Kilkenny was the tenth least worst affected by the Famine, as it had other agricultural pursuits to supplement the failing potato harvests (e.g. corn, fishing, livestock). This was scant consolation to urban residents, or the 'inmates' of the Kilkenny Union Workhouse – the fifth largest in the country during the Famine period – where a recent excavation unearthed a mass grave containing the remains of at least 970 famine victims; 60 per cent of which were under the age of 18 years.[4]

Over 50 per cent of the soil in County Kilkenny was classified as 'grade A', with the vast majority of the remainder classified between grades B to D and little of the least valuable grade E land. In *Griffith's Land Valuation* (1850s), the land in Mooncoin and Piltown in the fertile River Suir valley in the far south of the county had the highest valuation, followed by land around Kilkenny City.[5] The series of Land Acts from 1870 to 1903 triggered a vast social revolution in Kilkenny, as thousands of Kilkenny farmers gained ownership of their farms for the first time, albeit with long-term mortgages. In 1873, 98 per cent of the land in County Kilkenny was owned by just 828 landlords.[6] The five largest landlords were Viscount Clifden, based around the Gowran area, Captain Wandesforde in Castlecomer in the north of the county, the Earl of Bessborough in the south of the county based in Piltown, the Tighes in Inistioge, and the famous Butlers of Ormonde, with their land mostly surrounding Kilkenny City. Those five landlords alone controlled 21 per cent of Kilkenny's land between them, or in terms of land mass, 105,000 acres of County Kilkenny's 505,000 acres of arable land.[7]

The ownership of land changed drastically in Kilkenny prior to the revolutionary era. If land transactions are analysed from the Registry of Deeds in Dublin – using the five-year indexing format used there – the peak period of land transfers in Kilkenny occurred in the period 1910–1914. During that period alone, 4,347 land transactions occurred, with the vast majority assigned land folio numbers on the indexes.[8] This meant the land transactions took place between a landlord and the Land Commission, which was the governing organisation tenant farmers used to purchase their land holdings. On the eve of the War of Independence, therefore, 76 per cent of Kilkenny land had been purchased by tenant farmers.[9] The generous monetary terms offered to landlords in the 1903 Act, along with the reality that some of Kilkenny's largest landlords were in massive debt, induced the majority to part with their holdings with little protest.[10]

Furthermore, by 1911, County Kilkenny had the lowest percentage of farms classified as 'smallholdings' in Leinster, Connacht or Munster (excluding Dublin). Smallholdings were farms that were valued below £15 per annum. Just 38.6 per cent of Kilkenny farms were classified as this, which compared favourably to Mayo on the other end of the scale where 90.9 per cent of farms were defined as smallholdings. Therefore, as over 61 per cent of Kilkenny farms were considered middling or strong farms, it implies a higher standard of living in County Kilkenny.[11]

By January 1916, the RIC County Inspector (CI) made the following observation: 'The greater portion of the county has been sold under the Land Purchase Acts and the results have been excellent. The relationship between landlord and tenant on the few estates remaining unsold are good and also those between employer and workman.'[12] In tandem with the upsurge in land ownership, the new century also saw the introduction of agrarian co-operative movements throughout County Kilkenny. From 1900, creameries and their auxiliary branches began appearing mushroom-like around the county and by the revolutionary period there were thirty-six creameries in the county.[13] This provided a much needed and steady source of income for many. The creameries also provided employment locally, not just at the creamery building itself, but also in side enterprises such as butter-making. It now became more profitable for some farmers to focus on dairy farming, as opposed to crops. However, it often fell to the children or the females in the household to milk their cows twice daily, by hand. The creameries also became the main focal point for social interaction in a village or townland, a place where news could be transmitted or received. The creamery manager also gained a high social status, becoming a significant figure in the community, and coming close in the social hierarchy to the priests, RIC Sergeant, and national school teacher.[14]

It should be noted that farmers throughout Kilkenny had embraced the fight for agrarian and political reform from the 1870s. The Land League era was the first time tenant farmers – including women – were involved in political movements. Charles Stewart Parnell visited Kilkenny on a number of occasions during this period. In October 1880, in a speech he made on The Parade in Kilkenny City, he used 'what was undoubtedly the most revolutionary language ever heard on a public platform in County Kilkenny, to advocate the complete destruction of landlordism'. By 1882, some forty-six branches of the Land League, including six women's branches, were established in County Kilkenny.[15]

Some of those rebellious tenant farmers were the fathers, mothers, grandfathers and grandmothers of the revolutionary-era generation. However, it has also been argued that the lack of widespread consistent support from the farming community during the troubled years (1916–1923) was as a direct result of farmers having already completed their own social revolution. In other words, farmers had by and large won their fight, having gained ownership of their land prior to the commencement of the political revolution. For many farmers, the turmoil caused by the conflict of the revolutionary years was not a price worth paying if it impacted significantly on their livelihoods. While, for others, the unpredictability of an independent Ireland was also too high a risk to take.

The Gaelic Revival

What is termed the 'Irish Gaelic Revival' was said to have originated in the 1880s. This was a renewal of interest in the Irish language, culture and industry. This manifested itself in a number of different ways. For example, Irish music, language, dance and sport all became more fashionable, especially amongst the middle classes. Prior to this revival, many Irish cultural pursuits were seen as backward, and were associated with the poorer classes in the west of Ireland. Certainly the two most important organisations of this period were the Gaelic Athletic Association (GAA), focusing on the playing of Irish sports, and the Gaelic League, which was concerned with the Irish language, literature and theatre. The influence of the Gaelic Revival, with all its varying strands, had a multifaceted effect on many of the revolutionary generation.

The GAA

At the time of the foundation of the GAA in 1884, cricket was the most popular sport in Kilkenny.[16] Ironically, considering recent history, the first ever game of Gaelic football was played in Callan in 1885 between a local team and Commercials from Kilkenny City (the rules of this new game had been created by Carrick-on-Suir native Maurice Davin).[17] The popularity of handball also increased, especially in Kilkenny City, where a court was built during the early years of the GAA. However, it was the ancient sport of hurling which became extremely popular throughout the county, in a relatively short period of time. There had been a tradition of hurling in some parts of the county prior to the foundation of the GAA, especially in the northwest areas bordering County Tipperary. Kilkenny played in their first All-Ireland hurling final in the 1893 championship (held in 1894), losing to Cork. They proceeded to lose a further three All-Ireland finals before eventually winning their first title in the 1904 championship (played in 1906).[18] This unexpected one-point victory sparked their first 'golden era', as the team went on to win seven All-Ireland Championships between 1904 and 1913.[19] Some of the hurlers of this era became the first 'GAA celebrities', with Dick 'Drug' Walsh, Dick Doyle, Jack Rochford and Sim Walton, all becoming household names throughout the county. Sports and politics often sat side-by-side during this era. This was true even on the day of Kilkenny's first All-Ireland hurling victory, played in June 1906, near Carrick-on-Suir, County Tipperary. On the busy streets of the town that day, a group of people were distributing pamphlets describing a new movement called 'Sinn Féin'. Most of the Kilkenny and Cork fans found the words difficult to say, pronouncing it as 'Sin Feen'. For the bulk of supporters it was their first encounter with these two Gaelic words which would go on to dominate the next two decades. It may have been the first time they heard these words, but it would certainly not be the last.[20]

The Gaelic League

One of the primary functions of the Gaelic League was to offer Irish language classes. The number of people speaking Irish (Gaelic) in Kilkenny had been declining rapidly since the Famine. Yet, even in 1851, 15.5 per cent of the population of County Kilkenny was speaking Irish as their primary language, equating to 21,420 people. The Irish language was not part of the mainstream education system, and the speaking of the language in school was actively discouraged. Those that could speak Irish in Kilkenny were usually elderly and had grown up speaking the language in their youth. As recently as 1871, parts of rural south and west Kilkenny had the highest portion of Irish speakers in Leinster (where around 25 per cent of the population in those areas could speak the language).[21] The small fishing hamlets on the River Suir in the far south of the county and the remote homesteads on the Walsh Hills in the southwest, were the areas where the language survived naturally, spoken amongst the poorest classes in society.[22]

The Gaelic League clubs in Kilkenny also had a wider range of interests besides the language, including amateur dramatics, Irish history, poetry, Irish dancing, arranging Feiseanna, as well as organising trips to the An Rinn Gaeltacht in Waterford.[23] It was often members of the upper echelons of society – many from Anglo-aristocratic unionist backgrounds – who were the initial driving forces behind the formation of Gaelic League clubs around Ireland. There did not appear to be a conflict between being passionate followers of the Irish language and culture on one hand, while at the same time being loyal supporters of the Crown. It was a similar story in Kilkenny. One of the first Feis events to be organised in rural Ireland was held in Coon in north Kilkenny in 1895 – just two years after the organisation had been founded. There was a sizeable Protestant population in the area, some of whom were friendly with Douglas Hyde, one of the initiators of the organisation. Hyde made an appearance at the Feis as guest of honour. Showing how the Gaelic League crossed religious divides, the chief organiser of the Coon Feis was the local Catholic curate, Fr William Delaney.[24]

A Gaelic League club was established in Kilkenny City in 1897. Two of its most enthusiastic members were prominent local landowner Captain Otway Cuffe (1853–1912) and his sister-in-law, the exceedingly wealthy Ellen, Countess of Desart (1857–1933). Captain Cuffe was president of the Gaelic League in Kilkenny until his death in 1912, at which time the Countess took over the role. The Countess of Desart, Ellen Odette Cuffe (née Bischoffsheim), was independently wealthy due to her father's involvement in founding three of the world's largest banks. She was the second wife of William Ulick O'Connor Cuffe, 4th Earl of Desart, who had an ancestral home at Desart Court near Kilkenny. After her husband's death in 1898, the now Dowager Countess moved to Aut Even House, located 3 km north of Kilkenny City. Whereas her brother-in-law Captain Cuffe formulated many schemes inspired by the Gaelic Revival, it was the Countess who was usually responsible for supporting them financially (in addition to underpinning the overall monetary position of the Gaelic League in Kilkenny). In 1898 Captain Cuffe and the Countess helped secure the position of editor of *The Kilkenny Moderator* newspaper for Standish O'Grady (1846–1928). O'Grady had played a formative role in the Gaelic revival as a result of his publications on Irish history and mythology which were an inspiration to many – including one of the founders of the Gaelic League, Douglas Hyde, and later, 1916 leader Patrick Pearse. Although O'Grady only lived in Kilkenny for two years – he was removed as editor after he was sued for libellous editorials, including one which attacked the Marquess of Ormonde for his part in an embezzlement scandal – the presence of such an influential figure within the local community was invaluable to the fledgling Gaelic League Club.[25]

In addition, the Countess of Desart was responsible for founding the Kilkenny Theatre in 1902, located on Patrick's Street, as a venue for local dramatics. She also financed the building of a dance hall (known as Desart Hall), a recreation centre and a handball court at Talbots Inch in Kilkenny City. In 1910 she supplied the land and the books for the new Carnegie Library on John's Quay, while in 1915 she paid for the new Aut Even Hospital.[26] As the cultural revival was also concerned with Irish industry, the Countess established a number of local businesses including; a woollen mill, a basket factory and a tobacco-growing farm, with varying degrees of success. She was bestowed with the Freedom of Kilkenny City in 1910, the first female to receive such an honour.[27]

The original Gaelic League club, based in Rothe House, in Kilkenny City became known as 'Central Branch'. Many districts established their own clubs in subsequent years, with mixed levels of success. These included Castlecomer, Tullaroan, Johnstown, Goresbridge, Threecastles, Saint Canice's (in the city), Dunnamaggin, Knocktopher, Johnswell and Freshford.

Although the Gaelic League was financed by some of the wealthier people in the community, these did not represent the typical membership of the organisation in Kilkenny. If anything, the Gaelic League was unique locally in that its 100-plus members in Kilkenny City comprised a cross section of society. Membership of religious denominations came from the Roman Catholic, Jewish and Church of Ireland faiths. The League was not segregated on gender lines either – which was rare for the time – and it subsequently became recognised as a place where love could blossom. The political affiliations of the Kilkenny membership were similarly diverse. The backgrounds of its members included unionists (such as the Cuffes), nationalists (such as E.T. Keane of the *Kilkenny People*), IRB members (such as future Sinn Féin mayor Peter DeLoughry), sports figures (such as GAA President James Nowlan), and religious figures (such as the Catholic Bishop of Ossory, Dr Brownrigg).

The religious divide, however, was not going to be allowed to become too blurred. At Christmas 1904 the League in Kilkenny planned a Christmas show to take place in the Kilkenny Theatre, which was to include a performance of the nativity. A local priest discovered that two Protestants were to act in the play. He subsequently wrote a letter to the national media condemning this. A letter from the bishop was read at all Sunday masses in the dioceses the following week which was supportive of the priest's comments. The Gaelic League decided to cancel the Christmas concert to avoid any negative publicity.[28] Generally, there is no evidence to suggest there was any widespread resentment between opposing religions in Kilkenny. However, for some pious

Roman Catholics there was certainly an element of 'them versus us' when it came to important matters; the performance of nativity plays being one such example.

Thomas MacDonagh

Arguably the most famous member of the Gaelic League in Kilkenny was Thomas MacDonagh, future signatory of the 1916 Proclamation. From September 1901 to June 1903 he taught English and French at St Kieran's College, a boy's secondary school and Catholic seminary in Kilkenny.[29] In the latter stages of his time there, he attempted to include the Irish language on the school curriculum but found very little support among the college superiors. Evidently he was well liked by the students, as the following account by a past pupil attests:

> he taught us honours English for two years and gave us an appreciation of poetry, especially Wordsworth and Keats, which we never lost and often recall ... He was of a gentle disposition, and I cannot remember him ever being in a real temper, or even punishing any of us (a contrast indeed to many of his colleagues!). I liked and admired him very much, although he never was familiar with us or made friends among the boys. Sometimes he brought simple Irish textbooks to show us the paintings of Jack Yeats [brother of poet W.B. Yeats]. Though I belonged to High St., where he lodged, I cannot remember whether he went in much for social activities or not as I was incarcerated in St. Kieran's as a border at the time ... though the classes were pleasant nobody would dream of playing any pranks.

Another former pupil mentioned that MacDonagh used to play rugby in the college, in complete contrast to its renown currently as a hurling school: 'I do remember that rugby was played in St Kieran's College at that time and there was quite a respectable team – fit to meet any of the Dublin teams. Tomás MacDonagh had been in Rockwell College, and there he learned to play rugby, and I remember him playing with the college team.'[30] It was at a meeting of the Kilkenny Gaelic League at the end of 1901 that MacDonagh was first introduced to the Irish language and literature.[31] MacDonagh's purpose in attending the meeting was actually to ridicule the attendees, but he had a complete change of heart. In later life he was reported to have remarked that he had been 'the greatest West-Britisher in Ireland' prior to attending this meeting in Kilkenny. He subsequently became a passionate member and secretary of the Kilkenny branch.[32] In notes he wrote for a speech he gave in Kilkenny a number of years later, he recorded the following: 'Personal: My debt to Kilkenny. My baptism in Nationalism. My first experience'.[33] More recently his granddaughter, Muriel McAuley, referred to his time in Kilkenny as his 'road to Damascus moment'.[34]

Health of the Irish Language

The areas where Gaelic League clubs were founded had an immediate impact on the language, as was borne out by the 1911 Census of Ireland results when compared to 1901. At a time when the general population was declining, the number of Irish speakers in the Kilkenny City area rose from 532 to 776. Castlecomer District had the largest increase of Irish speakers in the county, increasing almost fivefold from 75 to 360. The most dramatic increase in Castlecomer was for those aged in their teenage years and younger.[35] Con Brennan, a Gaelic League member from Castlecomer, secured the services of a fluent Irish speaker for the national school which was the reason for the substantial increase. The teacher, Con Horgan, was a native Irish speaker from County Cork. The teaching of Irish had only been permitted within the British national school system, as an optional subject, in 1900.

It was not all positive news about the native language however. The southern district – which included parts of Mooncoin, Kilmacow, Mullinavat, Glenmore and Slieverue – saw a 61 per cent decline in the Irish speaking population, dropping from 1,226 speakers in 1901, to 479 in 1911. As the vast majority of the decline was in those aged 60 or over, it indicates that many of the older native Irish speakers had died, while the lack of active Gaelic League clubs in the area prevented the language being taken up by a younger generation.[36]

A Royal Visit: 1904

As mentioned, Kilkenny in the early 1900s did not have the appearance of an area that would rebel in the near future, although under the surface there were some murmurings of discontent. Kilkenny had a tradition of loyalism. The City of Kilkenny had been 'famously Anglicised' from an early stage due to the Norman conquest of the 1170s.[37] Notably, in 1366, the Irish Parliament met in Kilkenny City under Prince John, son of King Edward III. At this session, the infamous Statutes of Kilkenny Acts were passed – the main purpose of which was to stop the descendants of the Norman settlers taking up Irish customs. From 1395 up until the 1900s connections with the British royal family remained strong. The reason was the Butler family, who had their seat at Kilkenny Castle. The Butlers may be considered to be the 'great survivors' of Kilkenny history, as they managed to hold and maintain substantial land and power through many precarious centuries.[38] Besides the Butlers, other Kilkenny Anglo-Aristocratic landowners in the county received visits from princes and princesses of the British royal family, including the Bessborough family of Piltown and the Tighes of Inistioge.

At the end of April 1904, King Edward VII, his wife Queen Alexandra, and daughter Princess Victoria, spent two days in Kilkenny on a royal visit, residing with the Butler family at Kilkenny Castle. When they arrived over 150 soldiers provided a guard of honour for the royal family, while a substantial crowd also gathered to view the procession, although some felt it was 'not as large as generally was anticipated.'[39] 'Decorations of every kind' graced the 'principal thoroughfares' including streamers, bunting, Union Jack flags and a number of triumphal arches, with the *Cork Examiner* noting that the 'narrow winding streets of the city lend themselves to public decoration.'[40] A stage was erected at the railway station in Kilkenny, where a number of speeches were heard. An official address from the Corporation greeted the King with 'céad míle fáilte'. Notably, a number of banners on the royal party's route from the railway station to the castle also had words of welcome in Irish. The popularity of the Gaelic League was clearly evident. Moreover, there did not appear to be any conflict in using the Irish language to address the royal party.[41]

Not all people in Kilkenny were enthralled with the royal visitors however, particularly some members of the Corporation. Nominally 'nationalist' councillors occupied all but one of the council seats.[42] The nationalist members came from a number of parties but, predominantly, the United Irish League, which was the branch organisation supporting the Irish Parliamentary Party (IPP). The shades of nationalism obviously varied, as the Corporation approved an 'address of welcome' for the royal party by twelve votes to seven.[43] The Mayor of Kilkenny, Edward O'Shea, was one of the 'no' voters, and did not attend the welcome address. As this visit was – in theory – a private one, the members of local government were not required to participate in the formalities.

Amusingly the veteran Fenian John Daly of Limerick was due to receive the Freedom of Kilkenny on the same day that the royal party arrived.[44] John Daly was well known, having been in solitary confinement in an English jail for over a decade. Daly's niece, Kathleen Daly, would go on to marry his former prison mate, Thomas J. Clarke, of Easter 1916 fame. This embarrassing clash had been orchestrated by the more advanced nationalist members of the Corporation, which, since the Local Government Act of 1898 extended voting rights to citizens, had become a sizable minority within the Corporation. When the resolution to confer Daly with the Freedom of the City on the same day as the king's visit passed, spectators in the gallery sang *A Nation Once Again*.[45] To make matters more complicated, Daly had quickly accepted the invitation. But at a subsequent emergency meeting of the council a new resolution was passed to move the conferring ceremony to the night prior to the king's arrival, with this vote passing by fifteen votes to two.[46]

To highlight the ambiguity that existed in the Corporation, they also passed a motion decrying the oath the king had taken at his coronation, specifically the 'outrageous insult offered to us as Catholics by the abominable and insulting language [against Catholics used in the Oath]'.[47] This resolution had come about due to the editor of the *Kilkenny People* newspaper, Edward T. Keane, printing the entire text of the oath in the previous week's edition to stir up some nationalistic fervour. The Stallard and DeLoughry families, who would go on to play a pivotal role in the revolutionary period in Kilkenny, registered their protest when they hung black flags on St Francis's Abbey – at the site of the Smithwick's brewery – as a mark of protest against the visit. The flag would have been visible to their Majesties from Kilkenny Castle.[48] In general, the royal visit was considered a success. Queen Alexandra donated £50 to the 'deserving poorest of the City of Kilkenny'. The right to privacy of the near fifty individuals who benefited from the money was not commonplace at the time, and so the names and addresses of the 'poor' beneficiaries were announced in the local print media.[49]

Newspapers

In that era prior to radio and television, newspapers were a vital source of information and were frequently shared between families and neighbours. The last decades of the nineteenth century saw something of a 'reading revolution' as there was a huge upsurge in printed materials – including newspapers, periodicals and books. The younger generation read widely and possessed a high level of literacy, something that was not necessarily the case for their grandparents' generation. By 1911, nearly 93 per cent of Kilkenny's population was literate, up from just 39 per cent prior to the Famine. Kilkenny's illiteracy rate of 7.2 per cent was one of the lowest in the country (the national average illiteracy rate was 9.2 per cent). The largest proportion of people who could neither read nor write in Kilkenny were those aged 60 years or over. This was most likely due to schools not being founded in their immediate area when they were children, while non-attendance was also common. Callan town had the highest illiteracy levels. At 12.8 per cent this was nearly double the Kilkenny average.[50]

During this era, newspapers often maintained a clear ideology or agenda. They were usually not very impartial and offered strong opinions on the topics of the day. In the early 1900s, County Kilkenny was served primarily by three weekly newspapers. These were *Kilkenny People, Kilkenny Journal* and *Kilkenny Moderator*.[51] There was a general differentiation between the primary audiences for each of the Kilkenny newspapers, usually delineated along political and class lines.

From its inception, the *Kilkenny People* courted controversy with its staunch support of the Parnellite element of the Irish Parliamentary Party (IPP), which later translated into support for John Redmond after his unification of the warring factions of the party (this included the newspaper's support of the IPP's grassroots organisation, the United Irish League, which had clubs throughout Kilkenny). After the 1916 Easter Rebellion it became supportive of the republican cause, and was staunchly pro-Treaty during the Civil War. Its primary readership was the growing middle classes, both urbanites and farmers alike. The *Kilkenny Journal*, on the other hand, was supportive of the anti-Parnellite grouping in the 1890s, but after the merger of the opposing wings of the party, it too became supportive of Redmond and the nationalist movement generally. After 1916, the *Kilkenny Journal* became republican, and more supportive of the working classes following the appointment of Labour Councillor James Upton as editor. The *Kilkenny Moderator* was regarded as a Unionist newspaper as it was historically supportive of the British Conservative Party, and so was read by many in the upper classes of Kilkenny society. Although maintaining a unionist ideology throughout, it was usually measured and reserved in its journalism. During the most violent years of the revolutionary period it was often equally critical about the actions of the Crown Forces in the county, as it was about the IRA.

The spread of the Sinn Féin movement in County Kilkenny in its embryonic years was greatly aided by the *Kilkenny People*. Kerry native Edward Thomas Keane (1867–1945) helped found the newspaper at the age of 25 in 1892, initially with the help of his friend, the Fenian, P.J. O'Keeffe. 'E.T.' Keane, as he was typically known, was previously employed as a journalist by the *Kilkenny Journal* and *Moderator*. As full-time editor of the *Kilkenny People*, Keane played a pivotal role throughout the era of the troubles, eventually acting as the republican voice for the area. Keane's nationalistic views became more intense as each year of the early 1900s progressed. His evolution from Parnellite to advanced nationalist, to republican, could be considered an analogy of Irish society as a whole. He went on to become chairman of the Kilkenny City Sinn Féin Club in 1918. Future Kilkenny IRA Brigade Commandant Thomas Treacy remarked on the newspaper's importance in the 'moulding of public opinion':

> The Kilkenny People ... [was] full blooded in its support for Sinn Féin. It carried articles written by its editor in his own peculiar hard hitting style, interspersed with wit of a devastating quality all his own, which was a holy horror to, and the envy of, his opponents ... It would be difficult to measure the tremendous importance and value of this support to the cause in Kilkenny City and County.[52]

The republican cause in County Kilkenny was fortunate to have another staunch ally in the local media. The editor of the *Kilkenny Journal* from 1914, James W. Upton (1872–1956), was similarly supportive. Upton was born in Waterford City and was a founding member and first secretary of the Waterford Sinn Féin branch. He was editor of the *Waterford Star* for a period but was forced to resign as a consequence of his advanced nationalist views. Upton had played an important role during the 1916 Rebellion in Dublin when he was one of the men responsible for printing Patrick Pearse's *Irish War News*. This was a propaganda pamphlet published during Easter Week, and Upton contributed articles for that publication. He became a labour councillor in Kilkenny Council and devoted many of his editorials to the socialist cause generally. During the 1918 election campaign he was asked to speak on behalf of Kevin O'Higgins, the Sinn Féin candidate in Laois. He spoke on a number of platforms alongside O'Higgins, with one of those in attendance commenting that the 'crowds at the meetings preferred his speeches of ready wit and satire to those of Mr O'Higgins who was inclined to labour [points with] figures and statistics'.[53] He resigned his position as editor of the *Kilkenny Journal* in 1922, and eventually returned to his native Waterford.[54]

Both Keane and Upton went on to share public platforms on which they often introduced Sinn Féin politicians. The *Kilkenny People* became the biggest selling newspaper in the county during this period.

The First World War Years in Kilkenny

Notwithstanding the enormous loss of life, the First World War had a less negative effect on Kilkenny City and county compared to many other areas of Ireland. This was primarily due to relatively low levels of recruitment, especially after the first year of the conflict. In recent years a tremendous amount of research has been undertaken regarding Kilkenny's involvement in that war.

It is estimated that 3,129 people from Kilkenny served in the First World War (this includes women in the auxiliary services). This figure encompasses all participants who had a connection with Kilkenny. It incorporates those who were born in Kilkenny; recruits who lived there at the time of their enlistment; those from the county who enlisted in overseas regiments; and all those who enlisted in Kilkenny Barracks, irrespective of their place of residence. People joined from every parish in County Kilkenny to fight in the largest war the world had ever experienced up to that point. Many acts of bravery were attributed to Kilkenny soldiers, and a number of Kilkenny natives were awarded Victoria Cross medals for acts of valour. Kilkenny City itself was a garrison town, its barracks having been built a century before, at the time of the Napoleonic Wars. However, permanent regiments had ceased to exist in Kilkenny since the period prior to the Boer War in the late nineteenth century.[55]

Following an initial flourish, army recruitment figures for Kilkenny remained comparatively low throughout the war years. In their detailed publication, *Kilkenny Families in the Great War,* historians Niall Brannigan and John Kirwan offered a number of explanations for the limited enlistment. Farming experienced a boom during the war years which greatly benefited Kilkenny's mainly agrarian-based economy, while the local woollen industry, woodworkers' factory and horse breeders benefited from army contracts during the war.[56] Therefore, given that there was so little unemployment amongst the labouring class, many did not have an economic necessity to enlist. It was not all good news, however, especially for the working class who bore the brunt of wartime inflation, which saw the cost of living in Ireland rise by 100 per cent. For instance, a loaf of bread was nearly double the price in 1918 as it had been prior to the war.[57]

For those in Kilkenny who did not have a close relative fighting in the war, the trauma of the trenches seemed like a distant land, as described by James Comerford who lived in rural Muckalee during this period:

> Between 1914 and 1918, the World War I years, life went on quietly and smoothly in all parts of Muckalee Parish. A number of local young men who were serving in the British Army fought on the battlefields of France, Belgium and Gallipoli … Farmers as a result of good prices for their products were well off. The battlefields seemed a long distance away. No one in particular was fretting about a German invasion of Ireland.[58]

Another factor in the diminishing army enlistment figures was the public's questioning of the motives of the war; especially as the death toll continued to increase, with no end in sight. The first Kilkenny deaths occurred in month one in August 1914, but apathy increased considerably after Gallipoli in 1915 following the high casualty rate of Irishmen there. *The Kilkenny War Dead* lists 787 service men and women from Kilkenny – or with next-of-kin from Kilkenny – who died during the First World War (this figure has more recently been revised upwards to 870 deaths).[59]

Writing in 1916, the local Inspector of the Royal Irish Constabulary (RIC), Pierce Power, did not mince his words when he gave his reasons for the low recruitment in County Kilkenny: 'There is an undercurrent of disloyalty which hampers recruiting, in addition to which farmers' sons prefer self-interest and an easy life at home to the more strenuous and dangerous work in the trenches.'[60] The decade prior to the commencement of the First World War also witnessed a substantial increase in employment in non-agricultural industries. A number of notable construction projects had taken place, including the building of the new John's Bridge over the River Nore in the city (opened in 1910), while nearby, a public library was also constructed. Some industries outside the city were similarly thriving. For example, the large mill owned by William Mosse in Bennettsbridge expanded, and its machinery was upgraded in the years before the outbreak of war.[61] Kilkenny made international headlines in April 1912 when a local resident, Denys Corbett Wilson from Suttonsrath in Jenkinstown, became the first person to land a plane in Ireland having taken off from Britain. Wilson landed his Bleriot monoplane in County Wexford before flying onwards to the Polo Grounds in Jenkinstown near his home. He circled Kilkenny City on his return flight, with the resulting headlines bestowing a sense of modernity and glamour on the county. The achievement was all the more remarkable considering aircrafts had only been invented during the previous decade.[62]

The Nationalist Spectrum, and Competing Agendas in Kilkenny: 1900–1915

Generally the political scene in County Kilkenny in the first decade of the twentieth century was dominated by John Redmond's Irish Parliamentary Party (IPP). The IPP held all three Kilkenny seats in the House of Commons unopposed since 1900. Many of the local council seats were also held by members affiliated to the party. The IPP was the leading nationalist party in most parts of Ireland at this time, although the proximity of County Kilkenny to Redmond's home county of Wexford – and constituency of Waterford City – was an added factor in its popularity.

On the other hand, it was certainly not surprising that Kilkenny had elements of more radical nationalism in the 1900s. The Irish Republican Brotherhood (IRB) – a secret oath-bound society created to establish an 'independent democratic Republic' – was founded in Dublin by Kilkenny man James Stephens on Saint Patrick's Day 1858. Stephens was born in Blackmill Street in Kilkenny City in 1825. He first came to prominence in the ill-fated 1848 rebellion in Ballingarry, County Tipperary. During the revolt, Stephens acted as an aide to the Young Ireland leader William Smith-O'Brien. Stephens was only 24 years old at the time of the rebellion and in the aftermath he escaped to France.[63] His organisation instigated the failed 'Fenian rebellion' of 1867, and for a period in the mid-1860s he was the most wanted man in the British Empire. A total of eighty-two men with an address in County Kilkenny were arrested as part of a roundup of Fenian suspects between 1861 and 1871.[64]

Another Kilkenny City native, Joseph Denieffe (1833–1910), was instrumental in helping establish the fledgling IRB organisation. He was one of its first five members, having returned from New York to be present at its inaugural meeting in Dublin on 17 March 1858. He then accompanied his kinsman, James Stephens, in his 'ramblings around Ireland' when spreading the gospel of the new movement. John Devoy, later leader of the American version of the IRB (known as The Fenian Brotherhood or Clan na Gael), credits Denieffe more than Stephens for 'bringing Fenianism to Ireland'. This was because the Fenian organisation in New York had been established prior to the IRB in Ireland. Denieffe had been a founding member of both. Denieffe was helped considerably on his mission in establishing the IRB in Kilkenny by John Haltigan (1819–1884), yet another city native. Haltigan, a printer by trade, became the first IRB 'head centre' in the county.[65]

In 1894, the famous Fenian, Jeremiah O'Donovan-Rossa, to whom Patrick Pearse would bequeath a famous graveside oration in 1915, visited Kilkenny where a 'large crowd' greeted him in the City Hall.[66] Stephens himself died of old age in 1901, and although not at the peak of his popularity, his death ignited new mythologies and deference from some of the younger generation who were influenced by the Irish cultural revival then in vogue. Special trains from Kilkenny were provided to cater for the large crowds who wanted to attend his funeral in Glasnevin Cemetery in Dublin.

However, the IRB movement in Kilkenny existed in name only by the early 1900s, a state of affairs that was typical throughout the country. Peter DeLoughry (1882–1931) was the 'head centre' (leader) of the Kilkenny IRB. DeLoughry was from an old Fenian/IRB family and became leader after the death of previous head centre P.J. O'Keeffe in 1905. Peter's deceased father, Richard, was a contemporary of James Stephens and was associated with the Fenians in Kilkenny in the 1860s. Peter DeLoughry was born in Rothe House in Kilkenny City and his family later moved to another house on Parliament Street.[67] The family business was an iron foundry, a business Peter would later manage. The Kilkenny IRB met at irregular intervals, generally on Sunday evenings, either in DeLoughry's home or in the garden of his close friend Tom Stallard. The height of the group's activity was 'organisation and the admittance of new members'. There was a maximum of twenty members in the Kilkenny IRB at that stage.[68]

Similarly, the recently-founded 'Sinn Féin' movement looked like finishing before it had even begun. A branch of Arthur Griffith's Sinn Féin had been established in Kilkenny in 1908. Sinn Féin, which translates as 'ourselves', was initially not particularly involved in mainstream politics. At the beginning, it was most associated with promoting Irish self-sufficiency, hence the name 'ourselves'. One of its first activities in Kilkenny was a 'buy Irish' campaign. In the lead-up to Christmas 1908 it encouraged traders to sell only locally produced Christmas cards. Likewise, the selling of imported margarine was discouraged, while St Kieran's College secondary school was criticised by the local Sinn Féin branch for importing school desks from Scotland instead of sourcing them locally.[69] However, by 1910, an RIC County Inspector reported that the recently established Sinn Féin branches in Kilkenny City and Thomastown had 'collapsed', having only been founded a few years previously.[70]

This decline was about to change, however, as the IRB went through a period of rejuvenation both nationally and in Kilkenny. Around 1912, Thomas Furlong – an IRB member who was a native of Wexford but who had moved to Kilkenny – was asked by Seán MacDiarmada about the possibility of restarting the IRB in Kilkenny City. Furlong had been sworn into the IRB in Wexford in 1908 by Seán T. O'Kelly (who later became President of Ireland). MacDiarmada – a key IRB organiser who would later become famous as a signatory of the 1916 Proclamation – was put in contact with Peter DeLoughry. Following the communication from MacDiarmada, DeLoughry organised a meeting with the aim of revitalising the IRB in Kilkenny, at which MacDiarmada spoke 'a few words'. DeLoughry, then 30 years old, was re-elected head centre of the rejuvenated IRB, while Pat Corcoran was made deputy centre.[71] Similarly, in July 1912, DeLoughry was heavily involved in the establishment of a branch of Na Fianna Éireann in Kilkenny City. That movement was founded in 1909 by Bulmer Hobson and Constance Markievicz, and was essentially an Irish nationalist boy scouts movement, which was in direct competition to the recently established British scouting movement.[72] Liam Mellows, another Na Fianna organiser, cycled through north Kilkenny in 1914 and helped establish branches of the organisation there. Some of the older teenage boys were members of both the local Irish Volunteers and Na Fianna, subsequently training with both.[73]

On 5 March 1914 a local company of the Irish Volunteers was established in Kilkenny at City Hall. The Irish Volunteers had been founded four months previously in Dublin, and mirrored the Ulster Volunteer Force – but with the opposite aim of ensuring that a 'Home Rule' parliament *would* be established in Ireland. The IRB quickly infiltrated the movement, securing key positions in its organisational hierarchy. The chief speakers on the day the Volunteers were founded in Kilkenny were Roger Casement, who would later organise the shipment of arms from Germany for the Easter Rising, and Thomas MacDonagh, one of the seven signatories of the 1916 Proclamation. Both men were subsequently executed for their participation in the Easter Rising. MacDonagh's presence at the launch of the Volunteers was an obvious choice, given his close association with Kilkenny as a former teacher in the county. One of the men who enrolled that day, Tim Hennessy, reported that 100 men joined on that occasion, while the *Kilkenny People* mentioned that 200 joined.[74] The local RIC County Inspector put the figure at 250, while also giving his view on the class distinction and snobbery involved: 'The Volunteer Movement ... has made steady progress ... [The] respectable classes have held aloof from the movement so far as they are unwilling to be brought into the contact for drill purposes with persons whom they consider inferior to them socially.'[75] The Volunteer movement spread throughout the county, and by June 1914 British Intelligence reports estimated the total numbers of Volunteers in County Kilkenny to be 2,000.[76] This does not necessarily mean that they were all active, as this varied greatly throughout each district, but nevertheless it highlighted the far-reaching effect of the Volunteers, and that generally, class distinctions did not hold true.

It is also important to acknowledge that not all Kilkenny inhabitants were supportive of Home Rule. In 1912, after the introduction of a Home Rule Bill by the British Parliament, a meeting of over 300 'Kilkenny Unionists' convened at Kilkenny Castle. The Marquess of Ormonde presided, and the main speakers were ardent unionists Lord Middleton and Lord Kenmare. A resolution was passed at the meeting 'protesting against Home Rule'.[77]

Votes for Women

During this time another pressing social issue to the fore throughout Ireland and Britain was female suffrage (votes for women in general elections). In 1910, the Dublin-based 'Irish Women's Franchise League' requested the use of City Hall (the Tholsel) in Kilkenny for a meeting in support of female suffrage. The suffragist Mary Kettle – who was married to politician, poet and university lecturer Thomas Kettle – was the main speaker. The (all male) Urban Council in Kilkenny decided to approve the use of the hall for the proposed meeting, with most of the councillors stating they were in favour of votes for women.[78]

However, in subsequent years, attitudes to the suffrage movement became more hostile. There was a great deal of negative newspaper coverage about the actions of the militant suffragettes, as opposed to the more moderate suffragists. Furthermore, as the question of Home Rule and female suffrage were being debated at roughly the same time in the British Parliament (in 1912), many within the nationalist movement believed that votes for women would have to wait until after Home Rule was achieved. There was also the unfounded fear that female voters would be more cautious, and were therefore more likely to vote for the Conservative Party. As the IPP was supporting the Liberals in Government, it was in its best interests to keep them in power, to achieve Home Rule. Consequently, John Redmond – who was personally against votes for women – and the majority of the IPP were not supportive of the extension of the franchise to women. The campaign against female suffrage had an added dimension in Kilkenny as the popular local philanthropist Ellen Cuffe, dowager Countess of Desart, was president of the Irish branch of the 'National League for Opposing Woman Suffrage'. At one meeting of the organisation in Dublin in 1913, suffragettes were described as 'senseless hooligans' who were having a bad effect on the morals of women.[79]

When the Munster Women's Franchise League held a public meeting in Kilkenny City Hall in June 1913 they received an unsympathetic reception. The meeting was full to capacity with many eager to view 'a real life' suffragette in the flesh. However, when Dr Mary Strangman – co-founder of the Munster Women's Franchise League and the first woman to be elected to Waterford Corporation in 1912 – delivered her speech, she was heckled and jeered by the mostly male audience. The next speaker, 'Miss Cook', received similar laughter and hissing from the excited audience. Stating the case for the right of women to vote, she said: 'A woman's life was affected at every turn by laws made in the House of Commons. A mother could not say whether her child would be vaccinated or not, at what age it would go to school, what it would learn at school … or at what time it should leave school.' Her arguments for giving women the vote focused mainly on topics that were considered 'women's issues'. Her own political views may have been more complex but her line of argument was probably more out of necessity, as many suffragists realised that to obtain votes for women they needed to allay the fears of some men who believed women would 'interfere' in other issues if they were in parliament. As the meeting continued in disorder, Cook went on to state:

> I have attended meetings in Hyde Park, London, where I was desperately afraid of the men around me. Here [in Kilkenny] I felt confident that I had nothing to fear. I know quite well that there are plenty of men in this room ready enough to defend me if there happened to be any necessity … it is extremely difficult to speak when those lads at the back of the room – who are not old enough to appreciate what they are saying – will be [sic] creating a disturbance.[80]

Some of the audience were offended that the Franchise League had requested the attendance of the RIC at the meeting. The presence of policemen inferred that the women needed protection, which annoyed some of the locals. After the meeting ended, Strangman and Cook left the hall to 'hissing and cheering' and were 'accompanied by a large police escort' as they walked towards Patrick's Street. The general stereotypes of suffragists had evidently been accepted by some in Kilkenny.

Suffragettes were even parodied by local drama groups. In Dunmore village, during an amateur theatre production, 'determined and wicked' suffragettes stormed the stage. This was all part of the comical performance however, as the 'offending suffragettes' were actually local children, who went on to sing the satirical *Could We But Rule*. Similarly, Stoneyford National School children produced 'a most amusing' piece in their variety show entitled *The Suffragettes*.[81]

The Irish and National Volunteers (1914–1915)

At the formation of the Irish Volunteers in Kilkenny in 1914, the IRB received 'instructions from Dublin to capture as many key positions as possible [on the committee]'.[82] This was something that was happening nationally with the aim of 'pulling the strings' of the fledgling organisation, as the IRB relationship would be unknown to the other more moderate committee members. Kilkenny IRB members, Peter DeLoughry, Patrick Corcoran and Ned Comerford succeeded in doing so, and were the driving force in the organisation locally during its formative months. A former British soldier, Thomas Connolly, trained and drilled the Volunteers. The committee was involved in the purchase of obsolete Italian Martini rifles, nicknamed 'the gas pipes' because of their long barrel, for which it proved impossible to get ammunition. The sight of the Volunteers drilling and marching with these guns, or with hurls, caused the organisation to be ridiculed in the city.[83]

The split in the Irish Volunteers occurred publicly in September 1914, following the commencement of the First World War.[84] A full parade of all Kilkenny City companies met in the Market Yard.[85] In total there were around 650 men on parade. A number of people addressed the crowd. The majority 'favoured the policy of the Redmondites and Ancient Order of Hibernians', including two local clergymen Rev. John Rowe and Rev. Philip Moore. IRB members Peter DeLoughry, Pat Corcoran and Ned Comerford spoke passionately on behalf of the 'Irish side' (IRB/Sinn Féin). Thomas Treacy, who would eventually become head of the Kilkenny Brigade of the IRA during the War of Independence, stated that the following subsequently occurred:

> Peter DeLoughry then called on all those who stood for Ireland and the Green flag to fall out and line up at a point indicated by him ... and all those who stood for England and the Union Jack to stand where they were. Twenty-eight men left the ranks and lined up at the point indicated ... the balance on parade (over 600) stood on the Redmondite side.[86]

The approximate 95 per cent that did not heed DeLoughry's call became known as the 'National Volunteers' (sometimes referred to as the 'Redmondite Volunteers'). Some of these volunteers joined the British Army and fought in the First World War, but the majority stayed in Kilkenny and participated in neither movement. Just 4.3 per cent stayed within the ranks of the Irish Volunteers, which was below the reported 10 per cent figure of the split nationally.[87] The Irish Volunteers were often referred to colloquially as the 'Sinn Féin Volunteers'. By dividing in such a public manner, and in very small numbers, it was also very clear to the public – and the RIC – which families were supportive of the more advanced nationalist Irish Volunteer movement.[88]

The National Volunteers were initially very successful throughout County Kilkenny. From the early stages they mostly adhered to the social and class structures that were prevalent at the time. In rural areas the 'strong' farmers, or priests would usually fill roles on Volunteer committees. Another example of the class norms in Kilkenny involved the position of the 'County Inspecting Officer' of the National Volunteers. A number of local men from upper-class backgrounds were invited to take on the role. The esteem their names carried would appear to be the main qualifying factor for their consideration. Most, however, declined the offer. Major James H. Connellan of Coolmore in Thomastown, whose only son would go on to be killed in the First World War, declined stating; 'owing to my age (65) … [and] moreover as I have been retired from the service for many years I do not think I am professionally qualified to fill the position'.[89] Major Joyce, of Sion House near Kilkenny City, turned down the offer stating; 'owing to ill health, I am unable to undertake the duties therein mentioned … I left the service [army] in 1885 … and am 70 years of age'.[90] Similarly, Richard Prior-Wandesforde of Castlecomer House declined stating; 'unfortunately I have had no military experience & only know a little drill that I have picked up'.[91]

Nevertheless the National Volunteers were active throughout the county from the split in 1914 into 1915. In March 1915, the Callan National Volunteers reported a membership of 170, with 120 drilling regularly. They were well trained as they had the services of a former British Army drilling instructor, Captain Mahon, but lost his expertise when he re-joined the army. However, they only had one rifle between the 120 men for shooting practice., However, they had a variety of other equipment including eighty bandoliers (belt for holding ammunition), 170 haversacks, thirty water bottles, one hundred caps, and fifteen uniforms.[92] The Graiguenamanagh National Volunteers had 150 enrolled, with one hundred drilling regularly.[93]

The numbers of young men enrolled in the National Volunteers throughout rural Kilkenny was high. The Kells/Kilree National Volunteers had eighty men registered, with sixty attending regularly. In nearby Kilmaganny, there were eighty-five enrolled, with fifty attending regularly. Inistioge had one hundred National Volunteers with seventy attending regularly, while their Commanding Officer, Aidan Furlong, was a Boer War veteran. Kilmanagh National Volunteers had ninety members and forty-five drilling regularly.[94] These figures emphasise the popularity of the National Volunteers prior to 1916, relative to the unpopularity of the Irish Volunteers. It also highlights the large number of young men throughout Kilkenny who were eligible for the British Army, but who did not enlist to fight in the First World War. It is also notable how quickly the organisation dissipated. By the end of 1916, there was little evidence of any active National Volunteer Company in County Kilkenny; while in contrast, the Irish Volunteers were growing rapidly.

Regarding the Irish Volunteers in the county at the end of 1914, the local RIC inspector initially referred to the organisation in Kilkenny as a 'small clique in the City', and that they were looked on with 'contempt'. He also referred to those in the Irish Volunteers as 'rabble'.[95] In January 1916, the same inspector referred to men who joined the Irish Volunteers as 'mostly irresponsible youths without influence'.[96] They may have been young, but they were not irresponsible, and their influence would be felt in the coming months and years.

The Kilkenny City Irish Volunteer Companies were extremely well organised, and had regular drilling (with wooden rifles), manoeuvres, and field training, along with classes in history and the Irish language. This dedication involved them paying for their own ammunition for rifle practice, and they also purchased their own copies of *The Irish Volunteer*, the official newspaper of the organisation. The Volunteers also contributed money to the cost of procuring a dozen new Lee Enfield rifles and a dozen small revolvers, which they purchased from Volunteer headquarters.[97]

In the summer of 1915, five members of the Kilkenny Irish Volunteers, all from in and around the city, went to Galbally, County Limerick, for a week-long training camp, under the stewardship of J.J. ('Ginger') O'Connell. There were over sixty men at the camp, mostly from the Munster area. A rigorous training regime was taught along strict military lines. Ginger O'Connell went on to stay nearly three months in Kilkenny over the next year, training the local Volunteer companies. The largest procession of Irish Volunteers in Kilkenny occurred at the Manchester Martyrs commemoration on 23 November 1915. The Volunteers paraded with their new Lee Enfield rifles and afterwards heard an oration from Seán MacDiarmada in Rothe House. After his speech MacDiarmada and a number of the prominent IRB men retired to Peter DeLoughry's house on nearby Parliament Street. It was at this meeting that one local IRB member, James Lalor, heard MacDiarmada state that a rising would take place 'soon'.[98]

Thus, as 1915 drew to a close, few could have predicted the events that would unfold in the weeks before and after Easter 1916; or how these events would change the course of Irish history.

CHAPTER 2

Kilkenny 1916:
The Fight that Never Was

'Sure an old woman could take Kilkenny to-day' [1]

The interaction between the Irish Volunteers headquarters in Dublin and the Kilkenny City Battalion continued into 1916. One of the reasons for the close connection was because of the occupation of Peter DeLoughry. He owned a small foundry on Parliament Street in Kilkenny City and used his premises and skills to produce the casing for homemade grenades. Casings of this sort were difficult to get hold of, thus DeLoughry's skills were much sought after. In addition, as a side enterprise, he rented out motor cars, which were useful for communications and transportation for IRB and Volunteer work.

At the beginning of 1916, Lieutenant Ted (Edward) O'Kelly was sent from Volunteer HQ to reside in Kilkenny and train the local companies. Lieutenant O'Kelly was a Kildare native and an Irish Volunteer organiser who would go on to acquire injuries near the GPO during Easter Week.[2] Kelly was also involved in the establishment of the first Cumann na mBan Battalion in Kilkenny on 9 January 1916.[3] Cumann na mBan had been founded in Dublin in 1914 as a sister organisation to the exclusively male Irish Volunteers. Hanna Murphy (née Dooley) was elected Brigade O/C, and was also made leader of the Kilkenny City Battalion (battalions were also referred to as 'district councils' within the organisation). Winnie DeLoughry, wife of IRB head centre Peter, became president. Another member who joined on the inaugural night was Maisie Stallard, who would go on to replace DeLoughry as President of the Kilkenny Cumann na mBan Brigade during the years of the War of Independence.[4]

Judging by the police reports compiled by the Kilkenny RIC prior to Easter 1916, it is fair to say they were not expecting any disorder in the immediate future. In County Kilkenny the most senior ranking position in the RIC was the County Inspector (CI), a position held by 54-year-old Westmeath native

Pierce Charles Power in 1916. He had occupied that position in Kilkenny since 1910. One of the most important jobs of all County Inspectors was to forward monthly reports to RIC headquarters in Dublin Castle, stating any major incidences that occurred during the month. These records make for fascinating reading about life in Kilkenny in 1916.

RIC Report: January 1916

CI Power sent a list of 'political organisations' in Kilkenny, including their membership figures. They included the following; United Irish League (farmer-based, IPP-affiliated); 2,559. Gaelic League; 105. GAA; 632. National Volunteers (IPP-affiliated); 2,358. Irish Volunteers (split from National Volunteers); 105. Ancient Order of Hibernians (staunchly Catholic, IPP-affiliated); 709. Labour Association; 200. IRB; 3.

His report highlights the range of organisations that existed in Ireland, even in a small county like Kilkenny. It is also significant that the GAA was considered a 'political organisation', something it would have strongly denied. Here are some other extracts from Inspector Power's report for January 1916:

> The entire County continues in a peaceable satisfactory condition ... Recruiting for the Army has been poor and the sources which have supplied recruits, chiefly the labouring classes, are now almost exhausted. There are however in the County very many suitable men but they continue to be apathetic and indifferent to recruiting appeals and I fear will continue so ... There has been no serious crime during the month and only four arrests ... The Irish Volunteers have also been inactive this month ... Two pro German and Sinn Fein publications were found in the city during the month. One headed 'Stop the War' and the other 'How to help the Volunteer Movement.'[5]

RIC Report: March 1916

Inspector Power noticed an increase of activity in Kilkenny in March 1916, a month before the Rising:

> The Irish Volunteers still shows activity and have made some progress. On 17th March about 122 members assembled at their club in Kilkenny [Kyteler's Inn] and marched to Divine Service at St Johns R.C. Church, 14 members being armed with rifles and sword bayonets. The respectable people with very few

exceptions keep aloof from the Sinn Feiners and look on them with contempt & disapproval.[6]

It should be noted that there was nationwide Irish Volunteer drilling on St Patrick's Day 1916. This was a tactic on the part of the IRB, as when the Irish Volunteers announced more manoeuvres on Easter Sunday, the authorities and the public would have assumed it was more of the same and therefore not considered it suspicious.

Easter 1916: The Lead-Up

Considering the investment in terms of time and resources in the Kilkenny Battalion, it is no surprise that it featured very much in the plans for a national rising at Easter 1916. Cathal Brugha, in his capacity as a key IRB organiser, arrived in Kilkenny one week before Easter 1916 to meet Peter DeLoughry and Pat Corcoran. Brugha himself later gained fame during the Easter Rebellion after he single-handedly held back a British military advance in the South Dublin Union Hospital, while also being shot eighteen times in the process and surviving. Brugha met the Company captain, Thomas Treacy outside the Volunteer Hall on Kings Street, now Kieran's Street, Kilkenny. Volunteer Hall (also known as Banba Hall, named after a Celtic goddess) is more commonly known as Kyteler's Inn today.[7] This meeting was the first time Treacy heard that a Rising was to take place on Easter Sunday, and Brugha gave him the plans for Kilkenny. Firstly, Treacy was to arrange 'general manoeuvres for Easter Sunday', so the mustering of men would not appear suspicious. On the day, the whole company, with 'whatever arms and equipment' they possessed, were to proceed to the Scallop Gap on the Wexford/Carlow border, passing through Borris, with the aim of meeting the Wexford battalions there. No operations were to commence until they 'linked up with Wexford'. Captain Ginger O'Connell from GHQ would be 'in command of all units in the city and county and all orders … were to be taken from him'.[8]

The number of active Irish Volunteers in Kilkenny City at this time was around sixty. The total number of Irish Volunteers and IRB combined in the county was approximately 160, although the majority of the men outside Kilkenny City were less well trained.[9] The police intelligence was found wanting, as it suggested the Irish Volunteers numbered 105 men, while it also estimated there were only three members of the IRB in the county, and these three individuals were 'old men of no importance'.[10]

Upon receiving these instructions from Brugha, Treacy was quick to point out that he had only enough 'rifles and revolvers' to 'poorly arm' twenty-five of his men. Brugha told him a quantity of arms would be collected at Dr Edward Dundon's house, an IRB member and Volunteer organiser from Borris in Carlow, hence the reason for passing through there. Brugha also predicted that 'there would be sufficient arms and ammunition for all the available men' nearer the time, which was most likely a reference to the arrival of arms organised by Sir Roger Casement. Treacy subsequently issued the orders for Easter Sunday 'without of course giving the slightest indication of the main objective'.[11] Following Cathal Brugha's visit, it was decided by the Kilkenny IRB committee that some members would travel to Dublin to clarify aspects of the plan. Peter DeLoughry and Pat Corcoran went to Dublin to meet Eoin MacNeill, Chief of Staff of the Irish Volunteers. In relation to the upcoming Rising, MacNeill said 'the first he knew about it himself was when a few more lads from other parts of the country went to him on the same mission'. MacNeill had only become aware that the IRB faction within the Volunteers were planning a rebellion. This led to the 'on/off' nature of the Rebellion in the days leading up to Easter Sunday. Most importantly, the Kilkenny contingent agreed that the Kilkenny Irish Volunteers were to only follow orders that came directly from MacNeill himself.[12]

There was much activity in Kilkenny in the week prior to the Rising. On the Tuesday before Easter, three members of the company drove with Peter DeLoughry to The Swan, County Laois, where they collected gelignite fuses and detonators which they subsequently delivered to Portlaoise for onward transportation to Dublin.[13] Similarly, on Good Friday, Pat Corcoran, Peter DeLoughry, James Lalor and Thomas Furlong drove to Wexford where they picked up another batch of explosives. They packaged these explosives and sent them to Dublin.[14]

In the middle of Holy Week, Claire Gregan, fiancée of IRB committee member Bulmer Hobson, was sent to Kilkenny with a dispatch from him that contained a letter along with a copy of 'the famous document', meaning the Castle Document which was modified intelligence that incorrectly suggested that the British authorities were planning an imminent arrest of Volunteer organisers and the seizing of arms.[15] The purpose of her visit was to warn DeLoughry and the Kilkenny Volunteers that they might be arrested and disarmed; although there was no actual plan by the authorities to do this. The following day, Holy Thursday, Kitty O' Doherty was sent by Tom Clarke to deliver a message to DeLoughry in Kilkenny with Clarke stating; 'don't say that either Seán [MacDiarmada] or myself sent you. Say Pearse sent you'. She was to 'bring back some specimens' which were, in fact, homemade grenades DeLoughry had made. She was told by Clarke to tell DeLoughry; 'Pearse wanted all they had.'[16] When she arrived in Kilkenny on Holy Thursday morning, having travelled by the 6.40 am train from Dublin, she gave DeLoughry the message. She later recounted the following exchange which occurred between them: 'Who sent you?', he asked. I said, 'Pádraig Pearse'. He said, 'It was not. It was Clarke and MacDermott. I have my instructions and I am going to act on them.' DeLoughry was obviously not duped. She had to return to Dublin empty-handed and when she told Clarke what occurred he said; 'just as I expected'.[17] At a bare minimum from these exchanges it can be surmised that DeLoughry was now aware of the power struggle that was taking place in Dublin about initiating a rising. As DeLoughry had received instructions from MacNeill, it is fair to assume that he was looking to him as the main authority.

Easter Week in Kilkenny

On the morning of Easter Sunday, the entire Kilkenny Battalion, 'without exception', mobilised at Volunteer Hall at noon, even though 'practically everyone' was aware of the announcement which had appeared in that day's *Sunday Independent* stating that 'manoeuvres were cancelled'.[18] The Kilkenny Volunteers would seem to have preferred to arrive and find out further information, instead of accepting the advertisement in the newspaper verbatim. The company was then dismissed at 2.00 pm with orders to mobilise again at 8.00 pm that evening. When the company reconvened later, they waited for Ginger O'Connell and Pat Corcoran to return from Dublin. They arrived with news that the Rising was 'off' that day. Tom Treacy dismissed the battalion with orders to mobilise the following evening, Easter Monday, at 8.00 pm.[19]

On Easter Monday morning, Peter DeLoughry and Pat Corcoran drove from Kilkenny to Borris to retrieve the guns that the Volunteer company were supposed to have collected the previous day.[20] When Martin Kealy, leader of the Clara Company, arrived at Volunteer Hall at 8.00 pm for the mobilisation he noticed an 'air of tension' and that was the first time he 'heard that the Rising had commenced in Dublin'.[21] The main task for a number of the Volunteers that night was to unload the shotguns and ammunition from Peter DeLoughry's car. The number of guns they collected numbered around thirty.[22] If this was the case, it would give the company around fifty-five weapons in total for its approximately sixty members – although of 'poor' quality as previously outlined by Treacy.

The Kilkenny Volunteers mobilised on Tuesday, Wednesday, Thursday and Friday of Easter Week at 8.00 pm, with the discussing of rumour and counter rumour being the main activity. The *Kilkenny People* reported that the county had 'been practically isolated from the outer world since Monday [24 April 1916]', with no post, newspapers, telegrams or train services from Dublin.[23] At the beginning of the week, Ginger O'Connell – who was the Commandant of the southeast volunteer brigades – travelled between Waterford, Wexford, Carlow and Kilkenny to demobilise the Volunteers.

A number of different contradictory narratives exist in relation to the dynamic between DeLoughry and Ginger O'Connell on Easter Week – specifically about why Kilkenny did not play an active part in the Rising. On Tuesday of Easter Week, Dublin Cumann na mBan member Nancy Wyse-Power delivered a message to Peter DeLoughry from Ginger O'Connell, whom she had met in Carlow that morning. It included 'a long list of instructions' which she memorised and delivered to DeLoughry. She states that '[DeLoughry] did not appear to be pleased to see me' and 'altogether I felt that my room was more appreciated than my company'. She believed he was not keen to start a rising. She returned to Dublin and said that after her 'chilly reception in Kilkenny I felt down'.[24]

Another account by Dr Josephine Clarke (née Stallard) – who had been tasked with delivering a mobilisation message to Kilkenny on Easter Sunday from Lieutenant Ted O'Kelly, at the time her sister Maisie's boyfriend – suggests that on Easter Week 'Commandant O' Connell restrained them from going out to fight, while Peter and the others [Kilkenny IRB] were anxious to do their part in the Rising.'[25] Dr Clarke was a long-standing friend of the DeLoughry family and her brother Tom Stallard was DeLoughry's business partner in a cinema venture in Kilkenny.[26]

A differing statement of events in Kilkenny came from Maeve Cavanagh who travelled from Waterford to Kilkenny on Wednesday of Easter Week with a message from Seán Matthews, IRB Head Centre in Waterford and leader of the Irish Volunteers there. The Rebellion was at this stage in full throttle in Dublin, with Liberty Hall being pounded by the Helga gunship that morning. When she located DeLoughry and O'Connell she states the following exchanges occurred:

> He [DeLoughry] was very truculent and angry and began to give out about Sean McDermott coming down to Kilkenny and getting entertained and then pulling this off in Dublin. I felt that he was completely antagonistic to the Rising …

I gave him [O' Connell] the message. 'They should have waited till there was conscription [to the British Army]', [Ginger] O Connell said 'Look at that, it is all over already', showing me an English paper. I said 'Sure an old woman could take Kilkenny to-day'.[27]

The last statement was disingenuous, considering that the strength of the military and RIC in Kilkenny at that time was about 440.[28] The RIC inspector also drafted in seventy officers during the week, with 'most of them assigned to the protection of bridges in the district'.[29]

Judging by the evidence available, DeLoughry appeared to have been aligned to the Ginger O'Connell/Eoin MacNeill faction which was understandable, given that he had much more of a working relationship with them. He also had personally met MacNeill some days previously. It is difficult to comprehend how he could follow orders from Patrick Pearse or Tom Clarke having no relationship with either of them. Furthermore, Ginger O'Connell was based, for the most part, in Kilkenny City during the week of the Rebellion. His authority superseded DeLoughry's anyway, as he was on the headquarters staff of the Irish Volunteers as Chief of Inspection.[30] Although DeLoughry was an IRB member, he followed Irish Volunteers orders instead of following his allegiance to the IRB. Ginger O'Connell was not in the IRB. This highlights the complexity of the loyalties that existed, something which was mirrored across Ireland before and during Easter Week 1916.

Outside of Kilkenny City, the Volunteers in Crutt, Castlecomer – a rare example of an Irish Volunteer company still in existence in rural Kilkenny in 1916 – did mobilise on Easter Sunday, but were totally reliant on receiving further orders from Kilkenny City which did not arrive.[31] One other interesting facet of the week was that about a dozen new or lapsed members joined the Irish Volunteers in Kilkenny City, perhaps eager to join in some fighting.[32]

Thus, despite meeting every day from Sunday to Friday of Easter Week (23 to 28 April 1916), the Kilkenny Volunteers played no active role in the Rising. However, by just 'coming out' at Easter 1916 they were part of a very small minority who were willing to put their heads above the parapet, thus, leaving themselves and their families open to possible repercussions. Many of those within the IRB/Volunteer movement who did not actively participate in the fighting spent their lifetimes defending their actions – or lack thereof – during that historic week. It was impossible to know at the time that Easter Week 1916 would be remembered by many as the apogee, or high-watermark, of the Irish fight for freedom. The small numbers who had played an active role could always maintain the moral high ground.

It is unclear what sort of action the Kilkenny Volunteers would have been involved in had they mobilised to the Scallop Gap. It is quite possible the military and RIC would not have engaged them there and they would simply have surrendered once the Dublin rebellion ceased. Perhaps the major achievement of the Kilkenny Volunteers during Easter Week was that, unlike other areas which had a similar experience during the week, they lost none of their arms, having hidden the majority of them in the grounds of a local convent.[33]

For the local populace of Kilkenny, some of the boredom from the lack of communication was lifted with the launch on Easter Monday of the local cinema season after the Lenten break, with 'hundreds being unable to gain admission' to see the film *The Trumpet Call*.[34]

Easter 1916 in Kilkenny: The Aftermath

'The Felon's Cap is the Noblest Crown an Irish Head can wear'

On Wednesday, 3 May 1916, the same day as the executions commenced in Dublin with the Pearse, Clarke and MacDonagh deaths, the first arrest took place in Kilkenny. Ginger O'Connell was detained by the RIC that day, followed the next day by Peter DeLoughry. On the same evening, 4 May, James Nowlan, President of the GAA, was arrested having just arrived back from Dublin. By coincidence, Nowlan had been in Dublin since the weekend prior to the Rising – firstly for the funeral of Frank Dineen, a key GAA official who had famously purchased the land Croke Park is now built on, and secondly for the GAA Congress held on Easter Sunday.[35] Interestingly, the GAA Congress was held in Dublin City Hall on Easter Sunday which was one of the buildings taken by the rebels the following day in an attack on Dublin Castle. If the Rising had commenced on Easter Sunday as originally planned, the GAA men would have unwittingly become players in the unfolding drama.

The Kilkenny RIC evidently had outdated information about James Nowlan. He was a long-time member of the IRB, but had played little part in the rejuvenated IRB or the Volunteers, most likely due to his more mature age when compared to the younger generation leading the IRB (Nowlan was aged 54 in 1916). It was also likely he was not an advanced nationalist, as a month prior the Rising he had been at parliament buildings in Westminster, along with John Redmond, lobbying against the imposition of a proposed 'entertainment tax' on GAA gate receipts.[36]

On Friday, 5 May 1916, the day after Nowlan's arrest, Kilkenny was patrolled by about 800 military who had been drafted the previous evening from other parts of the country. A large roundup of men and arrests followed.[37] Considering the scale of the reinforcements, the authorities clearly believed that Kilkenny was a significant location for the movement. As Kilkenny was a small city, and the Volunteers few in number, the RIC would have known many of them by name. Similarly, the parades during the previous year would have advertised the members and leaders of the local Volunteers in a very public way.[38]

The *Kilkenny People* newspaper editor Edward T. Keane received a letter from Sir John Maxwell in May 1916 warning against the 'inflammatory' articles he had written in support of the Irish Volunteers and critical of the British Military authorities. Maxwell stated that he 'did not want to interfere unduly with the liberty of the Press', but contradictorily went on to state that all proofs of the *Kilkenny People* will have to be submitted to the County Inspector or the 'seizure and destruction' of their printing press could follow.[39] Keane's editorial in the newspaper on 20 May 1916 was the provocative piece in question. In it he derided Maxwell for selecting Kilkenny 'for an extra special dose of martial law', and in particular for the large number of arrests in comparison to Cork and Kerry which had actually seen some 'trouble'.[40]

The censorship imposed on the *Kilkenny People* appeared to have irked Keane even further. In June 1916 he referred to General Maxwell as the 'Military Dictator who rules Ireland' and stated that if he as editor could not 'speak free and untrammelled' he would 'not speak in the accents of slavery'.[41] This surprisingly passed the censorship, while blocks of blank, white space in the newspaper highlighted the sections that had been removed by the censor.

In all, a total of thirty-three men were arrested and held in Kilkenny Jail, a relatively large number considering there was no conflict in the area. On 9 May they were marched under heavy guard to Kilkenny railway station for transportation to Dublin. The reaction of the general public was 'silence and indifference',[42] unlike Dublin where prisoners had been jeered. By this point eight executions had taken place in Kilmainham Jail which perhaps had initiated some feelings of sympathy already. Likewise, many of the Kilkenny prisoners and their extended families would have been known locally, which was bound to elicit an empathetic response. A tragic event took place on this march to the station. One of the prisoners, John Kealy, collapsed and died just yards from his home on John Street (where the present day O'Gorman's public-house is located). He had been ill when arrested, probably suffering from tuberculosis or pneumonia. It was reported that he had to be 'literally dragged to the railway station'.[43] He collapsed near the entrance of Connell's

Lime Works and Elizabeth O'Connell ran to the aid of her stricken neighbour. She took the cushions from her baby's pram and put them under Kealy's head to give him some comfort but he died soon afterwards.[44] His death certificate gives his place of death as 'John St' and his cause of death as 'Heart Disease Probably – No medical attention,'[45] but does not mention anything about the circumstances surrounding his death. He was 33 years old and brother of another arrested man, Martin Kealy. Martin did not hear about his brother's death until after his release a month later, as his prison mates kept the bad news from him to avoid adding more despair to his situation.[46]

The prisoners spent two days in Richmond Barracks in Dublin before the majority were transferred to Wakefield Prison near Leeds. Most of the Kilkenny prisoners were released on 7 June, with the remainder released in August 1916.[47] Seven Kilkenny natives ended up in the infamous Frongoch prison camp in north Wales.

In the aftermath of the Rising, Kilkenny RIC County Inspector P.C. Power remained undeterred in his report about events in the county, despite extra soldiers having been drafted into the city the previous week. This can be put down to some self-preservation on his part. As the Rebellion had come as a surprise to many in authority, downplaying events was something a lot of individuals were endeavouring to do in its aftermath. Power's May 1916 Kilkenny RIC report contained the following:

I beg to report that the general condition of this County is peaceable so far as ordinary crime is concerned … No persons, so far as can be ascertained, took an active part in the recent rebellion and disgraceful scenes in Dublin & elsewhere, but the local Sinn Feiners appeared to be in thorough sympathy with it … I had made adequate police arrangements to deal forcibly and probably effectively with any hostile movement … The National Volunteers held strictly aloof from the I.V's [Irish Volunteers] and in fact a body of them turned out & marched through the streets [of Kilkenny] on the night of 27th [of April] headed by a piper in order, as they subsequently told me, to openly demonstrate their entire lack of empathy with the Sinn Feiners.[48]

The fact the National (Redmondite) Volunteers were still in existence in Kilkenny is interesting to note, as most throughout the country had become defunct. Their parading during Easter Week highlighted the rivalry that still existed between themselves and the Irish Volunteers. The *Kilkenny People* editor Keane called the National Volunteer parade a 'deliberately provocative act' and called the participants 'brainless nincompoops' who 'ought to be in trenches', while stating that the Irish Volunteers in Dublin, although 'misguided', were 'not afraid to die'.[49] Keane made an interesting comparison; the idea of likening the motives of Irish soldiers in the First World War with the Irish Volunteers regarding their willingness to die for their country, albeit in different ways. The National Volunteers were caught in the middle as they had fought nowhere. It was perhaps opinions like Keane's that provided the final death knell for the National Volunteers after Easter 1916.

County Inspector Power did not escape so lightly by having to provide just one report, as he was called before the 'Royal Commission of the Rebellion in Ireland' on 27 May 1916. Below are some extracts from his appearance before the committee, which shows a glaring lack of understanding of the situation within Kilkenny:

> CI Power: As the situation was rather threatening and I did not know what would happen I took immediate steps to concentrate a force of armed police in Kilkenny. I stripped all the stations in the peaceful districts of men and by Tuesday and Wednesday morning [of Easter Week]. It was necessary to hurry a force to protect the Barrow Bridge, which is very important and a very vital line of communication with Rosslare Port … Excitement at this time was running very high and a great number of respectable people made several applications for protection. On the 5th May [1916] we made a raid on the local Sinn Fein Hall [Banba Hall/Kyteler's Inn] at Kilkenny, and searched it very thoroughly … we found in it a number of pikes and old bayonets, an air rifle, 200 round miniature rifle cartridges … and a map of Kilkenny. Amongst the things we found in the hall was a large scroll which was hung across the wall, and had the words written on it, 'A felon's cap is the noblest crown an Irish head can wear'.
>
> Chairman: Was there any recruiting done in your district for the [British] Army?
> CI Power: A great deal. Kilkenny did extremely well.
>
> Chairman: Did the number of Sinn Feiners increase with the fear of conscription or military service?
>
> CI Power: It did.
>
> Do you attribute that to the [Sinn Féin] men being shirkers or to their having a conscientious objection [to the First World War]?
>
> CI Power: I should say shirkers.[50]

Nationally, the vast majority of 1916 prisoners were released by Christmas 1916 under an amnesty by the new Prime Minister, Lloyd George. By then, the majority of public opinion had swung firmly in favour of the Easter rebels, while recruitment and general feeling for the war effort had decreased substantially. In that light, the general amnesty can be seen as a peace offering to negate unhelpful public reaction, with one eye also on the possibility of introducing conscription to Ireland (which had already been implemented in Britain since January 1916).

The 1916 Rising: Kilkenny Connections

Besides events that occurred in Kilkenny during and after Easter Week, there were also many Kilkenny connections in the broader context of the Rising.

Francis Sheehy-Skeffington

St Kieran's College in Kilkenny City lost two former teachers following the events of Easter week. As mentioned, executed signatory of the proclamation Thomas MacDonagh had been a teacher of languages there until 1903. His colleague – and housemate for a period at 19 High Street – was Cavan native Francis Sheehy-Skeffington who was also a teacher of languages at the school.[51] People in Kilkenny remembered Sheehy-Skeffington going on marathon walks, just for the pleasure, which was fairly uncommon at the time.[52] Like MacDonagh, he fell foul of the more conservative ethos of St Kieran's and resigned after one year's teaching there in 1902.[53] Sheehy-Skeffington – who unusually took his wife's name, 'Sheehy', upon marriage – came to a tragic end during the 1916 Rebellion. During Tuesday of Easter Week, he was in Dublin city centre attempting to muster support to form a group that would stop the looting of businesses. He was arrested by a mentally unstable British army captain – Cork-born, J.C. Bowen-Colthurst.[54] On the morning of Wednesday 26 April, he was executed, without having a trial, in Portobello Barracks (now Cathal Brugha Barracks), along with two other innocent men.[55]

Father James Crotty

James Thomas Crotty (1867–1930) from Kilkenny City had an unusual association with the Rising. James was born in New Ross, but the Crotty family moved to Kilkenny when he was aged 3. James joined the Dominican order in 1884 and became Prior of the Black Abbey in Kilkenny City for a period before being transferred to Rome. At the outbreak of the First World War, he was sent to Germany to administer to the spiritual needs of the Catholic Irish soldiers in the British Army who were captured as prisoners of war. In the internment camp in Limburg, Germany, Fr Crotty came into contact with Joseph Plunkett and Sir Roger Casement. With the blessing of the German authorities, Casement was attempting to recruit an 'Irish Brigade' from the Irish prisoners. This was intended to be a force that would be sent back to Ireland to fight in a rebellion. Although Fr Crotty struck up a friendship with Casement, he did not approve of his plan and discouraged the prisoners from joining – although most of the 2,000 men had no intention of doing so anyway. Casement's small army of less than sixty were never sent to Ireland.[56]

Paddy Bealin

The death of Paddy Bealin (sometimes recorded as Baylon or Bealen) was representative of many of the tragedies that occurred in Dublin during the Easter Rebellion. He was born into a large family of ten in the townland of Loon, Clogh, near Castlecomer, in May 1890.[57] Paddy was employed at Bergin's grocery in Castlecomer before moving to Dublin where he held the position of foreman in Mary O'Rourke's public house, North King Street. Paddy was not involved in the fighting during Easter Week. He was executed by British soldiers in his place of employment on Friday of Easter Week, 28 April 1916, with no apparent reasoning offered for his killing.

In what was known as the 'Battle of North King Street', British soldiers fought Ned Daly's 1st Dublin Battalion of the Irish Volunteers. A repercussion of this battle was that fifteen civilians were shot or bayoneted to death by soldiers from the South Staffordshire regiment. The subsequent British inquiry caused consternation in Ireland. Nationalistic sympathy increased when the British Army accepted responsibility for the massacre but held no specific individuals to account.

Mary O'Rourke, the owner of the pub, stated herself and Paddy took refuge in the basement when British troops took over the pub at 177 North King Street on the Thursday night/Friday morning of Easter Week. She told the inquiry that Bealin and her 13-year-old son were searched by the military. O'Rourke and her son were removed from the house but Bealin was never seen alive again. He was actually shot six times and buried in the basement by the soldiers, but his body was only discovered two weeks later, on 10 May 1916; the day before what would have been his 26th birthday.[58] Another body was also found under the basement floor, that of James Healy, an employee of the Jameson distillery. He had no connection with the pub and was last seen trying to make his way to work. It was the discovery of these two bodies that put pressure on the British Government to establish an inquiry into what happened on that street during Easter Week 1916.

Rosanna Knowles, who was a neighbour of O'Rourke's on North King Street, told the inquiry how one of the British sergeants had discussed Paddy's death with her on the day. She stated:

> This soldier told me; 'I only felt sorry for the poor fellows at the corner [O'Rourke's pub] … I pitied him from my heart though I had to shoot him'. He said that he brought him downstairs [but] he had not the heart to shoot him straight and they told him to go [back] up the stairs and they let bang at him [shot him] from the foot of the stairs.[59]

Paddy Bealin was brought home to Castlecomer for burial and his remains lie in Castlecomer cemetery. A plaque was unveiled in Paddy's memory at Castlecomer courthouse on the centenary of his death in 2016.[60]

Kilkenny Men in the Thick of the Action: Dick Healy, Jack O'Shea, William Phelan, John Brennan and Patrick Whelan

As stated, thirty-three men were arrested in Kilkenny after the Rising, but there were at least five additional Kilkenny natives who were fighting in the thick of the action during Easter Week.

Richard 'Dick' Healy (1894–1982)

Dick Healy left his native Kilcollan in the parish of Conahy in 1910 to work in his uncle John Healy's shop and public house at 93–94 Great Britain Street (now Parnell Street), Dublin. His uncle was a member of the IRB and Healy's premises also neighboured Tom Clarke's shop – Clarke being one of the leaders of the 1916 Rebellion. Likely influenced by his uncle, along with the array of cultural organisations in Dublin at this time, Dick joined the Irish Volunteers from its inception in 1913. He was a member of D Company, 2nd Dublin Battalion, known as the 'Grocers Company' as most of its members were employed in the merchant trades and so had similar business hours which facilitated the arranging of training. This Battalion, led by Thomas MacDonagh, was based around the Jacob's Biscuit Factory during Easter Week. However, 22-year-old Dick Healy arrived late on Easter Monday and was instead assigned to the GPO area. He spent a large part of the week on the east side of O'Connell Street in the Hibernian Bank and Reis buildings, sniping in the direction of Trinity College.[61] He was present at the death of his Captain, Thomas Weafer, on the Wednesday of the Rebellion week. Dick, along with his comrades, retreated to the GPO on the following day. Tom Clarke personally appointed him in charge of the topmost section of the GPO on the penultimate day of the Rising, probably because he was acquainted with Dick through his uncle and the fact that Dick was in Irish Volunteer uniform, something many combatants could not afford.[62] The GPO garrison, including Dick, evacuated the building on Friday evening due to widespread fires, and moved to nearby Moore Street. A surrender was initiated the following day and Dick and his comrades were arrested. They spent the first night of their detention in the Rotunda Hospital gardens, now the Garden of Remembrance, which was very close to his home. Dick spent time in Knutsford Prison and Frongoch internment camp, before being released in September 1916. He re-joined his old Battalion and participated in the War of Independence in Dublin.[63]

Jack O'Shea (1898–1973)

Jack O'Shea from Knocktopher followed a similar path. He was born in the townland of Tullow (formerly known as Blackditch), into a family of eventually ten children.[64] He moved to Dublin in 1915 and gained employment as a hospital porter in the Royal Hospital on Upper Baggot Street, where he also resided. During the same year he joined B Company, 3rd Dublin Battalion Irish Volunteers. He was, in fact, working in the hospital when the Rebellion broke out on Easter Monday as he had not received a message to mobilise. During the afternoon a group of retired British soldiers, who were part of an Army Training Corps known as the Georgius Rex Brigade, were attacked by O'Shea's battalion on nearby Mount Street. As the hospital porter, he received the telephone calls requesting assistance. O'Shea, who was still shy of his 18th birthday, left his post to join in the Rebellion. He decided it was too dangerous to link up with his own Battalion and instead travelled to St Stephen's Green. It was there he fought during Easter Week, not with the Irish Volunteers, but with the Irish Citizen Army under the command of Michael Mallin. He was arrested following the surrender of the garrison at the Royal College of Surgeons on Sunday, 30 April 1916 and incarcerated in Richmond Barracks. When he left the hospital in haste on the first day of the Rising, he accidently took the key of the hospital mortuary with him. This had caused a great deal of trouble at the hospital as they eventually had to smash the door of the mortuary in.

After the Rising, a British soldier brought O'Shea – including the missing key – from his place of detention to the hospital, with the view of releasing him because of his youth. However, the hospital matron stated that Jack was 'in the movement' and so was rearrested.[65] He was jailed in England and later Frongoch from where he was released in August 1916. Suffice to say his position in the hospital was no longer open to him. O'Shea did not take an active part in the War of Independence or the Civil War. In addition to living in Dublin, he also spent periods of his life in Counties Tipperary, Donegal and Mayo. He passed away in Manchester in 1973 but was interred in his native Knocktopher.[66] O'Shea suffered the misfortune of losing his right hand in a sawmill accident in 1919, which greatly limited his ability of finding employment in later life and providing for his family of five. In 1935, frustrated at the amount of bureaucracy involved in the application process for his military pension, he wrote a compelling letter to the Pension Board referees stating: 'I am just one of those forgotten heroes, who have not the wit to secure a cushy job or the push to help himself in anyway. & in my own small way I played my part as unselfishly as any man.'[67] It took over ten years for Jack O'Shea to be finally approved for a military pension. His local community in Knocktopher did not forget him during the centenary commemorations of the Rising, unveiling a new plaque at his grave in October 2016.[68]

William O'Brien Phelan (1889–1971)

William O'Brien Phelan was born in Bishop's Hill in Kilkenny City.[69] He was given the middle name 'O'Brien' presumably in tribute to William Smith-O'Brien the nationalist hero and leader of the 1848 Rebellion.[70] William lost both parents at a young age. His father Thomas died at the age of 57 in 1897 from 'acute gastritis'. Just two years later, at the age of 10, William was orphaned when his mother Margaret (née Kirwan) died aged 54, from 'acute congestion of the liver'.[71] In 1911, when he was 21 years old, William was living with his four older brothers in the family home on Bishop's Hill. He was employed locally as a harness maker.[72] In 1915 he moved to Dublin and continued the same profession in Box & Co. Harness Makers on Dame Street. He joined the Irish Volunteers and was a member of the Commandant Éamonn Ceannt's 4th Dublin Battalion. He fought throughout Easter Week under the command of Con Colbert in outposts of the South Dublin Union, chiefly in the vicinity of the Jameson and Marrowbone Lane distilleries. On Sunday 30 April he stated that he left the post 'with some others to have something to eat'. When they returned they found the garrison had surrendered and so they decided to leave to avoid capture. He spent a number of weeks with his brother in Monasterevin and avoided arrest.[73] Another of his brothers, Michael Phelan, was very active in Kilkenny during the War of Independence.

For a man christened 'William O Brien', perhaps he was destined to be a revolutionary like his namesake. However, his story has been somewhat forgotten locally; perhaps because he was not arrested after the Rising, or possibly because from 1920, just like his namesake after an earlier rebellion, he emigrated to Australia. He spent the remainder of his life in Ayr, Queensland, raising a family of eight and passed away in 1971.[74]

Corporal John Brennan

There is even less known about one Kilkenny fatality of Easter Week, undoubtedly because this story was on the 'wrong side' of the historical narrative of 1916. John Brennan, a native of Gowran, was a Corporal in the 3rd (Special Reserve) Battalion of the Royal Irish Regiment. His Company was stationed in Richmond Barracks in the west of Dublin when the Rebellion broke out on Easter Monday, 24 April 1916. Unfortunately for Brennan and his comrades, they had not been permitted to travel to the Fairyhouse Races that day, unlike the majority of the other soldiers. They therefore made up the minimal garrison in the barracks and passed the morning of Easter Monday listening to one of the army bands. Brennan's unit was one of the first into action on the opening day of the Rising when they were ordered to attack the 4th Battalion Irish Volunteers who had seized the nearby South Dublin Union Hospital (now St James's Hospital). Brennan was killed in a ferocious gun battle in the early afternoon as his Company attempted to gain control of parts of the hospital complex. Brennan was one of the earliest fatalities of the 1916 Rebellion. Although his comrades took control of parts of the hospital, they were ordered by their superiors to retreat during the night; Brennan's death had been in vain.[75] He was later buried in Grangegorman Military Cemetery in Dublin.[76]

Although the Rising pitted Irishmen in the British Army against their fellow countrymen in the Irish Volunteers, most were not overly conflicted by the scenario. The foes of the Irish Volunteers were anyone in a British uniform, irrespective of nationality. Similarly for the British soldiers, they were attacking rebels who were committing treason during a time of war. They all had one thing in common however – both sides followed the orders of their commanders, as all soldiers vow to do. In a strange twist of fate, the section of

Irish Volunteers Brennan had been attacking was led by a man named William T. Cosgrave. Cosgrave would go on to represent Brennan's native Kilkenny as a TD in the years that followed.

Patrick Whelan (1878–1916)

Patrick Whelan (sometimes recorded as 'Phelan') was from Whiteswall in the parish of Galmoy, close to the Laois border. He joined the RIC at the age of 27 and was stationed in Galway City. He became the only fatality in the west of Ireland as a result of the fighting of Easter week. County Galway had the largest mustering of Irish Volunteers outside of Dublin during the uprising, led by their commandant Liam Mellows. In the early hours of Wednesday of Easter week, 26 April, a mixture of military and police – including Whelan – were sent from Galway City on a reconnaissance mission. Reports had reached the Crown Forces that the Irish Volunteers had attacked a number of RIC barracks in the east of the county. After moving about nine kilometres from the city, at approximately 5.00 am, they came upon a group of Irish Volunteers from the Castlegar and Claregalway companies, who were resting behind a wall at Carnmore Cross. A gun battle broke out, during which Constable Whelan was shot in the head and neck. He died ten minutes later from his injuries. He was 38 years old.

Whelan was mourned by his parents in Galmoy, Patrick senior and Margaret. Both were over 70 years of age, but they had been divorced for a number of years (although they were Roman Catholic, civil law permitted divorce at this time under British law). Patrick Whelan was also engaged to be married at the time of his death. His killing was very unpopular. His funeral and burial in Bohermore Cemetery in Galway was attended by thousands of people. Following his funeral, the *Connacht Tribune* newspaper remarked; 'he was especially popular with the children around the City [of Galway] to whom he frequently dispensed pennies and even their young minds have felt the sorrow which has been brought about by his untimely and tragic end'.

The Friar and the Fireman of 1916: Thomas (Fr Albert) Bibby and Captain Thomas Purcell

Thomas Bibby (1877–1925) was born in Bagnelstown, County Carlow and was raised in Kilkenny City where his parents owned drapery shops on Parliament Street and High Street. He became Brother Albert Bibby when ordained into the Capuchin Order in 1902. He was a fluent Irish speaker and was involved in the Gaelic League. During Easter 1916 his friary was thrust into the centre of the Rebellion as the 1st Battalion Dublin Volunteers took command of the street and the surrounding areas near Dublin's Four Courts. During subsequent weeks, Fr Albert and his Brothers found themselves placed at the epicentre of recent Irish history when they attended the spiritual needs of the men facing execution in Kilmainham Jail.[77] Fr Albert visited Michael Mallin and Con Colbert prior to their executions. He was also present at the executions of Seán Heuston and Michael O'Hanrahan, anointing their remains immediately after execution.

In the years that followed, Father Albert was sympathetic to the republican cause and was arrested by the British military following a raid on the Church Street friary during the War of Independence, but released soon afterwards. He was also present in the Four Courts when the Civil War commenced in June 1922, attending to the needs of the anti-Treaty Republicans. Father Albert's close relationship with the anti-Treaty side caused disquiet among some of his superiors and the new Free State Government. He was subsequently transferred to Cork by his Order but was denied 'exercising diocesan faculties' in the district.[78] This was probably the main factor in his transfer to a friary in California where he subsequently died in 1925, aged 48 years. His remains, along with another Brother, Father Dominic, were repatriated to Ireland in June 1958. After a large public funeral and ceremony they were laid to rest near the Capuchin Friary in Rochestown, just outside Cork City.[79]

The Chief of the Dublin Fire Brigade during the 1916 Rising was also a Kilkenny native; Captain Thomas Purcell (1851–1943). Purcell trained as a civil engineer and was also a member of Kilkenny City Volunteer Fire Brigade. He was awarded a silver medal from the Royal Society for the Protection of Life in London for saving the life of a woman from a fire at Hennessey's Drapers on High Street before Christmas 1875. He married Margaret Phelan of Oldtown, Ballyragget and they had three sons, with only one child, Pierce – later Professor of Civil Engineering at University College Dublin (UCD) – surviving infancy.[80] Thomas Purcell became chief of the Dublin Fire Brigade in 1892. He was a man ahead of his time. He travelled extensively in Europe and the United States studying the different fire-fighting technologies. Utilising his engineering background, he designed and built specialist vehicles needed for his brigade, most notably the horse-drawn turntable ladder and later, the motor fire engine in 1909.

For a man who had spent most of his working life studying and advancing fire-fighting technology, the sight of Dublin city centre burning during

Easter Week must have been his worst nightmare. Purcell had removed his fire-fighters from the more dangerous parts of the city early in the week for their own safety. The fires were started by looters and from the heavy shelling initiated by the British military. Purcell's team were mobilised into action almost immediately after the ceasefire was agreed between Brigade-General Lowe and Patrick Pearse. Purcell had two main objectives; to save the Pro-Cathedral close to O'Connell Street, and to save Jervis Street Hospital towards the end of Henry Street. His men had achieved that objective by the following morning, Sunday, 30 April 1916, with all major fires contained.[81]

Purcell received a £50 bonus for his work during Easter Week and retired following an accident with a horse in 1917. He lived to his 93rd year – decades beyond life expectancy for men at this time – and he was buried in Deansgrange Cemetery in Dublin under a Kilkenny limestone headstone made from his own design.[82]

Affected in a Myriad of Ways

A number of Kilkenny people were affected in different ways by the 1916 Rising. George Smithwick from Ballylinch, Thomastown, was attending the Fairyhouse Races on Easter Monday. Smithwick, who was a member of the famous brewing dynasty of the same name, was returning that evening to the Shelbourne Hotel when his taxi cab came under fire in St Stephen's Green. A lady who was in his company was wounded in the crossfire and required treatment by a local surgeon.[83]

In a less serious way, the burning down of the famous Hopkins and Hopkins Jewellers – located on the corner of O'Connell Street and Eden Quay – resulted in seven Kilkenny people claiming compensation for the loss of their jewellery, which was being repaired. Patrick T. Kelly and his wife from 1–2 Market Street, Thomastown, claimed £16 for the loss of a 'gent's massive gold chain with gold locket pendant', 'a lady's gold brooch set' and 'a gents silver watch'. He was eventually awarded £12.[84] This would have been several weeks' salary for the average farm labourer at the time. The Reverend James McCaffrey, from the Carmelite Priory in Knocktopher, claimed £3,10s for the loss of a 'silver watch'. He stated; 'the watch was a valued one, being a present, and though I cannot say what was the exact cost price, I consider the stated amount to be the minimum'. He was awarded £2,10s.[85] Others who lost valuables in Hopkins Jewellers included Norah Delaney, Freshford (claimed £1, awarded £1), Margaret Kealy, Kilcreene Villa (claimed £5, awarded £4), Julia O'Donnell, Bramblestown, Gowran (claimed 10s, awarded 10s), Margaret Byrne, Kilderry (claimed 10s, awarded 10s) and Gertrude Lowry, Bennettsbridge (claimed £5, awarded £4).[86]

Richard Woodlock residing at Bridge Street, Ballyragget was employed at Murphy's public house at 42 Henry Street, Dublin, a building burnt down during the Rebellion. Aside from losing his job, Richard also applied for compensation of £13,6s,9d for the loss of his personal belongings including; '1 best suit, 2 work suits, 2 aprons, half dozen collars, 2 pairs of boots, 1 razor' and a 'prayer book & beads'. He was awarded £9.[87] The garments of another Ballyragget resident received a much higher award. Major-General Sir Lawrence Dowdall of The Grange, Ballyragget, lost his 'uniform and decorations [medals]' when Scott and Co. Military Tailors, 2 Upper O'Connell Street Dublin, was destroyed, somewhat ironically, as a result of fires caused by his own army's shelling. Sir Lawrence was awarded his claim in full; £48, 9s, 8d.[88]

The events in Dublin during Easter Week 1916 caused much annoyance for a number of Kilkenny cooperative creameries. A consignment of butter sent from Glenmore Cooperative Creamery, destined for Belfast, was stalled at Amiens Street Station (now Connolly Station) on Easter Monday. Nine of the sixteen boxes of butter were looted from the station during the week. Glenmore Cooperative received compensation of £35, 2s, 0d for the missing butter.[89] Four other Kilkenny creameries, whose consignments were held up in Kingsbridge Station (now Heuston Station), were not so fortunate. Boxes of their butter, destined for the Dublin market, were sold by the Great Southern and Western Railway Company to the military authorities to 'prevent it from melting or going bad' in the unseasonably warm weather. However, the price paid was below the stated wholesale price set by the creameries. Much of the excess butter was then sold on by the military authorities to traders in Dublin who then sold it to the public at inflated price as supplies were low throughout the city. The railway company refused to give compensation for the full price stipulated by the creameries, while the Government compensation board (known as the Property Losses Ireland Committee) declined to reimburse the creameries, as technically the butter was not 'destroyed by fire or looting'. The Kilkenny creameries whose compensation claims were rejected by the board included; Tullaroan £27, 9s, 6d, Callan £11, Windgap £40 and Bennettsbridge £44.[90]

CHAPTER 3

By-Elections and the 'Big Flu': Brewing up a Storm (1917–1918)

'I was very glad to hear from Josie that you escaped the Influenza,
it is a dreadful disease and leaves such a weakness after it.'

Resembling most of southern Ireland after the Rising, the pendulum now swung firmly in favour of the Sinn Féin movement. The term 'Sinn Féiner' was a label used generally to denote anybody who was considered an 'advanced nationalist'. It was a catch-all term which referred not only to supporters of the political wing of the organisation, but often to those who were interested in a broad spectrum of Irish interests, including music, art, fashion and language. The sparks of revolution initiated by the Easter Rebellion of 1916 ignited during 1917 and spread like a gorse fire throughout the country. Kilkenny was one of the counties to the forefront of this movement, mainly because of the by-election held for the Kilkenny City constituency in August 1917. This was won by Sinn Féin, who, by the end of 1917, had consolidated many of the different strands of advanced nationalism under one political party umbrella. Nationally, the statistics regarding the number of Sinn Féin clubs tells its own story; they soared from 166 in the spring of 1917 to 1,200 by October 1917, with a membership of 250,000.[1] As historian Michael Laffan remarked; 'Sinn Féin was … the craze of 1917.'[2] County Kilkenny was no exception.

In Callan, an influential young priest, Rev. Father Patrick H. Delahunty (1880–1955), founded a Sinn Féin club, while simultaneously re-establishing an Irish Volunteers company. He had been heavily involved in the National Volunteer movement but became more radical in the aftermath of the 1916 Rebellion. Fr Delahunty, who was originally from Curraghmartin, Mooncoin, became regarded by many as the validating public face of the reinvigorated Sinn Féin movement locally. His brushes with the law – which included a warning from the RIC after he sang 'treasonous' songs about the executed Easter rebels at a New Year's Day concert in 1917 – merely added to his appeal.[3] As he made numerous public speeches during this period, Fr Delahunty became the chief protagonist in spreading the Sinn Féin gospel throughout south Kilkenny. He was aided and abetted by his friend and fellow priest, Father Thomas Henneberry, who was a curate in nearby Dunnamaggin. Delahunty also used his friendship with Michael Collins to purchase arms for the local Callan Volunteer Company from Volunteer GHQ.[4] Referring to Fr Delahunty in 1916, one local RIC sergeant reported that he saw:

> [Volunteers] digging a trench on the Fair Green at Callan and firing volleys in the air [while drilling]. They were led by Father Delahunty C.C. and I am informed, proclaimed their sympathy for John [Eoin] McNeill [Irish Volunteers] as opposed to Mr John Redmond [National Volunteers]. I have fully reported the incident and the steps I was able to take which apparently checked the zeal of the Rev.[5]

The 'zeal' of the said Fr Delahunty was not 'checked' for long however, as within the year he became President of the South Kilkenny Executive of Sinn Féin.[6] In addition, through Fr Delahunty's diplomacy, the National Volunteers in Callan disbanded and linked up with the local Irish Volunteers. They brought with them their equipment, including twenty-four Martini-Enfield rifles and ammunition.[7] Fr Delahunty's Superior, Dr Brownrigg, Bishop of Ossory, was not enamoured with his curate's ever-expanding role in an increasing separatist movement. Some years later it resulted in the Bishop prohibiting Fr Delahunty from performing his pastoral duties after he was arrested by the RIC during the War of Independence for the possession of 'seditious literature' in September 1920.

The GAA clubs also played their part in the aftermath of the Rising. They became involved in arranging hurling tournaments, allowing for the collection of funds at matches for the Irish National Aid and Volunteers Dependent Fund (INAVDF). This charity was established in the aftermath of the Rising to raise money for the families of those who died, were imprisoned, or lost their jobs because of the Rising.[8] It was chiefly women from local Cumann na mBan Companies who organised and collected the funds. In addition to GAA matches, variety concerts were also staged to raise money. By the end of 1917 the Kilkenny INAVDF had raised £1,500.[9]

The growing negative attitude towards British authorities – and equally the ongoing war effort – was becoming increasingly apparent as 1917 progressed. After the death of Willie Redmond MP – the brother of John Redmond – during the Battle of Messines in Belgium, Councillor Fogarty of Castlecomer Board of Guardians tabled a motion of sympathy for Redmond and his family.

The chairman, Councillor O'Brennan, spoke against the resolution asking the question; 'how many fellows from your own district died on the field of battle and you didn't pass a vote of sympathy with their people. Why should we make any distinction because he died?' Annie Laracy, a rare example of a female councillor – as women had been permitted to sit on Boards of Guardians twenty years earlier – agreed with the sentiments expressed; 'he died for England. I don't see why we should pass a vote of sympathy.' The motion of sympathy was rejected by six votes to five.[10]

In April 1917 three local Kilkenny volunteers, James Lalor, Pat Corcoran and Martin Kealy, attended a meeting in Dublin at which Michael Collins and Cathal Brugha spoke. The aim of the gathering was the reorganisation of the Irish Volunteer movement.[11] The following month, a meeting was called in Kilkenny City with the same purpose of restructuring the Irish Volunteers throughout the county. Three battalions were initially formed, roughly dividing the county into north, south and Kilkenny City. The Callan area later formed its own battalion. The Kilkenny Brigade was further divided in the following years to initially become seven battalions, which later increased to nine. Members of the original Kilkenny City Volunteers travelled around the county to organise the new battalions, with the aim of creating leadership and communication networks.[12] The Kilkenny City Volunteers took the leadership roles in the brigade, most likely due to their association with the movement since its origins in the county and their connections with GHQ in Dublin. Thomas Treacy became the first Brigade O/C (Commandant), James Lalor became Brigade Vice-O/C, Ned Comerford was Quartermaster, and Leo Dardis was Adjutant.[13]

Kilkenny City By-Election: August 1917

The establishment of Sinn Féin clubs and the reorganisation of the Volunteers arrived just in time for a by-election in the Kilkenny City constituency in August 1917, caused by the death of the sitting MP Patrick O'Brien who was a member of the IPP and an Offaly native.[14] At the time, Kilkenny City was the smallest constituency, not just in Ireland, but was also the smallest constituency for a House of Commons seat in the United Kingdom. There had been no election in the constituency since 1896, over twenty-two years previously, as the sitting MP was always returned unopposed.[15] The size of the electorate was small; around 1,700.[16] The majority of males were not allowed to vote as only men who owned or rented property/land above a certain value could vote. No women were permitted to vote either. Sinn Féin affiliated candidates had won three by-elections already that year. However, this was the first official candidate for the party and the first urban area Sinn Féin had contested. At the time, it was unclear how much support Sinn Féin had in urban areas.[17] William Thomas (W.T.) Cosgrave was chosen as the Sinn Féin candidate to contest the election. Cosgrave's connection with the constituency 'began and ended by accident … he had no Kilkenny links'. He was, however, a 'city man' having been born in Dublin.[18] His 1916 Rebellion credentials, which were evoked often during the campaign, appeared to be the main reasons for his selection. Cosgrave had participated in the fight in the South Dublin Union and subsequently received a death sentence, which was later commuted to penal servitude.

Cosgrave had the 'legendary political organiser' Dan McCarthy managing his campaign, along with the support of the *Kilkenny Journal* newspaper.[19] The *Kilkenny People* was suppressed by the military censor at the beginning of the campaign in July 1917. It is probable the authorities believed a pre-emptive strike on Keane's newspaper would dent the chances of the Sinn Féin candidate.[20] The newspaper remained suppressed for over three months. A notable aspect of the by-election campaign was the widespread interest throughout the country. Editorials were written in the *Ulster Herald*, the *Meath Chronicle*, the *Skibbereen Eagle* and the *Kerryman,* to name but a few. The death of the sitting Kilkenny City MP on 12 July 1917 had occurred just a day after Éamon de Valera was proclaimed the winner in the East Clare by-election. The eyes of the media were focused on Kilkenny to discover if this winning streak could continue. A number of Kilkenny volunteers had been in Clare assisting in the lead-up to that election. They, as well as the Sinn Féin movement in general, were by this stage becoming adept at running election campaigns.

Cosgrave's campaign was launched with a great publicity coup with the investiture of Countess Markievicz with the Freedom of Kilkenny City on 19 July 1917. Éamon de Valera and Eoin MacNeill also made speeches during the campaign.[21] Cosgrave attended a number of Gaelic League Irish classes in Kilkenny during this period to improve his competency in the language with the aim of opening his speeches in the native tongue.[22] The opposing Irish Party candidate, or as he was referred to, 'the anti-Sinn Féin candidate', was John 'Jack' Magennis.[23] He was a nationalist and had been Mayor of Kilkenny on eight occasions, including serving three terms between 1914 and 1916. His campaign focused on the successes of the previous IPP candidate, along with the fact that he would actually take his seat in the House of Commons, unlike Cosgrave who followed the Sinn Féin abstentionist policy. One of his main campaign slogans was 'Kilkenny for a Kilkenny man', an obvious jeer at Cosgrave's non-Kilkenny pedigree.[24]

On polling day, Friday 10 August, an *Irish Times* reporter 'could not fail but notice' the 'business method of the Sinn Féiners' where 'they brought up their supporters in motor cars and conveyed them back to their homes with wonderful regularity'. One Sinn Féin enthusiast, who was registered to vote in Kilkenny City, travelled from Donegal, while another came from Yorkshire. The same journalist also stated that he saw no aggression or intimidation with 'nothing more harmful than occasional shouts of "Up Cosgrave"'.[25] After the polls closed, local Irish Volunteers members guarded the premises where the ballot boxes were located overnight, for fear the boxes would be tampered with.[26]

The result was a resounding victory for Cosgrave on a poll of 772 votes to 392. The near double majority was higher than expectations.[27] Evidently disappointed with his defeat, Magennis called the result 'a victory for intolerance, low, mean, lying and scurrilous abuse, intimidation of the grossest type'.[28] The rejoicing that followed Cosgrave's victory, not just in Kilkenny, but countrywide, was unprecedented for a Kilkenny election. In Listowel, the 'town was ablaze' with 'lighted tar barrels', while in the midlands 'a number of women were bound to [the] peace for disorderly conduct in Athlone in connection with the celebrations after the Kilkenny election'. There were 'scenes of jubilation' in Waterville and republican flags were flown in Baltimore.[29] There was a parade in Derry, bonfires blazed in west Donegal, while in Kiltyclogher, County Leitrim – the home parish of Seán MacDiarmada – a torch light procession took place.[30] The publicity garnered from the election campaign was very beneficial to the local Volunteer movement, with many new recruits and the formation of Companies in districts where it had not existed previously.[31]

Conscription, Flu and More Elections: 1918

The experience of the Kilkenny Volunteers in the by-election was put to further use when another by-election was called in the Waterford City constituency in March 1918, following the unexpected death of John Redmond. About forty members of the Kilkenny Volunteers took part in the election campaign in Waterford, with their main responsibility being the protection of Sinn Féin meetings from attacks from IPP supporters. If the Kilkenny by-election was noted for its peaceful electioneering, the Waterford by-election was the polar opposite, with two Kilkenny Volunteers actually requiring a stay in hospital following one altercation. Thomas Treacy, who was in charge of the Kilkenny group, later commented that it 'was probably the hottest and roughest election of modern times'.[32] The Kilkenny Volunteers clashed with IPP followers outside the City in Sallypark. Fights broke out daily in the run-up to the election, while on polling day itself, shots were fired between the opposing sides.[33]

If 1917 could be classed as the 'year of the Sinn Féin clubs', due to their rapid formation throughout the county, 1918 could be regarded as 'the year of the Irish Volunteers'. The reason for the upsurge in Volunteer membership was as a consequence of what became known as the 'Conscription Crisis'. By April 1918, as victory for the allied forces in the First World War looked far from assured, it was decided by the British Government to extend the military draft to Ireland which would conscript all men between the ages of 18 and 41 into the British Army (conscription had been in place in Britain since 1916). The threat of conscription had the effect of uniting Sinn Féin, the Irish Parliamentary Party, the trade-unions and the clergy, under one banner. The membership of the Irish Volunteers in Kilkenny City quadrupled in the month of April alone, in protest against the proposed forced enlistment. The volunteer companies throughout the county experienced a similar uptake, where 'new Companies sprang up mushroom like'.[34] In total, the number of Irish Volunteers in Kilkenny increased from approximately 700 before the conscription crisis in April 1918, to around 3,500 by the summer of 1918. Instructions were issued by Volunteer leaders for guerrilla tactics if the British military tried to enforce conscription. During the month of April, anti-conscription meetings were held all over the county, including a monster meeting on The Parade in Kilkenny.[35] In addition, an estimated 5,000 people attended an anti-conscription meeting at The Square, in Castlecomer, on Sunday, 28 April 1918.[36] In Graiguenamanagh, local volunteers were assigned to collect signatures for the anti-conscription pledge, a form of petition. It was a similar story in Thomastown where 'practically all the men in the parish ... have taken the anti-conscription pledge'. The boarders of Saint Kieran's College in Kilkenny City were allowed to return home 'to make their own arrangements [to oppose conscription]', with many joining their local Volunteer company.[37] In June, some 1,500 women proceeded from the Callan Road to the Dominican Black Abbey in Kilkenny City while reciting the rosary, before signing the anti-conscription pledge at City Hall.[38]

At the peak of the Conscription Crisis, the North Kilkenny Irish Volunteer Battalion held a large 'manoeuvre' on Sunday, 12 May 1918. All Companies converged at The Swan, a part of Laois in the Kilkenny Brigade. There was a large mustering of 393 men and they were directed by their Battalion O/C George O'Dwyer, along with the nine individual company captains. All the companies then 'fell in' and marched to Clogh Church, in the far north-east of Kilkenny, where they attended 12.00 pm Mass. A separate Mass had to be held for some of the local parishioners in a nearby school, such was the overcrowding in the church. Afterwards, the men moved to a large field in The Swan which was known as 'the Camp' for the day. At their ad-hoc training camp, the Volunteers engaged in 'manoeuvres and sham battles'. They were dismissed after 6.00 pm and each Company trooped home separately while singing marching tunes such as *The Soldiers Song*. Most had marched a total distance of 30 km or more.[39]

Although conscription had 'brought new life and energy' to the Volunteer movement, many of the new recruits simply faded away once the threat had passed (the British Government decided not to enforce compulsory enlistment due to the turmoil it would cause and the fact the situation was improving for the Allies on the Western Front).[40] Simon O'Leary, Captain of the Paulstown Company, described the situation in his unit: 'About 1918, there was a terrible [big] crowd. There were 90 men the time of the conscription scare. They dwindled to 25 or 30, I think, – the active lads who would do the work for you.'[41] The crisis galvanised support for Sinn Féin and its then separatist/ republican agenda. For many, the threat of conscription was the final straw in any support they had for the Irish Parliamentary Party – their allegiance now lay with Sinn Féin.

On 18 May, there was a major round-up of leading Sinn Féin and Irish Volunteer members in Kilkenny under what became known as the 'German plot arrests'. This occurred throughout Ireland when Sinn Féin members were arrested and interned in response to an alleged conspiracy involving Germany, which was later found to be false and invented by the British administration in Dublin Castle. Peter DeLoughry and notably the sitting MP W.T. Cosgrave, were arrested and sent to prisons in England. The authorities also became severe in their hostility towards Irish Volunteer drilling in the county. For instance, at Castlecomer in July 1918, John Fleming and Martin Delaney were charged with 'illegal drilling and unlawful assembly' and sent to prison for two months.[42] In the same month, similar arrests for prohibited drilling took place in Graiguenamanagh in the east of the county. One Volunteer sounded the church bell when the raids were taking place which allowed many in the area to escape arrest. A baton charge by the RIC on crowds at Thomastown courthouse protesting against some of these arrests caused a great deal of bitterness towards the police in the area.[43] In October 1918, District Inspector Moylan recommended charging 16-year-old Patrick Holden of Callan for defacing a British Army recruitment poster, although he admitted that there was little chance of Holden being found guilty as 'the local justices at Callan [Petty Sessions] are more or less in sympathy with S.F. [Sinn Féin]'.[44]

The year 1918 ended with a general election just before Christmas. It was the first to be held in eight years due to the First World War, which eventually came to an end in November. It was the first general election where all males over 21 years of age were entitled to vote. It was also the first general election to include female voters – once they were over 30 years old and met certain property requirements (or had a university degree). This had the effect of trebling the electorate nationally.[45]

The Kilkenny North constituency, which now included the former 'Kilkenny City' constituency, elected W.T. Cosgrave unopposed. Cosgrave's success was considered to be even more of a sure bet than in the previous year's election – considering he was now incarcerated in an English prison. Thus, nobody ran against him. Therefore, all the attention on the election was focused on the Kilkenny South constituency which had just two candidates in the race in a 'first-past-the-post' voting system. These were the sitting MP Matthew Keating for the Irish Parliamentary Party (IPP) and James O'Mara, a Limerick businessman, for Sinn Féin. O'Mara had some public recognition as he was previously an IPP MP for another constituency until he resigned in 1907.[46]

O'Mara suffered a setback when the Bishop of Ossory published a letter in a local newspaper supporting the IPP candidate. Sinn Féin countered this by arranging a meeting which was addressed by Father Michael O'Flanagan, Vice President of the Sinn Féin National Executive, at which a letter of support from Dr Fogarty, Bishop of Killaloe, was read out.[47]

The election was held on 14 December 1918 but votes were not counted until 28 December because of the Christmas season and to allow time for the return of ballots from British soldiers based outside the country. The ballot boxes were kept in a 'sealed room' in Kilkenny City courthouse with an armed guard on duty at all times. Members of Sinn Féin also kept watch on this room for the two-week period, day and night, to confirm that no interference of the ballot boxes occurred. The result, on a turnout of 62 per cent, was a resounding victory for the Sinn Féin candidate O'Mara, gaining four times the vote of his opponent, with a poll of 8,685 to Keating's 1,855. For the IPP candidate, the margin of defeat must have come as a shock. Just two years previously he had visited the Kilkenny men imprisoned in England after the 1916 Rebellion, bringing them 'a large parcel of fruit, cigarettes and sweets'.[48] Now these 'felons', as they were often called, were largely responsible for the loss of his parliamentary seat.

The night the result was announced there was a torch-lit procession in Kilkenny City and the 'Sinn Féin flag [Irish Tricolour] was hoisted on the City Hall'.[49] Sinn Féin doubtlessly were confident of a victory in South Kilkenny as in the closing stages of the campaign the local director of elections received instructions to send all available spokespeople, money and transport, to County Laois for Kevin O'Higgins's election campaign there.[50]

The excitement of the election was tempered by the 'great flu' that swept through Ireland during the winter of 1918–19. The flu struck in three waves. The second wave, which hit from October 1918 to January 1919, was the most 'pervasive in its spread and gruelling in its length'. Kilkenny City was badly hit and registered the third highest proportion of flu deaths of any town in Ireland in 1918.[51] It is thought Kilkenny bore the brunt of this second wave because it had suffered little from the first wave, thus immunity amongst the populace would have been very low. The flu strain was unusual in that it was most lethal in strong and healthy adults, particularly those between the ages of 20 and 40. This was because in healthy hosts the disease could incubate and establish itself more vigorously.[52] On 2 November, the *Kilkenny People* described the ferocity and impact of the flu:

> The influenza epidemic made its appearance in Kilkenny about 10 days ago. At first it contained itself to the younger people but after a few days it claimed old as well. The death rate in Kilkenny is increasing daily. There is scarcely a family in the city that has not been touched by this disease … Several business premises have been shut for a week. All the streets of the city have been washed with carbolic acid.[53]

Kilkenny Battalion commander Thomas Treacy also mentioned the epidemic: 'What was known as the big flu was raging in the country. Many died. The daily funerals of young and old were numerous. There was practically no Volunteer work done while the epidemic lasted.'[54] Therefore, on the eve of the War of Independence in Kilkenny, there were many preoccupations on the minds of the local populace. The struggle for independence was perhaps not the primary concern for most.

The following letter, sent at Christmas 1918, between two former classmates, one now a nun, the other a farmer's wife in Dunnamaggin, highlights that a war for independence was not something they thought was imminent, or possibly, did not want to consider:

Convent of Our Lady of Mercy
St Mary's – Callan – Co Kilkenny
23rd December [19]18

My dearest Kattie,

Thanks very much for your good wishes for Xmas, which I heartily reciprocate.
I hope you and all your dear ones will spend a very happy Xmas and bright
and happy new year.

T.G. [Thank God] there is peace in the world after the horrors of the past four
years [First World War]. I was very glad to hear from Josie that you escaped
the Influenza, it is a dreadful disease and leaves such a weakness after it. I
enclose a few cards for the children. Fondest love and renewed good wishes
my dearest Kattie,

Yours sincerely in J.C. [Jesus Christ]

Sr. M. Bernard [55]

CHAPTER 4

War of Independence Part 1 (January 1919–December 1920)

'Kathleen Ní Houlihan is very different now to the woman who used to play the harp an' sing, "Weep on, weep on, your hour is past", for she's a ragin' divil now, an if you only look crooked at her you're sure of a punch in th' eye.'[1]

– Seamus Shields in *The Shadow of a Gunman* by Seán O'Casey

In March 1920, Hugginstown in County Kilkenny was the scene of an RIC Barracks attack, which was only the third IRA capture of a barracks up to then in Ireland. It was also the first successful RIC Barracks surrender recorded in Leinster.[2] However, from such an auspicious start, the remainder of the campaign in Kilkenny did not continue in such a vein.

In terms of the military structure, County Kilkenny had just one Brigade, made up of nine Battalions, which were further divided into Companies (the Kilkenny Brigade was made up of over sixty Companies). The Brigade essentially encompassed the entire county with a small number of additional Companies from just inside the bordering counties of Tipperary, Laois and Carlow – most notably Mullinahone Company in County Tipperary which was part of the 7th Kilkenny IRA Battalion.[3] The only area of County Kilkenny that was not part of the Kilkenny Brigade was Ferrybank in the far south, which overlooked Waterford City. The 8th and 9th Battalions were the last to be formed, in November 1920 and February 1921 respectively, following a reorganisation. These Battalions previously formed parts of the 6th and 7th Battalions. The 1st Kilkenny Battalion was centred on Kilkenny City and surrounding areas, with the other Battalions radiating from there. By the end of the War of Independence there were two Flying Columns – also known as Active Service Units (ASUs) – formed in the Brigade. One was based in the north and east of the county and was known as the 'North Kilkenny ASU' or '1st Kilkenny ASU'; the second was focused in the west and south of the county and was known as the '7th Battalion Flying Column' or the 'West Kilkenny Flying Column'.[4]

The Kilkenny Brigade O/C (Officer Commanding) from its formation in August 1918 until November 1920 was Thomas Treacy, a member of the 1st Battalion based in Kilkenny City.[5] Prior to the formation of the Kilkenny Brigade he was Captain of the Kilkenny City Irish Volunteer Company. After Treacy's arrest in November 1920, Peter DeLoughry, the Mayor of Kilkenny City, served briefly as Brigade Commandant until he was also arrested. George O'Dwyer from Castlecomer, a former Dublin Metropolitan Police Constable and O/C of the 3rd IRA Battalion, served as Kilkenny Brigade Commandant from January 1921 for the remainder of the War.[6] If all IRA members from Kilkenny Battalion companies are aggregated using the Military Service Pensions Collection (MSPC) records, the total nominal number of IRA members in the county was 2,988 men by the time of the Truce.[7] This does not necessarily imply they all took an active part in military actions against the Crown Forces, it simply means they were official members of the Kilkenny IRA Brigade. Most were 'part-time soldiers', doing their duties after they had completed their day's work. During the last months of the War of Independence, just over fifty of the most devoted IRA men were attached to one of the two ASUs operating in the county. The individuals attached to these Flying Columns could certainly be classed as 'full-time' soldiers, as they sacrificed their family life, health and livelihoods for a life on the run in aid of their cause.[8]

Regarding the social background of the IRA Volunteers, the synopsis of historian Peter Hart that they 'were neither very poor nor very well off, but came from the central stratum of "plain people" in between', is applicable to Kilkenny.[9] The occupations of Kilkenny IRA members who completed witness statements included chemists, corporation employees, shop assistants, farmers and brewery employees.[10] In historian Joost Augusteijn's study of IRA members, he highlighted that IRA officers 'tended to be older, more urban-based, and of a higher status – better educated, more skilled and financially better-off'.[11] This is also an accurate reflection of the Kilkenny IRA leadership. Focusing on the Kilkenny Brigade officers, their occupations included; owning a drapery business, owning a foundry and motor car hire firm, a factory manager, and a baker. All but one of the Brigade leaders was over the age of 30 and all were based in Kilkenny City.[12]

The Cumann na mBan Brigade in Kilkenny was formed into nine matching Battalions (also known as District Councils), although the number of Companies attached to each Battalion was less. The Brigade Commandant throughout the War of Independence (and later Civil War) was Hanna Murphy née Dooley (1891–1961) from Dunningstown. She was known as 'Joan of Arc' to the IRA men due to her boundless support for the cause throughout the revolutionary years. The total nominal number of women recorded as members of Cumann na mBan in Kilkenny in 1921 was 821.[13] Similar to their male counterparts, the strength and activities of each branch differed from district to district. The RIC vastly miscalculated their influence in 1921, giving an estimate of just seventy women in Cumann na mBan in the whole of County Kilkenny.[14] Although they had a relatively large membership, O/C Hanna Murphy said that many of the women were not inclined to take leadership roles; 'I found it hard to get officers to take charge. Although they were all willing to join up, yet none liked to take charge.'[15] Although she does not offer a reason for this, it may have been because of family responsibilities or the perception of their activities within the local community. Moreover, women – unlike the men – did not have the option of going on the run. Therefore they would be subjected to the full brunt of the repercussions of their activities, such as raids and intimidation.

A Historical Lineage

It was probably more than coincidental that the areas of County Kilkenny that experienced high rates of IRA activity during the War of Independence had a historical lineage of militant activity that spanned over a century. The town of Graiguenamanagh, where the 5th Battalion was based, was considered the birthplace of the Tithe War in 1830 when a local Catholic priest refused to pay his tithe tax, supported by many locals.[16] Arguably the most important battle of the Tithe era took place in Carrickshock, near Hugginstown, in 1831, where seventeen people were killed, including fourteen members of the Crown Forces.[17] John O'Gorman from Poulacapple, who was a member of the 7th Kilkenny Battalion during the War of Independence, had a grandfather who participated in the Battle of Carrickshock nearly ninety years previously.[18] Even earlier eighteenth-century anti-tithe movements, such as the Whiteboys and the Rightboys, had been particularly strong in County Kilkenny.

In a similar vein, Castlecomer in the north of the county was famous for the organisation of its coalminers who joined 'combinations', which were early forms of trade unions. From the early 1830s they went on strike on various occasions, requesting better working conditions. Many of these strikes took a militant direction and a mine manager was killed in one altercation in 1832.[19]

Lastly, the town in County Kilkenny where the most active unit of the IRA was based – Callan – was the birthplace in 1849 of the Tenant Protection Society. This society, which was a precursor to the Land League, was the first significant organisation established in Ireland to protect the rights of small landholders and labourers.[20]

The Land League would eventually play a vital role in gaining tenant rights, and ultimately land ownership, in the decades that followed. It could be inferred, therefore, that a disposition towards militancy appeared to have been part of the Kilkenny psyche.

The Combatants

So who were the enemies of the Irish Volunteers, or the Irish Republican Army (IRA), as they became known during the War of Independence? Any person who tried to subvert the Irish Republic in any way was considered a foe and this included informers. However, the chief adversaries were the British Crown Forces, which eventually consisted of four components, namely; the RIC (police), the Auxiliaries (ex-British Army Officers), the Black and Tans (usually ex-British soldiers, officially called the RIC Special Reserve) and the military (in County Kilkenny this was usually soldiers from the Devonshire Regiment). The Auxiliaries, who had the fiercest reputation, were at the time the most highly-paid uniformed police force in the world, earning one pound a day. They were made up of former First World War army men of the officer grade, who were 'more accustomed to giving than to receiving orders'.[21] Although working for the same 'side', these different strands of the Crown Forces sometimes acted independently – and sometimes in contradiction – of one another. It is also important to note that many of the general populace referred to the various sections of the Crown Forces under the umbrella term 'the Tans', even if they were members of other segments of the Crown Forces.

A Low-Key Start: 1919

At the beginning of the War of Independence period in early 1919 – the start date is generally considered as 21 January 1919 – some Kilkenny Volunteers were still in prison since the time of the 'German Plot' arrests of the previous May. There grew an enormous amount of sympathy for the prisoners from across the political divide; especially, as by then, the First World War had ended, so there did not appear to be a valid reason to keep them incarcerated.

This was illustrated at the Kilkenny City Council meeting on 23 January 1919 when the still imprisoned Peter DeLoughry was elected mayor. There were no dissenting voices in the Council due to a coordinated campaign of publicity and mass meetings initiated by E.T. Keane during the previous weeks. The IPP Councillors had wanted to elect one of their members as mayor but bowed to the overwhelming public support in favour of DeLoughry.[22] On the night, Pierce Wall, a Labour Councillor, asserted that 'it was the only fitting answer [in electing DeLoughry as mayor] that they in Kilkenny could give to the English government for taking away their fellow citizen and placing him in an English prison without making any charge against him or giving him a trial.' After DeLoughry had been elected, the Council meeting ended when the members proceeded to DeLoughry's house to present his chain of office to his wife Winnie.[23]

However, Mayor DeLoughry, who was interned in Lincoln prison in England's East Midlands, had other things on his mind at this time. Using his metalworking skills, DeLoughry played a pivotal role in the escape of his prison mates Éamon de Valera (who was then President of Sinn Féin), Seán Milroy and Seán McGarry from Lincoln prison.

DeLoughry secretly created a master key which opened all the gates and doors in the jail. The blank key had been smuggled into the prison inside a cake which was addressed to; 'Mayor DeLoughry, with congratulations and best wishes from a few Kilkenny exiles, J. Dardis'. He created a near-perfect key with just 'files and two stout pen-knives' as his tools. To the delight of all internees, the key 'opened the doors beautifully'. On the night of 3 February 1919, de Valera, Milroy and McGarry escaped from Lincoln prison by simply walking out of the prison under the cover of darkness. Michael Collins and Harry Boland were waiting on the other side of the prison wall and ferried the men to safe houses and to freedom. De Valera's escape made worldwide headlines and he became a real-life scarlet pimpernel with supposed sightings of him simultaneously in different continents.[24]

Just six weeks after the escape, the German Plot prisoners were released by the British authorities in a general amnesty, after ten months in confinement. On DeLoughry's return to Kilkenny in March 1919, a large crowd gathered on The Parade to welcome him home and to witness his formal investiture as Mayor of Kilkenny by Alderman James Nowlan, who said: 'I have the greatest possible pleasure in putting on DeLoughry, the felon, the mayoral chain of the City of Kilkenny.'[25] The release of the German Plot prisoners allowed other key players in the Kilkenny Volunteers – soon to be renamed the IRA – the opportunity to return home. Thomas Treacy, Brigade O/C, Jim Lalor vice-O/C and Ned Comerford the Brigade Quartermaster, had all been on the run for the previous ten months.[26] This new freedom allowed them to fully focus on the organisation of the Kilkenny IRA Brigade, although many of the brigade officers were required to lead parallel lives. For instance, Peter DeLoughry, in his capacity as Mayor of Kilkenny City was hosting the annual 'Mayoral Banquet' with many of the leading players in Kilkenny society in attendance, while at the same time he was privy to the planning of an RIC Barracks attack.[27]

What could be termed the military campaign in Kilkenny got off to a rather inauspicious beginning. In early 1919, the Sinn Féin National Executive imposed a ban on foxhunting throughout Ireland in protest over the aforementioned 'German Plot' prisoners.[28] The campaign against hunting was primarily aimed at disturbing the lives of members of the 'ascendancy', who were the usual conductors of foxhunting in the country, although the sport itself by then had a wider appeal. The Kilkenny Hunt was one of the oldest and most distinguished in the country.[29] Initial hunts in early February in Kilmanagh, Ballykeeffe and Freshford passed without incident. The first interference against a hunt occurred near Threecastles on a farm owned by the Hennessy family where 'a number of young men' blocked the route.[30] On 18 February 1919 members of the 7th Battalion caused consternation in the locality of Windgap when they prevented the Master of the Kilkenny Foxhounds, a Parisian-born American citizen named Isaac Bell, and his hunting party, from passing through the village. Both local and national newspapers reported that a crowd of '150 young men' blocked the hunting group and that they stated that they were 'against foxhunting while man hunting was the game of the British Government in Ireland'.[31] James Leahy, who was one of the IRA Volunteers involved, estimated that fifty men took part and they were armed with just 'sticks and ash plants'. Leahy also mentioned that their actions made them very unpopular in the locality as their behaviour was considered a source of embarrassment.[32] Isaac Bell wrote to a number of the local Sinn Féin clubs stating that foxhunting had 'always [been] kept free from all politics', while highlighting the devastation caused to the local horse breeding industry as a result of the First World War. He also caustically remarked; 'I am in no mood to be "stopped" and "started" like a Ford Car, although I am an American.'[33] On 22 February a meeting of all local farmers supportive of foxhunting was convened in Kilkenny City. Many Sinn Féin supporting members of the public also attended and there was heckling and angry exchanges throughout the meeting.[34] It is probable that some smaller farmers, in private at least, were supportive of the measure to stop the hunt, as it prevented large hunting parties trampling through their fields and damaging their land, something they had no power to prevent previously.

One of the main goals of the Kilkenny IRA from the spring of 1919 was the procurement of arms. The Kilkenny City IRA managed to acquire nine Lee Enfield rifles through a soldier named 'Williams' who was based in Kilkenny Military Barracks.[35] They passed him money over the wall of the barracks and he gave them the rifles, one at a time. The arrangement came to an abrupt end when his actions were discovered by his senior officers and he was court-martialled, receiving two-years imprisonment.[36]

During this period, the 3rd Battalion IRA from Castlecomer and its surrounding hinterlands used an ingenious method of warning each other about the movement of Crown Forces. They cut off the end of glass bottles and blew through the spout. This acted as an improvised horn which they all called 'bottle horns'. The noise from the horn could be heard for a great distance. The rule of the Battalion was that if any member heard a bottle horn, even faintly in the distance, they were to immediately blow theirs. Hence, a chain would be created and word would be spread quickly of approaching Crown Forces. Even some farmers who were not members of the IRA kept a bottle horn in their fields when they were working to help deliver the warning and keep their neighbours out of danger.[37]

The British Army in Kilkenny suffered misfortune within its own ranks in September 1919. During this period there was an armed military guard at the explosives store at Castlecomer Collieries. The explosives were required for the mining process. Due to the unstable political situation, it was decided by the military authorities to transfer all the explosives to Castlecomer Military Barracks for safekeeping. On Thursday, 25 September 1919, all barrels of explosives – which were essentially drums of gunpowder – were removed from the site by motor lorry. Five soldiers stayed behind to clean up the guardhouse. There were two 'dead' barrels of explosives left behind also. These were considered defunct, useless, gunpowder which the soldiers intended to bury in the ground. During the course of their tidying, the soldiers lit a fire to burn some documents. Unfortunately for them, they soon discovered that the 'dead' barrels of gunpowder were in fact very much alive. Sparks from the fire ignited the gunpowder which resulted in a massive explosion that could be heard for miles around. The soldiers were thrown a long distance. Two were severely burned, while three died from their injuries. The deceased were Private Frank Lord, aged 20, Private George Frederick Heppenstall, aged 24, and Lance-Corporal Andrew Walsh, aged 21. All were natives of England and members of the Yorkshire Hussars Yeomanry.[38]

Towards the end of 1919, an IRA organiser, Joe McMahon, came to work in Kilkenny City. He was originally from Kilmaley, County Clare but was on the run in Kilkenny. He was pivotal in the early successes of the Kilkenny Brigade and was known to many in Kilkenny as 'the Clare Wild Goose'.[39]

Beginners' Fortune: 8 March 1920, The Capture of Hugginstown Barracks

In January 1920, Tom Treacy, the Kilkenny Brigade O/C, was summoned by IRA GHQ to Dublin. He met Richard Mulcahy, IRA Chief of Staff, at St Enda's in Rathfarnham. He received instructions from Mulcahy that an RIC Barracks was to be 'taken'. When Treacy returned he called a Brigade meeting. An attack on Tullaroan RIC Barracks was decided upon.[40] Advanced plans were made for this attack but cancelled the day before, following information that the authorities were aware of the planned assault. Further plans were devised to attack Cuffesgrange Barracks but this location was deemed unsuitable. Eventually Hugginstown RIC Barracks, 25 km south of Kilkenny City, was chosen as the most opportune target.[41]

In preparation for the Hugginstown attack, Joe McMahon worked in Peter DeLoughry's foundry creating bombs that were to be used in the assault. The gelignite had been sourced from the Castlecomer mines – one of the only mines in Ireland licensed to hold gelignite at the time – from where members of the 3rd Battalion had been smuggling it out.[42] Luckily for the Kilkenny Brigade, McMahon escaped arrest just a week before the attack. The RIC had arrested him in his bedroom but while they waited for him to get dressed he escaped out of a window.[43]

The night of Monday, 8 March 1920 was chosen as the date for the attack. Arguably it was the Kilkenny IRA Brigade's most organised and effective attack of the entire War of Independence era. It was planned by the Brigade GHQ in Kilkenny City, with members of the 1st and 7th Kilkenny IRA Battalions comprising the attack party.

Arrangements were made for telegraph wire cutting, which was carried out exceptionally well as no other RIC Barracks would come to their aid during the night. The closest RIC Barracks to Hugginstown, in Stoneyford, had gunmen placed outside in case of movement of the police from there. A motor car was commandeered to transport combatants in the event of casualties.[44] Luck also played a part. On the night in question one of the RIC in Hugginstown Barracks, Constable Dockery, was having a retirement gathering in Cleary's public house next door, that night being his last on duty.

Dockery's final night of service would turn out to be the most eventful of his thirty-two-year career in the force. This was a lucky coincidence on the part of the IRA planners. Brigade O/C Thomas Treacy later noted the only negative was the 'bright moonlight which lit up the village', as the full moon had just occurred a few days before.[45]

Around thirty-five men took part in the actual attack. Beforehand, they symbolically congregated in the nearby townland of Carrickshock, the site of a previous Tithe War altercation.

The IRA attacking party was divided into four sections. Treacy was at the front of the barracks, another party was at the side, and another at the rear. Finally a 'bombing party' led by Joe McMahon assembled in an adjoining yard near the back of the Barracks with the aim of attacking the roof.[46]

All six RIC men had returned to the Barracks from the public house by 10.30 pm. The attack commenced at the planned time of 11.30 pm, with the bombing party throwing some of their fifty homemade grenades at the building. Brigade Commandant Treacy, using an 'improvised megaphone', informed the occupants they were under attack and would be given ten minutes to surrender. They were also told that the women and children inside would be given safe passage away from the Barracks. Sergeant John Neylin's wife and five children were living in the building at the time, which was not unusual for the era. The same message was given after the ten minutes had elapsed, but the reply was rifle fire from the Barracks. The attack then commenced fully with gun fire from all sides. The attackers were mostly armed with shotguns and homemade bombs. Although they had some rifles, Treacy believed his men were more familiar with the shotguns.[47] In the meantime, Joe McMahon climbed onto the roof using a ladder and by breaking the slates managed to drop grenades through the roof.[48] Many of the IRA that took part mentioned the tremendous volume of noise produced, as most had never heard a bomb explode before.[49] Inside the Barracks, Constable Ryan, who was considered 'an expert bomber', went upstairs and started dropping grenades through a small opening in the gable end of the Barracks. This opening had only been constructed the previous month with the express purpose of dropping grenades during an attack of this nature. After about fifteen minutes, Ryan came back downstairs and said, 'I am killed, they got me through the window', and subsequently became unconscious.[50] His upper right arm and elbow had been shattered from a blast and he was bleeding profusely.

After about forty-five minutes, the RIC surrendered. The IRA ordered them to take out all their arms and leave them on the street outside, with which the RIC complied. The RIC sergeant informed the IRA Commandant that one of his men was injured and he needed a priest and a doctor, which were sent for. The captured weapons included six much sought-after rifles, two revolvers, and three boxes of cartridges. These were transported 13 km north to the village of Ennisnag for hiding.[51] The IRA men dispersed and returned to their homes without difficulty and without suffering any casualties. The police reports to the media stated that 200 men had attacked the Barracks, which was more than quadruple the actual figure.[52]

The local priest, and Doctor James Marnell of Kilmaganny, arrived at the Barracks but they were unable to save 39-year-old Constable Thomas Ryan who died at 6.00 am. Ryan was originally from Limerick, but living in Waterford, and left a wife and five children.[53] The Coroner's inquest was held in Cleary's public house in Hugginstown two days after the attack. As was customary, the jury was made up of locals, but there was 'difficulty in securing a sufficient number of jury men'. In his summation the coroner stated that:

> this man died of shock and haemorrhage caused by a high explosive … forget that this man was a policeman. Just consider him as an ordinary neighbour and put yourself in his place and make the cause your own … You have ample proof that his house was attacked by men armed with deadly weapons, and like everyman he had the right to defend his house.

Whether through fear or loyalty to their local area, the head juror, Edward Tennyson of Boolyglass, announced the verdict which prevented a murder investigation commencing: 'Thomas Ryan died from shock and haemorrhage caused by a high explosive and there is no evidence to show where the explosive came from.'[54] The ordeal for Constable Ryan's wife Bridget was prolonged as the court case regarding compensation for her husband's death dragged on for over a year. At the first hearing in June 1920, Bridget Ryan claimed compensation of £8,000, which included her husband's predicted earnings and pension had he lived (his yearly wage was £240 at the time of his death), while also taking into account six dependent children under the ages of 10. Although having five children at the time of the attack, Bridget Ryan was five months pregnant when her husband died and was eight months pregnant at the time of the first hearing.

The main issue regarding the compensation was which Local Authority was liable. This was complicated by the fact that Hugginstown Barracks bordered three council jurisdictions, namely; Thomastown District Council, Kilkenny County Council and Carrick-on-Suir District Council. Men from all three districts were arrested after the attack. Subsequently, solicitors representing the three Councils defended against the claim. Michael John Buggy, a Kilkenny City-based solicitor representing Thomastown Council, argued that it was 'the [English] Government' who were liable as they had 'unreasonably placed this man in danger by allowing him, after an insufficient period of training, to use bombs'.[55] Mr Bacon, barrister for Kilkenny County Council, argued that 'Constable Ryan met his death in using one of his own bombs', which implied the Councils were not culpable.[56] This contradicted Dr Marnell's evidence which stated that Constable Ryan's right hand was fully intact – it was his upper arm that was shattered – which inferred that the grenade was not in his hand when it exploded. Finally, in April 1921, after a number of adjournments over the course of nearly a year, Bridget Ryan was awarded £4,500 which was 'to be levied off the County Kilkenny [revenue] at large'. Judge O'Brien, who presided at the case in Thomastown Courthouse, awarded £1,000 of the total amount specifically for the two youngest children, including Bridget Pauline Ryan, who was born in July 1920, four months after her father's death.[57]

In the aftermath of the Hugginstown attack, the RIC arrested a number of people from Hugginstown and surrounding areas who were mostly part of the IRA, but who were not the main instigators of the attack. Many of the prisoners subsequently went on hunger strike. Although there was no evidence against them, the Brigade O/C Thomas Treacy and the Mayor of Kilkenny Peter DeLoughry were arrested and sent to prison in England.[58] As no case could be built against the prisoners, they were released in June 1920 and received an enthusiastic welcome on their return, after two months incarceration. The majority arrived home by train and decamped at Ballyhale Station where a fife and drum band led them to Hugginstown. There was a bonfire at the crossroads in the village close to the ruins of Hugginstown RIC Barracks which had been burned down the previous month.[59]

Along with excellent planning, it was chiefly the element of surprise that was the principal contributing factor to the success of this attack by the Kilkenny Brigade. The fact that it was in a very remote and rural area allowed a large number of men to converge without being reported. Joe McMahon's actions on the night were as invaluable as his explosives. His bravery in attacking the roof under heavy fire was a strong factor in the success. Unfortunately for the Kilkenny Brigade, McMahon had to leave the county and go on the run as he was a wanted man. He subsequently was killed less than six months later while demonstrating explosives in Cavan. The Kilkenny Brigade IRA would not have such an uncomplicated success again. Within a few months of this attack the Auxiliaries and what the *Kilkenny People* called the 'embryo policemen',[60] commonly known as the Black and Tans, arrived in the county.

'An Air of Peace' in the County: Summer 1920

The withdrawal of the police from so many barracks has handed over stretches of the county to the disaffected.

– RIC CI Whyte, Kilkenny (June 1920)[61]

IRA Volunteer Nicholas Carroll, vice-O/C of 8th Battalion from Hugginstown, noted that in the summer of 1920 there was 'an air of peace and independence in the district'.[62] The primary reason for this was the British Government's decision to evacuate RIC police barracks throughout rural parts of Ireland. Following orders from IRA GHQ, much of the activity for the Kilkenny IRA Battalions during April and May 1920 was concerned with the burning of over twenty barracks and courthouses, with the majority occurring symbolically on Easter Sunday night, 4 April 1920, with any remaining barracks or partially burned barracks, destroyed on Ascension Thursday, 13 May 1920.[63] The list of destroyed barracks in the Kilkenny Battalion area included; Corbettstown, Kilmanagh, Loughbrack, Killamery, Windgap, Inistioge, The Rower, Rosbercon, Glenmore, Slieverue, Bennettsbridge, Garrylawn (Crosspatrick), Gathabawn, Clonmantagh, Johnstown, Paulstown, Railyard, Coolcullen, Stoneyford, Hugginstown, Slatequarries, Mooncoin and Clooneen.[64]

In Graiguenamanagh, the local IRA showed consideration to local businesses that were attached to the barracks by not burning it, but instead destroyed the building by hand.[65] In Templeorum, in the south of the county, the local curate moved into the evacuated barracks in an apparent attempt to prevent it from being destroyed.[66] Piltown Courthouse and Stoneyford Courthouse were burned down also, while raids took place on the Callan, Graiguenamanagh and Kilkenny City Income Tax offices, where all records were amassed and burned.[67] The Piltown Courthouse operation was considered important as it contained 'all the court registers for south Kilkenny'. To prevent similar fates, the Crown Forces seized Callan and Thomastown Courthouses.[68] Also in April 1920, the homes of 'rate collectors' for Kilkenny City were raided with their records and documentation destroyed.[69]

The comprehensive destructive of the vast majority of intended targets in County Kilkenny did not go far enough for Michael Collins, IRA Director of Intelligence. Living up to his reputation of constantly demanding more from his men, he questioned Kilkenny IRA O/C Thomas Treacy, as to why some buildings that were on the hit list were not destroyed. The main building in question was the Surveyors, Customs and Excise Office on The Parade in Kilkenny City. Treacy explained that the property had not been set alight as the female caretaker had recently suffered a stroke and was seriously ill. Seriously, Treacy defended not burning down one RIC barracks as the property was actually leased from a member of the IRA. These reasons did not wash with Collins as he remarked; 'the strategic merits of destroying the building should outweigh any personal connections'.[70]

Following the destruction of these buildings, there was a raft of claims for compensation in the local courts from the owners. In most cases, the proprietors of RIC barracks were not the RIC, or even the State for that matter. Due to a legacy regarding how the RIC police force was first established the previous century, the owners mostly comprised of the principal landowner in each area. In other words, they owned the barracks as they had given the land in the first place. Compensation would be paid by the 'county at large', meaning from the Council, who derived most of its income from local ratepayers. For instance, the trustees of the Tighe estate in Woodstock claimed £2,500 for the destruction of Inistioge Barracks (awarded £1,350), the Earl of Ossory claimed £2,142 for the destruction of Killamery Barracks and £1,764 for Slatequarries Barracks (awarded £1,500 and £1,200 respectively).[71] Richard Power claimed £1,000 for Mooncoin RIC Barracks but was awarded £500, with the judge in this case commenting; 'wouldn't you rather have £500 than a shed [the destroyed RIC Barracks]'.[72]

Many of the local prisoners who were jailed following the Hugginstown attack were on hunger strike in prison, so a general boycotting of the RIC was ordered by Sinn Féin in Kilkenny. Intimidation of RIC officers increased. The intimidation manifested itself in different ways and included new cadets receiving threatening letters,[73] while in Mullinavat the local sergeant's goat was killed maliciously.[74]

In August 1920, following a general communication from GHQ in Dublin, a general collection of arms was ordered. This order was carried out diligently throughout the county, with one member of the Dunnamaggin IRA Company, Denis Lahart, becoming the first Kilkenny IRA casualty of the war when he received a gunshot wound from a 'loyalist' in Kells who refused to part with his firearm.[75] Some farmers handed over their weapons without protest.

There was also some selectivity applied to the houses that were targeted. The home of Major McCalmont, who resided at the large Mount Juliet Estate near Thomastown, was not raided for arms by the local IRA even though he was an avid organiser of local hunts. He had been somewhat sympathetic to the nationalist cause previously and had used the newly established Sinn Féin courts, thus courtesy was shown in this case. However, in an unusual occurrence, an outside IRA Company from Holycross, County Tipperary, crossed into the Kilkenny Brigade area without approval and raided McCalmont's residence for arms. They found an array of rifles, revolvers and shotguns. Although the Tipperary No 2 Brigade Commandant James Leahy had not given his sanction for the raid, he did not feel compelled to return the weapons: 'I felt the material seized should have been taken long before that by the Kilkenny men themselves and that when they failed to do so they did not deserve to have it returned to them.'[76] The Holycross men could have had a bigger coup that day. When they raided the house, McCalmont was having lunch with a guest. They were unaware that this guest, wearing civilian clothes, was Major John Kirkwood, Commandant of A Coy, Auxiliary Division, based in Woodstock.[77] A kidnap of this sort would have been enormously embarrassing for the British authorities – while also being contentious for the IRA, as it was outside men taking action in the Kilkenny Brigade area.

While Kilkenny Brigade O/C Thomas Treacy was recovering from his hunger strike following his release from prison in London in June 1920, a Kilkenny man living there, James Delaney, visited him and offered his services. With the help of the local London Cumann na mBan, Delaney managed to post nearly twenty revolvers to Kilkenny over the following months. His actions were eventually discovered and he was arrested by police at Trafalgar Square in London. After he was released on bail, he discreetly returned to Kilkenny and joined an ASU, later taking part in the ambushes at Coolbawn and Uskerty.[78]

The 5th Kilkenny IRA Battalion, based in Graiguenamanagh in the southeast of the county, also used ingenious ways to acquire guns. Members made house-to-house collections, along with church gate collections, where a sum of 'between £110 and £120' was raised for the 'maintenance of the Volunteer [Republican] Police Force'. The purpose of the collections were a ruse however, as the money collected was for an arms fund. The battalion purchased ten guns from GHQ in Dublin using money they had collected. They transported their new weapons inconspicuously to Graiguenamanagh using a barge as their unusual method of transport; a journey that took over a week.[79]

In response to the pilfering of arms throughout the county, an 'anti-I.R.A. unit' was established by a small group of Protestant families in the Piltown area of south Kilkenny. These families were considered to be 'violently pro-British', and it was quite rare for such a unit to exist in this part of Ireland. Some members of the 7th Battalion launched a pre-emptive strike on these families and captured a number of weapons although they did not locate the much sought-after machine gun – which had been moved to a relative's house for safekeeping.[80] Generally, there is no evidence of sectarianism being an element of the War of Independence in Kilkenny. When George O'Dwyer, then 3rd Battalion O/C, was leading a group of IRA in burning Coolcullen RIC Barracks in June 1920, he told the IRA scouts that were going to be blocking the roads in the area, to make sure they were 'courteous to all local people on the roads and to remember that the large number of Protestants living within the area of the Barracks were friendly people and helpful to the IRA'.[81]

Some 8,000 km from Ireland, two Kilkenny men made their contribution to the cause of Irish freedom when they took part in what became known as the 'India Mutiny'. Lance-Corporal John Murphy from New Street in Kilkenny City, and Private William Bolger from The Mall, Thomastown, were members of the Connaught Rangers, a British Army regiment based in the city of Jalandhar, in India's Punjab region. Along with many of their comrades, they decided to mutiny in protest against the effects of martial law in Ireland. Both Kilkenny men were imprisoned for a number of months. In addition to the unpleasant incarceration – during which Murphy contracted malaria – their defiance also relinquished any claim they had to a British Army pension in later life.[82]

Following the success of the Hugginstown attack in March, and up to the autumn of 1920, there is no evidence to suggest that the Kilkenny Brigade was planning any further large-scale attacks.[83] Some battalions used their own initiative in progressing the military campaign. For their part, the Kilkenny Brigade leaders did not appear perturbed by the independent actions of the local battalions, although this was to change in the coming months as Dublin IRA GHQ attempted to assert more control nationally.[84] In June 1920, Jim Roughan, Commandant of the 7th Kilkenny Battalion, supplied riflemen and scouts for the Drangan Barracks attack in neighbouring County Tipperary. Roughan did not ask for, or seek permission, from any Kilkenny Brigade superiors.[85] The 7th Battalion was the only Battalion to complain about the lethargic progress of the military campaign during the summer of 1920. The military also had been ratcheting up tension in Callan. Two prominent Sinn Féin supporters in the town – J.J. Dunne a local auctioneer and Michael

Shelly a drapery store owner – were arrested and interned for a period. They were cheered out of the town as they were brought away. That night, Crown Forces in the area daubed their premises, and other businesses in the town, with pro-British graffiti, such as; 'To Hell with the republic' and 'God save the King.'[86]

William Kenny's Execution: August 1920

In July 1920, a party of fifty soldiers of the Devonshire Regiment were transferred to the town of Graiguenamanagh in the southeast of the county to reinforce law and order. The newly arrived military were helped in their searches by a local man and ex-British soldier, William Kenny. The 5th Battalion IRA were angry with Kenny for helping the enemy, as the soldiers would have been 'absolutely powerless' without his help as they 'did not know the district, nor the names of the people in the town'. In August 1920 the IRA decided to arrest Kenny. He was in hiding but was seen one day walking on a road in the direction of Thomastown. James Blanchfield, who would later become Assistant Intelligence Officer for the 5th Battalion, spotted Kenny at Thomastown railway station. He informed the officers in his Company and Kenny was captured by local man Thomas Kelly and brought back to Graiguenamanagh by IRA Lieutenant Stephen Lawlor.[87]

After Kenny was searched a ticket to Canada and a 'good sum of money' was discovered on his person. This was the payment from the Crown Forces for his help, with a passage to Canada arranged for his safety.[88] A court martial was held by the IRA and Kenny was sentenced to death as an informer. Kenny was held in a small hut known as Blanchfield's Eel House located on the banks of the River Barrow.[89] It was situated about 1 km south of Graiguenamanagh in the townland of Ballyogan. A local priest was brought to Kenny on the eve of his execution to administer spiritual rites. On 31 August 1920, Kenny suffered an unusual and presumably harrowing execution by drowning in the River Barrow. John Walsh, who later became O/C of the 5th Battalion, described the execution:

> Fr Gerry attended to Kenny in the eel house and then left, wishing us goodnight … We gagged and blindfolded him [Kenny] and, having bound his arms and legs, we dropped him into the River Barrow at a point just a few yards from the eel house. The water at this point would be eight or ten feet deep and, as an additional precaution, we tied a 56-lb [pound] weight to his body before dropping him into the river.[90]

The reason given for drowning, as opposed to shooting, was due to the proximity of the IRA's location to British forces, as a gunshot would have been heard. The execution of Kenny had not been sanctioned by IRA GHQ. James O'Hanrahan, Adjutant of the 5th IRA Battalion, was part of the group that detained and executed Kenny. He later remarked that he and his fellow battalion officers 'were threatened with court-martial [by IRA GHQ] for doing in the spy [Kenny]'.[91]

Local and personal animosities cannot be discounted regarding William Kenny's death. The family had been in conflict with some of their neighbours prior to the War of Independence. William Kenny was something of a 'black sheep' in the community, which was amplified after he began helping the Crown Forces during the summer of 1920. The Kenny's were also antagonistic to the IRA, or more specifically, the local men attached to the IRA in Graiguenamanagh where some bad blood appeared to have existed already. Thus, 'hitting-back' at those in his community he did not get on with was part of his motivation for helping the military. In addition, four sons in the family, including William, had fought for the British Army during the First World War. Kenny was asked to join the IRA in 1919 but had refused stating that 'he had fought for one flag and would never fight for the second one'.

On 5 April 1921, some eight months after Kenny's death, his sister Margaret and 'blind father' were stopped when driving their donkey and cart by members of the local 5th IRA Battalion.[92] The cart was destroyed and the IRA warned them; 'you will not go back to Woodstock [Auxiliary HQ], there are enough informing on us there already'. Margaret Kenny was apparently not intimidated as she reported the incident. The following day local IRA members Patrick Lanigan and Edward Naddy were arrested. Each were later sentenced to six months in prison for intimidation and malicious damage of property.[93] The acrimonies did not stop there. Kenny's father, 73-year-old William senior, moved to Waterford City. It was there he alleged he was kidnapped by the IRA and brought to an unknown location. He was told he had been sentenced to the same fate as his son and that he would be shot in the morning. William senior managed to escape from the place he was detained by breaking a hole through the thatch and unlocking the door from the outside. He walked barefoot to the nearest military barracks in Waterford using 'a blind man's keen instinct' and was subsequently placed under full-time military protection.

The most gruesome aspect of the episode was that William Kenny's body washed up some six weeks after his execution at the weir in St Mullins, just 4 km downriver on the County Carlow side. His sister was able to identify

Kenny's remains by the boots he was still wearing. Before the incident could be reported, three members of the 5th Battalion, James Ryan, James Mackey and John Walsh – who had taken part in the original execution – arrived at the location and put the body back in the river for the second time, weighing him down with heavy stones which were tied to the badly decomposed body.[94]

The fear of informers, or 'spies', as they were disparagingly termed, was something that was to the forefront of IRA battalions throughout Ireland during the War of Independence. In a hierarchy of misdemeanours, many within the IRA considered informing to be amongst the worst, especially if it was carried out by their fellow kinspeople. In small parochial areas, this often caused tensions between families and local communities that lasted for generations.

The Fight Becomes Bloody: Crown Forces Hit Back in Autumn and Winter 1920

In late summer of 1920, the British authorities launched its counter-offensive. The strength of military and RIC garrisons based in the county increased. The very first Auxiliary Company in Ireland, 'A' Company, was placed in Woodstock House in Inistioge in August 1920.[95]

Crown forces began arresting many known 'Sinn Féiners', sometimes on very innocuous charges. For example, the residence of Patrick Funcheon of Bridge Street in Callan was searched in November 1920 where 'a copy of *An Introduction to Volunteer Training* [manual]' was 'found in a hole in the wall in the back yard', along with 'two other copies of *An t-Oglach*' which were discovered in a bookcase. Funcheon was sentenced to six-months hard labour for possession of this material.[96]

In a similar vein, 22-year-old James Beck from Thomastown, who was a member of the 5th Battalion IRA, was picked up by Black and Tans during the course of his job delivering bread in the town. The following then occurred:

> I was taken to the bank of the River Nore [in Thomastown]. I was ordered under the threat of being shot to climb a tree and remove from the top [of the tree] the tri-colour flag of the IRA [Irish Tricolour]. I refused to carry out this order. For my refusal, I was badly beaten and thrown into the river.[97]

When he had swum to the banks of the river, Beck was ordered to remove the flag again, but refused for a second time. He was beaten with the butt of a rifle and because of his ordeal he contracted 'a severe illness' which lasted three months; which resulted in him losing his employment.

Woodstock and the Capture of Ernie O'Malley: December 1920

In November 1920, Dublin IRA GHQ summoned Brigade O/C Thomas Treacy, who had recovered from his hunger strike of the previous summer, to Dublin where he was informed that the Kilkenny Brigade would attack Woodstock House near the village of Inistioge. The stately home of the Tighe family had been commandeered by Auxiliaries as their headquarters for the southeast of Ireland in August 1920.[98] The Kilkenny Brigade was to gather reconnaissance on the Auxiliary post prior to the attack. James Lalor, Vice Brigade O/C, carried out this task and travelled to Dublin to meet Richard Mulcahy, IRA Chief of Staff. Lalor estimated the total amount of Auxiliaries in Woodstock by noting all the food that was delivered to the premises. However, he was somewhat taken aback during the meeting as Mulcahy already had much more detailed intelligence information:

> I told him first of all that I estimated the strength of the garrison as forty-five and explained to him how I arrived at that figure. He then more or less took the wind out of my sails by telling me that not only did he know the exact number of Auxiliaries in Woodstock, but that he had a list of their home addresses in England. His figure was, I think, twelve less than my estimated figure.[99]

Lalor told Mulcahy that he was pessimistic that the building could be taken without artillery. Mulcahy replied: 'All right. I will send down a man who will take it for you.' Ernie O'Malley from IRA GHQ was to lead the attack.

The Kilkenny IRA Brigade suffered a number of setbacks in the week prior to O'Malley's arrival in Kilkenny. Brigade O/C Treacy and Vice O/C Lalor were arrested and interned by Crown Forces. Peter DeLoughry, Mayor of Kilkenny City, who had not taken an active part in fighting to date, was elected Kilkenny IRA Brigade O/C in place of Treacy, due to his eminent position within Sinn Féin.

Ernie O'Malley arrived in Kilkenny City on Saturday, 4 December 1920, opportunely when a brigade meeting was taking place which allowed him to record all company captains and available weapons throughout the entire

Kilkenny Brigade. He would have been known personally by some of the Kilkenny IRA officers present who participated in the Drangan Barracks attack in County Tipperary six months previously. O'Malley stayed with the Stallard family of Danville, just 3 km south of the city.[100] On 8 December 1920 O'Malley travelled to Inistioge with the help of Edward 'Ned' Holland, a member of the Kilkenny IRA who was then on the run in Ballyouskill, attempting to avoid arrest. Holland had spent much time secretly making munitions at DeLoughry's foundry and had taken part in the Hugginstown RIC Barracks attack.[101] The two men stayed with local Company O/C, James Hanrahan, in Cappagh, near Inistioge.

The following morning, Hanrahan informed O'Malley on 'three occasions' that Auxiliaries were raiding houses in the area.[102] At about 10.30 am, the Auxiliaries entered Hanrahan's house. Although he had been warned of the raids, O'Malley later stated in his autobiography that the Auxiliaries were as 'unexpected as death'. When the Auxiliary Officer questioned him, O'Malley said he was visiting his aunt and that his name was 'Bernard Stewart'. However, he had left his mill bombs (grenades) on the windowsill and a notebook on the desk. After glancing through O'Malley's notebook one of the Auxiliaries stated 'we have the lot'. O'Malley tried to make a run towards a back entrance of the room, while simultaneously attempting to pull out his revolver. However, his gun got wedged in the lining of his coat and he was pinned against the wall by Auxiliary section leader Arthur Stopher. O'Malley was immediately disarmed, arrested, and taken to nearby Woodstock, ironically the place he was attempting to enter on his own terms.[103] All inhabitants of James Hanrahan's home were removed, including his 80-year-old mother who was sick in bed. In spite of the presence of a priest – Father Kearns who had arrived to administer the last rites to Margaret Hanrahan – the Auxiliaries burned down the house and adjacent farm buildings. Neighbours brought the ailing Margaret Hanrahan away from the house on a mattress, as she watched the home she had lived in for over sixty years engulfed by flames.[104]

The calamity of events in Inistioge, from a Kilkenny IRA Brigade viewpoint, was that the Auxiliaries obtained from O'Malley's diary the full list of names of all Kilkenny IRA captains, along with the number of weapons and ammunition in each area. As O'Malley sourced the weaponry information directly from the battalion leaders themselves, it is safe to assume it was accurate data. The County Inspector reported to his superiors in Dublin Castle using this captured data. He stated the Kilkenny IRA Brigade was in possession of 103 rifles with 4,900 rounds of ammunition and 471 shotguns with 3,490 cartridges of varying quality.[105]

O'Malley was subjected to extreme beatings by the Auxiliaries but never revealed his true identity to his interrogators. The Auxiliaries in Kilkenny also tried a less violent tactic to obtain information from him. Laurence Cody from Romansvalley, Newmarket, County Kilkenny was sheltering in Woodstock. His identity has only recently become known due to the release of files relating to this period from the British Archives. Cody had assisted the Auxiliaries in their arrest of local IRA member Daniel Holden the previous week and was now in fear of his life. The Auxiliaries decided Cody would have to earn his keep in Woodstock and he was placed in the cell with O'Malley and Holland under the pretence that he was also a prisoner. Cody reported to the Auxiliaries that the following occurred: '[One of the prisoners] stated he was on the shooting og [of] 14 police (Auxiliary) near Cork. The second prisoner stated he was on the shooting of three officers in Dublin. [The] Prisoners stated they came to Inistioge last night, 54 of them in number.'[106] Cody's story was entirely fabricated. The reference to Cork was in relation to the ambush of Auxiliaries at Kilmichael by Tom Barry's Flying Column the previous week. Cody was perhaps trying to show his usefulness to his hosts. O'Malley was not fooled by the subterfuge. He later wrote about the Woodstock incident in his autobiography:

> a man was kicked into the cell [Cody] whist the Auxiliaries spewed out a stream of curses ... He was placed near me. He began to talk, asked me what was my name, why I had been arrested. I said for carrying a gun ...The conversation languished. I managed by moving up my forehead to work the bandage [blindfold] off my eyes so that after a time I could see a form seated near me. I said, 'Do your ropes hurt you?'. 'Yes', he replied. 'Have they tied you on top of the handcuffs?'. 'They have, and my wrists hurt like the devil'. I rolled over, sat up and touched his arms with my fingers. He had no handcuffs and his arms were loosely tied ... Then I talked to him, told him extravagantly simple tales of my not being in much sympathy with the Irish Republican Army and of my being tired of it all. An hour later some Auxiliaries entered and told the prisoner to whom I had been talking to sit up ... they hustled him out ... Later I heard them [Auxiliaries] shouting outside the door. I was from Macroom, they said, where the big ambush of Auxies had taken place. They meant Kilmichael ... 'It looks as if they don't like me', I said to Holland, and we laughed.[107]

O'Malley was then sent to prison in Dublin (via Kilkenny Military Barracks) from where he escaped two months later. Ned Holland, who suffered similar beatings after his capture, was transferred to Spike Island prison having been sentenced to ten-years penal servitude.[108]

The net effect of O'Malley's capture was that during the following days there was a major round up of IRA members. Peter DeLoughry was once again arrested. Kilkenny lost its second Brigade O/C in a number of weeks. DeLoughry was used as a 'human shield' during Auxiliary searches in the days after his arrest.[109] In addition, Jim Roughan, O/C of the highly active 7th Battalion, was also arrested. George O'Dwyer (1884–1948), O/C of the 3rd Battalion in Castlecomer, was elected as the new Kilkenny Brigade O/C the following month.[110]

On 20 December 1920, just two weeks after this setback, the Kilkenny Brigade received a morale boost when the 7th Battalion Kilkenny IRA, acting on its own initiative, attacked a party of Auxiliaries and RIC on a road near the village of Ninemilehouse. Due to premature gunfire they did not cause many casualties. However, during the retreat, in the bleak December darkness, a party of soldiers from the Devonshire Regiment opened fire on RIC reinforcements who had made their way from Kilkenny City to help the soldiers. The District and County Inspectors barely avoided being hit. Sergeant Thomas Walsh was not so lucky and was struck in the head, dying soon afterwards. He was 40 years old and a native of Ballyragget. He was only a few months previously promoted to sergeant, having served in the RIC for twenty years.[111] Media reports directly after the Ninemilehouse ambush widely exaggerated the casualties, asserting that there were 'many killed and wounded'.[112] However, just one soldier was killed, with one badly wounded, losing an eye.[113] The London *Times* would seem to be responsible for the inaccurate and widely exaggerated reporting. The newspaper gave a large amount of coverage on the front page on 22 December 1920 to the 'hill battle' and the 'many ambushes' that took place, while even including maps of the area.[114]

The final months of the conflict saw a further escalation in the violence, with no end in sight.

CHAPTER 5

War of Independence Part 2: Martial Law (January–July 1921)

'The morale of this County Force is excellent thanks largely to the vigour and utility of the Auxiliary Division.'

– Kilkenny RIC County Inspector Whyte

Early 1921 brought Martial Law to County Kilkenny, with the crime of 'wearing or the unauthorised possession of uniforms' punishable by the death penalty.[1] There was a push to reorganise the Kilkenny battalions from the brigade leadership but also from GHQ in Dublin after the imprisonment of so many of their key leaders before Christmas. Following on from the formation of the 8th Battalion in October 1920, the new 9th Battalion was formed in early February 1921. A number of battalions were visited by Patrick Medlar, IRA Director of Organisation, who tried to 'hammer them [the battalions] into some kind of shape'.[2]

Michael Cassidy's Execution: January 1921

On 5 January 1921, Michael 'Micky' Cassidy, a 38-year-old bachelor labourer, was shot at the farm of his employer James Campion in Knocknadogue, 5 km south of Castlecomer. Cassidy had been antagonistic to a number of the local IRA members and had 'boasted that he would stop the Volunteers [IRA]'.[3] Cassidy and some of his friends were being observed by the IRA for a number of months, especially where they congregated on the main Kilkenny to Castlecomer road near the Dinin River, south of Castlecomer (also known as Dysart Bridge). Here they were seen conversing with Crown Forces on a number of occasions, while their presence at that location also alarmed the local IRA who suspected their movements on the main road were being noted and passed to Crown Forces.

Also at this time, the 3rd Battalion IRA often commandeered mail from the postman to examine the content of the correspondence. Once finished, the letters would be returned to the postman for onward delivery with 'censored by the IRA' written on the front. It was through this activity the IRA discovered that the Crown Forces in Castlecomer were obtaining information from Cassidy about IRA members in the area.[4] In addition, just a few days before Cassidy's shooting, the home of K Company (Muckalee) O/C, Jim Conway, was raided by Crown Forces and his hay barn burned down.[5] Conway was lucky to escape and again Cassidy was suspected of providing information.

Cassidy's fate was now sealed. A tribunal was held locally where Cassidy was found guilty of spying *in absentia* and the evidence against him was sent to IRA GHQ in Dublin. At around 7.45 am on Wednesday, 5 January 1921 two men arrived at the farm where Cassidy was employed. Elizabeth Olive Campion, wife of Cassidy's employer, stated that two individuals, who were wearing cloths over their faces, knocked on her kitchen door and asked to speak to Cassidy for 'a few minutes'. She pointed them to the outside barn loft where Cassidy slept.[6] The IRA wanted to remove Cassidy from the farm and execute him near Dysart Bridge as a warning to other informers, but Cassidy attacked the men with a four-pronged sprong. In the ensuing struggle, Cassidy was shot in the chest by one of the men, and then as he fled he was hit in the head by the other man, dying instantly. Before leaving, one of the men 'whispered the Act of Contrition in his ear' and left a placard on Cassidy's body with the following written on it; 'Spies beware – killed by the IRA'.[7]

Michael Cassidy's brother, Jack, passed the gunmen on the road some minutes later and stated they were 'both strangers to me', although he did give their description to the authorities. One was 'about 50 years of age' with a 'fat face' and about '5ft 6 inches'. The other was aged about 35 years, '5ft 10 inches', of 'slight build', with a 'dark brown moustache'.[8] As Jack Cassidy did not recognise the men, it implies it was an outside IRA Company who carried out the execution. Therefore, the strike was most likely arranged by IRA GHQ after Cassidy had been found guilty. Months later, the RIC issued detailed descriptions of the men in the official RIC magazine *Hue-and-Cry*, but to no avail.[9] The military from Castlecomer collected Michael Cassidy's body from the farm later that day and after an autopsy recorded the cause of death as 'a gunshot wound of [the] chest'.[10]

Friary Street Ambush: February 1921

Following the restructuring of the IRA in early 1921, it is notable that on the night of 12 February 1921 the first coordinated brigade attacks took place, when separate battalions attacked police Barracks in Gowran and Callan.[11] They also received help from the nearby Carlow Brigade who trenched roads to impede the arrival of British forces. Although the attacks were small in nature and no injuries were reported to the Crown Forces, it was nevertheless a propaganda coup for the IRA as it looked as if their numbers were numerous and well organised.[12]

The only attack that took place in Kilkenny City occurred on Friary Street on Monday morning, 21 February 1921. It was organised by Timothy Hennessy from Threecastles who was the 1st Battalion O/C. The plan was to ambush a patrol of seven soldiers from the Devonshire Regiment who transported food supplies daily from Kilkenny Military Barracks to Kilkenny Jail, passing through the city centre.[13] To avoid the problem of being identified, only men from rural Companies of the 1st Battalion, based outside Kilkenny City, were chosen for the attacking party, with the majority sourced from Kells, Bennettsbridge and Threecastles. Tim Hennessy himself was not part of the ambush group as the Kilkenny Brigade could not risk the capture of yet another Battalion O/C, while he also had recently received a severe beating by the Auxiliaries at his place of employment at Ennisnag. Surprisingly, given the violent ambushes that were occurring throughout Ireland at that time, Hennessy ordered his men not to shoot the soldiers but instead to physically attack and disarm them.[14] His logic may have been for moral reasons or was perhaps to save the inhabitants of Friary Street suffering the same faith as parts of Cork City two months previously, where the city centre was burned to the ground by Auxiliaries. Either way, the IRA men involved in the attack showed their loyalty to the cause when they knew they would be at an immediate disadvantage by not using their firearms.

As the military convoy was typically spaced some distance apart – with two soldiers marching out in front, three with the cart in the centre, and two at the rear – there was an elaborate plan to attack and disarm the soldiers simultaneously at the different positions throughout the length of Friary Street. The IRA men outnumbered the soldiers two to one. The convoy proceeded as per expected, turning from High Street onto the narrow Friary Street. However, the intervention of a terrified woman who shouted 'soldiers you are being attacked' put the plans into disarray.[15] Thomas Hennessy and Michael Dermody had attacked the two soldiers at the rear of the convoy somewhat prematurely, before James O'Brien, the IRA Commander on the day, had blown his whistle. Two of the soldiers in the main part of the convoy then turned around and saw their two companions, Private Harry Hawthorn and Private Stanley Gay, wrestling with the two IRA men close to the Capuchin Friary. One of these soldiers, Lance Corporal Ernest Higgins, shot Michael Dermody, while the other, Private Harley Turner, shot Thomas Hennessy at close range. Hennessy died almost instantly, the bullet having passed through his abdomen which severed an artery, while Dermody was critically injured following a bullet wound to the head.

A civilian, Thomas Dollard, who had unfortunately left the Friary Chapel at the exact moment the altercation was taking place, ran down the road towards High Street. He was shot by the soldiers who believed him to be one of the IRA party.[16]

The remainder of the IRA ambush party escaped. Timothy Hennessy, 1st Battalion Commandant, paid a high price as his own brother, Thomas, aged 31 years, was one of the IRA fatalities. Thomas's funeral was held two days later in Tulla Church near Threecastles. During the Mass the church was surrounded by Crown Forces. Despite the fact the chief celebrant was a brother of the deceased – Father Nicholas Hennessy – Timothy Hennessy was duly arrested, thus ending his participation in the War of Independence.[17] Michael Dermody, aged 25 years, who never regained consciousness after being shot, died on 4 March 1921 and was buried near Thomas in Tulla graveyard.[18]

The beginning of 1921 also saw the formation of two IRA Active Service Units (ASUs – also known as 'Flying Columns') in the brigade area. Similar to what was occurring in the broader conflict in Ireland, the establishment of the ASUs in Kilkenny was instigated by GHQ, but had also become a practical necessity more than a choice, as many of the IRA men were now wanted and would be arrested if they returned to their homes. Therefore, being permanently on the run while carrying out sporadic attacks was the only alternative to likely arrest.

Garryricken House: The Great Escape, March 1921

On 12 March 1921 a dramatic shootout occurred between the 7th Kilkenny Battalion ASU and a number of soldiers and Black and Tans at Garryricken House, 7 km south of Callan near the Tipperary border. The ASU were billeting at the house after returning from the funerals of Tipperary IRA members Patrick Hackett, Dick Fleming and Martin Clancy, who had been killed during an altercation with Crown Forces the previous week at Knockroe in Tipperary. Garryricken House itself was owned by the Ormonde family but had been vacant for many years. Instead, adjoining houses were occupied by the Luttrell family who acted as caretakers of the property and land. One of the Luttrell family, 27-year-old Paddy, was a member of the 7th Battalion ASU. Consequently, many IRA men would have frequented the house when lodgings were required. At around 3.00 am on the morning of Saturday, 12 March 1921, five members of the 7th Battalion ASU retired for the night to the main part of Garryricken House. These were; Battalion O/C James Leahy, Vice O/C Ned Aylward and Seán Quinn who slept upstairs, while Paddy Luttrell and Jim McKenna slept downstairs. A sixth member, Paddy Ryan, slept in one of the other buildings close to the house. Unbeknown to the IRA men, the military in Callan had been informed of their presence in the house.[19] A large group of Crown Forces, which included the RIC, military and Black and Tans, advanced to the vicinity of the house during the early hours of the morning from three different directions. One of these parties arrived late, which would benefit the IRA greatly. At 7.00 am, RIC District Inspector Baynham, Corporal Fisher and Lieutenant Williams (both Devonshire Regiment) knocked at the door requesting to be let in. John Luttrell, brother of Paddy, eventually let the men inside, but John's wife Annie had enough time to wake the sleeping IRA men upstairs. They quickly decided they would rather fight than be captured. The IRA men sleeping downstairs were still unaware of the imminent danger. The Inspector and two military officers searched the adjoining house first. Turning into the passageway that lead to the main house Aylward opened fire. The Crown Forces returned fire but retreated to the bedroom of caretaker John Luttrell where his wife and three children, who were under the ages of four, were sheltering. Inspector Baynham went to the window of the room to communicate instructions to his men located on the front lawn of the house.[20] When Aylward and Leahy saw him at the window from the room they were in, they opened fire. Baynham was hit in the neck and was bleeding profusely. He was moved to a bed and Luttrell and his wife bandaged the wound with sheets.[21]

Leahy knew the layout of the house and surrounding area intimately and he also had a good view of the various troop positions surrounding the house. After about thirty minutes they decided to make their escape by the rear courtyard, as this appeared less fortified. They descended to the bottom floor of the house. They had presumed the two other IRA men in the house, Paddy Luttrell and McKenna, had already escaped. After saying a prayer, they ran into the yard where luckily for them Paddy Ryan, who had slept away from the main house, was engaging in a gun fight with some of the Crown Forces. He joined with his three companions and all four shot at the various Crown Force positions as they ran through the courtyard. After passing through the yard and over a back wall they were confronted by one Black and Tan, Constable Riley. All four fired at him killing 26-year-old Ernest James Riley instantly. Quinn seized his rifle and the four IRA men escaped through the fields at the rear, eventually arriving at a safe house – Sinnott's of Mallardstown near Callan – which was about 9 km away.[22] When Quinn had taken the rifle from the dead soldier, he had unwittingly dropped his pocket watch. He had bought the watch from a person called 'Martin Gunn', whose name was inscribed into the timepiece. Gunn had to go on the run as his description appeared in the RIC periodical magazine where he was named as 'the murderer' of Constable Riley, even though he was never in Garryricken House.[23]

The two remaining IRA men inside Garryricken House, Paddy Luttrell and Jim McKenna, were not so fortunate, having been trapped in the downstairs bedroom with no view of proceedings. A Lewis machine gun was also positioned in the front of the house where they were located, making it impossible to escape.[24] They surrendered and were badly beaten by the military with the aim of extracting information. They were later sentenced to death, which was subsequently commuted to life in prison.[25]

From a British Administration point of view, the events at Garryricken House were highly embarrassing. One constable was killed, a District Inspector was severely wounded (although he survived), and four IRA men managed to escape against the superior numbers of nearly thirty members of the Crown Forces. The inquiry that followed attributed blame in a number of areas, with the most notable findings being:

- D[istrict]. I[nspector]. Baynham acted on reliable information, but a complete 'round up' of active rebels was spoilt by entering the house prematurely.

- 2nd Lieutenant Evans's party [a group of ten soldiers from the Devonshire Regiment] had not reached the scene at the time some of the rebels escaped.

- Constable Riley was left 'in the air' [exposed] as Constable Griffiths was not where D.I. Baynham intended him to be.

- The bullet which caused the wound [to Riley] was dum dum or some form of explosive bullet.[26]

The final point about the bullet that killed Riley was untrue as the IRA did not possess bullets of that kind. It was an accusation often made against the IRA in an attempt to taint their reputation to the general public by amplifying their brutishness. The large amount of damage caused to Constable Riley's forehead is the reason many believed an explosive bullet was used. Writing over thirty years later, the leader of the IRA ASU on the day, James Leahy, was keen to emphasise the reality of what had occurred, stating:

> At a subsequent British military inquiry into the [Garryricken] affair it was stated, and it appeared in the press at the time, that Constable Riley died from two bullet wounds in the stomach and one in the head, and that the wound in his head was caused by a dum-dum bullet. None of our men was in possession of dum-dum ammunition, and it is my opinion that the bullet which hit him in the head first hit his cap badge and, or perhaps, the wire of his cap, and it was thus he received such a jagged wound.[27]

This feat in escaping against overwhelming odds was complimented by IRA Chief of Staff Richard Mulcahy, which was conveyed to the Kilkenny Brigade Commandant.[28] District Inspector Hubert Leslie Baynham, aged 28 and originally from Wales, was awarded £6,000 compensation for his injuries – which had been increased from £5,000 on appeal. The high award was due to the fact that, as a result of his injuries, he would lose his £700 per annum salary. On the other hand, the mother of the deceased Constable Riley from Brighton was awarded £750. Riley had only joined the RIC (Black and Tans) three weeks previously. He had spent four and a half years as a prisoner of war in Germany during the First World War.[29]

The five men arrested at the house, namely; Jim McKenna, John, Patrick, James and Thomas Luttrell, were all tried by military court martial in Waterford. They were lucky to have 'only' received jail sentences, as similar occurrences in other parts of the country resulted in at least one execution. Besides the Garryricken five, only two other Kilkenny civilians were court-marshalled by the British military during the martial law phase of the War of Independence. These were Laurence Medlar from Paulstown and John McBride from Knockmoylan, Mullinavat. Medlar was sentenced to death after he was caught with '39 sticks of gelignite' after an attack on Gowran RIC Barracks (it was commuted to fifteen years' penal servitude), while McBride had been arrested on innocuous charges of not cooperating with the Crown Forces after he refused to help them unblock a railway crossing.[30] Both were released following the signing of the Treaty.

Attempted Assassinations of Foxy Officer and the RIC County Inspector: March 1921

The 7th Battalion ASU tried to assassinate an officer whom they referred to as the 'Foxy Officer' in a public house in Mullinahone on the night of 20 March 1921. This Auxiliary Officer, named Litchfield, was believed to have been responsible for the killing of the three IRA leaders shot at Knockroe at the beginning of the month. The assassination attempt in Mullinahone was interrupted when a local RIC man, William Campbell, stumbled across Ned Aylward and Jimmy Kelly of the 7th Battalion ASU, who were waiting in a doorway for the Foxy Officer to leave the pub. The IRA men opened fire thinking they were surrounded by RIC. Campbell was shot in the head and died instantly. Ironically, Campbell had been very friendly to the IRA in the area, often informing them when the RIC were planning raids in the district.[31]

In retaliation, the military under the instruction of Colonel-Commandant Cammeron, destroyed four houses in Mullinahone which were close to where Campbell was killed. The families residing in the houses were; Cuddihy, Moroney, Vaughan and Redmond. The military released a statement to the press following the destruction of the houses stating that the 'owners must have known of the intention of certain unknown rebels to murder Constable William Campbell'.[32] Campbell's widow and three children were awarded £5,500 compensation.[33]

During March 1921, an attempt was made to assassinate RIC County Inspector Whyte in Kilkenny City. Whyte was described as 'a daredevil type' as he continued to make the five-minute walk from his office on Parliament Street in Kilkenny City, to his fortified home just off the Callan Road, even in the midst of the War of Independence. He did have a party of military who accompanied him, nevertheless, it was dangerous and something most county inspectors would not have risked at this time. Whyte was not well liked as he was believed to be 'particularly obnoxious' and 'was known to have approved of the manhandling of prisoners'. Ned Aylward, 7th Battalion ASU O/C, was asked by 1st Battalion officers to come into Kilkenny City with some of his men and carry out an attack, which he agreed to do. CI Whyte usually left his office at 5.30 pm daily and walked with his small convoy of bodyguards to his home. However, for security purposes his convoy split in two, one travelling via College Road to his home, the other travelling by the Circular Road via Abbey Street, with Whyte himself alternating between which group he travelled with. On the day in question there was miscommunication between Aylward and the Kilkenny City scouts, which resulted in Aylward and his assassination party walking up College Road in the direction of Saint Patrick's Church, although Whyte had taken the other route. Aylward and his men walked alongside the lengthy boundary wall of Saint Kieran's College and saw the RIC patrol coming towards them. However, as they got closer to the RIC patrol, near the entrance to Saint Kieran's College, they realised Whyte was not present and aborted. The two groups of men then simply walked past each other on College Road, the Crown Forces unaware of the real motives of the men they just passed, and that one of them was Ned Aylward, a most wanted man.[34]

Beware of Inherent Dangers: April 1921

On 6 April 1921, one of the best fighters in the 7th Battalion ASU, Jackie (Seán) Brett, was accidentally killed. He was billeting at the Donovan household in Castlejohn, near the village of Windgap, and a young member of the household unintentionally fired Brett's revolver while he was in the process of cleaning his other weapons. The bullet passed through his chest and he died shortly afterwards. He was 19 years old. Brett had played corner-forward on the Tipperary team that played in the infamous 'Bloody Sunday' Gaelic football charity match just five months previously, when fourteen civilians were killed by Crown Forces.[35] After his death, Brett was first buried in a makeshift grave in a cemetery nearby. Then rumours began to circulate that his body was to be taken by 'the Tans', so it was exhumed during the night and brought to the home of Tullahought Cumann na mBan member Nano Meagher. She buried the remains of Brett in her field and then planted mangolds over the grave so it would not look suspicious.[36] Brett's remains were interred for the third time and final time during the Truce in August 1921, in the graveyard of his native Mullinahone village, following a massive funeral.

On 13 April, the same 7th Battalion ASU was involved in the Moonarch ambush on the Kilkenny/Tipperary border where two lorries of Auxiliaries were ambushed wounding a number of the soldiers, with all IRA escaping.[37]

Trenching of roads and making bridges impassable was par of the course for the average IRA member during the War of Independence. Sometimes they filled the roads in again or fixed bridges temporarily to allow locals pass through, once the imminent threat of Crown Forces had subsided. The roads around Mullinavat and its surrounding hinterland were subjected to much destruction to impede the movement of Crown Forces based in the barracks there, while also disrupting the movements of Auxiliaries travelling from Woodstock. On one occasion during the afternoon of 21 April 1921, an unsuspecting group of Auxiliaries and RIC crashed into a trench causing them to be thrown from their Ford Touring car near the townlands of Castlebanny and Knockmoylan – on the main road between Ballyhale and Mullinavat. Two of the party were badly injured, while the rest were incensed. One of the injured Auxiliaries, Francis White, later requested £10,000 compensation for his injuries.[38] The remainder of the Auxiliaries went on raids in the locality. At one stage, a man who was visiting his mother in the district, was used as a hostage. A Vickers machine gun was actually rested on his shoulder as the Auxiliaries fired at fleeing men who were running through fields to get away from the area.[39]

Whether on that occasion or sometime afterwards, the Auxiliaries placed two mills bombs (grenades) in the rubble they had used to cross the recently destroyed Knockmoylan Bridge. They knew the IRA would make the bridge impassable at some stage again or use the stones to build road blocks. Their trap would have life-changing consequences for one local man, 19-year-old William Aylward from Knockwilliam, Ballyhale, who was a member of the Knockmoylan IRA Company. On 21 June 1921, Aylward's F Company, under the command of Captain Patrick Kearns, was tasked with destroying the bridge and blocking the roads between Knockwilliam and Knockmoylan. The reason for this action was because of yet another planned attack on nearby Mullinavat Barracks – the third such major attack on the barracks. As the Knockmoylan Company began moving the stones, one of the bombs exploded, shooting dust and debris into the air. Luckily no one was injured. However, the second bomb soon exploded. This time a piece of shrapnel entered the left eye of William Aylward, while he had blurred vision in the other eye. He was brought away from the scene to a safe house, as the Aylward family knew there was a good chance their home would be raided in the aftermath of the Mullinavat Barracks attack (although the barracks itself was not captured in the attack). He was without medical attention for some time because bringing him to a hospital would have been too risky as Crown Forces would have suspected a young man to have picked up an injury of that nature during IRA activities. Having spent his 20th birthday in 'untold agony', Aylward was relieved that a truce was declared the following month, meaning he was then able to seek medical help. He travelled to Dublin on 17 July 1921 – the week the truce was declared – to have his eyes medically examined. He went to the Royal Victoria Eye and Ear Hospital but was told the inevitable – that the left could be treated but the right eye could not be saved. It was subsequently removed.[40]

On 23 April 1921, the 7th Battalion/West Kilkenny ASU moved to the south of County Kilkenny where they planned to ambush a Black and Tan patrol which usually passed between the villages of Fiddown and Piltown.[41] The ASU arrived early in the morning, taking up a position in an area called Beech Farm. One Black and Tan, who was out walking on his own, was captured. The IRA presence in the area was evidently discovered, as during the afternoon large numbers of soldiers began arriving from Carrick-on-Suir and Waterford. The ASU decided to retire through the Bessborough demesne. The captured Black and Tan was brought with them. However, before they got to the 'big house' on the demesne, fire was opened on them from a wood.[42] Machine-gun bullets flew over their heads. They were very fortunate the gun was positioned too high and they were on an incline, thus avoiding serious injury. The ASU split up and fled. Some moved north across the Bog Road and over the hills through Templeorum, the others east towards Mooncoin. Ned Aylward, leader of the ASU that day, described what happened after they had been surprised by the Crown Forces in Bessborough:

> None of us were hit, however, and as we jumped for cover we were encumbered by our prisoner, the Black and Tan we had captured earlier. There was nothing we could do with him except bring him along, but in the predicament we found ourselves, he was a bit of a nuisance. We took him with us, however, for a couple of miles across country [towards Mooncoin] and then faced with the alternative of either shooting him or letting him go, we decided to let him off at this point. He seemed to be a fairly decent sort of chap and we did not like to shoot him in cold blood. His name was Carrigan – a London-Irishman – and he volunteered that if we allowed him to go he would not give away anything he had seen, nor identify any of us. We heard afterwards that he had been as good as his word … he said he was too frightened to remember anything.[43]

Although this planned ambush was another non-starter for the ASU, geographically the IRA appeared to be spreading attacks throughout the county which alarmed British authorities. Moreover, this part of south County Kilkenny was one of the quietest areas up to that point, thus the publicity was good for the IRA campaign. The RIC erroneously reported to Dublin Castle that the failed Piltown ambush was carried out by the famous republican Dan Breen.[44] There is no evidence to suggest why the RIC made such a connection. It may have been local gossip or perhaps an excuse to save their blushes as no IRA men were captured after so many troops had been deployed to the area, leading them to assert it was Breen the great enigma.

Kilmanagh and Tullaroan: May 1921

The 7th Battalion ASU was to garner even more publicity for its next engagement. The column moved northwards to the village of Kilmanagh, 13 km from Kilkenny City. Here they joined with Seán Hogan's 3rd Tipperary Brigade ASU, making a combined force of upwards of sixty men.[45] This link-up was not premeditated and was only decided by the two ASU Commandants after they arrived in the same area at the same time.

In the village of Kilmanagh the combined ASU forces, under the joint command of Ned Aylward and Seán Hogan, had their most daring engagement when they took control of the entire village at 6.00 am on 12 May 1921.[46] Men were positioned at all entry points into the village. A number of the local houses were occupied and they even erected posters stating that the village was in a 'military area'. They purposely sent word to Kilkenny City and Callan through the post office telegram system that the village had been taken, with the aim of drawing Crown Forces to the area and engaging in what would have been the largest fight in the south east of Ireland during the War of Independence. Their bait did not work however, and by evening they felt obliged to withdraw northwards to safety, as the element of surprise had dissipated. It was a great publicity coup for the IRA nonetheless, with the *Irish Independent* headlining it 'the Invasion of Kilmanagh' with '300 Sinn Féiners' invading the village – which was over three times the actual number.[47]

Large sections of British Forces pursued in their wake. The ASUs were planning on travelling north to Urlingford and attacking the barracks there. However, they never got that far, as disaster struck. The day after the Kilmanagh takeover, 13 May 1921, two ASU members, Seán Quinn and Captain Patrick Walsh, were mortally wounded at Knocknagress, Tullaroan, after an altercation with Crown Forces. Soldiers had arrived at the house where some of the ASU had billeted overnight. The main party of ASU escaped through the fields. Quinn, Walsh and another column member, Paddy Power, had been asleep in an outhouse of the property, unaware of what was happening until valuable time had been lost. They attempted to follow their comrades through the fields but got trapped in a military cordon. They tried to escape through dykes but when they surfaced back onto the field a volley of bullets was fired, hitting them a number of times. Luckily for Power, he had slipped backwards into the dyke and missed the volley. He miraculously escaped being caught, as he hid in dyke water by covering himself in rushes until the military had gone. Pat Walsh, from the village of Dunnamaggin, had just completed a jail term for the possession of 'seditious documents' the week previously and had only been a member of the flying column for four days.[48] The two men, who were still alive at the point of their capture, were left in a military lorry for two hours on their way back to Kilkenny City when the British Forces visited a public house. The captured and badly injured men were denied food or water which locals attempted to provide them with.[49]

Seán Quinn, who was 22 years old, died shortly after arriving in Kilkenny Military Barracks and was subsequently buried in his native Mullinahone. He had been one of the party that made a dramatic escape from Garryricken House two months earlier. Pat Walsh was transferred to the main military hospital in Fermoy but died there five days later on 18 May 1921, during an operation to amputate his leg. He was 33 years old. He possibly could have survived if he had received earlier medical intervention. The two fatalities were widely reported and were even raised on the floor of the House of Commons when James Kiley, the Liberal MP for Whitechapel in London, queried the circumstances surrounding the death of the men. The question occurred during a debate on the military campaign in Ireland, with Kiley being critical of his own party's role in the war in Ireland.[50]

The funeral of Patrick Walsh was held in Dunnamaggin on Sunday, 22 May 1921. The previous day, two members of Dunnamaggin IRA, John Hickey and Pat Holden, rented a hackney car from Bill Egan of Callan, to drive them to Fermoy. It was a long arduous journey through damaged roads but they got there just in time, as the military had a grave already dug to inter Walsh if his body had not been claimed that day.[51] Walsh was popular in GAA and Sinn Féin circles and was a founding member of the Gaelic League in Dunnamaggin. Floral tributes on his coffin included wreaths from Sinn Féin and Cumann na mBan in Fermoy where he had passed away. Dunnamaggin Hurling Club also sent a floral token which contained a message commiserating with his father, Matthew. Pat Walsh had been one of the founding members of the hurling club. The Republican tricolour flag placed on the coffin was unceremoniously ripped off it by the Crown Forces present at the funeral. After the service 'no more than 40 people were allowed to follow the funeral to the graveyard' on the orders of the military officer present.[52]

In the aftermath of the IRA fatalities in Knocknagress, two local ex-British soldiers who aided the Crown Forces in locating the ASU, 41-year-old Martin Dermody and Michael O'Keeffe who was approximately 55 years old, were executed as informers by the IRA. The two men were taken from their homes three days after the event, in the early hours of Tuesday, 17 May 1921. They were brought to a nearby gravel quarry in Oldtown, Tullaroan, where they were executed. No trial took place as the local IRA Company had 'ascertained the guilt of the men' as they were seen 'going around with the British troops'.[53] Local man, Thomas (Tod) Ronan, made the grim discovery in a sandpit at the quarry that morning. O'Keeffe was still alive when he was found and was brought to the home of his employer but died shortly afterwards on that same afternoon. He had been shot in the abdomen. Dermody was shot through the heart and would have died instantly.[54] Both men had been employed as farm labourers in the area, though O'Keeffe had recently moved from Carrick-on-Suir. Dermody's body contained a note 'sticking out of his left hand pocket' which contained the words; 'convicted as a spy and traitor. All others beware of the IRA'.[55] When Ronan initially arrived at the scene, Dermody's dog was found lying across his body. The 'dog was very much attached to Dermody' and it 'was with the utmost difficultly that he could be separated from the lifeless form of his master – faithful even in death'. The dog was brought to Kilkenny Military Barracks by some soldiers who were 'anxious to adopt him as a mascot'.[56]

These executions were not sanctioned by IRA GHQ in Dublin. A stipulation that permission must be sought had been issued by GHQ some months earlier, although this 'interference' from Dublin was widely ignored around the country. Richard Mulcahy, IRA Chief of Staff, wrote to the Kilkenny Brigade O/C some weeks later stating that it was 'a very serious matter that a junior Officer [Ned Aylward] should take upon himself the responsibility for executing two alleged spies … Brigade Commandant's [George O'Dwyer's] authority is necessary before a spy can be executed. There must be no slacking in this regard to this order.'[57]

The Rower Altercation: 10 June 1921

The 5th Battalion, specifically The Rower Company, had its most important – and unanticipated – action on 10 June 1921.[58] Two Auxiliaries had been carrying out reconnaissance work in the area that day – in civilian clothes – before retiring to Butler's public house/hotel for food and refreshments.[59] The men had been observed and recognised as Auxiliaries. After leaving the pub later that evening, they were followed by local IRA men (C Company, The Rower), who were led by their captain, James Mackey. The two Auxiliaries made their way out of the village on the New Ross Road. When they discovered they were being pursued, they tried to make their escape over a ditch. There followed an exchange of gunshots from both sides. Auxiliary Intelligence Officer Roy Kirke escaped and eventually returned to Woodstock, but his companion, 26-year-old Auxiliary Cadet Leonard James French, was fatally wounded in the exchange. French was formally a Royal Air Force pilot during the First World War and was from Lancashire.[60] In reprisal, the following evening, the Auxiliaries terrorised a number of residents of the village of The Rower, while the home and public-house of Timothy Butler were burned down. His wife and young children were given five minutes to leave their home. Butler himself was brought to Woodstock House where he was incarcerated and badly treated by the Auxiliaries for five days.[61] There was initially ambiguity in British ranks about whether French was killed outright or wounded and captured. His death, however, was confirmed by the IRA in August 1921. His family received a total of £3,400 in compensation from the authorities.[62]

Coolbawn Ambush: 18 June 1921

On Saturday, 18 June 1921 the 1st Kilkenny ASU (Flying Column), under the command of Kilkenny Brigade O/C George O'Dwyer, attempted to perform the largest single IRA engagement of the War of Independence era in County Kilkenny at Coolbawn, approximately 4 km north of Castlecomer. The intention was to attack a military escort that conveyed gelignite explosives from Castlecomer Military Barracks to Wolfhill colliery. The mines in the area had a licence to use explosives, a rarity at this time in Ireland in case they would fall into the wrong hands. However, the day did not turn out as planned for the ASU.

Since its creation in the early months of 1921, the 1st Kilkenny ASU did not have a great deal of luck. In April and May it had participated in an unsuccessful ambush at Uskerty Woods and a failed attack at Bagenalstown RIC Barracks, County Carlow.[63] In the lead-up to the Coolbawn Ambush, the O/C of the 3rd Battalion, Michael Fleming, clashed with O'Dwyer about the planned ambush as he thought it too risky. All companies in the battalion area were expected to provide at least four men for the attack, but Fleming did not sanction the men of his Swan Company (A Company) to participate. O'Dwyer received a dispatch from Fleming on the morning of the planned ambush, which stated:

> To Brigade Commandant,
> Sorry. I don't believe in your action. Wishing you luck.
> Commandant, 3rd Battalion.[64]

Two reasons can be offered for the no-show of Fleming and A Company. At a meeting a few days earlier, Fleming and some of the other 3rd Battalion staff had objected to the plan. Firstly, they did not agree with the physical geographic location of the ambush and had suggested an alternative spot near the Anglican church in Castlecomer. In addition, there had been an agreement between the IRA and the local trade union secretary, Tom Campion, which avowed not to interfere with the workings of the collieries, as its closure would affect the livelihoods of many local inhabitants. The ambush would therefore break the agreement, with the consequences of such an action unknown. The hinterlands in the vicinity of The Swan Company would also have borne the brunt of the colliery closure. O'Dwyer, however, had got permission from IRA GHQ to attack the colliery delivery.[65]

Besides A Company, E Company (Loon) and K Company (Muckalee) also failed to report. The O/C of the former company received the dispatch but took no action as his men had already been out on IRA work earlier that week and thought 'one night in the week sufficient when they all had to work [the next] day'. The lieutenant of the Muckalee Company did not act on the order as the 'O/C was away'. These companies were not integral to the actual fighting – as the non-ASU contingent were to act as lookouts – however, it did indicate underlying problems in the command structure, as those that did not turn up were technically disobeying orders from their Brigade O/C, the highest-ranked IRA man in the county. In a similar way, the dispatches informing the ten local companies of the proposed attack mostly arrived late on the eve of the ambush, except those dispatches that were delivered by members of Cumann na mBan which arrived promptly (dispatches to H and L Companies). O'Dwyer was not best pleased with the non-appearance of Fleming and immediately dismissed him from his post as battalion O/C. Another company captain, Garrett (Gerald) Brennan, was appointed 3rd Battalion O/C there and then at the ambush site.[66]

Nevertheless, despite the discontent, over sixty men assembled at the designated area near the ambush site at 5.30 am. The majority of the ASU was made up of members of the 1st, 3rd, 5th and 8th Battalions.[67] Landmines were placed in the road which were to be detonated when the first lorry drove over them.

The day of the ambush was also mart day in Castlecomer, so a complex plan had to be enacted to hold all the travelling farmers in a field so as to not disturb arrangements at the ambush site where the mines had been laid. This arrangement backfired when a farm labourer, Sandy Bradley, was allowed through the barricade as he was late for work in the nearby townland of Finsboro. He subsequently told his employer Florrie (Florence) Dreaper, a loyalist farm owner, the reasons for his tardy timekeeping. She guessed that an ambush was in the offing and she subsequently walked into Castlecomer by an alternative route via the Loon road, having crossed over the River Dinin by footbridge, to inform the military of the risk to their lives. This footbridge was supposed to have been occupied by members of A or E Companies.

At about 11.30 am, unbeknown to the ASU, soldiers from the Devonshire Regiment made an encircling movement on foot, outflanking the ASU. The hunters had become the hunted. At the last moment the lookouts informed O'Dwyer that they were being surrounded. He subsequently sounded his whistle and ordered a hasty retreat. As he did so, the Crown Forces opened fire from the rear.[68] ASU member Seán Hartley was killed instantly from an initial burst of machine-gun fire from behind his location. Positioned on either side of Hartley when the machine gun was discharged were Nicholas Mullins and James Doyle. Both jumped over the wall they were hiding behind and crossed the road to the other ditch, while also attempting to return fire. They were unaware that a group of Black and Tans had moved into the field on the north side of the road in tandem with the military on the south side of the road. R.J. Gwinnell, a Black-and-Tan constable, shot at Mullins, with the bullet striking him on the finger. He then shot Mullins in the back as he attempted to escape up a dyke on the north side of the roadway.[69] James Doyle, who went to Mullins's aid after he was hit, was also shot by Gwinnell. Doyle almost immediately became unconscious. The rest of the ASU managed to escape. Many of the column laid low until nightfall in a 'grove of yew trees' near the ambush site. The military did not appear inclined to risk their lives by venturing into the woods. The Crown Forces suffered no causalities during the Coolbawn altercation.[70]

Nicholas Mullins died from his injuries two hours later at around 2.00 pm, the bullet having passed through his liver.[71] Mullins, who was 28 years old, was from Thomastown and a member of the 5th Battalion. Hartley, who was 23 years old, was originally from Glenmore in the south of the county but had been employed in Kilkenny City and thus was a member of the 1st Battalion. Hartley's funeral took place in Glenmore on 21 June 1921 while Mullins's funeral took place in Thomastown the following day.[72] At the two funerals, the military were present in large numbers and they removed the tricolour flag from both coffins. The councillors in Thomastown passed a motion at their monthly meeting tendering their heartfelt sympathy to 'the relatives of the late Mr Nicholas Mullins ... who willingly gave up his young life on the altar of his country. He died so that Ireland might live and in his death showed an example of heroic sacrifice and chivalry worthy of the man and the cause for which he died.'[73] The military were antagonistic in Glenmore at the funeral of

Seán Hartley. One local woman, Ellen Cassin, who was present at the funeral, described the events of that day:

> I was searched at the Chapel gate as I went in [by the Auxiliaries and Black and Tans]. One man … ordered me to put up my hands and to open my shawl … The Black and Tans were in the porch [of the chapel] as I entered. They stood around the coffin in the chapel. They did not take off their caps … they were using violent language. Their conduct during the service was not becoming … There was a glass panel at the side of the coffin. As the people tried to look in at the corpse, the Black and Tans made remarks such as, 'Who do you want to see?' and pushed the slide back.[74]

James Doyle, having been shot twice, survived his injuries. He had the unpleasant experience of waking from his unconscious state the following day to find he was lying between the lifeless bodies of his two comrades, the military presuming he would have passed away during the night also. He described what occurred: 'I became semi-conscious and saw I was lying between my two comrades and that both were dead. I was unable to move. Later in the day I saw Crown Forces come into the place where [they] were to remove the bodies and they were surprised to see that I was alive.'[75] It took Doyle many months to recover, which was not helped by his imprisonment with hard labour. However, this was more preferable than his original sentence of execution, which was suspended after the Truce was declared three weeks after the ambush had taken place.[76]

The 3rd Battalion staff under the command of O/C Gerald Brennan, along with Kilkenny Brigade O/C George O'Dwyer, held a meeting in the days after the failed ambush to decide the punishment for Florrie Dreaper. Emotions were high following the death of the two ASU members, and some in attendance were adamant Dreaper should be executed as an informer as a consequence for her actions. However, it was pointed out by Brennan that IRA GHQ had prohibited the execution of women, while in addition, they should avoid the adverse publicity that had been caused by the Cork IRA when they executed a female informer, Mary Lyndsey, three months previously. After a vote, it was decided to burn Dreaper's house down and demand she left the country.

About 11.00 pm on the night of the 7 July 1921, around thirty members of the 3rd Battalion IRA converged on the home of Florrie Dreaper. She lived in Finsboro House, Coolbawn, with her sister Rebecca. The IRA told Florrie that she had been found guilty of informing and that her house would be burned as a result. The sisters were given a few minutes to gather their belongings and money, and vacate the house. Rebecca quickly moved to the outside stable, with some of the IRA men helping to carry her clothes. Florrie however went out onto the roof of the main house with her dog and jumped into a steel water tank. She subsequently fired flares into the night sky from a verey gun the military had given her, with the hope of attracting their attention. The house, however, was quickly set alight and the IRA dispersed. If the Crown Forces in Castlecomer had not seen the flares, they could not have missed the inferno that was Finsboro House lighting up the horizon. When the military arrived nearly two hours later, the house was gutted by the fire but Florrie Dreaper and her dog had survived in the steel water tank.[77]

The Dreaper sisters soon moved to England after local threats and intimidation increased during the Truce period (cattle were run into their fields to trample on crops, while two of their horses were stabbed). Later, the sisters requested £3,099 for the destruction of their property and belongings from the Free State Government but were awarded £452. In a twist of fate, Rebecca Dreaper died three years to the day of the Coolbawn Ambush, 18 June 1924, aged 57. Florrie Dreaper died in 1930 at the age of 60. The 365-acre Dreaper farm was later divided and redistributed to local farmers by the Land Commission.[78]

Sinnott's Cross Ambush: 18 June 1921

The Kilkenny IRA Brigade subsequently received a moral boost, when, on the very same day of the ill-fated Coolbawn ambush, the 9th Battalion Kilkenny IRA successfully ambushed a patrol of Black and Tans at Sinnott's Cross in Tubrid, Mooncoin, in south Kilkenny.[79] A party of seven Black and Tan constables were cycling on their usual patrol from Fiddown RIC Barracks to Clogga Creamery, from where they often rendezvoused with another RIC patrol coming from the Kilmacow direction; after which both parties returned to their respective barracks. At 2.45 pm, after just passing Sinnott's Cross, they were ambushed, with firing coming from both sides of the road. One Black and Tan, 23-year-old Albert Lawrence Bradford, was hit a number of times and died ten minutes later. Another Black and Tan, Constable Sweetman, was shot in the arm.[80] The casualties for the Crown Forces could have been even greater, but the gun of IRA member Dick Brennan, who was to start the firing, jammed. This delayed the attack by vital seconds until Pat 'the Fox' Walsh took the initiative and opened fire. The Black and Tans quickly sped through the ambush point and returned fire from a nearby laneway. The IRA quickly withdrew. The 9th Battalion Quartermaster, Ted Moore, captured Bradford's rifle. It is noteworthy, in terms of propaganda, that even though this was a complete failure for the British Crown Forces, their report into the matter included 'positive spin' such as the 'rebels were driven off with it is believed casualties to them', while also stating that 'five guns and 200 rounds of ammunition' were captured.[81] These statements were totally false as the IRA suffered no injuries, while they did not possess that quantity of ammunition to begin with.[82] This incident had a sequel, when on the following day, the Crossley Tender carrying Bradford's remains was alleged to have been ambushed on the new bridge (John Dillon Bridge) in nearby Carrick-on-Suir, County Tipperary. One soldier from the Devonshire Regiment, Private William Smith, was killed. The IRA denied ambushing the Crossley Tender and it was believed a gun was accidently discharged by one of Smith's comrades.[83]

The Final Weeks

Minor incidents occurred in the Kilkenny Brigade area in the final weeks of the War of Independence. The longer days of summer were actually seen as a hindrance for the IRA as it was more difficult to move around with so much daylight. Mostly minor actions took place around the county, such as the stealing of twelve bottles of gin intended for Auxiliary headquarters from Thomastown railway station.[84]

The last major altercation of the Kilkenny Brigade took place in Mullinahone, County Tipperary on the evening of 10 July 1921, just fourteen hours before a truce was due to come into effect (at 12.00 pm the following day). The truce had been announced since the previous Friday, thus British authorities were afterwards angry with the amount of IRA attacks that took place around the country over the course of the weekend.

The attack in Mullinahone had been planned for some time and was led by Jim Brien of Poulacapple IRA Company. The plan was to attack a military patrol that marched up the street every night after the 'curfew bell' had rung. This signalled to inhabitants of the village that they had to be indoors. On the night of their final patrol, just two soldiers of the Lincolnshire Regiment, instead of the usual six, marched through the village. As the two men approached the ambush site, Brien ordered the men to open fire. A bomb was also thrown by John O'Gorman which exploded in front of the soldiers. Sergeant John William Reynolds, who was 21 years old, was fatally wounded having been hit in the neck and chest. His companion, Lieutenant Rowles, was also badly injured but survived. He made his way back to the safety of the barracks. The IRA took Reynolds's gun before they departed. Reynolds died the following day.[85] Thus ended the War of Independence in the Kilkenny IRA Brigade.

CHAPTER 6

War of Independence:
Civilian Fatalities and Analysis

'As the first lorry passed the door I heard one shot fired ...
Mrs Ryan then came into the Tap Room. I asked her
did she hear the shot; she said "Yes and I think I have
got it through the foot."'

– Josephine Delaney, inquest into the death of Margaret Ryan,
24 December 1920

A total of four civilians lost their lives in Kilkenny during the War of Independence. The deaths occurred between December 1920 and April 1921.

Margaret Ryan

The only woman to die in Kilkenny because of the troubles was the first civilian fatality. Her killing was connected to the death of RIC Constable Thomas Walsh in the aftermath of the Ninemilehouse Ambush, discussed previously. The day after his death, 21 December 1920, Constable Walsh's remains were due to leave Callan Barracks in a convoy of cars, Crossley Tenders and Lancer armoured cars, for onward journey to his home village of Ballyragget where his funeral was due to take place.[1] The Auxiliaries had informed all businesses to shut and civilians to stay indoors during the procession. Margaret Ryan, who ran a grocery shop and public house with her husband Michael on Bridge Street, had permitted a customer, Josephine Delaney, in 'for a jug of milk' at about 5.30 pm. Both women were watching the procession from inside the shop when a shot was fired from a Crossley Tender of Auxiliaries. The files of the private inquests relating to the event have only recently been released from the British National Archives. During the inquest, which took place on Christmas Eve, a distraught Josephine Delaney described what occurred:

> I was in the tap room which is next to the shop. I was looking out of the window watching the funeral of Sergt. Walsh. I saw the hearse go by. The hearse was followed by a small car and some lorries. As the first lorry passed the door I heard one shot fired. I got down from the window. Mrs Ryan then came into the Tap Room. I asked her did she hear the shot; she said 'Yes and I think I have got it through the foot'. I asked her did she fall. She said yes ... She then sat on a chair for a few minutes and then walked into the kitchen and asked for some hot milk. She then went upstairs [to her bedroom]. All doors had been closed while Sergeant Walsh's body was passing through Callan.[2]

The bullet hole was visible in the shop door after the event. The bullet passed through the door and hit Ryan in the abdomen. As she had seen blood at her feet she presumed she had been struck in the foot. She deteriorated afterwards and was taken to the Callan Workhouse Hospital by her husband who had been in the adjoining storehouse when the incident occurred.[3]

She died there two days later on 23 December 1920.[4] The bullet had passed through her bowel and lodged in her back. She was 36 years old. Her death certificate stated she died from an infection 'following perforation of [the] bowel by a bullet wound'.[5] To add to the tragedy, Margaret Ryan was also pregnant at the time of her death.[6] The couple had been married since 1911, having grown up as neighbours on Bridge Street in Callan. Margaret Ryan's maiden name was also Ryan. Ironically, the Ryans were not active Sinn Féin supporters and the Crown Forces had frequented their public house on a number of occasions. The 'RIC and Military called on the relatives and sent tokens of sympathy'.[7]

Margaret Ryan's death was embarrassing for the British authorities. Three inquiries were held into the circumstances surrounding her death. The files relating to this incident generated the largest volume of paperwork of any single event of the War of Independence in County Kilkenny. Ryan's death was also mentioned in an IRA propaganda pamphlet entitled; *Statement of Atrocities on Women in Ireland*. It was produced by Hanna Sheehy-Skeffington – widow of Francis – for her tour of America in 1921. The purpose of the tour was to highlight the violence committed as a result of the British military campaign in Ireland. Under the heading 'Wanton Terrorism of Young Mothers', Sheehy-Skeffington stated: 'all traders [in Callan] were ordered to close their premises during the funeral ... as [a] form of compulsory mourning and trade reprisal ... Mrs. Ryan ventured to open her door to let out a friend and was instantly shot dead [*sic*]. She was within a few months of her [pregnancy] confinement.'[8] Although the information is not totally accurate, it nevertheless highlighted how an event in rural Kilkenny could be used for publicity purposes to garner support for the republican cause on the other side of the Atlantic. This was, however, of little consolation to the relatives of Margaret Ryan.

In the aftermath of Ryan's death, an unease can be observed between the local RIC and the Auxiliaries. Constable Gildea from Kilkenny RIC, who was travelling in a Ford motorcar near the front of the convoy with the brother of the deceased RIC man, disassociated himself from the actions of the Auxiliaries. He stated to the inquiry; 'I could see no reason for the shot having been fired.'[9] Eventually the Crossley Tender motor lorry where the shot most likely originated was identified. The Auxiliaries in that vehicle were from J Company and were not based in Kilkenny but had arrived that day from West Cork. The Kilkenny Auxiliaries – A Company – who made up three vehicles in the convoy disassociated themselves from the actions of their colleagues with their Captain stating: 'I can personally vouch for the fact no shots were fired from any vehicle of our convoy [A Company] ... nor were we aware of the order that all doors were to be closed when the cortège passed through.'[10] Pressure was placed on J Company from British Military HQ in Dublin and Cork to assist in the investigation. In April 1921, J Company sent the following to their military superiors:

> There appears to have been some difficultly owing to the move of the Auxiliary [J] Company first to Cork and then to Macroom; also the officer at these Headquarters who dealt with the matter has now been transferred. The delay is much regretted, but all steps are being taken to clear the matter up as soon as possible.[11]

Eventually, a third inquiry was held in Victoria Barracks in Cork in May 1921 where, for the first time, a member of J Company – W.S. Adams – gave evidence. He contradicted the previous inquiries by stating that the shot was not fired from their motor tenders. He was therefore absolving his company from any blame. Thus, nobody was held responsible for her death.[12] As J Company provided no evidence to verify that their weapons had not been discharged – unlike the Kilkenny Auxiliaries and RIC – it must be assumed that someone on their tender was the most likely perpetrator.

The inquiries all found that the deceased died as a result of a wound caused by 'a .450 revolver bullet', by 'a person unknown'. The correspondence surrounding this event also points to a disjointed and sometimes frosty relationship between the different security forces in Ireland; specifically relating to the RIC, the Military and the Auxiliary Division. Margaret Ryan was also very unfortunate in the turn of events. All lights on the street in Callan and in Ryan's shop were extinguished that evening. Therefore, the perpetrator was firing into relative darkness which would have made aiming at a target difficult. The probable offender was also based in West Cork, where just a few weeks earlier, seventeen Auxiliaries were killed in the Kilmichael Ambush. Auxiliaries were also chiefly responsible for the burning of Cork City in the same month as Ryan's death. Hence, J Company of the Auxiliaries were battle-hardened and more used to extreme methods, safe in the knowledge they would be protected by their superiors from any repercussions of their actions. The Ryan family received no justice however. And no excuse could be offered for taking the life of a young woman for the 'crime' of viewing a funeral cortège. Callan town on Christmas Day 1920 was a very forlorn place, as the funeral of Margaret Ryan took place in the afternoon.[13]

Thomas Dollard

Thomas Dollard was caught in the crossfire of the botched Friary Street Ambush of 21 February 1921. It has usually been recorded that he was killed accidently by a ricochet bullet. However, recently released documents that were composed by the British military at the time, confirm Dollard was shot intentionally by a member of the Crown Forces as it was believed he was one of the IRA ambushers. Dollard had gone to the Friary Church for his usual morning prayer on his break from his employment as a Corporation labourer. When he was leaving the church he saw the two IRA men, Thomas Hennessy and Michael Dermody, attacking two military officers at the rear of a military convoy. He subsequently ran down Friary Street towards High Street to get away from the trouble.[14] Two other British soldiers opened fire on the IRA men, who fell to the ground mortally wounded. When Dollard was seen running away from the vicinity, Private Hawthorn, who was one of the rear party that had been attacked by Hennessy, opened fire on Dollard. In the private military inquiry that was held the following day, Hawthorn stated:

> While the affray was going on there were a good many people in Friary Street, men women and children. They all started running and after they got clear a civilian man suddenly appeared about 25 yards away as if he had just come out of a house. He ran away and several shots were fired at him, including one shot fired

by me. The man fell. I thought he was one of the attacking party. I did not hear anyone call on him to halt.[15]

Dollard had been shot in the head and died shortly afterwards. Private Hawthorn, in explaining the events of that sad morning, was unsurprisingly defending himself and his colleagues to their superiors. He was clear in stating that the women and children had left the scene before shots were fired. This would have been difficult to ascertain considering the events took place within seconds. In addition, no one had called on Dollard to 'halt'. This was the usual protocol used by Crown Forces before firing was supposed to commence. In the official statements released by the Military in the immediate aftermath of the Friary Street ambush, they maintained it was a bullet that ricocheted off a wall that killed Dollard.[16] They also attempted to discover if he had any links to the ambushers.

Thomas Dollard was 37 years old when he died, leaving his wife, Bridget, and five children, ranging in age from 6 months to 15 years.[17] The failed ambush also earned a strong reaction from Bishop Brownrigg of Ossory. In a letter read at 'all the Masses' the following Sunday, he declared that he was 'mainly concerned with the moral aspects of the case', and stated that he could not 'find words strong enough to condemn the folly and the crime'.[18] The Military did not accept responsibility for Dollard's death, with one of the findings of the inquiry stating: 'That the said deceased [Dollard] was himself to blame in as much as he ran away from the scene of the ambush.'[19] It is difficult to understand how else they expected a person to react when faced with an ambush situation; running hastily being the most obvious response.

James Hoban

It was a similar case of being in the wrong place at the wrong time for 23-year-old James Hoban, from Glendonnell, Mullinavat. On 19 April 1921 he was in the village of Mullinavat with his elderly uncle, James Walsh, selling pigs. A large military presence was positioned outside Mullinavat RIC Barracks as General Strickland, who was in charge of the military in Munster, Kilkenny and Wexford, was visiting the barracks. Around 11.30 am, bullets were fired from the turret of a Rolls Royce armoured car. Hoban, who was 100 yards down the street standing next to his uncle, fell wounded. He had been hit a number of times in both legs and was bleeding profusely. His uncle escaped injury. Some of the soldiers attempted to administer first aid by bandaging his wounds. The soldiers then lifted Hoban, with the help of his cousin Michael Hoban, to nearby Costello's grocery shop on the main street in Mullinavat. He was fully conscious at this stage and said he was 'alright', but his condition deteriorated over the next hour and he was transferred by military ambulance to Waterford Infirmary. Hoban passed away there later that evening at 7.00 pm.[20]

The soldier who discharged the weapon which led to Hoban's death, Private McCulla, was subsequently court-martialled. McCulla refused to give evidence or cooperate with the inquiry. Nevertheless, he was found not guilty of Hoban's death as the 'fuse spring was too light' on the machine gun and it was therefore considered an accidental killing.[21]

Thomas Phelan

Just two days after the Mullinavat tragedy, another sad incident occurred, this time in the far north of the county near the village of Ballyragget. Thomas Phelan, who was 18 years old, had departed his house in the townland of Oldtown on the morning of 21 April 1921 to purchase a newspaper in Ballyragget. Usually Thomas would have been helping his brother Michael on the family farm, but he had been confined to bed with the flu and this was his first time out of the house in a number of days. Michael was a lieutenant in the local Ballyragget IRA, while Thomas was also a member (G Company, 3rd Kilkenny Battalion). When Thomas returned from Ballyragget that afternoon, he saw two RIC men and two soldiers from the Devonshire Regiment in the field near his house. During the previous days the local IRA had trenched the road and felled trees in the vicinity in order to impede military movements in the area.[22] When Thomas saw the Crown Forces he panicked. He dropped his bicycle and ran in order to evade possible arrest or being forced to clear the trees from the roads. He attempted to run towards the fields at the rear of his house at which point the soldiers ordered him to halt.[23] He failed to stop and the two soldiers, Private Davis and Private Humphries, fired six shots at him and Thomas fell behind a hedge. In the meantime, Thomas's mother, Margaret, had come out of the house and appealed to RIC Constable Patrick Egan to stop the pursuit of her son. Constable Egan was living in the area and was known to the family. However, it was too late. The two soldiers went over to the lane behind the hedge. Here they saw Thomas struggling for breath on the laneway, but he died a few moments later, having been shot in the back.

Thomas's body was taken by the military to Kilkenny for an inquest before being returned to the family. His belongings were also returned. They included cigarettes, a pen knife, a notebook, a handkerchief, bicycle clips and the *Irish Independent* which he had purchased on the ill-fated day.[24] Thomas was the youngest of four children and his father, John Phelan, died when Thomas was just 2 months old from suspected tuberculosis, aged 62 years (in August 1902).[25] The findings recorded in Thomas's death certificate stated that he died from 'shock and haemorrhage caused by [a] gunshot wound fired by the military in the execution of their duty'.[26]

Analysis of County Kilkenny's Contribution to the War of Independence

Regarding the number of what the RIC termed 'political outrages', which were crimes reported as a direct result of the ongoing hostilities, the number of crimes peaked in September 1920 before decreasing by nearly 80 per cent the following month. This is evidence that the new Black and Tan/Auxiliary forces were having the desired effect. However, outrages reached the same levels as September 1920, by May and June 1921.[27] This emphasises that by the spring of 1921, the IRA successes – although many were minor in nature – were very much on an upward trajectory.[28]

A number of reasons can be suggested as to why the Kilkenny IRA Brigade was not more successful during this period. The Brigade command structure within the county – for varying reasons – was often non-existent, with the result that many Kilkenny IRA companies and battalions acted on their own initiative. John Walsh, O/C of the 5th IRA Battalion headquartered in Graiguenamanagh, remarked; 'from the time our Company was formed in 1916 until the end of 1920 we were like an isolated outpost left to act and carry on as best we could'.[29] This autonomy was beneficial in some areas of Kilkenny as the IRA were permitted to carry out their own operations on their own terms, with little or no interference. However, the success of this self-sufficiency depended largely on the strength of the local IRA leadership, which varied widely from district to district and which resulted in IRA units stagnating in some parts of the county.

As occurred to the IRA throughout Ireland, the majority of planned ambushes did not take place as the Crown Forces did not arrive as expected, or took a different route. With the mass closing of RIC barracks in March 1920 and the movement towards strongly fortified locations, 'softer' targets were not as available for the IRA. One theme that permeated the military campaign in Kilkenny was the lack of quality intelligence on the IRA side. The height of their intelligence-gathering would appear to be the regular seizing of post with an aim of gaining information on the Crown Forces through that correspondence. However, there is no evidence to imply that the Kilkenny IRA Brigade tried or succeeded in infiltrating the British Military in the county at any stage.

The Crown Forces on the other hand appeared to have been a step ahead of the IRA in many cases. Whether through fear, or disapproval of IRA actions, the Crown Forces often had an accurate supply of information from some locals about IRA members and their activities, which lead to the capture of IRA men and the failure of some ambushes. In Callan for instance, a place not noted for its pro-British sympathies, the 7th IRA Battalion tried to attack a military patrol on four occasions in early 1921. Each night they entered the town the patrol did not come as far as the ambush position, while on one occasion, even the local priest had heard of the planned attack before it was due to occur.[30] It is also accurate to state that the engagements where Kilkenny IRA Brigade men died were all due to the British military having been informed of the presence of the IRA in the area i.e. Coolbawn, Knocknagress, and to a certain extent, Friary Street.

The brigade leaders of the military campaign in Kilkenny also took on a multitude of roles, from IRA commandants, to court judges, to councillors. Many also attempted to hold down a full-time job. Although this was not uncommon throughout the country, concentration solely on the military campaign would have been beneficial.[31] In any case, most IRA military failures came down simply to bad luck. If one of the five major planned ambushes by the Kilkenny ASUs – namely Ninemilehouse, Coolbawn, Moonarch, Uskerty Wood or Piltown – had been successful, it is possible that Kilkenny's name in the pantheon of the War of Independence histories would have resonated much stronger.

Ironically, the fact that the Kilkenny IRA had the third successful attack in the country on an RIC barracks almost certainly had a negative effect on their contribution to the remainder of the War of Independence. The immediate consequence was the arrest of the main brigade leaders but the subsequent placement of the very first Auxiliary Company in Inistioge in August 1920 put massive pressure on the IRA campaign.[32] This prioritisation by the British authorities in locating the Auxiliaries and a number of military regiments in Kilkenny also had traumatic repercussions for the local populace.

Ned Aylward, O/C of the most successful 7th Battalion/ASU, offered his own verdict on Kilkenny's lack of success, stating that the Brigade

Headquarters leaders in Kilkenny City were made up of 'older men' and lacked 'the necessary ruthlessness'.[33] The Kilkenny City-based brigade leaders gave the impression that they were trying to avoid killings for the majority of the war. The 'no kill' policy of the ill-fated Friary Street ambush was the most obvious evidence of this. Historian Jim Maher refers to the Kilkenny Brigade officers earlier in the war as 'gentle revolutionaries',[34] which is perhaps an apt description.

Likewise, 5th IRA Battalion Adjutant, James O'Hanrahan, based in Graiguenamanagh, also had a more cautious approach to the war, which was in complete contrast to his IRA comrades in Callan who acted in a mostly independent manner. O'Hanrahan remarked, 'I did no fighting for the simple reason that though we applied for permission [to IRA Brigade GHQ] on several occasions to carry off small jobs … [it] was not granted.'[35]

In a similar way, in Castlecomer, the 3rd Battalion decided not to attack the Castlecomer collieries for fear of the workers losing their jobs, even though the mines had a large supply of explosives. They also rejected the idea of attacking a public house the military frequented due to the mental health of the owner's wife. Garrett Brennan, who was O/C of the 3rd Kilkenny Battalion at the time of the truce, was of the opinion that many of the RIC were of the 'harmless type' and subsequently that 'one coffin going back to England [Black and Tans/military] would be worth hundreds of police shot'.[36]

That is not to criticise the noble motivations of those who were putting their communities before the fighting. However, to make an impact during a war of independence, at certain times, admirable traits are required to be put to one side. As Michael Collins wrote to Brigade O/C Tom Treacy when trying to encourage him to be more unyielding; 'strategic merits … should outweigh any personal connections'.[37]

An obvious exception was the 7th Battalion which was highly active and certainly contained the tough streak which was more in common with their neighbouring Tipperary counterparts. By June of 1921, however, some of the other battalions in Kilkenny, such as the 3rd, 5th and 9th Battalions, were showing increasing signs of moving towards a more aggressive course of action. It is not implausible to suggest that if the war had continued for longer, some of these battalions would have made further and more effective contributions to Kilkenny's military effort.

Finally, the capture of Ernie O'Malley in possession of the listing of all the Kilkenny battalion and company officers was a major setback for the Kilkenny Brigade and the effect of this cannot be underestimated, especially as it occurred in December 1920 at such a pivotal point in the war. The main leaders of the brigade were arrested while, more importantly, a number of the battalion commandants were also captured. The effect this had on the organisation and morale of the Kilkenny IRA Brigade was profound.

One aspect of the military conflict the Kilkenny Brigade excelled at was the manufacture of munitions. Peter DeLoughry's foundry was used throughout the period to make grenade casings and to refurbish old weapons and ammunition. In addition, Daniel 'Dan' Stapleton was appointed Kilkenny IRA Brigade Chemist by Brigade O/C George O'Dwyer. Stapleton owned a medical hall (pharmacy) at 23 High Street in Kilkenny City and as a trained chemist he was asked to join the IRA to make explosives, to which he readily agreed. Stapleton not only supplied the Kilkenny Brigade with explosive materials and ammunitions, but also provided munitions for other areas of the 2nd Southern IRA Division in Tipperary and Limerick. Stapleton's work was much regarded. During the Truce in September 1921 he was invited to the Leinster Hurling Final by Harry Boland who subsequently introduced him to Michael Collins on the pitch in Croke Park at half-time during the game. Stapleton was impressed with Collins's intricate understanding of his profession, later remarking; 'He [Collins] asked me several interesting question[s] which showed me that he had quite an intimate knowledge of explosives.'[38]

Fatalities in the Kilkenny Brigade Area during the Irish War of Independence

As historian Eunan O'Halpin has noted, establishing an accurate figure for fatalities during the revolutionary period 'is a very crude index of the intensity of disruption experienced by people and communities'.[39] It also does not take cognisance of the physical and psychological scars that were endured, which often had long-lasting repercussions. Although a grim barometer, it does at least highlight, to some degree, the suffering of the families and extended families that lost loved ones. All available evidence suggests that a total of twenty-two people were killed in the Kilkenny Brigade area as a direct result of War of Independence activities (two of these deaths were inside the Tipperary border in Mullinahone).

How deaths are defined and attributed has also been an area of debate, but the scope used here are fatalities caused as a direct result of the political violence, by either the IRA or Crown Forces, within the Kilkenny Brigade area (it includes those who received their fatal wounds in Kilkenny but died elsewhere). The fatalities include seven IRA combatants, three RIC, two Black and Tans, one Auxiliary, one military, four informers and four civilians. Excluding the two Mullinahone fatalities, this is still one death more than O'Halpin's estimate of nineteen deaths. It places Kilkenny in joint twentieth position in the gloomy ranking of War of Independence deaths in Ireland's thirty-two counties.[40] All but two of the total twenty-two deaths occurred in the violent eight-month period between December 1920 and July 1921. Contradicting the national trend, the number of IRA fatalities in Kilkenny was equal to the number of Crown Forces fatalities in the county (nationally, Crown Force fatalities were higher than IRA fatalities). The four people killed as informers were all members of the Roman Catholic faith, which was in contrast to Hart's research in Cork where a material proportion were of the Church of Ireland faith, which indicates that there was no evident sectarian element to the conflict in Kilkenny. However, three out of four of the informers were ex-British Army soldiers and all were farm labourers. It is far more likely, therefore, that a class factor was at play, alongside some local animosities.[41] The average age at death, encompassing all twenty-two fatalities, was 30.6 years.

The table below lists those who died as a result of the political violence in the Kilkenny Brigade area during the Irish War of Independence. In addition, the total amount killed is contrasted against the national statistics.

Table 1. Kilkenny Fatalities versus National Fatalities

	Kilkenny Brigade	%	National	%	% Difference
Total Deaths	22	100%	2141	100%	
Civilian (incl informers)	8	36%	898	42%	-6%
IRA	7	32%	467	22%	+10%
RIC/Aux/Black and Tans	6	27%	514	24%	+3%
Military	1	5%	262	12%	-8%

National deaths sourced from Eunan O'Halpin, 'Counting Terror, Bloody Sunday and the Dead of the Irish Revolution' in *Terror in Ireland 1916–1923*, ed. David Fitzpatrick (Dublin, 2012), p. 152. (Note: the two Mullinahone deaths are included in the Kilkenny Brigade.)

Table 2. Fatalities within the Kilkenny Brigade area as a direct result of the Irish War of Independence

Date of Death	Name	Age at Death	Category	Native Place	Details
9 Mar. 1920	Thomas Ryan	39	RIC	Limerick	Died following wounds sustained in an attack on Hugginstown RIC Barracks by IRA.
30 Aug. 1920	William Kenny	36	Executed as Informer	Graiguenamanagh	Ex-British soldier, he was executed by drowning by the 5th Battalion IRA for accompanying the military and helping guide them during raids in the Graiguenamanagh district over the course of summer 1920.
20 Dec. 1920	Sgt Thomas Walsh	40	RIC	Ballyragget	Accidently shot dead by a soldier(s) from the Devonshire Regiment during a search of an area south of Callan following an IRA ambush at Ninemilehouse earlier in the day.
23 Dec. 1920	Margaret Ryan	36	Civilian	Callan	Died from abdominal bullet wounds suffered two days previously in Callan, following firing from a lorry of Auxiliaries as the funeral cortège of RIC Sergeant Thomas Walsh passed through the town. She was pregnant at the time of her death.

The Parade junction, Kilkenny City, *c.*1900, with the Imperial Hotel at the corner of Rose Inn St (centre background), important locations during the Battle of Kilkenny, May 1922 (National Library of Ireland, L-ROY-10037).

Thomas Treacy (1885–1975), Captain of the Kilkenny Irish Volunteers (1914–8); O/C Kilkenny IRA Brigade from 1919 until his arrest in November 1920 (courtesy of the Treacy family).

Peter DeLoughry (1882–1931), New Buildin[g] Lane/Parliament St, Kilkenny City. Head-Cent[re] (leader) of the IRB in Kilkenny (courtesy [of] Páidrigín ní Dhubhluachra).

21 May 1914: St James Park. Lady Desart (1857–1933) talks to All-Ireland 3-in-a-row-winning Kilkenny hurling team. She was a millionairess, philanthropist, Gaelic revivalist, anti-female suffrage campaigner and Free State Senator. Right to left: Cllr John Slater, F.J. Biggar, Desart, Jack Keoghan, Dr J.J. Brennan, Dick Grace, Denny Brennan (courtesy of John Kirwan, not to be copied without permission).

ter DeLoughry with the Mayoral robes,
ain of office and ceremonial mace and sword
the City of Kilkenny (courtesy of Páidrigín
Dhubhluachra).

ctober 1914: members of Kilkenny National Volunteers parading down High St, Kilkenny,
n the occasion of John Redmond's inauguration as Freeman of the City (courtesy of James
ephens Barracks Museum).

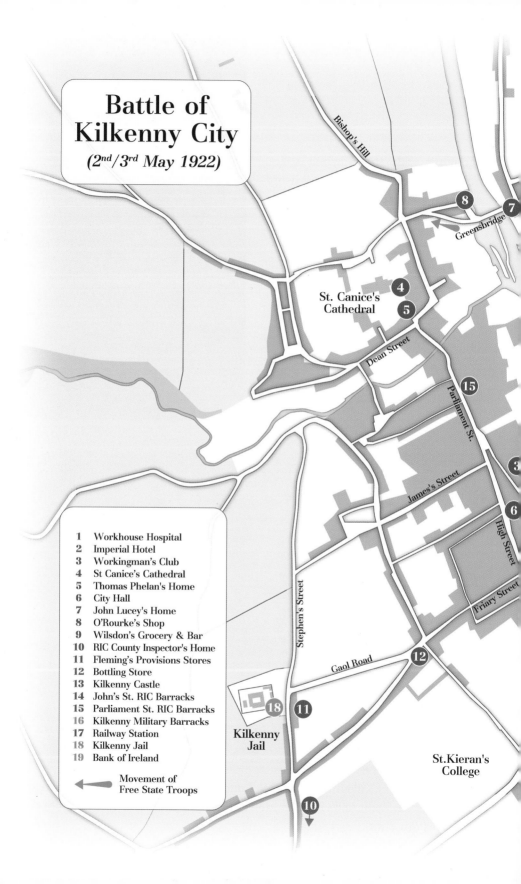

Battle of Kilkenny City
(2nd/3rd May 1922)

St. Canice's
Cathedral

Bishop's Hill

Greensbridge

Dean Street

Parliament St.

James's Street

High Street

Friary Street

Stephen's Street

Gaol Road

Kilkenny
Jail

St.Kieran's
College

1 Workhouse Hospital
2 Imperial Hotel
3 Workingman's Club
4 St Canice's Cathedral
5 Thomas Phelan's Home
6 City Hall
7 John Lucey's Home
8 O'Rourke's Shop
9 Wilsdon's Grocery & Bar
10 RIC County Inspector's Home
11 Fleming's Provisions Stores
12 Bottling Store
13 Kilkenny Castle
14 John's St. RIC Barracks
15 Parliament St. RIC Barracks
16 Kilkenny Military Barracks
17 Railway Station
18 Kilkenny Jail
19 Bank of Ireland

← Movement of
    Free State Troops

1917/1919: *Kilkenny People* newspaper office on James Street is raided by British authorities and the printing press confiscated. The paper popularised the ideas of Sinn Féin (courtesy of Jim Maher).

Albert (Thomas) Bibby OFM (1877–1925) was present at the executions of 2 1916 Rising prisoners in Dublin and became strong supporter of the republican cause ourtesy of the Irish Capuchin Archives).

Known as Kilkenny's rebel/jailbreaking priest, Fr P.H. Delahunty spread the gospel of the Sinn Féin movement in Callan (where he was curate) and Kilkenny generally (courtesy of Ms Frances Delahunty).

July 1916: 29 of the 33 people arrested in Kilkenny after Easter Week including many leaders of revolutionary-era Kilkenny. Tom Treacy (bk row, 3rd from r), Peter DeLoughry (2nd row from bk, 1st from r), Deputy IRB Head Pat Corcoran (bk row, 3rd from l), IRA Vice-O/C James Lalor (2nd row from bk, 3rd from r), Brigade QM Ned Comerford (3rd row from bk, 3rd from l), GAA President James Nolan (bk row, 4th from l) (courtesy of James Stephens Barracks Museum).

19 July 1917: Victoria Hotel (now AIB, 3 High Street), Countess Markievicz becomes Freewoman of Kilkenny City. Back row l to r: D. McCarthy, Darrel Figgis, Rev. Browne, Ald. T. Kelly, E. Fleming, É. de Valera, S. Milroy. Front row l to r: L. Ginnell, Markievicz, W.T. Cosgrave, A. Ginnell, with Rebel the dog (Military Archives of Ireland, BMH P-11-b).

11 August 1917: Parliament St. W.T. Cosgrave makes his victory speech on the balcony of Kilkenny Courthouse (Grace's Castle) following his success in the Kilkenny City by-election with 66 per cent of the vote (Military Archives of Ireland, BMH P-11-c).

Date of Death	Name	Age at Death	Category	Native Place	Details
5 Jan. 1921	Michael Cassidy	35	Executed as Informer	Castlecomer	Shot dead in his place of work by an outside IRA unit as he was found guilty of aiding Crown Forces in the area.
21 Feb. 1921	Thomas Hennessy	31	IRA (1st Batt.)	Threecastles	Shot dead by the military while attempting to disarm a soldier in Friary Street in Kilkenny City. The ambush was planned by Hennessy's brother Tim.
21 Feb. 1921	Thomas Dollard	36	Civilian	Kilkenny City	Killed from a bullet fired by the military during the Friary Street ambush as they believed he was one of the ambushers as he fled from the scene of the fighting.
4 Mar. 1921	Michael Dermody	25	IRA (1st Batt.)	Threecastles	Shot in the head by the military while attempting to disarm a soldier during the Friary Street Ambush. He remained unconscious after the incident, passing away two weeks later.
12 Mar. 1921	Ernest Riley	26	Black and Tan	England (Brighton)	Shot by the IRA at Garryricken House, west Kilkenny, during an escape by the 7th Battalion ASU who had been surrounded by Crown Forces at the place they were resting.

Date of Death	Name	Age at Death	Category	Native Place	Details
20 Mar. 1921	William Campbell	37	RIC	Leitrim	Received fatal wounds to the head in Mullinahone by members of the 7th Battalion ASU. He was not the intended target but accidentally stumbled across the men at the rear of his house. Instead, another officer known as the 'Foxy Officer', was the assassination target.
6 Apr. 1921	Jackie Brett	19	IRA (7th Batt.)	Mullinahone	Shot accidently by a teenager in whose house he was billeting in Castlejohn, near Windgap.
19 Apr. 1921	James Hoban	23	Civilian	Mullinavat	Shot by a Crown Force solider on Main Street, Mullinavat, dying later that evening in the Waterford City infirmary.
21 Apr. 1921	Thomas Phelan	18	Civilian	Ballyragget	Shot by soldiers near his home in Oldtown, Ballyragget, when he failed to halt.
13 May 1921	Seán Quinn	22	IRA (7th Batt.)	Mullinahone	Mortally wounded in Knocknagress, near Tullaroan, having been shot by soldiers while trying to escape from a military cordon. Died in Kilkenny Military Barracks later that day.

Date of Death	Name	Age at Death	Category	Native Place	Details
16 May 1921	Martin Dermody	41	Executed as Informer	Tullaroan	Two ex-British soldiers, who had served during the Boer and First World War, were executed by the local IRA for informing the Crown Forces of the location of the IRA, leading to the deaths of Patrick Walsh and Seán Quinn.
16 May 1921	Michael O'Keeffe	56	Executed as Informer	Carrick-on-Suir	
18 May 1921	Patrick Walsh	33	IRA (8th Batt.)	Dunnamaggin	Mortally wounded in Knocknagress, near Tullaroan, on 13 May 1921 while trying to escape from the military. He died in the military hospital in Fermoy, Co. Cork.
10 June 1921	Leonard James French	26	Auxiliaries	England (Lancashire)	Fatally shot while trying to avoid being captured by the 5th Battalion IRA when dressed in civilian clothes on a reconnaissance mission at The Rower.
18 June 1921	Nicholas Mullins	28	IRA (5th Batt.)	Thomastown	Mortally wounded by a Black and Tan while trying to retreat from the failed ambush at Coolbawn, near Castlecomer.
	Seán Hartley	23	IRA (1st Batt.)	Glenmore	Shot dead during an attempted ambush at Coolbawn, near Castlecomer, by the initial burst of machine-gun fire by Crown Forces.

Date of Death	Name	Age at Death	Category	Native Place	Details
18 June 1921	Albert Bradford	23	Black and Tan	England (Essex)	Shot by members of the 9th Battalion IRA during an ambush of a Black-and-Tan patrol at Sinnott's Cross, Tubrid, Mooncoin.
11 July 1921	Sgt John William Reynolds	21	Military (1st Lincolnshire Regiment)	England (London)	Received bullet and bomb injuries while on patrol in the village of Mullinahone, Co. Tipperary, on the evening of 10 July 1921 following an attack by members of the Mullinahone Company of the 7th Kilkenny IRA Battalion.

Note: Kilkenny natives who died as result of political violence during the War of Independence outside of the county are not included. For example, the following are not listed: Constable James Phelan, a native of Lisdowney, Ballyragget, who was killed in an ambush at Rathmore, Co. Kerry (see *Kilkenny Moderator* 16 May 1921). Peter Freyne from Thomastown, who was a member of the 2nd Battalion Dublin IRA, was killed in Dublin on 11 April 1921 in an attack on Crown Forces at a Dublin hotel. An informer named 'Hackett' who was reported as captured near Paulstown is not included as no record exists of his death which most likely took place in Co. Carlow. Similarly, the death of three British Military personnel in an accident in Castlecomer in 1919 are also not listed.

CHAPTER 7

Kilkenny's Political and Civil Counter-State (1919–1921)

'It is fairly obvious that an Irishman cannot serve two masters.'

– W.T. Cosgrave, September 1920

Kilkenny's contribution to the War of Independence in matters of Local Government and Civil Authority followed a similar pattern to the military side, in that adherence to republican efforts to establish a counter-state – in direct competition to the British state – varied throughout the county. This side of the War of Independence has often been overlooked as it was believed to be of lesser importance in comparison with the sacrifices of the military side. However, the building blocks of a new state, such as the administration of law and order by the Republican Courts, along with the establishment of local government, are factors that brought the new state into wider public knowledge in a practical manner. This chapter examines the other face of the War of Independence in Kilkenny – the Counter-State.

Following instructions from Dáil Éireann, the Kilkenny republican movement was quick to respond to the establishment of Republican Courts, or 'Sinn Féin Courts' as they were commonly known, in May 1920.[1] The Republican Police Force was also set up at this time to aid the work of the courts. Thomas Treacy, the Kilkenny IRA Brigade Commandant, stated that the Republican Courts were 'more concerned with dispensing justice than with dispensing law'. This perhaps explains how the new Republican Courts grew and gained popularity in a relatively short period. Regarding the new police force, Treacy gave details on how individuals were recruited stating that 'all members of the Republican Police Force were IRA men specifically selected for the work',[2] which was not unusual when compared to other counties. A 1st Battalion IRA member, Thomas Walsh, had overall responsibility for the Republican Police Force in Kilkenny.

The Republican Courts and Police

The success in establishing the Republican Courts and Police Force was greatly aided by the power vacuum that existed in County Kilkenny due to the closure and destruction of the majority of rural RIC barracks between March and May 1920. This was also evident in Kilkenny City where the first Republican Court was boldly held in City Hall on High Street, most likely due to the fact that it was presided over by the Mayor of Kilkenny, Peter DeLoughry.[3] In Callan, the initial court sessions in May 1920 were similarly held in the local town hall, with even the RIC turning a blind eye. The sentences handed down included fines, banishment from the county, or for the more serious cases, imprisonment for a number of weeks where the 'prison' was usually an abandoned house.[4]

The most common cases heard in the Republican Courts in Kilkenny involved stealing of some form or other. This was one of the negative effects of the decline in law and order, as non-politically motivated thieves found this an opportune time to ply their trade, while others merely thought it an apt time to break agreements or not fulfil obligations. Unlike other counties in Ireland, land disputes were not a common feature of cases heard in County Kilkenny.[5] The most valid reason for this, as discussed previously, was the success of the land Acts in transferring ownership of the majority of the land to tenants during the previous decades.

The first cases in Republican Courts in Kilkenny City were somewhat surprisingly initiated by Unionist members of the local community. Two former British Army majors had 'jewellery stolen from their houses' which was recovered by the Republican Police. Another case dealt with the 'stealing of cattle from the lands of Sir Wheeler-Cuffe, Lyrath', with the end result being the recovery of the animals. There was a 'gang of burglars' operating in Kilkenny at the time, who were responsible for many robberies and the Republican Police/ IRA eventually apprehended and jailed them at an abandoned house.[6]

Similarly, in Callan, one of the first cases heard was brought by Unionist, Major McCalmont, who owned the large Mount Juliet Estate near Thomastown.[7] His case was against a farmer from whom he had purchased a 'bull-calf'. The animal had not been castrated, which was part of the sale agreement. McCalmont won his case in the Republican Court, with the seller having to fulfil his original obligation. Many other cases in this district dealt with the stealing of farm stock, with the outcome usually the return of the animals to their rightful owners.[8] Another case in Callan involved the larceny of a bicycle near the village of Mullinahone. The accused, while in possession of the stolen bicycle, was arrested by members of the 7th Battalion IRA and 'marched' through the streets of Callan to the Town Hall for trial. He subsequently pleaded guilty after the owner of the bicycle identified it as his own. The guilty party was fined £1 and ordered to leave the district for six months.[9]

In Moneenroe, near Castlecomer, the local curate presided at the cases, which gave weight and respectability to the proceedings. The courts were generally held in a disused blacksmith's forge.[10] Offenders that were found guilty were usually 'sentenced to work at turf cutting, hay saving, or harvesting work for so many days'.[11] In Graiguenamanagh, a local Justice of the Peace was brought before the Republican Court for threatening to use his influence to bring back the RIC and military to the local area. However, during the trial, the case against the man was deemed weak as the majority of evidence was based on hearsay and gossip. In an indication of the even-handedness of the court, the presiding officer dismissed the case.[12]

The fair and balanced manner of the Republican Courts was a propaganda bonus for Sinn Féin locally. The fact that several traditionally Unionist families were utilising the Republican Courts and ignoring the British courts system enshrined general acceptance amongst the populace. In June 1920, the *Kilkenny Moderator*, a newspaper that had a Unionist pedigree, contained articles about the new Republican Courts. While not openly praising the courts, it did not criticise them either:

> Several Sinn Féin Courts have been recently held in County Kilkenny. Following the perpetration of a number of outrages on the property of some protestants in the districts of Gurteen, near Castlecomer – the fences, gates and piers were broken down ... – by a party of men who are described as irresponsible and belong [sic] to no political organisation, local [IRA] Volunteers assembled in large force and effected eight arrests. The prisoners were brought before a court constituted of three judges ... One of the accused pleaded not guilty ... The other seven pleaded guilty and expressed regret. Six of them were fined 1 pound each and the other 25s which they readily agreed to pay. The President of the Court ... told them to bear in mind that the [IRA] Volunteers were determined to protect the property of all persons, irrespective of religion or class.[13]

A witness statement by a Kilkenny IRA member gives a rare mention of probable sexual violence during this era – referred to as 'an attack on a girl'. The victim identified the accused man in court and his punishment involved being tied to the gates of the local church in Clogh so he could be seen – and presumably be shamed – by the local people attending Mass.[14]

The most public engagement for the Republican Police force was at the Gowran Park Races in June 1920 where the new police marshalled the grounds during race day, having been invited by the management committee. The police apprehended a pickpocket, fining him £2 for his misdemeanour, while they also arrested a man selling tickets for admittance that had previously been stolen. The police force garnered very positive publicity for the manner in which they conducted themselves. Under the headline 'Delinquents Summarily Dealt With at the Gowran Park Races', the *Kilkenny Journal* newspaper complimented the police under 'who's [*sic*] supervision the best of good order prevailed'.[15] It is important to bear in mind that during this period in spring and summer 1920 most of the rural RIC barracks in County Kilkenny had closed, while the Black and Tan and Auxiliaries had yet to arrive.

Raising Money

To run the new counter-state, the fledgling Dáil Éireann government needed money. To raise funds they launched a bond drive where the general public could subscribe and purchase bonds. It was usually referred to as the 'Dáil Loan'. James Lalor, the Kilkenny IRA Brigade Adjutant, was the person responsible for gathering the money collected in north Kilkenny (including Kilkenny City). All monies had to be accounted for, with the name and address of each subscriber to the Dáil Loan Fund noted and sent to the Dáil Éireann Department of Finance. Consequently, during the first half of 1920, James Lalor was much more likely to be found with a pen in his hand than a gun, as he battled to obtain money from the different districts and complete accurate records. Trying to tally the cash with the individual name and addresses was also a bureaucratic nightmare.

Nonetheless, Michael Collins was not overly pleased with the efforts in Kilkenny. The general public in the county had given a lacklustre response to the bond scheme. Wearing his Minister for Finance hat, Collins personally wrote a letter to Lalor on 24 February 1920, encouraging greater effort. He mentions that the money collected was 'fairly good' relative to the number of subscribers, which implies those who had bought the bonds gave an above average amount of cash (bonds were available to purchase in incremental values between £1 and £100). However, Collins also compared Kilkenny unfavourably to other areas of the country:

Mr Eamon Fleming [organiser and secretary of the Dáil Loan Fund] has mentioned to me that you have taken charge of Loan operations in North Kilkenny ... although fairly good from the money point of view, it is not what it should be. He instances that there have only been 33 Applications [subscribers] received from Kilkenny City. I know you are taking steps to remedy this ... If there is any assistance I can give you, either in the way of sending you literature, or getting printed and sending out for you any special circulars you may desire, I shall be only too glad to do so ... We have received £12,500 from west Limerick ... Leix and Ossory [County Laois constituency] has registered promises amounting to £10,000.[16]

Collins wrote again the following month, this time chastising Lalor on his bookkeeping. It is notable that at the same time as Collins was leading a war against the British, he was also involved in the tiniest of details, including trying to balance Dáil Loan money sent from north Kilkenny. Amongst Collins's strengths, perhaps his greatest was his administrative mind and his ability to multi-task. Evidently, he did not have much tolerance for those who did not possess the same traits. Writing on 15 March 1920, Collins stated:

> I have had a great deal of trouble in making this statement agree with the forms, but I have to some extent succeeded. Believe me, I appreciate all the difficulty that accompanies this work but I would ask you to see that in future a statement accompanies any amounts, showing exactly how it is made up ... [17]

By the end of the bond drive, the North Kilkenny area – which was the district fully under James Lalor's remit – had raised £2,912.[18] The south Kilkenny district fared better. The bond drive there was spearheaded by the redoubtable rebel priest, Fr Patrick H. Delahunty, raising £5,281. This ranked it in fourth place of the highest amounts raised in the constituencies in the province of Leinster.

Local Government Elections: 1920

One of the major factors in the rise of Sinn Féin and the challenging of British Government authority in Ireland was the takeover of Local Government by Sinn Féin at the urban (municipal) elections in January 1920, and the county and district council elections in June 1920. These were also the first elections to use the Proportional Representation (PR) voting system nationally, the method still used in Ireland today.[19]

The results of the urban elections for Kilkenny City, in January 1920, did not give Sinn Féin the rampant victories it had experienced in other parts of the country.[20] Sinn Féin made considerable inroads as it was the largest single party but did not have a majority, winning just nine of the twenty-four seats available.[21] The remaining seats were taken by Nationalists (previously allied with the IPP) and Independents who won eight between them, Labour who won five, while a Unionist and a Gaelic League associated councillor acquired one seat each.[22] Nevertheless, Sinn Féin nominally controlled the council, relying on an informal pact with the Labour councillors. It should be noted that the Labour movement had a large following in the county. The RIC reported that membership of the largest trade union in the county, the ITGWU, had reached 4,296 in 1920.[23] The membership would have included many of the county's farm labourers. The total number of ITGWU branches in the county by 1920 was thirteen.[24]

The election results indicated that many voters in the Kilkenny City district were not wholly supportive of the Sinn Féin movement. One illustration of this was the number of votes received by the mayor, Peter DeLoughry. He took the second seat in St John's Ward for Sinn Féin, however, in the two previous elections – when he ran as an independent – he topped the polls with record majorities. An explanation for this reduction in popularity may be attributed to a position he took during the course of the previous year. During a number of local strikes DeLoughry had not actively supported the workers. He was therefore considered more sympathetic to employers which most likely cost him ballots among certain voters.[25]

The precarious nature of the Sinn Féin majority on Kilkenny City Urban Council prompted W.T. Cosgrave, Minister for Local Government and North Kilkenny TD, to write to the local Sinn Féin branch secretary, James Lalor, to insist on all Sinn Féin councillors writing a 'form of resignation' but to 'leave blank the date of [the] resignation'. If a councillor was arrested or incarcerated for any reason, the letter would then be used so another Sinn Féin nominee could be co-opted into that seat, with the result that Sinn Féin would hold its majority in the Council.[26]

The coupling of the Labour Party and Sinn Féin was not without its tensions. In May 1920, prior to the council elections, a labour candidate was asked to stand down in favour of a Sinn Féin candidate. Sinn Féin described their candidate as 'a labour man as well as Sinn Féin', but eventually both candidates ran. There was also some evidence of class tensions between the parties. Many of the rank and file in the Labour Party locally did not believe that Sinn Féin was supportive enough of the working class.[27] The leadership of the Labour Party in Kilkenny, many of whom were also leading members of the local branches of the ITGWU, were similarly divided. When they voted on 'coming to a working arrangement' with Sinn Féin prior to the urban election, ten voted in favour with six against.[28] Also, some months prior to the elections, in October 1919, Sinn Féin and Labour councillors took different stances regarding the sale of the local O'Sullivan's Brewery to the Smithwick family, with Sinn Féin supportive of the sale.[29] The manager of Smithwick's Brewery was a local Sinn Féin councillor and when subsequently many of the employees of O'Sullivan's were dismissed, it caused a great deal of tension between the parties in the lead-up to the local elections.[30]

The County Council and District elections in June 1920 were much more successful for Sinn Féin. This suggests something of an urban versus rural divide relating to support for Sinn Féin. However, while this may partly explain the differences, it should also be noted that events, both locally and nationally, in the intervening six months between elections had a considerable effect on public opinion. On the national scene, for example, the Mayor of Cork Tomás MacCurtain, was shot dead by Crown Forces in March 1920. Locally, many Kilkenny natives were interned and went on hunger strike in the aftermath of the Hugginstown RIC attack in March; some of these men actually ran in the district elections in June. Events like this – along with the reaction of Crown Forces – substantially increased public sympathy for Sinn Féin throughout 1920. Editor of the *Kilkenny People*, E.T. Keane, left no room for ambiguity, expounding his position in the newspaper in the week prior to the election in June 1920:

> [Sinn Féin] is enforcing the principles of justice and maintaining law and order in the real sense of the term. Even those who do not agree with the objects that Sinn Fein seeks to achieve are driven to confess that its tribunals [courts] are dealing out even-handed justice, repressing crime and punishing evil-doers. The fount and origin of all crime and outrage in this country is the existence of an alien Government, maintained by an Army of Occupation whose ranks are being daily increased.[31]

The Kilkenny County Council and District elections were held on Monday, 7 June 1920. A notable feature of the elections was the complete absence of RIC at the voting stations, which had previously been the norm. Instead, IRA members filled the role of the RIC at polling stations, as the council officials conducted the voting, indicating just how much Irish society had changed in such a short period of time. Thirty motor cars, organised by County Council secretary Thomas Drew, transferred the ballot boxes from the different parts of the county to Kilkenny City Courthouse that evening. The ballot boxes 'were accompanied in most cases by an escort of [IRA] Volunteers, who witnessed the safe deposit of the boxes' to 'the custody of the returning officers'.[32] They were sealed in a room at the courthouse until counting began the following day.

The following evening, there were jubilant scenes outside the courthouse where the counting had taken place. James Comerford, who had cycled the 16 km from Muckalee to hear the results, described the anticipation:

> it was a hot June evening … A big crowd of men, women and some youngsters, waving small Sinn Féin [tricolour] flags, stood in front of the courthouse balcony. The St Patrick's Brass and Reed Band was playing in the middle of the crowd. Putting it politely, ladies perspired and men sweated while waiting in the crowd … Someone brought out plenty of lighted bicycle lamps. They lit up the scene. The crowd applauded. As the time closed in for us to hear the election count, we held our breaths. Slowly, but clearly, the count of votes for candidates was shouted out – one by one – by someone on the balcony. Cheers went up – particularly for the winning Sinn Féin candidates. The crowd was jubilant. The band played 'Wrap the Green Flag Round Me, Boys'.[33]

If all election results in Kilkenny were aggregated, the outcome was that Sinn Féin won 77 per cent of the seats, Labour won 13 per cent, Independents won 5 per cent, while candidates under the 'Sinn Féin–Labour' banner also won 5 per cent.[34] As Labour and Sinn Féin had an agreement at the time, the national media reported County Kilkenny as having over 95 per cent 'Republican' representatives.[35] It was also possible during this period for councillors to simultaneously hold seats on different councils of local government. In the June election, Peter DeLoughry won a seat on the County Council, with his margin of victory being much more impressive than his urban election win six months earlier. DeLoughry topped the poll, with nearly double the first preference vote of the next nearest candidate.[36]

This emphatic victory for Sinn Féin was something the RIC District Inspector was keen to stress as he underscored part of his report to Dublin Castle: 'The recent L.G. [Local Government] Elections have put all the public boards in the hands of Sinn Féin. At all the meetings of such new bodies; resolutions pledging their adherence and support to Dáil Éireann have been passed.'[37]

Ambiguous Councils

When the District Councils and County Council met for the first time in the week after the elections, all 'declared allegiance to Dáil Éireann'.[38] Matters were not as clear-cut as this would suggest, however. Resolutions pledging support did not necessarily translate into total adherence. Although ostensibly supportive of Dáil Éireann, this allegiance had varying degrees and was inconsistent throughout the county. In other words, while nominally a member of a political party, some Councillors practised a good deal of independent thought. Local concerns – most notably regarding finance – were often prioritised over other affiliations.

The principal evidence for this were delays in the District and County Councils communicating with the Dáil Éireann Local Government Board (DELGB) and more importantly, the timetable associated with the severing of all ties with the British Local Government Board (BLGB). The table below outlines the dates of the first communication with the Dáil Éireann LGB by each of the fifteen electoral divisions in County Kilkenny and when they confirmed that they had ceased communicating with the BLGB.[39]

The most noteworthy aspect was the gap of over a year between the first communication of Kilkenny Urban District Council, in July 1920, and Callan Rural District Council, which did not send its first communication to the DELGB until August 1921.[40] Following a decree by Dáil Éireann in September 1920, councils were told to cease communication with the BLGB. Castlecomer and Callan Councils, and Kilkenny County Council did not break their connections until the summer of 1921, making them some of the last in the country to do so.

There are a number of explanations for the disparity in the approaches of the different councils. Judging by the available evidence, one of the most obvious reasons lies in the personalities that made up the various councils. If the chairperson or clerk was opposed to breaking off communications with the BLGB, this usually caused dissention and prevented a decision being taken, which occurred in the case of Castlecomer. At first glance, it seems ironic that Callan, which was to the fore in terms of the military campaign against British rule, should have one of the worst records in relation to the political aspect. However, the two were linked. Many of the members of both Callan councils were either on the run or in jail for IRA activities. This meant that the council meeting was held without these 'die-hards' in attendance and so less devoted republican members made up the majority.[41]

The final reason for the bureaucratic foot-dragging by the councils was centred on money, specifically the receiving of grants from the British LGB. This was the main reason Kilkenny County Council did not fully sever links until June 1921. Sinn Féin relied on Labour for its majority on the County Council. When the pressure was on to respond to the Dáil LGB, Labour Councillor

Table 3. Councils within County Kilkenny: date they initiated contact with Dáil Éireann LGB and ceased contact with British LGB

Council/Union Areas	Date of First Communication with Dáil Éireann Local Government	Date that citation of communication with British LGB confirmed
Callan Poor Law Union	12 August 1921	August 1921
Callan Rural District Council	12 August 1921	August 1921
Carrick-on-Suir Rural District – No. 3 (Piltown, Fiddown)	8 January 1921	February 1921
Castlecomer Poor Law Union	30 September 1920	July 1921
Castlecomer Rural District Council	2 September 1920	July 1921
Kilkenny Poor Law Union	12 August 1920	April 1921
Kilkenny Rural District Council	17 June 1921	May 1921
Ida Rural District Council	25 September 1920	October 1920
Thomastown Poor Law Union	7 August 1920	November 1920
Thomastown Rural District Council	13 August 1920	November 1920
Urlingford Poor Law Union	21 October 1920	April 1920
Urlingford Rural District	30 September 1920	October 1920
Waterford No. 2 – Rural Kilkenny District (Kilmacow, Mooncoin)	28 August 1920	Unknown
Kilkenny Urban District Council	26 July 1920	June 1921
Kilkenny County Council	25 April 1920	June 1921

NAI DELG 14/1-15.

Alderman Upton stated that the BLGB 'owe us some money'. He also stated that the council 'were defending malicious injury claims in the courts' and so would require as much money as possible. The majority of the councillors eventually relented and agreed to cut ties with the BLGB as the money did not seem forthcoming, and presumably because of mild embarrassment, because they were one of the last 'public bodies in the country' to do so.[42] In March 1921, during a speech in Dáil Éireann, Kevin O'Higgins, the Assistant Minister for Local Government, used the news that Kilkenny County Council had finally 'decided to break' with the BLGB to emphasise the achievements of his Department that month.[43]

After declaring allegiance to Dáil Éireann, the guardians of the Callan Union 'got the bright idea' to recommence communication with the BLGB at the beginning of 1921 as they were 'short of money'.[44] The Dáil LGB had to write to them as late as September 1921 to remind them they had 'definitively declared their allegiance to Dáil Éireann'.[45] Callan District Council, which had a number of overlapping members with Callan Union Council, was equally unresponsive to instructions to break and after submitting its records for audit to the BLGB in late 1920, was visited by the IRA who 'carried away their books'.[46] Urlingford Rural District and Union Council decided to allow the BLGB audit its accounts in January 1921. They justified this action by pointing to the example of Kilkenny County Council which had its books audited and the fact that 'a considerable part of the expenditure' had occurred under 'the term of the old [British] board'.[47] The following month, its offices were duly raided by the IRA and its record books taken. To perhaps demonstrate the ambiguity that existed at the time, the Council reported the matter to the RIC, even though there were seven Sinn Féin members on the local council.[48]

Castlecomer Council: New Blood Versus Old

Although Castlecomer Rural District and Union Council initiated contact with the Dáil LGB at an early date, they too had council members who only gave nominal support to Dáil Éireann. There was a long-running saga about Denis O'Carroll, who acted as clerk of both the Rural District Council and Union Council (Board of Guardians) in Castlecomer for the previous twenty-seven years. The job of clerk was a salaried position within the councils, thus the upheaval could affect his wages. Consequently, O'Carroll was determined to keep both the British and Dáil Éireann LGBs on side. O'Carroll was not by any means a loyalist, on the contrary, he was a prominent nationalist in the area 'since his thirteenth year' and had acted as assistant secretary to the Land League in Castlecomer in his youth. He was, however, not willing to relinquish his position.

After Dáil Éireann decreed that all district magistrates should resign, O'Carroll sent a letter to William T. Cosgrave asking him if it was necessary for him to resign his position as Justice of the Peace – even though Castlecomer Council had approved the resolution to do so. O'Carroll received a curt response from Cosgrave, which was perhaps not helped by him referring to Cosgrave as 'Mr

Cosgrave MP' rather than 'TD': 'I have to state that for those who accept the will of the nation there should be no necessity for the occasion of such a resolution. It is fairly obvious that an Irishman cannot serve two masters.'[49] O'Carroll did not follow Cosgrave's advice of 'not serving two masters' as over the following months – somewhat unusually – he sent the minutes of the Council meetings to both the BLGB and the Dáil Éireann LGB, while also reading and actioning communications from both boards. In October 1920, O'Carroll allowed the BLGB official to audit the books. However, members of the IRA intervened and escorted the auditor from the premises while also taking the 'accounting books' with them.[50] Kevin O'Higgins, Assistant Minister for the Dáil Éireann LGB, wrote to Castlecomer Board of Guardians in frustration, stating:

> your Board must choose between Dáil Éireann and the English Government … It is a perfectly ludicrous position for the Guardians [Councillors] to take up to receive and take orders and communications from two absolutely conflicting authorities and to endeavour to delude themselves into the belief that they are acting up to their responsibilities as citizens and as public representatives in a national crisis.[51]

Tensions continued to rise in November 1920 when O'Carroll requested a pay rise from the council. Members insisted that a proposal of this nature would not be entertained until O'Carroll resigned his position as Justice of the Peace for the Castlecomer area. This role was considered 'part of the slavery of the British Government'.[52] O'Carroll refused to be coerced into resigning this position and his request for extra pay was not granted. O'Carroll also soured relations with the board of Thomastown Union at this time when he used the absence of the accounting books as a reason not to pay that Union for a number of children they had boarded there.[53]

Matters came to a head during the Castlecomer Board of Guardians meeting, held in Castlecomer workhouse, on 4 April 1921. Six were present at the meeting. Besides O'Carroll and Prior-Wandesforde, four Sinn Féin supporting councillors were in attendance. These were; James Butler, Ballyragget, John Lacey, Firoda, Patrick Mulhall, Castlecomer, and Thomas Conroy, Jenkinstown. A number of Crown Forces soldiers were also in attendance and scrutinised the proceedings, noting what was being said. James Butler, a 28-year-old Sinn Féin councillor, was elected chairman and he proceeded to ask O'Carroll whether he would 'obey the instructions of the Board' and 'forward all communications to Dáil Éireann [LGB] only'. O'Carroll responded that he 'would not comply with any rules or regulations except those laid down by the [British] Local

Government Board by whom he had been appointed'. O'Carroll then handed in his resignation.[54]

Minister for Local Government, Kevin O'Higgins, was irate, however, when he was informed about the course of events; specifically that O'Carroll was allowed to resign instead of being sacked. O'Higgins was indignant that the 'Board professedly loyal to the Republic did not even dismiss him [O'Carroll] but accepted his resignation thereby acknowledging his rights to a pension'. He finished by saying that 'the failure of the Board to form any conception of the man's offence gives one a very poor idea of the political convictions of the members'.[55]

A week after the Truce in July, the new clerk of the council, George O'Dwyer who had previously been on the run, 'had the great pleasure' in signing the order which dismissed O'Carroll.[56] Some months later, a directive was sent from the BLGB awarding O'Carroll a pension of £145 per annum, which the Council duly directed to be 'burned'.[57]

From 52-year-old Denis O'Carroll's perspective, the altering landscape of Irish society would have been a source of great anguish. It was presumably difficult for him to relinquish the influence and esteem he had held in the local community which was now being usurped by the younger radical generation. He was certainly not the only member of an older generation rowing against the tide of those changing times.

Belfast Boycott Committees

One exception to the various degrees of disagreement in the councils was the order by the Dáil Éireann LGB to establish 'Belfast Boycott' committees.[58] This was a ban on the selling of Belfast-produced goods in County Kilkenny in support of Catholics and Nationalist Protestants who had been expelled from their employment in Belfast City. The religious element was a major factor in the widespread support from the councils, with most denouncing the 'Belfast pogrom' against Catholics in that city and the 'imposition of religious and political tests as a condition of industrial employment'.[59] It is fair to say, however, that most in Kilkenny would not have had a clear understanding of the sectarian tensions in the north, as that type of division simply did not exist in the same way in Kilkenny, as Catholics made up 95 per cent of the population. On the other hand, the Belfast Boycott offered the opportunity for the different groupings to unite under one banner. Moreover, boycotting was an acceptable form of protest for the clergy and moderate nationalists alike, as well as the more ardent Sinn Féin supporters.

In Thomastown the whole Belfast Boycott committee was arrested by the Crown Forces, including the chairman who was the local curate. They were charged on grounds of being 'the authors of a conspiracy for the destruction of Belfast goods', in reference to an attack on a storage depot in Thomastown railway station.[60]

The local media gave widespread attention to the problems occurring in Belfast and in October 1920 Kilkenny City Hall held a public meeting to discuss the unrest there.[61] The IRA played its part also, which mainly involved raiding trains or rail stores, as occurred in south Kilkenny where a consignment of goods from Belfast 'were burned at Ballyhale railway station'.[62] In Ballyragget, posters appeared around the town listing all the products which were made in Belfast and which should therefore be boycotted. The list of over one hundred Belfast companies encompassed a range of household products to be shunned, including flour, candles, sweets, twine, starch and towels.[63]

Some self-interest was also evident. Richard Smithwick, whose family owned the Smithwick's Ale brewery in Kilkenny City, wrote to Kilkenny Corporation to insist on the addition of 'Bass Ale to the list of boycotted products', even though it was officially an English company.[64]

Work of Local Government: Varying Priorities

The social and economic realities of daily life dominated the correspondence between Kilkenny local authorities and the Department of Local Government. In April 1921, for instance, just as the IRA military campaign was reaching its apogee in Kilkenny, the clerk of Thomastown Union was writing to the Dáil LGB requesting permission for the master of the workhouse to keep a pony on site. In further correspondence in June 1921, a map of the proposed location of the stable was sent.[65]

The War of Independence was having a negative effect on the Thomastown Union Workhouse and Hospital in a number of ways. In December 1920, parts of the complex, including the Fever Hospital, were taken over by the military.[66] In January 1921 the Auxiliaries 'commandeered the provision store and took away 50lbs of bread' without payment. In the same month, two Auxiliaries were admitted to the hospital but their subsequent bill of £6 also remained unpaid.[67] As was common in that era, a workhouse complex often contained an adjoining hospital or fever infirmary which was accessible to

Table 4. Classification of 'inmates' in Thomastown Workhouse/Hospital (now known as St Columba's)

Inmates and Patients Total	Patients in Hospital	Tuberculosis cases	Aged & Infirm	Children under 15 years	Mothers with Infants [usually widowed or unmarried mothers]
	48	2	77	23	19

	Other classes of Inmates	Officials [Employees] (Outdoor & Indoor)	Qualified Nurses in General Hospital	Qualified and trained nurses in fever hospital	Fever patients (exclusive of Influenza) during past twelve months
172	5	12	4	1 (Nun)	10

BMH WS 1413 (Tadhg Kennedy) – Appendices A–F, 'Commission of Inquiry into Local Government'.

the public, usually if they could not afford to pay for healthcare elsewhere. The sick, elderly, infirm and women who had children outside marriage, often found themselves relying on 'the workhouse'. The table above gives the classification of all 'inmates' in Thomastown workhouse/hospital in August 1920:[68]

The most noticeable aspect of Local Government in Kilkenny was the sheer volume of the correspondence and wide range of subject matter with which the local authorities had to deal. The records also clearly demonstrate that during this time of military struggle, ordinary life continued unabated in many respects. For example, on the same week that the successful IRA ambush took place in Mooncoin in June 1921, the local sanitary officer informed the council that the pump was out of order in the village and would require 'immediate attention'.[69]

Members of the local councils dealt with a range of topics, including rent collection and arrears, dog licence collections, 'illegitimate' babies in the workhouses and farm inspections. Ironically, much of the time was taken up by claims for compensation that were as a direct effect of the parallel war that was taking place. Some of the most common claims were for personal injury, commandeered property, damaged telegraph wires and dug-up roadways.

Lastly, to emphasise the range of subject matters councillors were required to deal with, a letter from Patrick Walsh of New Building Lane in Kilkenny City to the board of the Kilkenny (Workhouse) Union offers an unusual example:

> Gentlemen – Having had the misfortune to lose my wife a short time ago I have decided to again enter the matrimonial state. I have looked outside for a suitable person and have not been so far successful. I have now decided to apply to your honourable board to assist me in this matter. I now write you to know if you will give me permission to select a wife from amongst the inmates of the [work] house. I require a steady, sober, clean woman who will look after my meals, and I promise to do my best to make her comfortable and give her a good home. I am well-known to most of the members of your board ... as well as the county priests. I hope you will give me your kind assistance, and grant me my request. Thanking you in anticipation – I am, gentlemen, your obedient servant, Patrick Walsh.[70]

It was not recorded if a 'lucky' woman was chosen for Patrick or if he ever re-entered the matrimonial state.

CHAPTER 8

A Truce: In Every Which Way but Loose (July 1921–March 1922)

The two most wanted things in Ireland today are
peace and rain; we may be within sight of both.

– Kilkenny Moderator, 16 July 1921

The Truce between the IRA and Crown Forces came into effect at 12.00 pm on Monday, 11 July 1921 and the truce period lasted nearly twelve months. Little did the public know that when hostilities recommenced, it would not be the Crown Forces that were the foe, but their fellow kinsfolk.

It is fair to say that news of the Truce was greeted with a mixture of relief and delight by most of the Kilkenny populace. For some, the British Government agreeing to a truce was as good as them declaring the IRA victorious against an empire. For others, a return to normality was their only desire. The definition of a truce meant different things to different people. As will be discovered in this chapter, some blatantly flouted it, while others stuck to it rigidly, with few in between.

An Air of Confidence Returns: Summer and Autumn 1921

An air of positivity prevailed for the remainder of summer 1921. Kilkenny IRA members who had been on the run were able to return home; many to heroes' welcomes. For parents and loved ones it was a huge weight lifted. Similarly, members of the Crown Forces could breathe a sigh of relief, as the threat of attack every time they left the confines of their barracks was now withdrawn. It also allowed them to socialise more freely, while still receiving pay.

With the Truce in place, the Sinn Féin and Republican movement consolidated the position they had garnered during the War of Independence. Republican Courts continued to be convened, while Republican Police patrolled the streets and districts. This was especially true throughout rural Kilkenny where there was a lack of RIC stations and where the British troops were mostly confined to barracks. The continued holding of Republican Courts in Kilkenny was raised by some English MPs in the House of Commons as a possible breach of the Truce, but it appears no heed of this warning was taken in Kilkenny.[1]

On the Monday night the Truce came into effect there was general rejoicing throughout the county. A large bonfire was lit in the City and dancing continued in the streets well into the early hours of Tuesday morning. The Republican tricolour flag was raised above City Hall. However, not all were enamoured with the turn of events. The following day a shot was fired at the City Hall flag as a convoy of Crown Forces passed by. The Councillors in Kilkenny Corporation were not pleased with the actions of the military. At that night's meeting a motion was passed which stated they took 'strong exception to the uncalled for and highly provocative conduct of two lorries of Crown forces', while they called for 'an explanation of this breach of the truce' from the military authorities. Similarly, the following day, a number of Crown Forces soldiers climbed onto the roof of the home of Sylvester Nolan in Walkin Street and removed a flagpole flying the tricolour, much to the amusement of people on the street outside.[2]

In practical terms, the suspending of martial law restrictions was the greatest benefit of the Truce. Two days after it came into effect, Lieutenant-Colonel Naper, commander of the Crown Forces in Kilkenny, issued the following decree lifting many of the sanctions: 'All restrictions on fairs and markets at Callan, Castlecomer and Ballyragget and restrictions on the use of pedal bicycles in the County of Kilkenny, will be temporarily suspended as from noon, July 13th, 1921, until further orders.'[3] Aside from politics, it was the weather that occupied the minds of many in Kilkenny in July 1921. Thus far, the summer had been hot and dry which was a major concern for farmers as the drought began to affect their crops. In addition, during the week the Truce commenced, the Corporation in Kilkenny City was required to cut off the water supply to the City daily between 6.00 pm and 7.00 am as the reservoir in Muckalee was extremely low. The Corporation also prohibited the use of water for gardens, while it also ceased watering down streets (the watering down of streets was common at this time due to the large volume of dust and animal droppings).[4] Rain at the end of July relieved matters greatly.

In an obvious breach of the Truce, the IRA drilled and established training camps. During August and September 1921, nearly 1,000 IRA members from all over the county took part in camps held at Knocknamuck near Urlingford, Crutt, Tullogher and Garryricken near Callan. Some young men, who were not involved in the IRA during the War of Independence, joined during the Truce. This was a development that was often derided by veterans of the IRA, who believed it was cowardly for them to join when the risk of danger had subsided (they were nicknamed 'Trucers').[5]

The Truce also allowed for public commemorations. A crowd gathered in Carrickshock for the ninetieth anniversary commemoration of the 'Battle of Carrickshock', a tithe war altercation. The procession was led by a number of local IRA and Cumann na mBan companies, as well as the Hugginstown Fife and Drum band and the Ballyhale Pipers band. Speeches at the event included many comparisons between the Tithe War and the recently ended 'Anglo-Wars [War of Independence]'.[6]

It was not just the buoyant IRA that were breaching the Truce. Although fighting had officially ceased, safety from gunfire was not guaranteed. On Sunday evening, 28 August 1921, 22-year-old Robert Burke was playing cards at the crossroads in Ballybur, near Cuffesgrange, with his father, uncle and two cousins. A Crossley Tender carrying around seven Black and Tans in civilian clothes, along with 'four or five young ladies', described as being of the 'flapper variety', was passing through 'on a joy ride' to Kilkenny.[7] A shot was fired from the vehicle and Burke immediately fell, having been hit in the thigh. A Franciscan nun who was home from America visiting relatives administered first aid and then drove Burke by motor car to the Kilkenny Infirmary where the bullet was removed. He survived his injuries.[8]

Non-Political Gripes to the Fore in Truce Time

The Truce also allowed space for non-political grievances to be aired, which may not have been countenanced during the War of Independence. The farm of Mary Shortall from Urlingford was targeted in July when seventy-one 'cocks of hay' were burnt in an apparent family dispute over the inheritance of a farm. She also received letters threatening consequences if she did not give up the land.[9] In a similar vein, in September 1921, cattle belonging to James Cottrell from Inistioge were prohibited from proceeding to the fair in New Ross by a group of armed men. Cottrell had brought his neighbour before a Crown Court in a grievance over land. A Republican Court then judged in the neighbour's favour with expenses awarded. Cottrell had refused to pay the expenses and subsequently the IRA warned that he would not be permitted to sell his cattle until his neighbour's expenses were paid.[10]

In addition to localised quarrels, a number of labour strikes broke out in September 1921. If supporters of the labour movement in Kilkenny believed that the new era of Irish independence would bring the utopian 'socialist republic' as envisaged by James Connolly, they were quickly brought back down to earth. When the labourers employed by Kilkenny Corporation went on strike in September 1921, appealing for an increase in pay, it was now the Republican Police forcing them back to work, as opposed to the RIC in previous times. Generally, unemployment was high, with '600 men idle in Kilkenny [City]'.[11] The protracted Corporation strike lasted ten weeks. The dispute caused considerable tension between local councillors, with Peter DeLoughry of Sinn Féin frequently clashing with James Upton of Labour, who was supportive of the workers' cause. On 25 October, the water mains that supplied Kilkenny City was maliciously damaged at Radestown, resulting in the stoppage of the water supply throughout the City. The Corporation water inspector, James Davis, was forced to come off the strike by members of the Republican Police and fix the damage. Davis was then reinstated to his position by Mayor DeLoughry. Davis however was called 'a scab' by the rest of the men still on strike. He was prevented from going to work and his tools and bicycle were thrown into the River Nore. Additionally, the grates of the sewers around Kilkenny City were deliberately blocked using manure, apparently by some of the strikers. The aim was to force the Corporation into settling the dispute as the excess water and sewage on the streets caused a foul stench to build up.

Eventually arbitration discussions commenced. Kilkenny IRA Brigade O/C George O'Dwyer was one of the mediators, resulting in little relief to the employees. At the end of November 1921 they were reinstated on their old pay rate and given back pay of £7, although their income would have been £22 higher if they had not been on strike. The chief instigators of the strike did not receive the back pay.[12] E.T. Keane of the *Kilkenny People,* who was not supportive of the striking workers, looked on the bright side of the dispute:

> The net saving to [the Kilkenny] Corporation would probably work out at between £300 and £400, but on the other hand, of course, the condition of the streets and particularly the lane ways, had become very bad, though happily no epidemic occurred … The Corporation staff were busy on Thursday morning [after returning to work], and the streets underwent their long-delayed toilette consisting of haircut, shave, shampoo, wash and brush-up … It is hoped that whatever bitterness may have risen … will now be forgotten.[13]

Similarly, approximately 530 employees of Castlecomer Collieries went on strike after management announced a reduction in pay due to a decrease in the price of coal. On 24 September 1921, during the second week of the strike, the general manager of the collieries, John Whitaker, and the assistant manager James Hargreaves, were kidnapped by 'armed and masked men'.[14] Both men were told to leave the country, which they refused to do, and were consequently held captive for nearly two months until 17 November.[15]

Initially both of these strikes had much support. There was a mass demonstration on The Parade in Kilkenny City in October 1921, with the bulk of the crowd made up of the striking Corporation workers and the coalminers from Castlecomer. Alderman William O'Brien, a Dublin City Labour Councillor and ITGWU member, addressed the meeting. His speech highlighted the class tensions within the Republican movement that had been somewhat supressed during the War of Independence era, but which were now bubbling to the surface:

> The Mayor of Kilkenny [Peter DeLoughry] swore allegiance to his National Government [the Dáil], and he was the first man in Ireland to repudiate that allegiance when it was a question of paying a few cents more to the poor unfortunate labourers of Kilkenny. Kilkenny Corporation [is] composed principally of shopkeepers, butchers, and as many more robbers as could be found. It is up to the workers of Kilkenny to make up their minds whether they were going to be slaves or not.[16]

Tensions increased further in Castlecomer when the management of the collieries brought three locals to court for stealing coal; a crime that was a fairly regular occurrence at the time. Two of the accused, James Morrissey and Thomas Doolan, were in fact employed by the collieries as miners. All pleaded guilty but were released on grounds of good character.[17] Eventually the strike ended before Christmas with little success for the miners.

Republican Police versus the RIC during the Truce

The usurpation of civil authority by the IRA – which was reinforced further after the Truce was established – was difficult for RIC members to accept. As the RIC's influence waned even more amongst the populace, morale within the force continually ebbed away. By September 1921, CI Whyte of the Kilkenny RIC, was clearly not happy with the unrelenting rise of the Republican Police and IRA:

> this county has been peaceable, this of course is due to the existence of the truce which is being loyally observed by the Crown Forces. The IRA, though

not resorting to violence, cannot be said to be doing likewise, but are more or less aggressive. Drilling, picketing by Sinn Fein 'police', and kidnapping alleged thieves are some of the IRA activities reported during the month.[18]

The power struggle between Republican Police and the RIC manifested itself in an unusual way in October 1921 when there was a showdown over the ownership of a dead body. William Shea, originally from County Kerry and who was described by the newspapers as being from the 'tramp class', was arrested by Republican Police for an 'attempted assault on a young girl' near Kells, County Kilkenny. He was brought to Callan hospital due to ill health; but escaped from there after a few days. The following week, his body was discovered near Garryricken, Shea having committed suicide by hanging from a tree. His remains were removed to Callan hospital morgue by Republican Police. The RIC arrived subsequently and locked the body into the morgue building, 'taking the key with them', with the apparent intention of preventing the Republican Police from carrying out the usual inquest into the death. The Republican Police, however, eventually forced their way into the building and brought Shea's body to another location in Tipperary where the inquest was held. A doctor found the deceased had died as result of 'a fracture of the cervical spine due to hanging'.[19]

The Republican Police force had their own unique methods of dispensing justice, while the Truce also gave them the scope to carry out their duties more freely. For example, early on Sunday morning, 25 September 1921, William Hayes and John Renehan were taken from their homes in the parish of Danesfort by a party of ten armed Republican policemen. They were brought to the nearby village of Bennettsbridge where, at 8.00 am, they were tied to the railings of the parish church, just as people were arriving for first Mass. This public embarrassment was punishment for the men who were accused of stealing an unspecified amount of porter stout from Walsh's public-house in Bennettsbridge.[20]

The upheaval and ambiguity regarding the maintenance of law allowed petty criminals to carry out their misdemeanours, using the political turmoil as a disguise for their motives. In November 1921, the home of John Fitzpatrick of Gathabawn was entered by four armed and masked men claiming to be 'IRA police in search of stolen greyhounds'. Fitzpatrick was rearing two pedigree pups, the offspring of *Harmonicon*, winner of the 1916 Waterloo Cup, then a world-famous coursing event in England. *Harmonicon* was 'the most important stud dog imported into Ireland' up to that time and cost £1,500 (the pups and *Harmonicon* were owned by Denis J. Gorey of Burnchurch, later leader of The

Farmers' Party).[21] A struggle ensued between Fitzpatrick, his daughter and the intruders. The pups were however, eventually stolen by the men and brought away in a motor car, their fate unknown.[22]

The Great Kilkenny Jail Break: November 1921

'Stone Walls Do Not Prisons Make'

– *Kilkenny Moderator*, 26 November 1921

County Kilkenny found itself in international news headlines after the audacious escape of forty-three political prisoners from Kilkenny Jail on 22 November 1921. The escape of so many prisoners was deeply embarrassing for the British authorities in Ireland, especially after many of the escapees had been moved to Kilkenny from other prisons as it was deemed more secure. The prison escape also occurred at a politically sensitive time for Sinn Féin. While it was considered an obvious breach of the Truce, the escape occurred as the treaty negotiations were entering their final critical weeks in London. A diversion like this was something Michael Collins and Arthur Griffith could probably have done without.

The Victorian-era Kilkenny Jail was located at the end of Gaol Road, about 1 km from the centre of Kilkenny City (the building no longer exists, and St Francis Terrace is in the location today). For the political prisoners languishing in Kilkenny Jail, all of whom were arrested before the Truce, the lack of any political progress in securing their release was understandably frustrating. If they had avoided arrest, like many of their IRA comrades who had been on the run, they would have been free to return home uninhibited after the Truce in July, four months earlier. Many prisoners probably felt forgotten, although the local Cumann na mBan launched fundraising initiatives to raise financial support for their families.[23]

Life within the jail had improved for the prisoners since the Truce, with the inmates treated better than 'ordinary criminals'. Martin Kealy from Blanchfield Park, Gowran, had been elected 'Commandant' or spokesperson for the political prisoners in Kilkenny Jail. Kealy was 4th IRA Battalion O/C until his arrest by Auxiliaries in September 1920 while he was engaging in Volunteer inspections. The political prisoners were mostly kept in 'A' wing of the prison, which was also known as the 'short-term wing'. On the whole, Kilkenny prison governor, John Boland, tolerated the special status of the prisoners in that wing and often gave into their demands. This was an understandable attitude for Boland to have, as when he was governor of Mountjoy Prison in 1917, Thomas Ashe – a 1916 Rising Commandant – died during a hunger strike as a result of force-feeding, resulting in Boland becoming 'public enemy number one' and a scapegoat for the prison authorities. A similar episode in Kilkenny was therefore to be avoided at all costs. Kealy described his interactions with Boland and life inside the prison:

> I had several interviews with the prison governor [Boland]. I soon realised that he was anxious to avoid anything in the nature of prison disturbances or hunger-strikes, and before long we had the Rules and Regulations of the Prison modified and altered to our satisfaction … A number of prison warders were sympathetic towards us and were very helpful, with the result that we were able to procure from outside sources, messages and articles which would not be allowed through regular channels.[24]

Another prisoner, Edward Balfe from Enniscorthy, County Wexford, was permitted to have his camera in prison where he indulged in his passion for photography, taking photos of the inmates.[25]

The prison population in Kilkenny Jail was growing steadily as a result of prisoner transfers from Rath Internment Camp in The Curragh and Spike Island Prison. One of the recently arrived prisoners, Tom McCarrick of the Sligo IRA, along with Kealy, decided on the idea that a tunnel should be dug as a means of escape from the prison. A plan was quickly formulated.[26]

The prisoners gained access to a long-disused punishment cell, which was directly below one of the occupied prison cells, by sawing through the floorboards and dropping down through the hole. Once access was made to the disused underground cell, it took a number of attempts and a lot of brawn to break the keystone of the prison block wall to enable the men to commence digging a tunnel underneath the yard and, thus, out beyond the perimeter wall. Kealy arranged for three shifts a day, of three men in each shift. Just one would work in the tunnel, the other two acted as a lookout and removed the excavated earth.[27] Their main implement for excavating the tunnel was a trowel that had been stolen from the prison tool store, while fire pokers, knifes and sharpened spoons were also used. Pillow cases and blankets were used to extract earth from the tunnel using improvised ropes. The would-be escapees worked relatively unhindered as the prison authorities had no idea that tunnelling was taking place, literally beneath their feet. As the tunnel developed it was also vital to reinforce it so it would not collapse. Improvised supports were made using planks of wood from the bed-boards of prison beds. The distance from the underground cell, to the nearest point outside the prison perimeter wall was approximately 40 feet (12 metres).[28] Conditions within the ever-expanding tunnel were far from ideal. The three-feet high, by two-feet wide tunnel was not ventilated, thus the cramped conditions meant it became unbearably hot, while there was also a constant stench of perspiration. In addition, during the course of the excavation, the prisoners came across human bones, most likely the graves of convicts of an earlier era.[29]

During the week before the escape, a number of unforeseen incidents occurred that had the potential to thwart all the plans. Fr Patrick H. Delahunty – the republican curate who was arrested in Callan the previous year and who was half way through a two-year sentence for the possession of 'seditious literature' – attempted his own escape bid. At that time Fr Delahunty was located in the hospital wing of the jail. As happened on occasion, gifts were sent into him from supporters outside. One day a loaf of bread was delivered, which he soon discovered contained the additional ingredient of hacksaw blades. Fr Delahunty subsequently proceeded to saw through the iron bars of his cell window but his handy work was discovered by a vigilant warder just before he could escape. Surprisingly, Governor Boland did not punish Delahunty, or increase security in the jail, but instead sent him back to the short-term wing. Luckily for Fr Delahunty, his arrival was just in time for the completion of the escape tunnel.[30]

Another potential threat to the planned escape attempt occurred just a few days before the estimated completion of the tunnel. The population of Kilkenny prison swelled when seventy-five prisoners were transferred from Spike Island prison to Kilkenny on Friday, 18 November 1921.[31] As the long-term wing of the prison was overcrowded, about twelve of these prisoners were placed in the short-term wing.[32] The addition of new inmates caused another headache for Kealy. Security was substantially increased, and military personnel were drafted in to augment the prison warden staff. This included a number of Black and Tans who patrolled outside the perimeter wall of the jail – which would most likely scupper the planned escape even if they got outside the walls. Kealy sent for his friend, Peter DeLoughry, Mayor of Kilkenny. He pointed out to DeLoughry that the placing of a military guard outside the walls of the prison, in full uniform, was a breach of the Truce. DeLoughry subsequently complained about this to the Military authorities and the guard was removed the day of the planned escape attempt.[33]

After nearly a month of digging, with unerring willpower and resolve, the amateur miners burrowed through the stone foundations of the perimeter wall and by Monday evening, 21 November, they reported to Kealy that they believed they were about 10 feet outside the prison wall. After a hastily arranged meeting it was decided to plan the escape attempt for 6.00 pm the following evening, with the hope that the November darkness would aid their escape.

As the day of the planned escape dawned, Tuesday, 22 November 1921, another unpredictable event arose. That morning, in an unrelated occurrence, John Boland was replaced as governor of Kilkenny prison by Captain Hubert Burke, former governor of Waterford jail. It was feared that the new governor would change the daily routine, while furthermore, prison warders would probably be more alert, eager to impress their new boss. At 6.00 pm, the time scheduled for the escape, Burke made an impromptu inspection of the prison. He thoroughly examined the cells but luckily for the prisoners he did not discover the entrance to the underground cell that led to the tunnel.

Just before the evacuation commenced, the warden on duty, Tom Power, was distracted by a prisoner who invited him to his cell to play draughts. This was a regular occurrence as Power was liked by the prisoners.[34] Before 7.00 pm, almost an hour later than scheduled, the prisoners made their way to the entrance of the tunnel. Kealy gave each prisoner the number of their place in the escape queue. Tom McCarrick was the first into the tunnel. He would be responsible for breaking through the upper layer of clay at the end of the 50-foot long tunnel. Fr Delahunty was offered the prime position of the next person to enter the tunnel but he refused, stating that prisoners with death or life sentences should go before him.[35] After breaking through the final 18 inches of earth, McCarrick pulled himself to the surface. He was shocked to discover that the tunnel exit was much closer to the main gate of the prison than anticipated – approximately eighteen metres – and was also near the junction of Gaol Road and St Rioch's Street. After McCarrick, the next five prisoners out were William McNamara from Clare, Frank Pyne, Edward Punch and Patrick O'Halloran from Limerick, and Laurence Condon, from Cork. McNamara was tasked with helping the evacuees out of the tunnel. However, just as Condon came out, a warder appeared behind him. Using a piece of pipe he had in his hand, Condon pretended to have a gun. Because of the poor visibility, the warder assumed it was real and quickly surrendered. With the help of Pyne, Punch and O'Halloran, Condon brought the warder to a nearby house where he was tied up.[36] Paddy Donoghue, who lived on St Rioch's Street, was walking home from work when, to his astonishment, he saw men coming out of a hole in the road. One of the Kilkenny escapees recognised Donoghue who was at that time a prominent Dicksboro and Kilkenny senior hurler and appealed to him; 'Paddy will you help us.' Donoghue immediately enlisted the help of his friend, Mattie Power, another Kilkenny hurler who lived nearby, and both men helped lead the different escapee groups from the area. By this time, women had come out of the nearby terrace houses and helped pull the prisoners from the tunnel, while also pointing them in the direction of the countryside.[37]

Meanwhile, inside the prison, the warden, Tom Power, became suspicious, having noticed a lot of men entering the cell that accessed the tunnel. He went to investigate and when he saw what was happening said; 'aw, lads, you shouldn't do this while I'm on'. He was quickly captured and gagged.[38] His warder colleagues noticed that something was awry and an alarm was soon raised. In the meantime, forty-three of the fifty-five prisoners in the short-term wing had escaped. This included Kealy, the prison O/C, along with Fr Delahunty, James Hanrahan from Inistioge, who had been O/C of the 5th Kilkenny Battalion, and Joe O'Connor, O/C of the 3rd Dublin Battalion. More prisoners could have escaped, except one of the escapees, David Connolly from Mayo, brought his suitcase with him. This eventually blocked the tunnel for the remainder of the prisoners. Connolly was clever enough to drag his suitcase behind him, so when it got stuck he still managed to escape. Behind the wedged suitcase was the unfortunate 18-year-old Maurice Walsh, from Limerick, who had to reverse back towards the prison where he was quickly apprehended by waiting warders. McNamara, who was still managing the exit of the tunnel, could hear the shouts of the prison warders through the tunnel and knew no more prisoners would be making their exit.[39]

At about 8.00 pm, the alarms were sounded and over 200 Crown Forces personnel converged on the prison from the military barracks in Kilkenny and the RIC barracks on Parliament Street. Although the prisoners had only began escaping about an hour beforehand, they had dispersed into the countryside by crossing fields at the end of St Rioch's Street.[40] They spread out in groups of between four to eight people, with one leader having been pre-assigned, with groups delineated usually by their county of origin. Some prisoners were lucky to get a lift by pony and trap which had been provided by Denis Treacy of the Dunnamaggin IRA Company. He had been tipped off about a possible escape attempt by Aly Luttrell of Garryricken, who had been thrown a message from a window of the prison earlier in the day.[41]

Edward Balfe and his group of four escapees, tracked east in the direction of their home county, Wexford. By the following morning, after an arduous journey through fields and dykes on a dark, wet, cold night, they reached Ballymurphy, County Carlow (about 35 km from Kilkenny). Here they located friends and were driven the rest of the journey to Enniscorthy.[42] Having walked some distance west of Kilkenny City, Tom McCarrick's group of escapees took the risk of asking for food and water at a farmhouse they came upon. In a stroke of good fortune, it was the home of Kitty Teehan, a member of Cumann na mBan, whose brothers were also part of the local IRA. She helped usher the men to safe houses later that night.[43] Another group of eleven exhausted escapees arrived at Duckett's Grove, County Carlow – about 45 km from Kilkenny Jail – where they received assistance from the local Cumann na mBan. Condon and a large number of escapees ended up on a farm near Cuffesgrange (8 km south of Kilkenny), where they were later smuggled by pony and trap via Ballingarry, County Tipperary, to their home counties (Fr P.H. Delahunty went into hiding in Mullinahone).[44] Unlike the War of Independence era, the Truce meant that the public, in general, were not afraid of the consequences of helping fugitives. None of the prisoners who escaped that night from Kilkenny jail were recaptured.

As reports emerged of 'the great Kilkenny jailbreak', the majority of the local populace greeted the news with a sense of delight. The humiliation caused to the British authorities was also a source of amusement. The escapees were natives of thirteen Irish counties, and as such, were seen as heroes by those in their local area. The news of a jailbreaking priest added to the extraordinary story, while even the conservative *Kilkenny Moderator* newspaper reported the story in a humorous light: 'The escape of the popular priest [Fr Delahunty] caused intense delight in Kilkenny, especially as it is believed he is the first clergyman in the present movement who won his way without leave or licence to freedom.' The *Moderator* also commented on how one escapee, Laurence Condon, visited 'a house immediately opposite the Gaol' and 'impressed on them the necessity for absolute quietness'; but this 'was quite unnecessary as everyone was friendly'. It went on to praise the escape as 'one of the most cleverly planned and daring instances' of a jailbreak in history.[45] The *Kilkenny People* called it 'the greatest prison-breaking exploit on record', and commented that 'all cinema stunts [were] knocked into a cocked hat' when compared to the real-life feat of the Kilkenny escapees. It was not only the Irish media that reported the event. The *Kilkenny People*'s assertion that 'the name of "Kilkenny"', was featured in the Press throughout 'the civilised world' was not a gross exaggeration. Evidently, stories involving jail breaks and escape tunnels appeared to have universal appeal. For example, in far-off Australia, most of the national and local newspapers reported on the exploits of the Kilkenny fugitives. Similarly, the Kilkenny jailbreak featured in *The New York Times* on 23 November 1921.[46]

In the aftermath of the breakout, the governor, John Boland, who had initially been transferred to Dundalk prison, was suspended from duty as a penalty of his management of Kilkenny jail and was later forced to retire.[47] During the official inquiry into the escape, Boland stated his life since 1917 had been 'a living hell' and that in public he was treated as a 'living leper' because of his occupation.[48] The remaining prisoners in Kilkenny jail were transferred to Waterford or Limerick prisons. Kilkenny jail was closed on 10 December 1921.[49]

The twist in the whole jailbreaking affair was that on 6 December, just two weeks after the Kilkenny escape, the Treaty was signed between the British and Irish delegations in London, resulting in an immediate general release of most political prisoners. The Kilkenny escapees were not to know this. Besides, the excitement of attempting a jailbreak must have relieved the boredom of prison life.

Taking No Chances: November–December 1921

On the national political scene, the Treaty negotiations between the Irish delegation (headed by Arthur Griffith and Michael Collins) and their British counterparts, commenced on 11 October 1921 and lasted nearly two months, culminating with the signing of the Treaty on 6 December 1921. Some within the IRA in Kilkenny were taking no chances about a successful outcome of the talks. The risk of a breakdown in negotiations without agreement, with the subsequent resumption of hostilities, was believed to be a real risk. The IRA did not have the same luxury as the Crown Forces who had a vast and ever-replenishing arms and ammunition reserve. Consequently, some within the Kilkenny IRA Brigade continued to locate and procure arms where possible, in an obvious breach of the Truce. This backfired in November 1921 when Ned Halley and James Maher from Callan, both members of the 7th Battalion, were arrested while attempting to buy 300 rounds of ammunition from two corrupt members of the Oxfordshire and Buckinghamshire Regiment. As the rendezvous of the four men was taking place in McEvoy's public house in Callan, the military raided the premises and all four were arrested. It was another embarrassment for the Crown Forces, as the two soldiers arrested were a sergeant and a corporal in the regiment.[50] The event had been something of 'a sting' operation on the part of the Crown Forces. They had become aware of the motives of the corrupt soldiers and permitted the meeting to take place. The local 7th IRA Battalion subsequently claimed the actions of the British authorities was a breach of the Truce as it lured the IRA members into 'a trap'. The IRA decided they would kidnap some British military officers in retaliation for the arrest of Halley and Maher.

On the night of 1 December 1921, three off-duty military officers left the barracks in Callan and went to Callanan's Hotel in the town, a place where they often socialised. Just after 9.00 pm, six members of the 7th Battalion IRA arrived at the hotel. They entered the small smoking room just off the main hallway and shouted 'hands up' at the three British officers sitting by the fireplace. One of the soldiers had his loaded revolver on the table beside him and quickly turned and opened fire on the IRA, missing one of them by inches. The IRA retreated to the hall of the hotel and returned fire, with the resulting gun battle lasting a number of minutes.[51] Eventually the IRA men withdrew from the hotel and escaped. Miraculously, no one was seriously injured in the shootout, although there was much damage to the hotel, including the destruction of a large mirror in the hall, arousing feelings of superstition.[52]

Although a truce was in place, Kilkenny IRA companies continued to meet regularly to drill and attend classes. On the evening of 9 December 1921, Michael Byrne of the 5th IRA Battalion, was demonstrating how to use bombs (grenades) at his home in Kiltown, The Rower, when one of the bombs exploded unexpectedly. Byrne was blown backwards and suffered dreadful burns. He also badly fractured his thigh bone in the blast. He was quickly brought to New Ross workhouse hospital by motorcar, but he passed away the following day. He was only 20 years old. His funeral service took place in The Rower on 12 December, with a large contingent of IRA and Cumann na mBan members from the Kilkenny Brigade present.[53]

The Treaty: December 1921–January 1922

*But the Republican ideal has not died, nor will it die, even
though there be but fifty men left in Ireland to carry it on*

– Ned Aylward TD (7th Battalion IRA)

As the Kilkenny populace arose from their slumber on the morning of Tuesday, 6 December 1921, news and rumour began to circulate that an agreement had been reached in the early hours of the morning in London between the delegates representing Britain and Ireland. Telegrams first brought the news to Kilkenny, with late editions of Tuesday's newspapers confirming it. Although the details of the Treaty (officially known as the 'Articles of Agreement for a Treaty between Great Britain and Ireland') were not yet analysed, the news of a settlement brought relief and joy to many. The threat of hostilities resuming had been the major worry, but with the signing of the Treaty, this danger appeared to have dissipated.

The relief quickly swelled to elation throughout the towns and villages of the county when it was confirmed that nearly all the political internees would be released within a few days. The first groups of freed prisoners arrived in Kilkenny on Friday evening, 9 December 1921, just three days after the Treaty was signed. An initial group of Callan internees arrived in Kilkenny at around 3.00 pm. They made the three-hour trip from Portlaoise prison by 'char-a-bane' – an opened-top motor bus – which was driven by Callan Cooperative secretary James Lyons. It was decked out for the occasion with Irish tricolours. They stopped in Kilkenny City for several hours where they were greeted by ever-expanding crowds and where they waited for some of their fellow internees to arrive by train. The *Kilkenny Journal* vividly described the scenes at Kilkenny railway station that evening:

> On Friday night Kilkenny City paid a fitting tribute to the patriotic men from our midst who had been held in British dungeons without charge or trial … The explosion of fog signals marked the arrival of the train … Touching scenes followed as the men embraced dear ones whom they had not seen for so long – mothers and sisters whose duty it had been to wait and watch … A large number of [IRA] Volunteers formed into processional order and marched to The Parade, headed by St Patricks Brass Band and Kells Piper Band; there were scores of motor cars and buses.[54]

Amongst the released men were Callan residents J.J. Dunne, Michael Shelly and Jim Roughan – former O/C of the 7th Battalion – who was arrested exactly one year previously after the capture of Ernie O'Malley's documents by Auxiliaries. As the twenty-eight men of the Callan contingent made their way towards their hometown later that evening, they were guided along the route by numerous bonfires lit in their honour. They were accorded an even greater welcome on arrival in Callan:

> As was befitting the occasion, the day [Friday 9 December] was observed as a general holiday [in Callan], and all business houses were closed. Outstanding features of the demonstration in Callan were the display of banners inscribed with words of welcome, one that immediately caught the eye bearing the motto; 'Welcome to the Felons of our Land' which spanned the street at the Central Hotel. The Christian Brothers' schools and residence … the Augustinian Convent,

Mill Street, and the convent at Bridge Street were prominent in the matter of decorations, the tricolour being much in evidence.[55]

It was a similar story in Thomastown, where all shops closed to welcome home their interned citizens. The previous day, Thursday 8 December, local Sinn Féin Councillor Liam Forristal was officially the first Kilkenny prisoner to arrive home and was the centre of his own special party. A motor car, with an accompanying IRA and Cumann na mBan guard-of-honour, paraded him from the railway station around the town. The following day, the four remaining Thomastown and Inistioge internees; Tom Ryan, William Cotterell, William Lee and Patrick White, arrived home to similar festivities. The celebratory atmosphere also continued in Kilkenny City on Saturday, 10 December, with the return of more prisoners, including former Kilkenny Brigade O/C, Thomas Treacy. He had been arrested over a year previously and was imprisoned in Ballykinlar internment camp in County Down, where he held the rank of prison Commandant.[56]

It is accurate to state that the Treaty was widely accepted across many sections of the community in Kilkenny. Mayor Peter DeLoughry said the Treaty would 'receive the endorsement of the Irish people and the Irish race'.[57] The Catholic Bishop of Ossory, Dr Brownrigg, announced a Triduum (three days of thanksgiving) to be held in all parishes in the diocese, commencing Thursday, 15 December 1921. In a letter read throughout the county at Sunday Mass on 11 December he gave his approval of the 'bountiful' deal reached in London. Understandably, from his viewpoint, there was only one being responsible for the outcome and it was not Michael Collins or the IRA:

> For the last two years in the sad history of our country, calamities of a dreadful nature have forced us to go in prayer to God … At last … relief has come … We should now show our gratitude to Him who has prospered us in such a bountiful and unexpected way.[58]

The Church of Ireland Bishop of Ossory, Dr Day, similarly accepted the terms of the Treaty, while also indicating that some 'sacrifices' would be required by his flock: 'I think we have reason to be profoundly thankful. Of course all are called on to make sacrifices, but I do feel that these terms are a basis on which a true and lasting settlement can be made.'[59] The terms of the Treaty were published in the local newspapers, with all three newspapers supporting it. The *Kilkenny Journal* stated the deal reached was 'honourable to both Ireland and Great Britain' after 'the long struggle of bitterness and suffering stretching back throughout the past seven and a half centuries'. Alluding to the events of the previous years that led to the current agreement, it noted; 'the fight for freedom was not inspired by hatred of England, but by a love of Ireland'. There was also an acknowledgement that the joy felt by many, would be tinged with sorrow for some; 'there is no victory without suffering ... this will be a happy Christmastide in Ireland even though there may be some vacant places in many homes'.[60]

E.T. Keane of the *Kilkenny People* was even more enthused by the Treaty deal. Without any guilt that he was bordering on hyperbole, he declared:

> One of the greatest and most heroic fights for freedom ever put up in ancient or modern history by any small nation has ended in a victory as complete and as striking as any nation, great or small, has ever achieved ... It [the Treaty] makes the Irish people masters in their own house ... what is good enough for Mr Arthur Griffith and Mr Michael Collins is good enough for us. It may be that there are people who claim to be better Sinn Feiners than the Founder of Sinn Fein [Griffith], just as there may be people who claim to be more Catholic than the Pope, but we doubt the validity of their claim.[61]

The *Kilkenny Moderator*, which traditionally had a largely Unionist readership, was mainly supportive of the terms of the Treaty – as the only real alternative was a return to fighting. They had long since given up on the idea that society would revert to the pre-1914 era, or as historian Roy Foster put it; 'Southern unionists had long forecast their eventual abandonment [by the British Government] (as they saw it)'.[62] The *Moderator* did issue words of caution on the question of Ulster however, something which was generally ignored by other publications. Although the Northern Ireland state and parliament were already in existence six months prior to the signing of the Treaty, the unionist population of Kilkenny was understandably worried about their fate, as they were now a very small minority within a proposed Free State. Many southern Unionists expected – or hoped – Northern Ireland would eventually have to merge into the Free State:

> we have not yet fully realised that the people of Ireland have stepped from the darkness into sunshine ... There seems to be but one fly in the ointment – the unity of Ireland. That Ulster [Northern Ireland] will come in [to the Free State] now or later we cannot doubt. If Ulster decides to maintain her present isolated position she will have to consent to a new boundary line, she will pay her taxes to the Imperial Government, and will doubtless[ly] remain boycotted by the rest of

Ireland ... it is only a matter of time [until she joins the Free State]. It is too early
to indulge in wild enthusiasm; much yet has to be done.[63]

Kilkenny County Council held their meeting about the Treaty behind closed
doors, obviously expecting some vigorous exchanges. The result of the meeting
was a resolution requesting the local TDs to vote in favour of the Treaty in Dáil
Éireann. The resolution stated that the Council could see 'no alternative to the
ratification of the Treaty but chaos' and it was passed by fifteen for, with one
against. The only dissenting voice was James Donovan from Thomastown.

Similarly, the South Kilkenny Sinn Féin Executive voted overwhelmingly
in favour of the Treaty by thirty-six votes to six against.[64] The North Kilkenny
Sinn Féin Executive, chaired by Seán Gibbons, met in the New Year after the
hostile 'Treaty debates' had commenced in Dáil Éireann. The Executive voted
unanimously in favour of the Treaty but the resolution they forwarded to the
Dáil was cognisant of the storm clouds that were gathering:

> having in mind all the circumstances that led up to the signing of the Treaty, and
> the alternative in case of rejection, [North Kilkenny Sinn Féin] are of the opinion
> that while the Treaty falls far short in satisfying Ireland's national demand, it
> secures for Ireland a large measure of freedom, by which we believe the Irish
> people can gain full and complete independence.[65]

The matter of the Treaty was considered of such importance that the County
Kilkenny Farmers Union broke with one of their 'cardinal principles' of not
getting involved in politics when they convened at Kilkenny Courthouse to
discuss the agreement. The Union obviously had a loose definition of the term
'politics', as by their very existence they were inherently politicking for the
rights of farmers. Following a debate, in a 'very largely attended meeting', there
was a show of hands with the result that 'all' persons present voted in favour of
the Treaty. The large Farmers Union had a membership of approximately 6,000
people in County Kilkenny at this time.[66]

A meeting of ex-British Army servicemen from Kilkenny, the majority of
which had fought in the First World War, met in City Hall, in December 1921.
The Chairman, John O'Neill, encouraged the attendees to support the Treaty,
stating: 'it was up to ex-soldiers of Ireland who had fought for the freedom
of small nations [in the First World War] to show their appreciation at being
citizens of a free Irish State, and to feel jubilant with every other section of the
community.'[67] The Anglo-Irish Treaty was ratified by Dáil Éireann on 7 January
1922. At that time, a four-seat Carlow–Kilkenny constituency had replaced the

previous Carlow, North Kilkenny and South Kilkenny constituencies. All four seats in the Carlow–Kilkenny constituency were held by Sinn Féin TDs, who were elected unopposed the previous year. However, they were divided on the Treaty, with two voting in favour and two voting against. The two who voted for the Treaty were W.T. Cosgrave, the Minister for Local Government, and Gearóid O'Sullivan, who was originally from Cork and a cousin of Michael Collins, but who also had connections to Carlow as he was a former teacher at Knockbeg College there (he was also a member of the Carlow IRA Brigade staff). The local TDs who voted against the Treaty were James Lennon from Borris, County Carlow, and Ned Aylward from Callan – O/C of the 7th Kilkenny IRA Battalion at the time of the Truce. Aylward had only discovered he was put forward as a candidate after he was elected unopposed to Dáil Éireann in June 1921 while he was leading an ASU.[68] The two TDs in favour of the Treaty clashed fiercely with the two that opposed it during the Treaty debates in Dáil Éireann. Ned Aylward's contribution contained the following:

> I was elected by the people of South Kilkenny; and the people who elected me know what views I had because at that time I was fighting [in the IRA] for the realisation of those views. Should my constituents change their mind then they can remove me at the next election and put in a politician [Aylward saw himself as a fighter – an IRA man – and not a politician]; but they cannot change my personal opinion or my principles … if their willingness to become British subjects with a British Governor-General to look after them, and to take their allegiance to the British Government and all that – if that is not compromise I don't know what compromise is. Not only do they become British subjects but they take an oath to a British King. I did not take it that the Republic had been let down at any time until I saw the terms of the Treaty in the public Press … But the Republican ideal has not died, nor will it die, even though there be but fifty men left in Ireland to carry it on.[69]

In a highly controversial speech, Deputy Gearóid O'Sullivan strongly rebutted those against the Treaty, who he believed had a green-tinted view of an old mystical Ireland:

> … I would like to draw your attention to the effect of Gaelic culture and Gaelic civilisation on the world. What has it done? The greatest Anglicisers of the world have been the Irish. We, the Irish people, have been Empire builders for England all over the world. We have built her railways and her roads; we have shot down troops who attempted to secure freedom from that Empire … the reason I give in

support of the ratification of the Treaty is that I believe it is the wish of the people who sent me here that I should support it.[70]

It was not surprising that the majority of Kilkenny citizens were undoubtedly in favour of the Treaty. The fear of returning to the turmoil of war against Crown Forces was a major factor in the Treaty's general acceptance; while there was also an acknowledgment that the terms of the agreement conferred a measure of freedom that was unimaginable just a few years previously. Furthermore, since the Truce came into effect, the people of Kilkenny had experienced a life largely unhindered by British rule. This 'trial-run' of self-governance, although less than six months in existence, had not seen a descent into anarchy that some had predicted. For the majority, life continued relatively unchanged. For others who were active in the War of Independence years, their exploits and sacrifices had thrust them into positions of authority, while, in addition, they also became highly regarded members of their local communities. As the Treaty bestowed wide-ranging powers to an Irish government, many were now satisfied to work along non-militant lines in developing the fledgling state; and were therefore not overly perturbed whether it was termed a 'Free State' or 'Republic'. Not all veterans of the War of Independence era were of the same opinion however, and they were to make their feelings known in the coming months.

Clouds Form on the Horizon: January–March 1922

Even after the Treaty was ratified in the early weeks of 1922, it was not a forgone conclusion that the country would be facing a civil war just six months later. For much of the Kilkenny populace it seemed the Treaty was now a *fait accompli* and those against would need to accept the decision of the Dáil and move on. Accordingly, attention turned away from the national stage and focused on issues closer to home.

A number of farmers took the law into their own hands when, in January 1922, they kidnapped a Crown Solicitor named Dr Lewis J. Watters from his home, Tinnypark House, which was located 5 km south of Kilkenny City. Watters was representing a landlord in the prosecution of a number of farmers for the non-payment of rent. The farmers abducted the 70-year-old Watters at gunpoint, although they did allow him to get warmer clothing before leaving. The purpose of the abduction was to prevent him from attending the court cases that were pending against the farmers. The incident was reported to the Republican Police who quickly located Watters on a farm 'on the borders of Kilkenny and Tipperary'. He was returned to his home by his abductors two days after he was kidnapped 'looking none the worse for his exciting experience', but the court case had to be delayed.[71]

Also in January, the IRA in Callan visited the homes of ardent loyalists, and those who had previously provided services for the Crown Forces. The families were told they had 'six days' to leave the area. This warning had not been sanctioned by IRA GHQ and subsequently a proclamation was issued by the Provisional Government countermanding these orders. This event in Callan reached the floor of the House of Commons where Winston Churchill, Secretary of the State for the Colonies, was forced to defend the Provisional Government and their response to the Callan incident stating; 'none of the persons intimidated has since been molested in any way'.[72]

Hostility at Castlecomer Collieries was still evident in early 1922. In the early morning of Thursday 9 February, an estimated £10,000 worth of damage was done to the 'aerial ropeway between [the] Rockbog and Vera pits' with the corresponding engine and boiler destroyed. In addition, the engine-house, which powered this transportation system, was also burnt down. The night staff had been detained by a number of 'armed and masked men' during the attack. The elaborate aerial ropeway covered a length of 11 miles and this was cut in a number of places. There was outrage locally, as the destruction of the coalmine's transport network resulted in the closure of one of the pits, leaving over 250 people out of work for a number of months.[73]

In response, Kilkenny IRA Brigade Commandant George O'Dwyer, placed parts of Castlecomer parish under martial law and enforced a curfew between the hours of 10.00 pm and 5.00 am. The IRA subsequently arrested fifteen people believed to be involved, but none were ever charged. All of those suspected of having caused the damage were 'carters'. These were men who had previously carted the coal from the mines to the train line which was four miles away. After the aerial ropeway system was installed the previous year, all twenty-five carters lost their jobs. Hence, this was believed the most likely motive for the act of sabotage. The colliery owners later received compensation of £8,750, which was levied against Kilkenny and Laois County Councils (some of the former carters resided in the latter county).[74]

Hospital Closures

Another major issue in the public sphere involved a directive by Dáil Éireann to close down the workhouses in Castlecomer, Urlingford and Callan. This was a countrywide 'amalgamation' strategy by the Dáil government to shut many of the Victorian-era workhouses which they perceived to be a draconian legacy of British Imperial rule. Moreover, the cost of running the workhouse and their adjoining hospitals were a drain on the local exchequer. The problem, however, was there was no plan to replace the services provided by the workhouses, or more specifically, the hospitals attached to them. For many who could not afford to pay for their healthcare in privately run hospitals, the workhouse hospital was their sole option. The same was true for many incapacitated or elderly people who were unable to fend for themselves. However, there was less sympathy for some of those who availed of the services of the workhouse who were frequently stereotyped as 'idle' people of the 'tramp class' who refused to work for a living. Many of these were homeless or suffered from addiction to alcohol and were therefore considered 'undeserving' of ratepayers' money.

In Callan Workhouse and Hospital, all 'inmates' of the workhouse were to be transferred to Thomastown, while 'all hospital cases' were to be transferred to Kilkenny Central Workhouse Hospital by 31 December 1921. If a patient was from County Tipperary, they were to be transferred to that county. There was also an assurance by the Dáil government to provide a motorised ambulance service for the Callan area to transfer people to Kilkenny City speedily when required. These suggestions were scoffed at by many of the local representatives. A number of the members of Callan Workhouse Board of Guardians said, 'the feeling in their respective districts was that the hospital should be retained'. However, Councillor Jim Roughan, the former 7th Battalion IRA O/C who had just been released from prison, agreed with the Dáil government's policy of saving money, commenting that the local Council should be 'delighted to be getting rid of the hospital', as only 'one-eighth' of the hospital building was occupied, and it contained just thirty-eight patients. In his view, the hospital was very costly as staff and board officials had to be paid from local rates. Councillor John Molloy retorted; 'It is all right for you [Roughan] who are a big farmer to say that but what about the poor population of Callan, Killamery, [and] Mullinahone … What are the poor living in these districts going to do when they get sick?'.[75]

Castlecomer Board of Guardians refused to close the local hospital. The people of Castlecomer had reasonable grounds for keeping it open. Although the town itself had a population of less than one thousand, there was multiples of this figure living in the surrounding areas, with many engaged in the physical and dangerous work of mining. So an unusual agreement was reached between the owners of the collieries and the miners to keep the hospital open, where each would pay 50 per cent of the cost of running the hospital.[76]

Crown Forces Move Out: February 1922

Definitive proof that Kilkenny was indeed in the midst of a new era occurred on Tuesday, 7 February 1922, with the withdrawal of British soldiers from Kilkenny Military Barracks, just two months after the signing of the Treaty. For the ordinary person, witnessing the departure of Crown Forces from the country was perhaps the most tangible and visual effect of the Treaty. Special trains were required to transport the 214 men, 145 horses, seventy-five wagons, six eighteen-pounder artillery guns and about sixty tons of baggage from Kilkenny to Dublin, for onward embarkation to England through Dublin Port. It was Kilkenny IRA Brigade O/C, George O'Dwyer, who formally took control of the barracks on behalf of the Provisional Government of Ireland. Less than a year earlier, he was attempting to attack some of these same soldiers as leader of the 1st Kilkenny ASU.

The event undoubtedly was tinged with emotion for many – on both sides – as they were now coming face-to-face with the people that killed or injured their friends and comrades during the troubles of the previous years. For the general public, the evacuation of Crown Forces during that Tuesday afternoon in February 1922 was a joyous occasion, with most shops shutting their doors as if it was a public holiday. It was also somewhat of a family occasion, as parents travelled from different parts of the county, not just to watch the British military leave, but to witness their sons marching in to take over the barracks.[77] Some of the business owners on John's Street were perhaps happier than most to see the departure of the Crown Forces, as a number of inebriated soldiers had smashed windows along the street two nights previously, in an over-zealous response to finally leaving Kilkenny. James Comerford, an IRA captain who marched into the barracks that day, recalled the events over fifty years later:

> That span of fifty four years does not dim my memory of that event … Right now, I again can see the joyful faces of the packed crowds, of men, women and children on High Street, Rose Inn Street and John Street. Again I can hear the clapping of thousands of hands and the ringing cheers – from hundreds of throats … The noise from the cheers and the applause grew louder in a rising crescendo.[78]

For some, it must have been a time to reflect on events. Many of those marching to Kilkenny Barracks on that day in February 1922, had journeyed much the same route six years earlier when they were arrested by the military after Easter Week 1916. Martin Kealy had been one of those prisoners in 1916 and his brother John had died on that enforced march. Now Martin was leading a group of IRA men into Kilkenny Barracks to take possession. The events of the day were reported in the *Kilkenny Moderator*:

About 3.30 o' clock [pm] a detachment of I.R.A. went into occupation of the military barracks. The men … were in [the] charge of Commandant O'Dwyer. They formed up in St James Park [in the west of the City at about 1.00 pm] and headed by St Patrick's Brass Band, marched through the city to the military barracks … The scene along the route from St James Park, and especially at the entrance to the Barracks, was one of jubilation and enthusiasm. Crowds thronged the streets and the arrival of the Irish soldiers at the barracks was the signal for a great outburst of cheering from the assembled crowd. Inside the Barracks the soldiers were put through various evolutions by Commandant O'Dwyer, and the precision with which they executed the different orders of their Commandant impressed the crowd who had gathered in the square of the Barracks. The walls and doors in some of the sleeping apartments, which were left in anything but a tidy condition, bore various inscriptions. One was: 'Erin-go-Bragh – when the fields are white with daisies we'll return' [which was a quote from a popular First World War song]. Another was, 'Gone but not forgotten'.[79]

The following month, a celebratory party was held in the barracks with many of the local dignitaries invited. Mayor DeLoughry summed up the swiftness of the changes taking place; 'I do not think that any of us a few short months ago ever thought – not even in our wildest dreams – that Irish soldiers would so soon occupy the Kilkenny Military Barracks.'[80] Mayor DeLoughry's brother, Larry, provided some of the singing entertainment, with the accompaniment of an orchestra.[81]

Some weeks prior to the evacuation of Kilkenny Military Barracks, the abode of the infamous A Company of Auxiliaries, Woodstock House in Inistioge, was also evacuated. The RIC police were also disbanded by the British Government. By mid-March 1922, George O'Dwyer issued a proclamation stating that 'as the forces of the British Crown, [both] military and police, and every vestige and symbol of enemy power and authority have disappeared from Kilkenny City and County, the onus of maintaining law and order devolves for the present on the Irish Republican Army'.[82]

The Slide to Civil War: February–March 1922

While many were optimistic about the future, clouds of discontent had been gathering on the horizon since the Dáil Treaty debates the previous December.

Many of those who were angry with the agreement had been at the coalface of the War of Independence in Kilkenny. As they had sacrificed much to 'fight for a Republic', the demotion of this to a 'Free State' – with the reigning British monarch as head of that State – was too much of a compromise to bear. Consequently, by February 1922, as opinions and attitudes were formulating at a rapid pace, there were efforts by those against the Treaty to prepare for the recommencement of hostilities. At this time however, it was not fully clear who the combating participants would be. The best scenario for those against the Treaty was the continuation of a fight against the Crown Forces, which would avoid a civil war. But as the British forces began to withdraw from the country, it became increasingly likely the combatants would be Irish people supportive of the Treaty (pro-Treaty), versus those against (anti-Treaty). Ireland was slipping towards civil war.

On the night of Friday 25 February, the arms store of John's Street RIC barracks was raided by a group of anti-Treaty IRA men. Most of the weapons had only been moved there the previous night. All the arms had been handed in by the recently decommissioned Black and Tans who had left the previous week. Clearly the anti-Treaty IRA did not want this treasure trove of arms returning to England and therefore stole the haul, including; ninety rifles, one hundred revolvers, a Lewis machine-gun, and 9,000 rounds of corresponding ammunition. They left a note 'expressing thanks for the way the rifles had been oiled and otherwise cared for'.[83] Local members of Cumann na mBan, led by Maisie Stallard, distributed the arms to safe houses around the city for storage.[84] Overall, the anti-Treaty IRA in Kilkenny were now much better armed than the IRA had ever been at any period during the War of Independence era.

In addition to the arms procurement, as the anti-Treaty IRA had no source of finance, they began raiding countywide to help fund the presumed impending conflict. On 31 March a total of £239, which was the amount of dog tax collected locally, was taken from the General Post Office on High Street and the sub-post office on John's Street in Kilkenny City, by four anti-Treaty IRA men. The day in question had been the deadline for paying the dog tax, and the Republican Police – soon-to-be known as 'The Civic Guard' (An Garda Síochána) – had placed posters around the City warning of fines if the tax was not paid.[85] When raiding the post offices, the anti-Treaty IRA were forthright in demanding only the proceeds of the dog tax and not any other funds. In this way they were emphasising that they were solely taking tax owed 'to the Republic' and were not stealing private monies. This was a courtesy they could not afford when civil war eventually broke out. In addition, a number of cars and bicycles were stolen at this time, usually from persons associated with the new Free State Army or the old RIC.[86]

It was becoming clearer as each day and week passed by, that something would have to give, and the spark that would ignite civil war was closer to being lit.

The list of combatants who died during the Truce era are listed in the following table:

Table 5. Fatalities of combatants in Kilkenny during the Truce era (July 1921–June 1922)

Date of Death	Name	Age at Death	Category	Native Place	Details
20 July 1921	Major Cyrus Hunter Regnart	42	Auxiliaries	England (London)	Committed suicide by shooting himself at Woodstock House, Inistioge. He had only joined the Auxiliaries six weeks earlier having been demobilised from the British Army. His remains were returned to England for burial.
10 Dec. 1921	Michael Byrne	20	IRA (5th Batt.)	The Rower	Byrne was demonstrating how to use bombs at his home in Kiltown, The Rower, when one unexpectedly exploded. He died the following day in New Ross as a result of burns and a fractured thigh.

CHAPTER 9

Civil War in All but Name: The Battle of Kilkenny (April–June 1922)

'The sharp crack of rifle shots and the noise of machine gun fire began to resound all over the City.'

– *Kilkenny Moderator*, May 1922

The Irish Civil War, for understandable reasons, often stirs up emotive and unwavering opinions. Although many decades have passed since the Civil War took place, the perspectives of older generations have often influenced the opinions passed down to younger generations who were informed 'what side the family was on' in the Civil War. In attempting to understand the conflict however, it is important to recognise – as objectively as possible – the various motives, aspirations and actions of both the pro and anti-Treaty sides. It is also essential to discern why the Civil War occurred in the first place.

Contrary to established faux history, the Civil War was not fought because of the partition of Ireland. The six counties in the north-east of the island had already been partitioned by the British Government under the Government of Ireland Act (1920). Moreover, the Parliament of Northern Ireland – led by Prime Minister Sir James Craig – had officially opened in June 1921, six months prior to the signing of the Treaty. The principal cause of the Civil War was one of sovereignty; specifically, the loss of 'the Republic' (albeit this was never accepted as in existence in the first place by the British Government), to be replaced by an 'Irish Free State' as a dominion within the British Empire; meaning the Monarch was still head of state. To add fuel to the fire, members of Dáil Éireann would be required to take an oath of fidelity to the reigning British Monarch. From a British political perspective, having the Crown in any settlement with the Irish was all but mandatory. For some TDs however, promising to be 'faithful to HM King George V' and 'his heirs and successors' was something they could not bring themselves to do, particularly as all Dáil politicians and members of the IRA had been required to swear an oath of allegiance to the Republic during the War of Independence era.[1]

From a present-day perspective, giving one's allegiance, or promising one's fidelity – whether that is to a republic or monarch – may appear to be just a few superficial words. However, during this period of history, 'giving your word' meant more than mere semantics. This explains why Michael Collins believed he had achieved a small victory in the Treaty negotiations when he succeeded in watering-down the final oath. Instead of an oath of allegiance to the monarch, there was firstly an oath of allegiance to the 'Constitution of the Irish Free State', with 'just' a promise of fidelity to the monarch.[2] Thus, the intricacies of language, and where words were positioned in a sentence, were of utmost importance.

It is helpful to assess the perspectives of the two opposing factions in the Civil War to discern why they took their respective positions. There were a myriad of reasons in choosing a particular side. Firstly, to outline generally the pro-Treaty/Free State view; the terms of the Treaty gave Ireland a measure of freedom unfathomable just a few years previously and was therefore much more than had been expected by many. This new autonomy included control over defence, domestic and foreign affairs, while in addition, the Crown Forces would evacuate the country. The Treaty also received widespread public support, although the fear of returning to the war against the British was a big factor in this. Furthermore, many people in Ireland, both political and non-political, did not have a clear-cut definition of what 'independence' meant; they had flexible attitudes. Therefore, there were many different shades of green on the scale between the most hard-line and the most moderate interpretation of 'independence', with people on the moderate side of the scale being mostly satisfied with the Treaty.

From the anti-Treaty perspective, the Republic had been diluted and the Irish people were still to be subjects of a British monarch. Many of those opposed to the Treaty had been IRA combatants or Cumann na mBan members who were at the frontline of the fighting during the War of Independence. They had made many sacrifices regarding their livelihoods, family life and their health, for the cause of the Irish Republic. Some had also witnessed comrades and family members terrorised or even killed. From their vantage point, all they had sacrificed was now diminished. Many anti-Treatyites placed the blame for the capitulation firmly on the shoulders of the politicians, many of whom who they did not respect, as they were perceived not to have been at the vanguard of the fighting during the War of Independence. In addition, from the point of view of the IRA, restarting the fighting from where they left off prior to the Truce was not going to be overly difficult as many had become hardened fighters as a result of their experiences in the War of Independence. Moreover, they had also become accustomed to operating as semi-autonomous groups with little direction from above. This toughness and self-sufficiency was required in times of civil war.

At this juncture, it is advantageous to outline the various terminology used to define the two opposing sides in the Civil War. The pro-Treaty combatants, supportive of the Provisional Government (and later the Free State Government), were officially called 'The National Army'; but became better known as the 'Free State Army'.[3] In the early days of the Civil War, they were also referred to as the 'Regular IRA' or the 'GHQ Forces'.[4] On the other side, the anti-Treaty IRA were disparagingly referred to as the 'Irregulars' by the Free State side (which implied the 'regular' position of the National Army). In addition, they were sometimes called the 'IRA Executive Forces' or simply the 'Republicans'. Both sides attempted to maintain ownership of the title 'IRA' at the beginning, but it became most associated with the anti-Treaty side after the commencement of civil war.

Although the Irish Free State did not formally come into existence until December 1922, for consistency purposes and ease of understanding, the combatants on the pro-Treaty side will mostly be referred to throughout as the 'Free State' forces, while the anti-Treaty side will be denoted as the 'anti-Treaty IRA'.

Splitting Up

It is correct to say that not everyone was persuaded to join a particular side by scrutinising the complexities of oaths or ideologies; many simply followed the crowd and joined their respective faction to be alongside their closest friends or family. This can be clearly illustrated by examining the IRA membership in County Kilkenny at the end of the War of Independence in July 1921, compared to the anti-Treaty IRA membership at the start of the Civil War one year later. There was very much a 'follow the leader' approach at play. This is best exemplified by the 3rd Battalion, headquartered in Castlecomer, which witnessed the largest reduction in IRA membership in the county. At the end of the War of Independence in 1921, the total nominal membership of the 3rd IRA Battalion was 621 men. By the start of the Civil War in 1922, this had decreased to 253, a reduction of 59 per cent. In other words, just 41 per cent took the anti-Treaty IRA position at the commencement of the Civil War in the Castlecomer area (to put this into context, on a national scale, an estimated 70 per cent of IRA Brigades were opposed to the Treaty[5]). The motivations of the 3rd Battalion can most likely be explained by the approach of leaders in the district. George O'Dwyer, the Kilkenny Brigade O/C and former 3rd Battalion O/C, took the pro-Treaty side. In addition, the 3rd Battalion O/C at the time of the Truce was Gerald Brennan, who also took the pro-Treaty side and both men later became officers in the Free State Army. Hence, it is not difficult to understand why the majority of the IRA in the 3rd Battalion chose the pro-Treaty side, as they were heavily influenced by the position of their leaders.[6]

In stark contrast, it was unsurprising that the membership of the 7th Battalion – the most active and experienced battalion in the county headquartered in Callan – remained steadfast. All its prominent leaders took the anti-Treaty side, or at a minimum, remained neutral. At the time of the Truce in 1921, the number of 7th Battalion IRA was recorded as 366. This remained relatively static by the outset of civil war, with 355 taking the anti-Treaty position. There were also interesting developments in quieter areas of the county. The 9th Battalion, headquartered in Mooncoin, saw its IRA membership hold firm at approximately 250 men. Its entire battalion staff took the anti-Treaty IRA position. The 9th Battalion had just found its feet by the end of War of Independence. Moreover that battalion only had their first taste of the fighting three weeks before the Truce with the successful ambush of Crown Forces at Sinnott's Cross. Thus some companies in the 9th Battalion actually increased their membership by the beginning of the Civil War. This implies that some men joined the anti-Treaty cause during the Civil War who had not enlisted during the War of Independence.[7] There was a similar phenomenon occurring around Ireland where some of the least active areas during the War of Independence were at the forefront of the action during the Civil War. The parochial nature of the IRA split goes a long way in explaining the geographical pattern of the Civil War in County Kilkenny. As will become apparent, aside from the initial opening salvos, the majority of the hostilities were focused in the south and west of County Kilkenny, with the least amount of fighting in the 3rd Battalion area in the north of the county.

The Kilkenny Brigade Cumann na mBan also split. At a national level, Cumann na mBan were the first organisation to reject the Treaty, doing so overwhelmingly. The leadership of the Kilkenny Cumann na mBan Brigade also voted to reject the Treaty. However, this was not reflective of the membership in Kilkenny as a whole. Maisie Stallard, President of Kilkenny Cumann na mBan Brigade during the Civil War, stated the average membership in her company was approximately thirty, of which 'only about 10' voted against the Treaty.[8] Hence, there was a drastic two-thirds reduction in the average membership of each branch. Thus, the depleted Cumann na mBan was then a wholly anti-

Treaty organisation. The geography of the split followed along similar lines as their male counterparts in the anti-Treaty IRA, where the membership in the south and west was more active than in the north of the county, with the health of the organisation in the latter described as 'very bad'.[9]

After the split in Cumann na mBan, many of the women who were in favour of the Treaty established branches of the new pro-Treaty female organisation; Cumann na Saoirse (The League for Freedom). At the inaugural meeting of the Kilkenny branch of the organisation in City Hall in April 1922, Winnie DeLoughry, wife of the mayor, was elected president. This organisation received the unflattering nickname of 'Cumann na Searchers' from their former comrades in Cumann na mBan. This was because members of Cumann na Saoirse often accompanied Free State soldiers on raids of homes of suspected anti-Treaty supporters. Along with pointing out the houses to Free State soldiers, the women were sometimes asked to physically search the females in the household being raided. During the War of Independence the searching of females by men of the Crown Forces was a major source of controversy. The Free State Army could do without this form of attention and so were grateful to have Cumann na Saoirse women helping them. It no doubt caused great bitterness between the women in opposing factions, who knew each other so well in a small place like Kilkenny. The Cumann na Saoirse members in Kilkenny also provided medical assistance and entertainment to the Free State soldiers who had been injured or were convalescing.[10]

The Battle of Kilkenny City: May 1922

The official commencement of the Irish Civil War is recorded as 28 June 1922, when the Free State Army attacked the Four Courts in Dublin which was held by the anti-Treaty IRA. The commencement dates and finishing dates of wars and battles are usually defined retrospectively, long after hostilities have ceased. But if events in Kilkenny City at the end of April and beginning of May 1922 had ended differently, it is possible that the commencement date of the Civil War could have been brought forward by historians by nearly two months – with the history books recording Kilkenny City as the location where the Irish Civil War commenced.

The Build-Up to Battle

From February 1922, anti-Treaty IRA forces around Ireland had sporadically raided and occupied buildings in a number of locations, most notably in

Clonmel and Limerick, which at times came close to initiating civil war. Tensions ratcheted up following the IRA 'Army Convention' which was held in Dublin on 26 March 1922. This event was mostly attended by anti-Treaty IRA members who denounced the terms of the Treaty and voted to establish a new sixteen-person Army Executive and to pass on control of the IRA to that Executive. In other words, this anti-Treaty IRA Executive was now attempting to seize control of the IRA, usurping the power from Dáil Éireann which had previously been – in theory at least – in command of the IRA.[11]

The week before the national Army Convention in Dublin, representatives from all nine battalions of the Kilkenny IRA Brigade met in Kilkenny Military Barracks on 16 March 1922 for their own local convention. It is interesting to note that in announcing the meeting George O'Dwyer referred to the location of the meeting as 'Kilkenny Brigade IRA Barracks' (James Stephens Barracks today). He was putting forward a united front within the IRA. At this meeting were men who, in less than two months from then would be firing bullets in each other's direction.

The Kilkenny convention was very representative, as there was at least one delegate from each of the sixty-two IRA companies that made up the nine battalions of the Kilkenny IRA Brigade. After the initial formalities, which were conducted with 'much dignity', the burning question was asked. The substance of this question was should the Kilkenny IRA follow 'the old Executive' under Dáil Éireann, which was pro-Treaty, or should they follow the 'new [anti-Treaty] Executive' which would most likely come into existence the following week in Dublin. Colonel-Commandant Prout, who was sent from Free State GHQ in Dublin to command the barracks in Kilkenny, spoke in favour of the Treaty. He used the theme of taking a 'rest' from the fighting against the British. He said; 'the Treaty is all right for the time being. It gives us a rest and a chance to get rifles and other guns which we could not get last year or before'. He carried on his theme about the IRA needing some respite by using an analogy of a farmer whose horse was drawing a heavy load; 'the farmer decides half way up the hill to stop the horse for a rest ... the horse has a chance now to get its wind'.

Dick Brennan from Mooncoin, a member of the 9th IRA Battalion, was given permission to reply to Prout. Brennan was strongly against the Treaty and would go on to be a leading member of the anti-Treaty IRA in Kilkenny during the Civil War. One person present, said Brennan's 'appearance and voice impressed people' and whether 'they were for or against the Treaty, [they] liked him and wanted to hear whatever he [had to say]'. Brennan's contribution included the following; 'Last December, it was not the will of the people that was expressed in Dáil Éireann when a small majority voted for and accepted the Treaty. What was really expressed was the fear of the people, instead of their will. As for me, I took an oath to support the Irish Republic and I intend to keep that oath.'[12] The entire meeting took about five hours. No vote or decision was made about the Treaty. Tensions were far too high and officers of the Kilkenny IRA Brigade were trying to keep the small threads of unity that still remained intact.

However, once the IRA split publicly at a national level, it forced many within the Kilkenny IRA to make a decision as to what faction they would support. Most of the Kilkenny IRA Brigade Officers during the War of Independence – including George O'Dwyer, Thomas Treacy and Peter DeLoughry – either remained neutral or joined the pro-Treaty side. Therefore, the anti-Treaty IRA had to reorganise the leadership in Kilkenny. Ned Aylward from Callan – the 7th IRA Battalion and Flying Column O/C at the time of the Truce – became the Commandant of the anti-Treaty IRA Brigade in Kilkenny. This followed a similar pattern of what was occurring nationally, where the majority of leaders who had been most active in the war against the British, took the anti-Treaty position (most notably Liam Lynch and Ernie O'Malley).

On the pro-Treaty side, Colonel-Commandant Prout was the leader of the Free State forces for the South-East Division, known also as the 2nd Southern Command. The headquarters for this division was Kilkenny Military Barracks. Colonel-Commandant John Thomas Prout (1880–1969) was born near Dundrum, County Tipperary. He emigrated to New York in 1904 from where he joined the United States Army, fighting in the First World War and reaching the rank of captain. He returned to Ireland during the War of Independence to offer his military expertise to the IRA in the fight against the British.[13] He was given the rank of Commandant – and later Colonel-Commandant – in the fledgling Free State Army and was stationed in Kilkenny in February 1922. Kilkenny became an important military centre, as it was used as 'an equipment and supply depot for the south of Ireland'.[14] His deputy was Kilkenny native George O'Dwyer, who had been O/C of the Kilkenny IRA Brigade at the time of the Truce.

On Tuesday, 25 April 1922, the Kilkenny anti-Treaty IRA followed the lead of their comrades in other parts of the country – including the anti-Treaty forces led by Rory O'Connor who took over the Four Courts in Dublin in the middle of April – when they seized possession of several buildings in Kilkenny City. These were the fortified RIC police barracks on Parliament Street and John's Street, which had recently been vacated by the disbanded RIC. They also occupied Kilkenny jail; ironically the same building a group of IRA men were attempting to break out of five months previously. The takeover of the prison was relatively easy, as at this time the only people inhabiting the jail was the governor and one warder, both of whom were quickly ejected. The number of anti-Treaty IRA in the City increased over the coming days as they were supplemented by members from south Tipperary anti-Treaty IRA units who joined their Kilkenny compatriots (south Tipperary and Kilkenny were in the same IRA Division; the 2nd Southern Division). The consolidation of anti-Treaty forces at Kilkenny City was a strategic move by Ned Aylward and the other leaders, as Kilkenny was becoming a frontier county; it divided the Free State stronghold of Leinster, from the largely anti-Treaty supporting province of Munster.

Buildings were also occupied outside Kilkenny City. On the same night, Tuesday 25 April, the former Thomastown RIC Barracks, along with the courthouse and the unoccupied fever hospital, were requisitioned by anti-Treaty IRA forces. The Free State Army also began occupying buildings that were formerly under the control of the Crown Forces, with the principal aim of stopping the anti-Treaty IRA doing likewise. Most notably, pro-Treaty forces were stationed at Woodstock House in Inistioge.[15]

Following the takeover of the old RIC barracks and jail by the anti-Treaty IRA, there was a tentative unofficial truce maintained with the Free State Army – located in the nearby military barracks – as no side wanted to engage the other and be responsible for the outbreak of trouble. The uneasy tension was breached on the evening of Friday, 28 April 1922 when a group of anti-Treaty IRA, who were based in the Parliament Street barracks, took possession of an adjacent bonded warehouse at Chapel Lane. The purpose of the takeover was to confiscate a consignment of forty casks of whiskey as part of their commitment to the Belfast Boycott.[16] Later that night, the anti-Treaty IRA removed the whiskey by motor lorry and horse and trap to Kilkenny prison.[17]

The following morning at 6.00 am, Colonel-Commandant Prout issued an ultimatum demanding the whiskey be returned and the jail evacuated. At 2.00 pm, Prout led a group of Free State troops to High Street where they distributed a proclamation that was placed in the windows of business premises. The decree gave an ultimatum to the anti-Treaty IRA forces to leave the prison by 6.00 pm, while instructing the public to stay indoors after that time. Prout's proclamation went on to say: 'I shall proceed at 6 o' clock pm to take such steps as I deem necessary and to use all military force in my command to compel the restoration of all stolen property [whiskey] to its rightful owners, and to reinstate the Governor of the Prison ...'[18] It was discovered that the whiskey had not in fact originated from Belfast, but was actually from Power's Distillery in Dublin. Free State troops were posted on the roof of the Bank of Ireland on The Parade and soldiers were also sent to St Canice's Church of Ireland Cathedral, where they occupied the 1,000-year-old round tower. The Free State soldiers had commanding views from the summit of the tower as it was one of the highest points in the City. This was the purported location from which Oliver Cromwell surveyed his attack on Kilkenny City in March 1650, hence the local title; 'Cromwell's chair'. The soldiers placed a machine gun on top of the round tower in order to hinder the possible movement of anti-Treaty soldiers around the City and to monitor the anti-Treaty garrison at Parliament Street RIC Barracks, just 300 metres away. As the hours passed on what was a busy market day, there was a palpable nervousness in the City. Some of the anti-Treaty IRA forces took it in turns to go to Confession 'in case anything might happen'. The mayor, Peter DeLoughry, and two priests were involved in negotiations with the anti-Treaty forces inside the jail. It was then communicated that the anti-Treaty IRA would return the whiskey but that they intended to remain occupying the prison. This was rejected by Prout and he stated that the building would need to be evacuated. Eventually, just before the arrival of the Free State forces at the jail at 6.00 pm, the anti-Treaty IRA men departed and marched back to Parliament Street RIC Barracks, which they had occupied before the whiskey incident. Prout's soldiers took over the jail and armed guards were placed on duty. As the angelus bells rang around Kilkenny at 6.00 pm and fighting had not broken out, a loud cheer arose from the crowds who had gathered on The Parade – obviously taking little heed of the proclamation which instructed them to stay indoors.[19] These celebrations were premature, as the real storm would hit two days later.

The Battle of Kilkenny: Day One

The Kilkenny anti-Treaty IRA, commanded by Aylward, were not happy with the heavy-handed approach adopted by Prout and his Free State troops in forcing them from the jail. They believed they had as much right as the Free State Army to occupy it. Consequently, over the course of the next two days, the number of anti-Treaty IRA personnel in the city swelled to over one hundred as additional anti-Treaty men arrived from other parts of the county. Then, at about 2.00 am on the morning of Tuesday, 2 May 1922, the anti-Treaty IRA launched a dramatic takeover of Kilkenny City by occupying several strategically located buildings. These positions were the Workhouse Hospital (located close to the military barracks); the centrally located Imperial Hotel on the corner of Rose Inn Street and The Parade; The Workingman's Club on Kieran's Street; St Canice's Cathedral and round tower (which just two days earlier had been occupied by the Free State forces), the home of Thomas Phelan in Canice's Place near the Cathedral, City Hall,the residence of John Lucey and the adjacent O'Rourke's shop (both of which fronted onto Green's Bridge which was situated approximately 500 metres from the military barracks). Also included were Wilsdon's grocery and public house on Upper John Street (which faced the railway station and was located at the junction of the Castlecomer and Dublin Roads, the former residence of the RIC County Inspector at Rose Hill, Fleming's provisions stores on St Rioch's Street, known locally as 'The Lighthouse' and the nearby bottling store (situated close to Kilkenny jail) and finally – and most sensationally – Kilkenny Castle, owned by the Marquess of Ormonde but usually inhabited by his son and daughter-in-law, Earl and Lady Ossory, which dominated the centre of the City, including John's Bridge. The anti-Treaty IRA also maintained control of the two previously occupied positions of John's Street and Parliament Street RIC Barracks, bringing the total number of buildings occupied to fifteen.

Each location was held by between two and fifteen anti-Treaty IRA men. All positions were fortified and a barrier was erected across Green's Bridge. As daylight was beginning to break, the anti-Treaty forces 'visited various shops, commandeering food supplies, culinary utensils, sacks to be used as sand bags, mattresses etc., all of which were conveyed by motor lorries' to the various garrisons.

Colonel-Commandant Prout, commander of the Free State forces, was awoken from his slumber in Kilkenny Military Barracks and kept up to date with developments. He telephoned the Free State Army HQ in Beggars Bush Barracks in Dublin for assistance and they confirmed they would deploy 200 reinforcements to the City which would arrive later that day. In addition to the military barracks, the Free State Army also had soldiers based in Kilkenny jail and Bank of Ireland on The Parade – these buildings having been occupied during the standoff of the previous Saturday.

As most businesses opened for trade as usual on Tuesday morning, much of the general populace of Kilkenny City went about their typical daily routines. If they had slept through the night's events, they were quickly brought up to speed with the rumours and gossip, as the news of the anti-Treaty seizure of the City was the only topic of conversation.

Late in the morning, just hours after the siege began, Prout began a counter-offensive to dislodge the anti-Treaty IRA. Understandably, it was the positions closest to the military barracks which were his immediate priority, specifically the anti-Treaty strongholds near Green's Bridge, which was less than 500 metres west of the barracks. Just after 11.00 am, a party of Free State soldiers left the military barracks and established a machine-gun position in St Maul's Cemetery, close to the occupied home of John Lucey, adjacent to Green's Bridge. They called for the anti-Treaty forces inside to surrender, but the response was rifle fire. The morning din in the City was then pierced by the unfamiliar sound of machine-gun and rifle fire, as bullets began showering Lucey's home. After about twenty minutes of fighting, a white flag of surrender was raised from one of the windows. Six anti-Treaty IRA were arrested.[20]

The machine gun was then positioned close to Green's Bridge and trained on O'Rourke's provisions store on the other side of the bridge. After a much shorter burst of machine-gun fire, the garrison there also surrendered. Four anti-Treaty IRA were arrested and joined their comrades who were sent to the military barracks. There had so far been no casualties, although there was extensive damage done to both buildings, both internal and external.[21] It should be remembered that both sets of combatants, both pro and anti-Treaty, were not familiar with this type of urban warfare. Those who had fought during the War of Independence were more accustomed to guerrilla fighting. Thus, being restricted inside buildings as they are barraged with gunfire – with the resultant amplified noise that entails – was a new and unpleasant experience for most.

After the first altercation had commenced, the echo of gunfire began to reverberate throughout the City, as snipers on both sides engaged each other from various positions, including City Hall, the jail and the castle. Shopkeepers quickly began locking up their premises, while the townsfolk, 'when they were not seeking shelter in doorways and arches, were taking advantage of short lulls in the firing to get to their homes'.[22] Colonel-Commandant Prout took a hands-on approach. From his position on the walls of the military barracks, a distance of over a kilometre, he began firing at the anti-Treaty snipers based in St Canice's Cathedral, evidently utilising his marksman skills gained during the First World War.[23] The Free State troops on the ground, who had by now dismantled the barricade and crossed Green's Bridge, also began firing at the snipers situated in the belfry of the cathedral and round tower. The anti-Treaty snipers were unable to return fire due to the concentration of bullets hitting their position from differing directions. Around 2.00 pm, they surrendered by waving a white towel. All anti-Treaty IRA combatants in the cathedral and at the nearby St Canice's Close were arrested.

The focus of the Free State forces then shifted to Upper John Street, specifically to the anti-Treaty IRA based inside Wilsdon's grocery and public house, which was situated less than 400 metres south of the military barracks. The owner, Arthur Wilsdon, later described how the anti-Treaty IRA men – who were mainly members of the 4th Battalion from the Paulstown, Gowran and Clara areas – had commandeered the premises in the early hours of the morning and requested provisions for themselves and their comrades in the nearby workhouse. The bill for all the supplies came to 'upwards of £23' which was to be charged to the '4th Battalion IRA'. During the course of the morning, 'a lorry with a load of iron shutters arrived', which were used to barricade the windows of the store in anticipation of an assault. Tea-chests, sacks of produce and furniture, were also used to barricade the premises. Wilsdon himself was then told to leave the building. Just before 3.00 pm the attack by the Free State Army commenced. George O'Dwyer, the former Kilkenny IRA Brigade O/C but now Free State Commandant, led the attack. He cut his honeymoon short, having just returned to Kilkenny in the previous days due to the escalating tensions. The Free State forces positioned themselves on a railway bridge that spanned across the Castlecomer Road, directly in front of Wilsdon's grocery. From this position the Free State troops began pummelling the facade of Wilsdon's with machine-gun fire; while rifle fire was also aimed at the building from various Free State positions from the nearby railway station. The anti-Treaty IRA members inside, having barricaded themselves more effectively than in other garrisons, were able to return fire in kind. One of the employees of the store jumped inside a large sugar bin and put the lid down to protect himself during the battle.

An unusual incident occurred when an ambulance, driven by William Oakes, travelled up John's Street in the midst of the ferocious gun battle. That morning, Oakes had been sent by his employers at the County Hospital to collect the body of 36-year-old Joseph Brennan, a native of Maudlin Street, whose body had been recovered from the River Nore. Brennan was believed to have drowned the night previously, with his death recorded as suicide. He had been a prisoner-of-war in Germany for most of the First World War and his death was attributed to a psychological 'disease contracted while on active service [in the First Word War]'; more accurately understood nowadays as Post-Traumatic Stress Disorder (PTSD).[24]

Ambulance driver Oakes was Captain of A Company (1st IRA Battalion) during the War of Independence. Clearly, he was not happy with the actions of the Free State forces that day and decided to help the anti-Treaty men. He drove straight through the combat zone at the top of John's Street and began firing his revolver at the Free State soldiers from the ambulance. Eventually he ran out of ammunition and the ambulance was surrounded. He was arrested by the Free State men and taken to the military barracks – along with the remains of the unfortunate Joseph Brennan who was still in the back of the ambulance.[25]

Notwithstanding this assistance from Oakes, the anti-Treaty IRA in Wilsdon's were forced to surrender after about thirty-five minutes due to the sheer volume of fire assaulting their position. The nine anti-Treaty men inside the building left with their hands raised and were swiftly arrested. It was estimated that up to £468 worth of damage was caused to the premises and stock, of which £386 was later reimbursed by the Free State government.[26] A member of Cumann na mBan, Nell Gibbs (née Cahill) from Callan, who had been inside Wilsdon's cooking for the men, managed to escape through the back of the premises after the surrender. She brought with her as much ammunition as she could carry in her garments. She then walked to Callan and delivered the ammunition to the anti-Treaty IRA based in the barracks there.[27]

During the same time as the barrage on Wilsdon's, a number of Free State soldiers and civilians had a near escape at the other end of John's Street. After the takeover of Green's Bridge by Free State forces earlier in the day, the second river crossing in the City, John's Bridge, was also commandeered by Free State soldiers and civilians were prohibited from crossing. From the roof of Healy's house that faced John's Bridge, a mill bomb was thrown by an anti-Treaty IRA soldier. The Free State troops underneath, along with some local residents who were loitering at the bridge, dived for cover before the loud explosion was heard. Fortunately for those present, there were no serious injuries, with just the parapet of John's Bridge being damaged, as pieces of concrete fell off into the River Nore. However, soon afterwards, a Lewis machine gun fired at the Free State forces on the bridge from the direction of the castle – the machine gun having been stolen two months previously by the anti-Treaty forces from John's Street RIC Barracks. The soldiers took shelter in buildings on either side of the bridge. After a lull in the fighting, a young boy could be seen crawling across John's Bridge in the process of collecting shrapnel, empty gun cartridges, and parts of the exploded mill bomb; evidently eager to obtain souvenirs of the historic day.[28]

Following the surrender of Wilsdon's, the Free State forces switched their attention to John's Street RIC Barracks, which was located halfway down the street beside the entrance to Kilkenny College (now known as County Hall). A Free State armoured car, with a fixed machine gun, attacked the building from the front, while Free State soldiers besieged the building from the rear. The barracks had been reinforced to protect Blacks and Tans just two years previously, so it took some time before the anti-Treaty forces surrendered as they had ample protection. They eventually yielded and the garrison of twelve was captured.[29]

As the evening progressed, those occupying the anti-Treaty positions in City Hall and the Workingman's Club evacuated to the relative safety of their stronghold at Parliament Street RIC Barracks. The abandoned locations were swiftly retaken by the Free State Army. The final – and perhaps fiercest – battle of the day was launched by Prout on the anti-Treaty IRA based in the Imperial Hotel, on the corner of Rose Inn Street and The Parade. The hotel had been taken over by anti-Treaty forces at around 3.00 am that morning. Guests in the hotel were permitted to 'remain until breakfast' but had to vacate the building after that. The proprietress, 61-year-old Margaret O'Neill, refused to leave and remained in the building with the IRA men throughout.[30] At about 8.00 pm, Prout himself coordinated the attack on the Imperial Hotel from the upper floors of the Bank of Ireland, located opposite the Imperial on the other side of The Parade. The Free State soldiers used a Thompson machine gun to attack the windows of the hotel. The rapid-fire weapon all but prohibited the anti-Treaty men from responding, as they were required to block the windows with mattresses to prevent bullets entering and ricocheting. However, their anti-Treaty comrades in Kilkenny Castle, just up the street, came to their aid by firing at the Bank of Ireland. The three-way battle continued for over an hour. Then Prout and a group of Free State soldiers charged across The Parade, narrowly avoiding being shot and broke into the hotel using their rifle butts.[31] The IRA inside were captured, although some escaped through the rear of the hotel into the Rose Garden of Kilkenny Castle, from where they joined their companions. Having secured the hotel, the fighting continued for about another hour. During the heavy gunfire, Hanna Dooley (Murphy), Cumann na mBan O/C, entered the Castle and delivered ammunition to the anti-Treaty men, while also treating the wounded inside. As the street lights remained unlit, the fighting began to fade in sync with the onset of nightfall.

The hostilities did not conclude early enough for one local woman. Throughout the day, there had been an ongoing sniping battle between Free State forces in Kilkenny jail and the anti-Treaty soldiers based in Kilkenny Castle, nearly 1 km away. There was also sporadic shooting from anti-Treaty IRA based in Fleming's and the Bottling Store close by, although these positions had also been abandoned. Just before 10.00 pm, 28-year-old Margaret Loughman was walking home with friends on Walkin Street, close to the vicinity of the prison, when she was shot in the leg by a ricochet bullet. Having lost a lot of blood, she was transferred to the military hospital where she underwent an operation. She survived her injuries, although she suffered from the wounds for the remainder of her life as her leg had to be amputated.[32] Thus, ended a surreal and frightening day in the annals of the City, with no one quite sure what the following day would bring.

The Battle of Kilkenny: Day Two

The following morning – Wednesday, 3 May 1922 – began much the same as the previous evening had concluded, as the anxious citizens of Kilkenny were awoken by a morning chorus of gunfire. Proceedings got underway just after 10.00 am, when Colonel-Commandant Prout left the military barracks to resume his command in the Bank of Ireland on The Parade. At nearly all times, Prout was accompanied by his 12-year-old son, Jack, who carried two Webley revolvers.

Free State soldiers took every available vantage point around the City to attack the castle, but the siege of Kilkenny Castle – the first such event there in many a century – was going to take longer than the relatively swift operation of the previous day. Sniping and machine-gun fire from the Free State Army was unrelenting throughout the day. By this stage, nearly every window on the outer walls of the large castle had been broken by gunfire.

In the early afternoon, a group of Free State reinforcements, which was travelling to the scene of the action from the military barracks, had a miraculous escape. As they were proceeding over John's Bridge in an uncovered lorry, there was a burst of machine-gun fire aimed at them from the castle. Luckily for the soldiers, the machine gun was aimed slightly too high and the only damage it did was to knock the caps from the heads of the tallest soldiers.[33]

Just after 2.00 pm, the first ground assault on the castle occurred. Five Free State soldiers made their way up The Parade under the cover of the wall of the castle gardens. They ran to the large wooden entrance of the castle and began hacking the wooden panels. They eventually got inside the courtyard but were immediately met with machine-gun fire from the anti-Treaty men inside. Sergeant Fennelly and Cadet James Kennedy were shot in the shoulder and the leg, respectively. The party retreated and the injured were brought to the military barracks.[34]

At about 4.30 pm, there was a second ground attack on the castle. A number of Free State soldiers advanced to the main entrance behind an armoured car, which had an attached machine gun firing at the anti-Treaty positions. As the battle raged around them, three Free State soldiers crawled along the ground towards the large wooden doors of the Castle. Just as one of the party raised his arm to throw a grenade at the entrance, he was hit by a rifle bullet. The Free State party quickly retreated once again, bringing their injured comrade with them.

Later that evening, it became apparent to the attacking Free State forces that ammunition inside the castle was running low, as the amount of gunfire returned from the anti-Treaty IRA inside had reduced dramatically. At 8.45 pm, a large group of Free State troops charged up the street, led by an armoured car which crashed through the entrance door of the Castle and into the inside courtyard. There was a brief exchange of gunfire but the anti-Treaty IRA eventually surrendered after about fifteen minutes, having fought a battle that had lasted nearly twelve hours. They believed they would have lasted much longer if they had had more ammunition.[35]

As the gunfire ceased, large crowds began to congregate near The Parade to see for themselves what had occurred. The anti-Treaty IRA were escorted from the Castle by Free State soldiers. To everyone's surprise, only fifteen anti-Treaty IRA were led away. The small number of men was the total castle garrison. All were from County Kilkenny and were led by Richard 'Dick' Brennan of Mooncoin who acted as O/C. The rest of the group were from Kilkenny City, Kilmacow, Mooncoin, Kilmanagh, Clara and Ballyfoyle.[36] The *Kilkenny Journal* described the scenes on The Parade:

> Everyone was confident the number [of anti-Treaty IRA] was large. Judge then the amazement of the huge gathering assembled on the Parade when fifteen prisoners were marched out between two single files of armed G.H.Q. [Free State] Troops! As the gallant defenders of the Castle turned into Rose Inn Street, cheers were given and portions of the crowd expressed their admiration with shouts of 'Up the Republic'.[37]

Next to leave the castle was Lord Ossory, son of the Marquess of Ormonde, who received an equally enthusiastic cheer from the amassed crowd. Lord Ossory spoke in complimentary terms about his IRA visitors, stating; 'they were courtesy itself, and fought with much bravery. I had permission to leave the castle if I chose to do so, and was also guaranteed a safe escort'. However, he decided not to vacate his home 'as it would look as if we were funking it'. He went on to say; 'they [the anti-Treaty IRA] did not go into any room that was not necessary for their military operations, and they obtained their own food'.[38] To recover from the ordeal both himself and his wife were going to take some time to holiday in England, commenting; 'I have been through the

European war [First World War] and did not mind it; but Lady Ossory has not had that experience and her nerves are somewhat upset. We have been here for 700 years and we are going to stay here.'

Lord Ossory was less upbeat after he surveyed the damage to the castle and its furnishings, for which he later claimed compensation of £3,310.[39] In an article written by a local journalist, Ossory described the events and the destruction caused over the course of the two days:

> The Executive [anti-treaty IRA] forces entered that [Monday] night very quietly and told the night lodge-man that nobody was to be disturbed. He [Lord Ossory] did not learn of their presence in the Castle until about seven o'clock on Tuesday morning ... the attack opened about 10 o'clock on Wednesday morning and lasted until 8 p.m. that night. Lady Ossory and he had breakfast in his sitting-room in the wing facing The Parade that morning, and remained there all during the day until 4 o'clock. 'We had no food during that time ... and during the lull in the firing we dodged along the corridor between the windows until we got to another quarter of the castle ... The sitting-room mentioned is one of the four rooms not damaged by the firing. Practically all the bedrooms and sitting-rooms are now uninhabitable. All the windows are shattered and chunks of plaster and glass are strewn all around ... practically all the bookcases were pierced with bullets. In one panel alone I counted twenty bullet holes. In all, nearly a dozen paintings were pierced with single bullet holes ... Practically all rooms will need repairs of one sort or another.'[40]

The anti-Treaty IRA garrison in the RIC station in Parliament Street also surrendered that evening. Three members of Kilkenny Cumann na mBan; Maisie Stallard, Hanna Dooley (Murphy) and Una Egan, who were acting as dispatch carriers for the anti-Treaty forces, were arrested on High Street while in possession of a revolver. They were all released once the fighting had ceased.[41]

In total, 108 anti-Treaty IRA members were captured in Kilkenny over the course of the two-day altercation, although an unknown number escaped. They were incarcerated in Kilkenny Military Barracks. Overall, eighteen people were reported as having been physically wounded during the fighting in the City, with fourteen of the total classified as 'slight' wounds to the arms or legs, with the remainder described as 'serious'. The Free State casualties numbered twelve of the total, most having received their injuries during the two failed ground assaults on the castle. The vast majority of the Free State soldiers injured were natives of Dublin City, as they were part of the reinforcements that arrived on

Tuesday afternoon. Four anti-Treaty IRA men were recorded as having received wounds. Besides Margaret Loughman, the only other civilian injury reported was 'a young boy named Kavanagh', who received a ricochet bullet wound to his foot when playing hurling near the Fair Green on Wednesday evening.[42]

The Battle of Kilkenny: The Aftermath

The following morning, Thursday 4 May, leading representatives of the Free State and anti-Treaty factions, six representing each side, met in Dublin's Mansion House with the aim of coming to an arrangement that would calm the situation.[43] They wanted to avoid a replication of events that had engulfed Kilkenny the previous days from spreading to other areas of the country.

Back in Kilkenny, Colonel-Commandant Prout was not yet finished with the fighting. In solidarity with their comrades in Kilkenny City, on Tuesday 2 May, twelve members of the anti-Treaty IRA had taken over the vacant RIC Barracks in Gowran along with the adjoining courthouse. The Free State forces, under the command of Captain Joyce, attacked the building early on Thursday morning. The anti-Treaty IRA responded and a gun battle ensued. After about twenty minutes the Free State forces stormed the building and arrested the men. They also captured ten rifles, some grenades and gelignite.[44]

The Free State Army had a matter of even greater concern in the southwest of the county. Nearly 500 anti-Treaty IRA soldiers, under the command of 33-year-old Dinny Lacey from Attybrick, County Tipperary, had mustered around the town of Callan. They were made up of 'a good many Kilkenny and Tipperary fellows'. Kilkenny anti-Treaty IRA leader Ned Aylward was a native of Callan parish. He had left Parliament Street RIC Barracks in Kilkenny City before the surrender and was now in command of the Kilkenny contingent mustering in Callan. They were also joined by Séamus Robinson, later O/C of the 2nd Southern Division anti-Treaty IRA. They gathered in Callan with the objective of helping their comrades who were under siege in Kilkenny City. To pay for provisions, they took a 'considerable sum of money' from the Callan branch of Bank of Ireland, with the bank teller commenting that they were 'as courteous as possible under the circumstances'. A receipt for the amount taken was charged to the IRA Army Executive.[45] The local parish priest was not best pleased with the new arrivals. Bill Quirke from Tipperary, who was an officer in the 2nd Southern Division anti-Treaty IRA, described an altercation he had with the priest. A party of anti-Treaty men were in the act of dismantling walls and using the stone to build barricades on the road to impede Free State forces:

The local priest in Callan kicked up a row over the building of the wall and Elwart [Ned Aylward] had it removed in consequence. I ordered them to replace it. The priest asked who was responsible for building the wall. I told him I was. He said did I not know the wall was the property of the people of Callan. I told him he was there to look after their spiritual welfare while I was there to look after their corporal welfare.[46]

On Wednesday 3 May, Free State troops, under the command of one of Michael Collins's most trusted comrades, Joe Leonard, travelled towards the Callan area in armoured motor cars. They stumbled upon the main anti-Treaty IRA column – including column leaders Séamus Robinson and Bill Quirke – erecting a barricade on the road between Cuffesgrange and Callan. The Free State soldiers immediately opened machine-gun fire on the anti-Treaty men who scattered in every direction. A number of the men were wounded, seven seriously, with Quirke later remarking; 'it was miraculous no one was killed'.[47]

On Thursday afternoon, 4 May, to the surprise of many, the pro-Treaty and anti-Treaty leaders reached a truce agreement in the Mansion House in Dublin. The deal called for a ceasefire for a number of days with the hope of 'discovering a basis for army reunification'. In addition, the agreement permitted the anti-Treaty IRA in Kilkenny to retain control of one of the local RIC barracks. Representatives of the Free State and anti-Treaty forces, including local TD Lieutenant-General Gearóid O'Sullivan, Brigadier-General Seán Moylan TD and Commandant Dan Breen, all arrived in Kilkenny on Thursday night by motor car. They met the local leaders of both camps in the badly damaged Imperial Hotel, where they informed them of the truce agreement. The delegation then travelled to Hayden's public house in Callan to meet Séamus Robinson, who then stood down the anti-Treaty forces there.[48] As a result of the agreement, on Saturday evening, 6 May – just three days after the surrender of the castle – all 108 anti-Treaty IRA were unconditionally released. They marched from the military barracks, led by their officers Richard Brennan and Dan O'Neill, to City Hall on High Street, where they retired to various restaurants for refreshments and where they were greeted by their families.[49]

The peace agreement had the desired effect as it diffused the situation throughout the county. The large party of anti-Treaty IRA soldiers mustered in Callan dispersed and returned to their homes by motor vehicles.[50] Most of their transport had been taken from Clonmel Barracks some months earlier, before the departure of Crown Forces.

In addition, all proclamations issued in County Kilkenny in May and June 1922 were jointly signed by Colonel-Commandant Prout, representing the pro-

Treaty side, and Kilkenny Brigade O/C Eamon Aylward, representing the anti-Treaty side.[51] For the most part, the ceasefire agreement lasted longer than the intended period of a few days and was superseded two weeks later by a political deal between Collins and De Valera, which lasted until the June elections.

After the conclusion of a remarkably eventful week in Kilkenny, it was not all positive news for Colonel-Commandant Prout. He received an unsigned letter from 'Kilkenny's True Republicans', in which the author(s) made their feelings crystal clear:

Dear Prout, the traitor!

Just a line to say I must congratulate you on [a] paultry (sic) victory of cowardice you and big George Dwyer [Free State Commandant], the ploughman, showed in taking two days to capture 15 men [in Kilkenny Castle] ... I may inform you there is a few .45 Webley's [guns] oiled waiting for you, your brat of a son, [and] big George the coward ... And Prout, I promise you sooner or later you will fall, You are marked.[52]

Prout obviously did not take the threat seriously, as he read the letter out in jest to his assembled troops in the days after the battle. He also made light of the danger to his 12-year-old son, Jack, who was an accomplished shooter, commenting; 'the threat to murder my son I disregard, for he is able to protect himself'.[53]

Considering the thousands of rounds of ammunition that were expended from both sides over the course of the two-day 'Battle of Kilkenny', perhaps the biggest shock was that nobody was killed. If people had died, it is likely there would have been a different narrative to the story, which could thereupon have sparked an escalation of the conflict nationwide.[54] Hence, Kilkenny avoided an infamous reference in the history books. Civil War had been contained – for the time being.

The 'Pact Election': June 1922

A general election was held in Ireland on Friday, 16 June 1922. Just as occurred with the army, the political wing of the revolutionary movement, Sinn Féin, also fragmented into two camps; pro and anti-Treaty. The 1922 election is often referred to as 'the pact election'. This was in reference to an arrangement reached in the weeks prior to polling day between Michael Collins and Éamon de Valera, who represented the pro and anti-Treaty wings of Sinn Féin respectively. The pact agreement was a last-ditch attempt by the two men to avoid a civil war by arranging for a form of 'power-sharing' coalition government after the election, with the proposed government consisting of members from both factions of Sinn Féin. In practical terms, this was to be achieved by having a 'panel' of Sinn Féin candidates, consisting of representatives for and against the Treaty. Then, as a single entity, Sinn Féin would run enough candidates to fill all seats in each constituency. Each wing of Sinn Féin would nominate as many candidates as it then had TDs in the Dáil. In other words, with the Pact deal in place, there would be enough seats to go round. The overall intention was to stop a fractious election campaign which would have seen the pro and anti-Treaty sides competing against each other for seats.[55]

It was not to be that straightforward, however. From a Sinn Féin perspective, the ideal scenario would have been that the panel candidates would take all Dáil seats without an election contest. Indeed, when Michael Collins and Éamon de Valera issued a 'joint manifesto' at the beginning of June, they said the 'spirit of the pact' was the hope that contested constituencies 'would be reduced to a minimum'.[56] However, the Pact allowed for non-Sinn Féin candidates to run.

The Labour Party, which did not put forward candidates in the previous two general elections for the sake of national unity, decided to contest the election in the majority of constituencies, including in Carlow–Kilkenny.[57] In addition, the newly formed Farmers' Party – under the auspices of the Irish Farmers' Union – also decided to put forward a candidate in the area. The Carlow–Kilkenny constituency therefore became one of the important contested battlegrounds. The Sinn Féin panel of candidates consisted of the four sitting TDs, two of whom were in favour of the Treaty – W.T. Cosgrave and Gearóid O'Sullivan – and two of whom were against it – James Lennon and Ned Aylward. The two additional contenders competing for the four Dáil seats were Carlow native Patrick Gaffney, representing the Labour Party, and Denis J. Gorey, a substantial farmer and councillor from Burnchurch, Kilkenny, who contested for the Farmers' Party. Gorey had additional pressure and expectation as he was leader of the party. This was also the first general election using the PR voting system, although it had been used in the local elections in 1920.[58]

There were some within Sinn Féin that regarded any group or individual running against their candidates as being self-serving and disloyal, as they believed having to contest seats endangered national unity. They could just about tolerate the Labour Party contesting the election, as it had been historically supportive of the republican cause, however, the decision of the Farmers' Party to follow suit was believed by some to be blatantly selfish as it prioritised the demands of farmers above the national interest.

It was most likely persons of this viewpoint who attempted to kidnap 48-year-old Denis Gorey, the Farmers' Party leader, on 6 June 1922, the day election nomination papers were due to be submitted. A group of about eight men arrived at Gorey's home, Burnchurch House, near Cuffesgrange, at 5.30 am. From an upstairs window Gorey asked them what they wanted, to which they replied to have 'a few words'. Gorey declined to go down, at which point the prospective kidnappers said they would give him two minutes to present himself or he 'would have to bear the consequences'. Gorey did not go downstairs but instead returned to the window with a shot-gun and opened fire. The men retreated for cover but then returned fire on the house. In the meantime, Gorey's wife, Elizabeth, had run to a neighbouring farm for help. By the time they arrived the intruders had left. Gorey himself was unscathed but the windows and outside walls of his house were damaged. All four local Sinn Féin candidates – Aylward, Cosgrave, O'Sullivan and Lennon – condemned the attack on Gorey and released a joint statement stating that it was 'an infringement of the Collins–de Valera pact' which accepted that non-Sinn Féin candidates could run in the election. Evidently Gorey was not intimidated by the actions of the men, as later that day he lodged his elections papers.[59]

Although presenting a unified face publicly, on the ground, both wings of Sinn Féin in Kilkenny usually canvassed separately during the campaign. On Wednesday 14 June, two days before polling day, there was a large rally for the anti-Treaty candidates held in Kilkenny which was chaired by J.J. Dunne from Callan. The speakers were Ned Aylward, the local candidate, along with Éamon de Valera, Austin Stack and Harry Boland – unbeknown to the latter, he had less than two months to live, as he died after being shot by Free State soldiers in a hotel bedroom at the end of July. In his speech, Éamon de Valera warned about 'the immediate need' for 'a strong Government'. Harry Boland said; 'if the country was to be saved, the forces that led it for the past five years should be returned to the third Dáil'. He was then interrupted by a member of the crowd who asked; 'At what cost?' in reference to a looming civil war. Boland responded; 'the people or the man who would give up liberty to purchase a little safety, deserves neither'.

The two pro-Treaty candidates, Gearóid O'Sullivan and W.T. Cosgrave, held a large public meeting on The Parade the following day, which was presided over by the Mayor, Peter DeLoughry. In his speech, O'Sullivan said that the 'labour and farming interests' had every right to put forward candidates and 'the people who were going to vote for them had a perfect right to do so', which was greeted with applause from the crowd.[60] The comments by O'Sullivan would not have pleased the anti-Treaty supporters, as Sinn Féin candidates were supposed to encourage voting transfers between themselves and not to other parties. Evidently, there were some who did not agree with the attempted show of harmony, as prior to election day, a number of walls around Kilkenny City were daubed with the words; 'Collins the Traitor'.[61]

The amicable front generally presented by both wings of Sinn Féin ended abruptly on the eve of polling day. During a speech in Cork, Michael Collins told the audience they should 'vote for the candidates you think best of'. This was understood by some to be a repudiation of the Pact, as it accepted that voters could give preferences to non-Sinn Féin candidates. If Collins's words were ambiguous, the publication of the draft 'Free State Constitution' – which appeared in the national newspapers on the day of polling – scuppered any hopes of the Pact agreement surviving after the election, as the constitution did not meet the fundamental desires of the anti-Treaty side.

An editorial in the *Kilkenny Journal* – a pro-labour newspaper – gave an insight into what some of the voters were feeling when it criticised the narrow focus of the election campaign by the Sinn Féin candidates who it said were fixated solely on the Treaty 'to the exclusion of every other matter'. It was equally unimpressed with the undemocratic nature of the Pact, and commented that 'the country seems sick and tired of politicians, whether Treaty or anti-Treaty … The Collins–de Valera Pact has of course rescued many of them [politicians] from well-merited obscurity … But their immunity from obliteration is, at best, only temporary.'[62] As the results of the election were announced, it became clear that many voters in Carlow and Kilkenny were indeed suffering from 'treaty-fatigue'. On a turnout of 61 per cent, Gaffney of the Labour Party topped the poll with nearly double the quota, followed by Cosgrave (Sinn Féin, pro-Treaty), while Gorey of the Farmers' Party came a close third. The final seat went to O'Sullivan, the other pro-Treaty Sinn Féin candidate. Therefore, the two sitting anti-Treaty candidates, Aylward and Lennon, lost their seats. The results gave a number of interesting perspectives on the attitudes of the Carlow–Kilkenny voters. Perhaps most surprising was the fact that non-Sinn Féin candidates, namely the Labour and Farmers' Party, took over half the first preference vote (54 per cent). The total Sinn Féin vote – both pro and anti-Treaty – was 46 per cent, which was well below the national average of 60 per cent. Although the election was not specifically a referendum on the Treaty, it was significant that nearly 86 per cent of the first preference votes were for pro-Treaty candidates (including Labour and The Farmers' Party), which was even higher than the national average. Aylward could have taken the fourth seat if the votes of the other anti-Treaty candidate had transferred better to him – as on the first count, Aylward was actually fourth overall, ahead of O'Sullivan.[63]

Table 6. Vote share by candidate/party in Carlow and Kilkenny Constituency in 'Pact election' – June 1922

Party	Name	1st Pref.	1st Pref. % of Vote	Elected
Labour Party	Patrick Gaffney	10,875	34.8%	1st Count
Sinn Féin (Pro-Treaty)	W.T. Cosgrave	7,071	22.6%	1st Count
Farmers' Party	Denis J. Gorey	6,122	19.6%	3rd Count
Sinn Féin (Pro-Treaty)	Gearóid O'Sullivan	2,681	8.6%	4th Count
Sinn Féin (Anti-Treaty)	Edward (Ned) Aylward	3,365	10.8%	Eliminated
Sinn Féin (Anti-Treaty)	James Lennon	1,113	3.6%	Eliminated
Total Votes		**31,227**	**100.0%**	

Table 7. Vote share of main parties in Carlow and Kilkenny Constituency in comparison to national share in 'Pact election' – June 1922

Party	Total Votes Carlow-KK	% Total Carlow-KK	% National Total	Difference Carlow-KK vs National
Pro-Treaty Sinn Féin	9,752	31.2%	38.5%	-7.3%
Anti-Treaty Sinn Féin	4,478	14.3%	21.8%	-7.5%
Labour Party	10,875	34.8%	21.3%	+13.5%
Farmers' Party	6,122	19.6%	7.8%	+11.8%
Independents	NA	NA	10.6%	+10.6%
Total Votes	**31,227**	**100.0%**	**100.0%**	

The newly elected TDs were due to sit for the first session of the new Dáil on Saturday, 1 July 1922. It never took place however, as by then, Ireland was gripped by civil war.

CHAPTER 10

Civil War Officially:
A Summer of Discontent
(June–August 1922)

'Unholy fratricidal strife'

Although the Irish Civil War officially lasted less than a year – from 28 June 1922 to 24 May 1923 – the repercussions lingered much longer, dividing friends, families and politics in Ireland for generations. Just like the War of Independence, few would endure the conflict unscathed. Indeed, as will be discovered, the turmoil caused by the Civil War affected the lives of those in Kilkenny even more so than the previous war.

The Civil War in County Kilkenny differed from the War of Independence in a number of ways. Most obviously, the adversaries changed. The geographical spread and type of warfare also altered, especially in the opening stages. Previously, the fighting against the Crown Forces had been relatively localised – with small, mostly independent IRA battalions, planning and executing their own individual offensives. The Civil War on the other hand was much more fluid. During the early period of the conflict, groups of anti-Treaty IRA mustered and travelled together in relatively large columns, often moving from district to district, while crossing over county boundaries.[1] However, by the final months of the fighting, the anti-Treaty combatants had reverted to the more familiar guerrilla style warfare. In addition, those on the anti-Treaty side had even less places to hide than during the War of Independence era, as they were well known to their Free State opponents.

Furthermore, the Free State contribution by soldiers based in Kilkenny were not necessarily locals, but instead hailed from various counties. In a similar way, Kilkenny natives who were members of the Free State Army were stationed in other parts of the country. Thus, unlike the War of Independence, examining Kilkenny's contribution to the Civil War is not as clear-cut, as will become apparent. The fact that County Kilkenny initially acted as a buffer zone between the Free State forces in Leinster and the anti-Treaty strongholds in counties Tipperary and Waterford in the 'Munster Republic', also adds to the complexity.

Civil War Commences

The Civil War started with a bang – both literally and metaphorically – in the early hours of Wednesday, 28 June 1922, when artillery shells began raining down on the Four Courts in Dublin. Kilkenny natives were in the midst of the conflict in Dublin – on both sides of the divide.

During the afternoon on the first day of the Civil War, large numbers of Free State soldiers stationed in Kilkenny City were sent to Dublin to reinforce the garrisons there. For two of these men, it would be the last time they saw their native county. James Walsh, aged 22 and from Killaloe, Callan, was one of the Free State soldiers manning a barricade on Church Street during the second day of the attack on the Four Courts. During the course of the heavy firing, Walsh was shot in the forehead. He died after being transported to Jervis Street Hospital and was later interred in Glasnevin Cemetery.[2]

After three days of intense fighting, the Four Courts garrison surrendered. The focus over the weekend shifted to O'Connell Street, where the anti-Treaty IRA had commandeered a number of buildings. Daniel 'Dan' Brennan was part of the Free State Army which was attacking the anti-Treaty IRA located in Upper O'Connell Street. Brennan was in the Ballast Office on the south side of the River Liffey, which faced towards O'Connell Bridge. At about 2.00 pm on Saturday, 1 July, Brennan was hit by a sniper's bullet. He died almost immediately. He was 18 years old and from the Dublin Road area of Kilkenny City. The following Wednesday his funeral, with full military honours, took place in St John the Evangelist Church in Kilkenny City (also known as O'Loughlin Memorial Church). 'Thousands of people thronged the streets' as his funeral cortège passed, and the local businesses shut their doors as a mark of respect.[3]

There were also Kilkenny natives on the opposing side, two of whom were administering to the spiritual needs of the anti-Treaty combatants. Fr Albert Bibby, the Capuchin friar who had been present during the final moments of some of the 1916 leaders, and Fr Patrick H. Delahunty, the jail-breaking priest, were firmly on the republican side. They performed their duties at the anti-Treaty strongholds in Upper O'Connell Street, including the Gresham and

Hamman Hotels. On Monday 3 July, as the shelling and fighting intensified, they were ordered to withdraw for their own safety.[4]

Conflict Commences in Kilkenny

The battle raging in Dublin triggered an increase in tensions closer to home. It prompted the Free State Army in Kilkenny to strengthen their control of strategically important buildings throughout the City in an effort to avoid a repeat of the May conflict, including; the Bank of Ireland on The Parade, St Canice's Cathedral, the General Post Office on High Street, and Kilkenny Castle.[5] County Kilkenny largely became isolated from Dublin on the day the Civil War broke out, as the telephone and telegraph lines were cut in many areas by anti-Treaty forces, while the railway lines to Dublin had been damaged in Kildare.[6]

The first tragedy of the Civil War within County Kilkenny however, was not as a result of a clash between the opposing sides. On the morning of 28 June, just as hostilities were commencing in the Capital, 23-year-old Free State soldier John Moran met an unfortunate end. Moran – who was a native of Moneenroe – was killed in a tragic accident in his bed in Kilkenny Military Barracks. His comrade, Sergeant Christopher O'Brien, who slept in the opposite bed, was in the process of unloading his revolver having returned from an early morning excursion into town. He had just called on all his roommates to rouse them from their sleep. As he unloaded his gun his 'finger slipped off the lever … and a shot rang out', just as Moran was rising from his bed. O'Brien later explained; 'he [Moran] was shot through the head … he fell back and moaned a little … he died almost immediately… we were the best of friends'. The coroner recorded the cause of death as 'shock and laceration of the brain as the result of a gunshot wound'. Moran's coffin, draped in the tricolour, was transferred to Castlecomer for his funeral. He was the eldest of a large family and had previously worked as a coalminer.[7] He wouldn't be the last such 'friendly-fire' fatality of the conflict.

Events then began unfolding around the county at a rapid pace. On Saturday 1 July, Free State forces travelled to Callan with the aim of dislodging the anti-Treaty IRA in the town. Anti-Treaty men had largely been in control of the district since the standoff in May, a situation tolerated by the Free State authorities – until now. The Free State soldiers began taking advantageous positions around the town. They then proceeded to open fire on Callan Barracks, which was occupied by local members of the anti-Treaty IRA. Those inside the barracks responded but after an hour evacuated and escaped into the countryside. They had set the building alight before they left, so the barracks was completely gutted, making it uninhabitable for the Free State Army (which had been the objective of course).[8]

The Free State Army, therefore, had no safe base in the town and returned to Kilkenny City later that evening. The anti-Treaty IRA returned to Callan just a few days later and reasserted their control over the town, which would last for the next month. Less complicated for the Free State Army was the seizure of Thomastown and Mullinavat Barracks, where they met little resistance from the small numbers of anti-Treaty IRA inside.

The Destruction of Woodstock House: 2 July 1922

The eruption of hostilities around the country had serious repercussions for the Tighe family, who owned Woodstock House in Inistioge. The Palladian mansion – built by architect Francis Bindon in the 1740s – had been occupied by the Auxiliaries during the War of Independence and then by Free State troops from April 1922. As the fighting broke out, these soldiers were desperately needed to reinforce garrisons in Kilkenny and Dublin, instead of this remote part of County Kilkenny. Hence, the approximately thirty-five Free State soldiers stationed there left the house on the first night of the Civil War, 28 June. The events surrounding the sudden departure were described by Woodstock Estate manager William Rogers in a letter he sent to Major Edward G. Hamilton, who acted as agent for the Tighe family who were based in England:

> The Free State Forces that were in occupation of Woodstock house left quite suddenly at 10 o c[lock] last night [Wednesday, 28 June], they went off in Lancia's & motor cars. From what I can learn they were urgently called to augment the forces in Dublin to take over possession of premises occupied by Rebel [anti-Treaty] forces. They left no one to guard the house inside, they just locked up the doors & took away the keys. Neither did they give any notice here [at the estate office] that they were leaving. I am informed that they arranged with local Volunteers to patrol about the house until they return ...

> Of course there is a good deal of valuable property at Woodstock and it is strange that they did not leave a guard inside to mind the house ... However I don't apprehend [sic] any danger from rival [anti-Treaty] forces, as nearly all round here are for the Provisional Govt.[9]

Rogers's belief that there was no immediate threat to the house proved to be greatly misguided. Just three days later, in the early hours of Sunday 2 July, the anti-Treaty IRA, led by local man Patrick White from Kilkieran, set fire to the house.[10] As daylight broke, the building was a smouldering ruin with only the skeletal structure of the outer walls remaining. The objective in destroying the house was to make sure the recently departed Free State Army could not return and reoccupy the building, thus depriving them of a stronghold in the area. Rogers had to write once again to his Superior:

Malicious burning of Woodstock House

I have to report that at 7.45 am this morning Duggan Hall, steward at Woodstock, reported to me that Woodstock House was burnt down. I went up immediately & found that the main building was totally destroyed, every room in it was burnt to the ground including the library. The Bachelors Gallery was on fire & some furniture was saved from that. The servants wing escaped so far. I got Hall to collect our men to save what we could and some of the Free State men helped … There was an immense lot of valuable property in the House a good deal of it was in those rooms reserved for Mrs [Viola] Tighe and the library contained a lot of very valuable books. All have been destroyed … men here heard marching up towards the main gate at 1 o'c[lock] a.m. & a quantity of petrol was stolen from Mr Kenny's Garage at Inistioge.[11]

Rogers later wrote about the reaction of the owner of the house, Viola Tighe; 'I had a letter from Mrs Tighe. She did not get my report about Woodstock until last Thursday [13 July]. She appears greatly upset about it and now regrets that she did not come over [from England] last summer.'[12] The family estimated the cost of the house and its contents to be £26,000. However, the Free State government later paid just £3,744 as it believed most of the valuables had been removed from the property in September 1920 after the Auxiliaries moved in, while much of the remainder were saved by workers on the morning of the fire and which were later auctioned.[13]

Urlingford Barracks Attack: 5 July 1922

In the early hours of Wednesday 5 July, there was a major confrontation between the pro and anti-Treaty forces in Urlingford, in the far northwest of the county. It was a reverse of the situation of the previous weekend in Callan and Thomastown Barracks. This time it was the anti-Treaty IRA who attacked the Free State forces who were garrisoned at Urlingford Barracks. A large group of approximately 300 anti-Treaty IRA, mostly natives of Tipperary, Cork and Kilkenny, converged on Urlingford in the early morning having crossed over the Tipperary border nearby, from the direction of Templetuohy. They were under the command of 33-year-old Tipperary native Dinny Lacey, who was O/C of the 3rd Tipperary IRA Brigade (he would soon become leader of the entire 2nd Southern anti-Treaty IRA Division). They began attacking the barracks at 3.45 am with rifle and machine-gun fire, with the Free State troops inside responding in kind. Some of the anti-Treaty men managed to get close enough to throw grenades inside the building. After a battle that lasted over three hours, the seventeen Free State soldiers within the barracks, under the command of Captains James Holohan and Ned Holland, surrendered. The anti-Treaty men captured eighteen rifles and some revolvers.[14] Three Free State soldiers were wounded in the attack, including Michael Loughman who received a foot wound. In an unfortunate coincidence his sister had also been shot in the leg in the crossfire during the Battle of Kilkenny City just two months previously.[15]

All the captured Free State soldiers were placed into lorries and driven away. The barracks was then set alight. However, the fire never took hold and after the anti-Treaty forces had departed, some locals extinguished it. The anti-Treaty IRA men were 'stood down' near Longford Pass, which is a townland in County Tipperary, 5 km from Urlingford. Some of the anti-Treaty IRA party then retired to the local public-house, known as 'Marys Willie's', to have a drink to calm themselves after the long battle. The lorries containing the Free State prisoners were sent in the direction of Templetuohy but they had only moved a few hundred metres when fire was opened on them by a group of Free State soldiers who had made their way from Thurles to help the Urlingford Barracks garrison. In the confusion, the seventeen Free State soldiers captured in Urlingford ran from the lorries and made good their escape. Under intense fire, Dinny Lacey gave orders to retreat. While this was happening, anti-Treaty IRA fighter Paddy English from Rehill, County Tipperary, was shot and fatally wounded.[16]

July 1922

In the midst of the turbulent month of July 1922, Colonel-Commandant Prout, leader of the Free State troops in the southeast of the country, found time to get married. At 8.00 am on Wednesday 12 July, Prout, who was then 42 years old, married 25-year-old Mary Conba of Kilmallock, County

Limerick, in a ceremony in St John's Church in Kilkenny City. The marriage – which was his second, his first wife having passed away – had been arranged prior to the outbreak of the fighting, and the event was kept secret. On her way to County Kilkenny through Limerick and Tipperary, the bride was stopped on a number of occasions by anti-Treaty IRA men who wanted to know the reason for her trip to Kilkenny – the true reason for which she did not disclose. There was 'a large gathering' in attendance at the ceremony and as 'the bride and bridegroom left the church they passed under an arch of crossed rifles'.[17]

Although the local newspapers were unambiguously supportive of the pro-Treaty side – of their own volition – it is important to note that censorship was in operation throughout the country. This was introduced by the Free State Provisional Government in order to prevent positive publicity for the anti-Treaty side.[18] Just over two weeks in, the *Kilkenny Journal* believed the fighting was 'practically over' and that the country was 'within reasonable distance of the end of the Irish [Civil] war'. The relative 'blitzkrieg' by the Free State Army in affirming its control of Kilkenny meant that, by mid-July, it was only the Callan district and the areas in the south of the county that bordered the River Suir – from Waterford City to Carrick-on-Suir – which were considered to remain under 'republican' (anti-Treaty) control.[19] The confidence of the *Kilkenny Journal* proved to be overly optimistic however.

The Free State Army now focused their attention on the south and south-west of the county. In the early hours of Monday, 17 July 1922, a party of Free State soldiers under the command of Brigade Adjutant James O'Hanrahan of Kilkenny Military Barracks, surprised a group of anti-Treaty IRA men who were camped near Windgap. Machine guns attacked their position and the anti-Treaty IRA, which numbered thirteen men, quickly surrendered. The Free State forces captured a number of rifles, shotguns and pistols – and they discovered two landmines which had been set on the road, which were subsequently disarmed.[20] One of the men captured – Éamon MacCluskey – had been wanted for some time as he was believed to be responsible for sending threatening letters to Colonel-Commandant Prout. MacCluskey made an audacious escape from Kilkenny prison just two weeks later. He disguised himself as a woman using clothes smuggled into the prison by Hanna Murphy. He then simply walked out of the jail with a group of females who had been visiting.[21] By the middle of July, it was apparent the anti-Treaty held Waterford City was going to be the next battlefront. The Free State Army needed to take that city if they wanted to push west into Munster.

A group of anti-Treaty IRA swept through the east of County Kilkenny from the Wexford/Carlow direction, on their way to rendezvous with the anti-Treaty forces in Waterford City. Their presence in the village of Inistioge was described by a local man:

> We had a very anxious night here on Sunday [16 July 1922]. At 10 o c[lock] from [about] 80 to 90 Republicans arrived in the village in motor lorries & an armoured car & some motors ... They placed sentries all round the place & then tea was demanded ... which they got. They were very civil & in no way offensive. They were fully armed & equipped. They left at 10 o c[lock] a.m. & caused no disturbance, but what would we have done if there was an opposing [Free State] force. Why the village would have been wrecked.[22]

On Tuesday, 18 July 1922, Colonel-Commandant Prout, fresh from his nuptials, departed Kilkenny City accompanied by a large column of over 500 Free State soldiers, and made their way south towards Waterford City. At around 1.00 pm they reached the village of Kilmacow – which is just a few kilometres from Waterford City – where they had dinner and refreshments. While there, the large group of Free State soldiers received General Absolution from Rev. Thomas Greene, the chaplain of the local De La Salle novitiate, lest anything should happen to them during the impending battle.[23]

At around 6.00 pm, they reached the outskirts of Waterford City. Prout then divided his forces into three columns under the command of Captain Heaslip, Captain Paul and himself. As the anti-Treaty forces had raised the only bridge that crossed the river, the Free State Army could not access the city. Instead, they took strategically advantageous positions in the hills which overlooked Waterford City from the north bank/Kilkenny side of the river at Mount Misery, Sallypark and Ferrybank. From these locations they began sniping and firing Thompson machine guns at the anti-Treaty IRA positions in the city. The battle raged in Waterford City for the next three days. On Thursday, from a position on Mount Misery that overlooked the railway station, an eighteen-pound artillery gun was placed. Prout gave the order to commence the shelling of the city. The missiles were fired over the River Suir and began raining down on specific anti-Treaty positions, most notably the Military Barracks and Waterford jail.[24]

Under the cover of darkness on Wednesday night, Free State soldiers discreetly crossed the river in boats further downstream at Little Island. They attacked the city from the eastern flank on Thursday and Friday. The anti-Treaty forces eventually surrendered on Friday evening, 21 July, with many making their escape in the direction of west Waterford. Some looting occurred before the Free State troops reinforced law and order.[25]

One of the Free State soldiers, 25-year-old Private Michael Costello, who was part of the Ferrybank column, died having been shot through the lung during the fighting. Costello had taken part in the attack on the Four Courts in June. He was a farm labourer before joining the Free State Army and had twelve siblings. His funeral took place in his native Dundrum, County Tipperary, on Sunday 23 July.[26]

Death of Samuel Oakes: 29–30 July 1922

At the end of July 1922, the Free State Army in Kilkenny City was embroiled in a great deal of controversy following the death of an unarmed local man. In the early hours of Sunday, 30 July 1922, Free State soldiers were raiding houses in the vicinity of Blackmill Street in Kilkenny City, looking for arms and certain wanted individuals. Passing Dowling's public house at 1.00 am, they heard voices from inside. During the Civil War era in Kilkenny, the licensing laws prohibited the sale of alcohol after 10.00 pm. Dowling's was a 'centre for communication' for the anti-Treaty IRA during the Civil War.[27] The leader of the Free State raiding party, Lieutenant Peter Ratcliffe, knocked on the door and ordered it to be opened immediately. He also sent three soldiers to the rear of the building to cover the exit there. Maria Dowling, owner of the pub, refused to open the door for a number of minutes until she eventually relented.

As the Free soldiers entered the premises at the front, shots were heard from the rear. Two Free State soldiers had opened fire on men they saw running through the back garden. One of these men was found lying face down in a drill of potatoes, with a gaping head wound. He was 21-year-old Samuel Oakes, an employee of the Smithwick's Brewery, who was living with his parents in nearby Waterbarrack. He was a brother of Bill Oakes, who was the ambulance driver who fired on Free State forces during the siege of Kilkenny three months earlier. Bill, the captain of the local anti-Treaty IRA Company, had sent his younger brother to the pub with .303 rifle ammunition. Sam was to rendezvous with two other anti-Treaty IRA men, Robert Kenny and James Morrissey. The latter were to convey the ammunition to Kilmaganny.[28] The wounds Sam suffered were severe and he passed away in Dowling's kitchen a few minutes after being shot. His body was brought to St Canice's Church in the City and later interred in Ballycallan.

The inquest concerning his death was held the following day, with the jury brought to St Canice's Church to view the remains before the funeral. The

Free State officers in charge of the party on the night of the raid, Lieutenant Ratcliffe and Captain Leo Duffy, were unable – or most likely unwilling – to identify the two Privates positioned at the rear of the building who fired the shots. Undoubtedly this was to protect them from revenge attacks. They stated that the solider who fired had done so with 'the intention of frightening the parties' and not 'with the intention of killing'. The verdict returned stated that Oakes 'died from shock and haemorrhage as the result of gunshot wounds accidentally inflicted by the military in the discharge of their duty'.[29]

The Assault on Carrick-on-Suir: August 1922

Having surrendered Waterford, the anti-Treaty IRA now shifted their attention to maintaining control of the town of Carrick-on-Suir, County Tipperary (located just over the Kilkenny border in the southwest of the county, close to the village of Piltown). From the Free State perspective, the town acted as a gateway to the Munster region – specifically south Tipperary and north Cork – and was therefore vital to overcome. The anti-Treaty IRA in Carrick-on-Suir, which numbered about one hundred, were under the command of Brigadier Dinny Lacey. Dan Breen, Quartermaster of the 3rd Tipperary Brigade, was in charge of another party of nearly one hundred anti-Treaty IRA in an area north of the town, close to the villages of Ninemilehouse and Windgap on the Tipperary/Kilkenny border.[30]

The Free State forces, once again under the charge of Colonel-Commandant Prout, planned a two-pronged strategy. The troops based in Waterford City would sweep across south Kilkenny and attack the town from the east. Simultaneously, another party of Free State soldiers, under the command of Colonel-Commandant Thornton, Commandant Joseph Byrne and Commandant McCarthy, would travel southwest from Kilkenny City. The aim of the latter party was to take control of the town of Callan, along with the villages of Mullinahone, Killamery, Ninemilehouse and Windgap, where anti-Treaty outposts were located, before eventually arriving in Carrick-on-Suir from the northern flank.

Just after midnight on Tuesday 1 August, a detachment of approximately 200 Free State soldiers left Kilkenny City Barracks and travelled towards Callan. Engineers were required in a number of locations to fix damaged roads and remove felled trees. Reaching the town of Callan after 4.00 am, it was discovered that the anti-Treaty IRA had withdrawn the previous evening in the direction of Carrick-on-Suir. However, it was not all good news for the Free State soldiers, as the main bridge in the town which crossed the King's

River – known locally as 'the Big Bridge' – had been blown up by the retreating anti-Treaty forces. The soldiers had no alternative but to wade across. The vehicles were also driven and pushed across the river – the low level of the river in summer helping their cause.[31] The convoy stopped in the Green Street area for the remainder of the day in order to consolidate their position and garrison the town permanently. As the RIC and Military Barracks had been destroyed some weeks previously, part of the Workhouse complex acted as their temporary barracks.

The following morning, Wednesday 2 August, the majority of the Free State party continued their journey towards Carrick-on-Suir. At around 10.00 am, outside the village of Killamery, they had their first clash against a column of anti-Treaty IRA men under Dan Breen's command. Under the shadow of the famed Slievenamon mountain, a raging gun battle lasted a number of hours. Eventually the Free State forces took control of the village at approximately 2.00 pm. All the anti-Treaty IRA escaped over the hills towards Carrick-on-Suir.[32]

The eastern flank of the Free State attack, under the charge of Colonel-Commandant Prout, also began their manoeuvres on Tuesday morning, 1 August. They travelled from Waterford and mustered in the village of Mullinavat some 15 km north. They took this circuitous route to Carrick as some bridges along the usual route through Mooncoin and Piltown had been destroyed or blocked. At 8.00 am, the convoy of ten lorries and over 500 Free State soldiers departed Mullinavat, proceeding southwest across the Walsh Hills, through Templeorum and down into the village of Piltown. This village had been an outpost of the anti-Treaty IRA based in Carrick-on-Suir but when the Free State Army arrived they were told by locals that the anti-Treaty forces had evacuated the area earlier that day after they became aware of the movement of soldiers from Mullinavat.[33]

There had been upwards of fifty anti-Treaty IRA in Piltown. Many of them billeted in the servant's quarters of Bessborough House, just outside the village. The house was owned by the Earl of Bessborough. Five sheep and one bullock from the demesne farm were slaughtered to feed the hungry anti-Treaty troops. The local GP, Doctor James Quirke, had his house commandeered by Doctor Kathleen Lynn – the republican suffragette who was a native of Mayo and who had fought in the 1916 Rising. Dr Lynn was aided throughout by Hanna Dooley (Murphy), Kilkenny Cumann na mBan O/C. A newspaper journalist, who wrote for the pro-Treaty Freeman's Journal, was travelling with the advancing Free State Army and wrote that the people of Piltown gave them 'a glad smile and a cheery welcome'. He quoted a local woman as saying; 'we are robbed and ruined' and that she had been 'saying Hail Marys that we might see their backs'.[34] As the anti-Treaty IRA had no stable source of funding, most of their money, provisions, and shelter had to be commandeered. This often annoyed the people whose possessions were seized 'in the name of the Republic' – hence the reaction of the lady in Piltown.

The attack on the town of Carrick-on-Suir by the Free State Army commenced at 8.00 am the following morning, Wednesday 2 August. It began at Killonnery, on the Kilkenny side of the small Lingaun River, about 3 km east of the town, in an area known locally as 'Three Bridges'. The attack was focused around Tinvane House, on the opposite side of the river, which was the main position held by Brigadier Dinny Lacey and about one hundred anti-Treaty IRA. The stillness of the summer morning was broken with the deafening rat-a-tat of machine-gun fire. At one stage, the anti-Treaty IRA tried to outflank the Free State troops but were driven back by rifle fire. They had, however, come very close, as the Free State soldiers could hear them shouting 'up Tipp' and 'up Cork', as they attempted to throw grenades. During the afternoon, eighteen-pound shells were fired by the Free State forces into the woods and fields surrounding Tinvane House.

One of the anti-Treaty IRA leaders, Bill Quirke, later praised his side's part in the battle, describing it 'as the best piece of line fighting done during the [Civil War] campaign'. He also commented on events that day on the Piltown/Tipperary border:

> Here we were under fire from an eighteen powder [sic] in addition to what appeared unlimited rifles and machine guns [from the Free State Army]. The big gun was rather demoralising but as an effective weapon it proved harmless. It was only weeks later we learned that we could in fact easily have captured 'the big gun'. I don't know what use we could have made of it except for the moral effect, which at a time when 'moral victories' were the fashion, would have been a matter of considerable importance. At this stage I found Mick Sheehan [another anti-Treaty officer] calmly reading a novel and when one of the big shells dropped in the same field [near Tinvane House] he just turned down the corner and closed the book.[35]

The heavy fire did eventually have the desired effect, as the anti-Treaty IRA secretly pushed back towards the town that evening and made a strategic retreat.[36] It was not all good news for the Free State Army. Private Patrick Murphy, who was 22 years old and from Enniscorthy, County Wexford, was killed in the assault. He died 'instantaneously' in Killonnery, Piltown, having been shot in the head. He was hit standing beside his Captain, Edward Balfe, who was also his neighbour and mentor from Shannon Hill, Enniscorthy. A number of cattle and a horse were also killed in the altercation.[37]

The following morning, the Free State Army under Colonel-Commandant Prout's command, made their way cautiously towards the town centre of Carrick-on-Suir. Arriving on Main Street, they realised that all the anti-Treaty IRA – both Lacey's eastern section and Breen's northern section – had evacuated the town during the night, travelling in the direction of Clonmel. Amongst the nearly 200 anti-Treaty members escaping was Éamon de Valera, who had been billeting in the town. He was just an ordinary IRA soldier throughout the Civil War; the Chief-of-Staff of the anti-Treaty forces was Liam Lynch. Hence, de Valera played little or no part in organising the overall military strategy of the anti-Treaty forces. However, one IRA column leader said that de Valera was heavily involved in the military tactics at the fighting in Carrick-on-Suir and directed operations along the River Pill.[38] Éamon de Valera had passed through County Kilkenny on his way to Tipperary. He crossed into Kilkenny from County Carlow and billeted in nearby Paulstown.[39] Either way, capturing de Valera would have been a major propaganda coup for the Free State Army if it had been achieved this early in the Civil War.

The departing forces destroyed large parts of the two bridges in Carrick that crossed the River Suir, to stop the Free State soldiers giving chase. This caused an additional headache for the local inhabitants, who were sheltering in their homes, as the main water supply to the town was also cut in the explosion. During their stay in Carrick-on-Suir, the anti-Treaty IRA were not made welcome by some locals, especially former soldiers who had fought in the First World War. One anti-Treaty soldier described an exchange with them on 1 August, the day prior to the main battle:

> The ex-[British] soldiers in Carrick are inclined to get nasty. I suppose they expect their friends [in the Free State Army] there in a few hours. We have taken up positions at the bridges and given them a few 'salutes' [shots] with the machine guns. Ex-soldiers were ordered off the streets but remained and jeered us. We coaxed them off with the butts of our rifles, and after a few strokes they did run.[40]

The outcome must have been a huge relief for the general populace of the town as the fighting had taken place mostly on the outskirts, thus, they avoided being caught up in the middle of an urban battle – along with the material damage that would entail. The Free State troops that came from the

Callan direction arrived in the late afternoon and linked up with Prout and their comrades. Later that night, the Free State Army GHQ issued a statement from Dublin affirming its success in the area; 'The [Free State] troops now occupy Carrick-on-Suir. An advance party entered the town at 2 pm today [Thursday, 3 Aug 1922] … The Irregulars [anti-Treaty IRA] in Carrick-on-Suir, estimated at about 300 [actually less than 200], crossed the river and retreated hurriedly across the mountains … The town has not suffered any appreciable damage.'[41] One of the anti-Treaty IRA leaders in Carrick-on-Suir, Dan Breen, later commented on the episode:

> As it was evident that the small Republican columns could never hope to hold their positions against such a formidable enemy, superior both in numbers and equipment, the leaders wisely decided to retreat. The Free State forces from Kilkenny, advancing through Nine-Mile-House and Windgap, were delayed sufficiently long [by Breen's anti-Treaty IRA column] to allow the main body of the Republican Army to withdraw from Carrick in safety.[42]

Prout and his Free State Army – including many Kilkenny men – continued to push west and attacked the town of Clonmel in County Tipperary, which was captured a week after Carrick-on-Suir.

Mishaps and a Tragic 21st Birthday: August 1922

Just before midnight on 13 August 1922, the Free State garrison in Urlingford Barracks received reports that there was a group of anti-Treaty IRA in nearby Crosspatrick. Six soldiers under the command of Captain James Holohan travelled by motor car in search of the anti-Treaty party. As they did not find anyone in that area, they travelled a further 3 km to the townland of Baunmore, to the home of a suspected anti-Treaty sympathiser. As they were dismounting from the car at the intended house, a gun was accidently discharged by one of the Free State party. Lieutenant Edward Maher, who was 26 years old and from Gortnahoe, County Tipperary, fell wounded. Captain Holohan described what happened next: 'We immediately ran to Maher's assistance. I asked was he hit, "He said he was", "but he didn't think it was much" … blood was running down his leg. We immediately laid him down on the road. I found the wound and bandaged it tightly, which stopped the bleeding.'[43] Maher was taken to a doctor in Johnstown and then back to the barracks in Urlingford. He did not appear to be suffering. However, at 5.00 am, 'he got a change for the worst'. A doctor was sent for but Maher died a few hours later at 12.30 pm, on 14

August. The doctor discovered that the bullet had entered his upper leg and lodged in his abdomen.

Meanwhile, Prout and the main body of Free State troops were still located in Clonmel. Some Free State soldiers were sent to supplement the Free State garrison in Cahir. This journey would have tragic consequences for one Kilkenny man. On 16 August 1922, Free State soldier Joseph Bergin, from Castlecomer, was part of a military convoy of three lorries heading towards Cahir. About 10 km outside Clonmel, the Free State party were required to travel through the grounds of Woodroofe Demesne – a large farmstead in the Kilmurry area – as the main road had been blocked and a bridge had been destroyed. The Free State soldiers alighted from their lorries and progressed in extended formation up the avenue that crossed through the estate. Having reached the other side of the demesne, the soldiers were in the process of mounting their lorries when machine-gun fire was opened on them from behind a barn and surrounding woods. An anti-Treaty IRA column, under the Command of Jack Killeen, had been placed in the area by Brigadier Dinny Lacey, in anticipation of Free State troop movements towards Cahir. Killeen called on the Free State men to surrender – which they refused to do. A rifle and machine-gun battle raged for nearly an hour until Killeen's column retired from the area.[44] There were no fatalities to the anti-Treaty soldiers during the altercation, however, the Free State troops were not so lucky, as three of their party were killed. These were; Cornelius Roche and Daniel Fogarty – both from Tipperary – and Joseph (Joachim) Bergin, a native of Skehana, Castlecomer, who died instantly having been shot in the head. Bergin was from a family of eleven siblings and trained as a carpenter with John Kelly of Castlecomer prior to joining the Free State Army. He was a member of the 3rd Battalion IRA during the War of Independence. Bergin's father, Thomas, was a farmer, while his mother, Annie, was a teacher in Firoda National School near Castlecomer. Bergin's parents received £50 compensation from the Irish Government as a result of his death.[45] They only received £50 – half the discretionary amount of £100 – as Annie's school wages/ pension was deemed to be a substantial source of income. Without doubt, the most heartbreaking aspect of Joseph Bergin's death was that, on the day he died – 16 August 1922 – he was 'celebrating' his 21st birthday.[46]

Sporadic Fighting Continues

As the large groups of anti-Treaty IRA had now left the Kilkenny area, the county was – in theory at least – wholly under Free State control. However, this did not stop small, local anti-Treaty IRA units throughout the county from launching sporadic attacks on the Free State Army. This type of warfare was similar to the guerrilla tactics employed by the IRA during the War of Independence. The chances of hitting Free State troops were minimal, but it let them know there were still anti-Treaty IRA soldiers in the county.

Kilkenny folk were not endearing themselves to the people of Waterford in August 1921. A civilian, John O'Keeffe from Waterford City, was killed in the crossfire of an ambush at Mullinavat on 15 August 1922. Just four days after his death, another Waterford native was shot dead in Kilkenny jail in controversial circumstances. John (Seán) Edwards was an anti-Treaty IRA member who had been arrested in Waterford the previous month during the attack on that city by Free State forces. He was incarcerated in Kilkenny jail, which had been reopened by the Provisional Government to cope with the large amount of anti-Treaty IRA prisoners. Edwards and his prison mates frequently conversed with people on the street outside from the window of the toilets on the top floor of the prison. They often got messages and even received sweets thrown through the window by friends and relatives below. On the particular evening in question, Saturday, 19 August 1922, Edwards was communicating with a friend who was outside the prison wall. A Free State soldier on sentry duty told him 'two or three times to get in from the window'. Edwards ignored him, before telling him in no uncertain terms that he was not going to stop talking. This appeared to have incensed the Free State sentry and he fired a 'snapshot' at the window. Edwards was shot in the head and died instantly, the bullet having entered through the bridge of his nose and exiting over his right ear. The Free State soldier responsible – whose name was not permitted to be printed in the official reports at the time for fear of his safety – said he had only meant to 'frighten him' and not kill him. He added; 'this man abused me and called me some filthy names'. The accused Free State soldier had been in the British Army for twelve years, which led to some accusations that he would have been a good shot and therefore had aimed at Edwards. Either way, the inquest found that Edwards 'died as the result of a bullet wound fired by a sentry in the discharge of his duty', and so he faced no punishment. At the inquest, Edwards's mother, Annie, who was from Summerhill in Waterford City, was understandably angry with the prison authorities. She had just been to view the remains of her 22-year-old son. She talked about the last time she saw him the previous week:

> I saw him last this day week [on Monday 14 August] through the prison window. That was the last time I saw him alive. I hadn't seen him before that since March

or April [as he was on the run]. I went to the barracks this day week and asked for a permit to get into the prison ... but I could not get it. When I was outside the prison I was threatened to be shot for speaking to him.

At this point Annie Edwards was stopped from speaking any further, as her comments were deemed to be 'outside the inquiry'.[47] Some months later, a Free State Intelligence Officer in Waterford observed sardonically that Annie Edwards had become something of 'a notable personality amongst the "Die-Hards" [republicans]'. They also raided her house on a number of occasions as they believed the anti-Treaty IRA were storing weapons there.[48]

Back in south Tipperary, another Kilkenny Free State soldier was at the receiving end of a deadly ambush on the morning of Monday, 21 August 1922. An anti-Treaty IRA column in Redmondstown received intelligence information that a large body of Free State soldiers would be passing through the area on their way to Clonmel, which was less than 4 km away. It was decided to ambush it. The site chosen was 'about two hundred yards' beyond the railway bridge that passes through Redmondstown. The anti-Treaty IRA began cutting down trees to block the road. They had only felled the trees when they were surprised by a Ford car carrying five Free State soldiers, including Frank Thornton, one of Michael Collins's foremost Intelligence officers. Driving the car was 22-year-old Private Richard Cantwell from Toortane, Clogh, Castlecomer. The following is an account of what occurred at the ambush from the perspective of the anti-Treaty IRA men, who were not expecting them to arrive so early:

The machine gun section was actually beside the tree when the car appeared. The occupants of the car were immediately called upon to halt, but they were, in fact, already pulling up and were actually jumping down from the car, having seen the obstruction on the road. Both parties opened fire almost simultaneously. The whole affair was over in a minute. The driver [Cantwell] and another soldier were mortally wounded, being literally riddled with bullets and their legs actually reduced to pulp owing to the close range at which they were shot and the concentrated nature of the fire. Colonel Thornton himself was desperately wounded ... Improvising a stretcher, four of the [anti-Treaty IRA] men carried the wounded officer [Thornton] to the nearest house (Kiely's) while one of their number, a doctor, rendered first aid ... The [anti-Treaty] Column Commander held up a passing cyclist and gave him a note addressed to the Free State Commander at Clonmel informing him that a wounded officer was laying on the roadside ... and asking that an ambulance be sent out. A passing priest (Rev.

Fr. Warren, C.C., Gambonsfield) administered the Last Sacraments to Colonel Thornton and the two dying soldiers [including Cantwell].[49]

Thornton actually survived his injuries. Richard Cantwell from Castlecomer was not so lucky. He died within a few minutes of being shot. He was the fourth oldest of a family of twelve children. His parents, Michael and Sarah, received £100 for their son's death.[50]

It was not just the Free State Army who were having bad luck with 'friendly fire' incidents. On 21 August 1922, a small column of five anti-Treaty IRA were resting on a haystack at the farm of the McGuire family at Crutt, Clogh, near Castlecomer. The five present were Frank Byrne, Thomas McGuire, John Brophy, Thomas Brennan and John Keenan. They had been carrying out raids for arms in the area earlier in the day. The men had been part of the Free State forces stationed in Castlecomer Barracks up until 28 June, at which point they decided to desert to the anti-Treaty side, taking their guns with them. While in the process of cleaning a revolver in McGuire's field, one of the anti-Treaty men accidentally discharged the weapon, hitting Frank Byrne. A witness to the tragedy, Thomas ('Mike') Brennan, described what happened: 'One of the company was repairing a revolver by turning some screw with a knife. Suddenly a shot went off and Frank, who was sitting directly opposite him, fell shot about the heart. He was part of a Column billeted at Thom McGuire's Crutt, Castlecomer, under who's [sic] orders he was at the time of the accident.'[51] Byrne passed away almost immediately. He was 21 years old and from Montheen, Crettyard – just inside the Laois border – which was about 7 km from where he was fatally wounded. He was previously employed as a miner up until February 1922, when one of the coalfields closed down.

More Deaths, on the National Stage: August 1922

On the national political scene, two other deaths during August 1922 had major repercussions. Firstly, the 'President of Dáil Éireann', Arthur Griffith, died at the age of 51 from a 'cerebral haemorrhage', just nine months after he had returned from negotiating the Treaty. The Mayor of Kilkenny, Peter DeLoughry, said they had been 'personal friends for a number of years', their friendship having been 'cemented while they were together for quite a long time in British prisons [after the German plot arrests of 1918]'.[52] The Mayor attended the funeral in the Pro-Cathedral in Dublin, along with Thomas Treacy, former O/C of the Kilkenny IRA Brigade. As the funeral was taking place in Dublin – from 1.00 to 3.00 pm on Wednesday, 16 August 1922 – all businesses in Kilkenny City closed as a mark of respect. James Ryan, a national school teacher from Gowran, composed a poem in memory of the late Griffith, entitled; *Dirge on Arthur Griffith's Death*. As well as memorialising Griffith, he criticised the present civil conflict. The poem included the following verse:

> Alas' that they for whom he gave,
> In premature decay, his life,
> Should wage against brother o'er his grave,
> Unholy fratricidal strife.[53]

Less than two weeks after Griffith's death, the 'fratricidal strife' claimed another victim; Michael Collins the Commander-in-Chief of the National Army and Chairman of the Provisional Government. The three Kilkenny newspapers all contained photographs and biographies of the deceased leader, along with a detailed synopsis of his final hours in Cork. Even the *Kilkenny Moderator* had black borders around the print columns to symbolise mourning. A range of public bodies passed votes of sympathy for Collins.[54]

At the time Collins's funeral was taking place in Dublin, on Monday afternoon, 28 August 1922, a High Mass was celebrated in St Mary's Cathedral in Kilkenny City for the repose of his soul (along with the soul of Arthur Griffith). The Cathedral was full to capacity and there were 'many hundreds [outside] who were unable to gain admittance'. There were thirty-eight priests or religious brothers in attendance at the ceremony. Colonel-Commandant Prout led a detachment of Free State soldiers to the service from Kilkenny Military Barracks. Afterwards, there was a military procession through the City, led by the army band who played 'funeral music'. Upon reaching The Parade, the Free State soldiers fired three volleys of shots into the air in honour of their dead chief and the *Last Post* was then sounded by the buglers. All businesses in Kilkenny shut for the entire day. About 500 people, including most of the County Councillors left by train on the morning of the funeral in order to attend the ceremony at the Pro-Cathedral in Dublin. However, they had just left Kilkenny when they were required to turn back. This was because the anti-Treaty IRA had dug up the tracks.[55] Mayor Peter DeLoughry and Councillor Thomas Butler did manage to make it to Collins's funeral in the Pro-Cathedral, as they had travelled to Dublin the previous evening.[56]

In Thomastown, the local businesses closed during the hours the funeral was taking place in Dublin, while in addition, a novena (nine days of Masses) took place for the 'repose of the souls' of 'President Griffith and General Collins'.[57] National school teacher James Ryan once again put pen to paper, this time in memory of Collins. This poem was simply called *Michael Collins* and the verse below was perhaps an early example of the devotion and admiration Collins evokes to this day:

> For in every home was Ó Coileáin a son,
> Every heart in the land, young and old, he had won,
> And lights in the pathway of all Erin's youth,
> Were his bravery, kindness, honour and truth,
> The prince of the forest, the stately young oak,
> Untimely has fallen; Oh, cruel the stroke.[58]

CHAPTER 11

Civil War: Executions and the Return to Guerrilla Fighting (September–December 1922)

'P.S. I am quite satisfied to meet my God'

– From John Murphy's last letter to his mother
on the night before his execution in
Kilkenny Military Barracks

The Free State Army had made much progress over the summer months of 1922 in regaining control of the towns and villages. To some, the Civil War appeared to have been won. This confidence was premature however, as the conflict would drag on for another nine months. Just like the War of Independence, guerrilla tactics meant it would be difficult to defeat rural, mobile units of anti-Treaty IRA. From the perspective of those in the Provisional Government and the Free State Army, the deaths of their leaders in August seemed to harden their resolve and any patience they had for anti-Treaty supporters appears to have died along with Griffith and Collins.

The anti-Treaty IRA within County Kilkenny were able to survive in the rural areas where there was little presence of the Free State Army. As the Civil War progressed, the anti-Treaty IRA units became more and more isolated, which meant they acted mostly on their own initiative. In addition, by the second half of the Civil War, it is evident that County Kilkenny was functioning as two mostly independent brigades. Whether this was by choice or necessity is unclear. One brigade operated in the south and southeast of the county with the remainder of the county functioning as its own brigade.[1]

Civil War ASUs

The anti-Treaty Active Service Units (flying columns) operating in Kilkenny fluctuated throughout the Civil War. Generally, however, there were five main ASUs in operation in the county. These ASUs linked up and sub-divided on occasion, while personnel often changed, depending on arrests and so forth. In addition, the ASUs were not continuously active as the combatants needed periods of rest.

Ned Aylward, Kilkenny anti-Treaty IRA Brigade O/C, was in command of an ASU which was mainly located in the west of the county, although this column continuously crisscrossed the Kilkenny/Tipperary border. For large parts of the Civil War, Aylward and his west Kilkenny ASU combined with Dinny Lacey's 2nd Division ASU. Lacey was Aylward's commanding officer as the Divisional O/C, thus Aylward was following his lead when they joined forces. During the Civil War, this flying column travelled as far south as Piltown and as far north as Johnstown. Aylward was often assisted by Martin Mulhall's 1st Battalion ASU, which was made up of men from the Kilkenny City vicinity. This ASU moved east and west across the county, linking up with other ASUs as opportunities arose.[2]

There was a third ASU column in the south of the county, encompassing the areas of Mooncoin, Piltown, Kilmacow, Hugginstown and Mullinavat. It had between fifteen and twenty members at any one time. For the majority of the period, this South Kilkenny ASU was under the command of Richard 'Dick' Brennan from Mooncoin.[3] A fourth ASU was based in the east of the county and covered a large area, including Castlecomer, Paulstown, Gowran, Thomastown and Graiguenamanagh. It sometime passed over the border into County Carlow. It was commanded by Martin Medlar of Paulstown. Lastly, an ASU of between thirty and forty-five men, under the command of O/C Martin Bates, was active in the 6th Battalion area.[4]

Autumn 1922

It should be noted that the Free State Army were in a much better position than their adversaries in one specific way. When they captured a member of the anti-Treaty IRA – or a suspected member – they arrested and interned them, usually without trial. The prisoners were generally sent to Kilkenny or Waterford jails, with many later transferred to internment camps in The Curragh. In this way, the Free State forces were able to round up scores of assumed anti-Treaty IRA or their supporters. Throughout September and October 1922, large-scale arrests occurred.[5] Understandably, the anti-Treaty IRA did not have the same advantage in capturing Free State soldiers and holding them for indefinite periods.

The Free State Army was not blind to the anti-Treaty ASUs roaming the countryside. They received many reports about the whereabouts of flying columns but often chose not to engage unless it was strategically important and they had ample backup. A Free State intelligence officer in Carrick-on-Suir had a novel way of keeping tabs on an anti-Treaty ASU as it passed through nearby Piltown. He hired a scout, who was a young boy who was most likely getting paid, to follow the anti-Treaty men and report back. In that way the Free State Army in the area knew the position of the constantly moving ASU, while the boy would not arouse suspicion. The intelligence officer in Carrick-on-Suir reported the following in October 1922:

> I sent a scout to locate them [the ASU], with instructions, if it were necessary to remain near them if they were on the move, and report to our nearest Garrison on the Column [ASU] if they happened to go far from here. Last night he [the scout] located the Column at Newmarket [near Hugginstown].[6]

The Free State intelligence network was also aware of the 'on foot' communication network provided by the women of Cumann na mBan. A report from the Mooncoin Free State garrison described in detail how the anti-Treaty IRA lines of communication stayed open in south-west Kilkenny, which implies that Brigade O/C Ned Aylward was in regular communication with his comrades in the south of the county. It also revealed how a dispatch could be transmitted a distance of over 30 km in a relatively short space of time by utilising a chain of couriers:

> Despatches are carried every day by a girl [Cumann na mBan woman], from Kiltrassey, near Newmarket [sic], travelling by cycle by Jamestown to Powers' of Brenor [Piltown]. From Powers' another girl goes to Donovan's of Dowling. From Donovan's to Brennan of Knockanure near Killinaspick Church [Mooncoin]. A middle aged man, named Brennan, [then] walks through Silverspring, Grange to Mooncoin.[7]

There were signs in September 1922 – in Kilkenny City at least – that life was beginning to return to something regarding normality. Since the disbandment of the RIC earlier in the year, the Free State Army (and the anti-Treaty IRA in some places) were providing the policing duties in the county. On Wednesday 27 September, the first batch of the Civic Guard (later known as An Garda Síochána) took up their posts in Kilkenny City, as was described by a local journalist:

> On Wednesday evening 22 members of the Civic Guard, including three sergeants, in command of Superintendent Lynch, arrived in Kilkenny [City] ... and marched to the old [RIC] police Barracks in Parliament Street ... Their presence in Kilkenny is most heartily welcomed by all classes of citizens ... The Civic Guard is a purely civil force. Its members carry no firearms.[8]

The youngest Kilkenny fatality of the Civil War occurred on 30 September 1922. William Purcell, who was 16 years old and from Kellymount, Paulstown, had enlisted in the Free State Army a few months earlier. He was accidently shot in the stomach the previous day by one of his comrades in Templemore Barracks, County Tipperary. He survived for a number of hours after the shooting but subsequently passed away as the bullet had severed a main artery. His mother, Annie Purcell, ran a public house and grocery in Paulstown. Only four years previously, in November 1918, she lost her husband William senior. He was just 37 years old when he succumbed to the great flu epidemic of that year, leaving Annie to provide for their seven children, the youngest being just 2 years old. The Free State Army reported his age as being 18 years old, with this age also recorded in his death certificate. The reasoning for this was most likely to avoid any adverse reaction that would accompany such a young death.[9]

Although the Civic Guard had arrived in County Kilkenny, law and order were a long way from being restored. During autumn 1922 lawlessness continued to escalate. Some of the incidents were as a result of anti-Treaty IRA larcenies as they needed supplies and money to continue the fight. For instance, in Muckalee, the local creamery was raided by anti-Treaty men in the quest for new boots; good footwear was a valuable commodity considering the huge distances travelled on foot. The anti-Treaty IRA were also attempting to discommode the Free State Army by destroying public infrastructure. This usually meant attacking railways, roadways and bridges. However, in Gowran, there was an attempt to burn down the grandstand at Gowran Park Racecourse, but luckily for the racetrack owners, the fire never took hold.[10]

These destructive activities caused severe annoyance to the Free State authorities, while also exposing them to large compensation claims. The attacks on the county's infrastructure irked ordinary members of the public just as much as it irritated the Government. As their daily hardships increased, sympathy for the anti-Treaty forces amongst the general public correspondingly decreased.

In the aftermath of the Civil War, nearly 400 claims for compensation were lodged to the Free State Department of Finance regarding the loss or destruction of property in County Kilkenny during the civil strife. The claims had a broad scope. For instance, the Oxo Company wanted reimbursement after a consignment of soup was stolen by the anti-Treaty IRA at Mullinavat railway station. In an unusual claim, Francis Bailey from Waterford City requested compensation after '5,000 artificial teeth' were seized from a train at Dunkitt, Kilmacow (he claimed £135, was awarded £85). In another case, Arthur Curran, from Warrenstown, Johnstown, requested reimbursement when his cow was shot dead by a Free State solider. The animal had been grazing close to Urlingford Barracks when the soldiers were at rifle practice, with 'bullets whizzing through the air'. One soldier's aim evidentially went very much astray. Curran requested £50 compensation but was eventually awarded £35.[11]

Most of the post office larcenies in the county were carried out by the anti-Treaty IRA. The most opportune time to raid a post office was after the postmaster/postmistress had cashed the cheques to pay the old-age pension. As this money came from the public exchequer, the IRA considered its actions as taking from the enemy i.e. the Free State Government. During September and October 1922, the post offices in Knocktopher, Tullaroan, Freshford, Inistioge, Mullinavat, Fiddown and Piltown were robbed, with various quantities of cash and stamps taken.[12] Not all involved in the postal service were on the side of the Free State, however, as this intelligence report regarding two south Kilkenny postmasters attests:

There are two postmasters, employed in the Waterford Postal Area, who have strong 'Die-Hard' [republican] sympathies. One of these men is Mr Williams of Kilmacow, and the other Mr A[ndrew] Wall, Clogga Post Office [Mooncoin]. Wall is a most bitter 'Die-Hard', but I don't believe he is active. It would be advisable from every point of view to have the Post Office taken from him. Williams ... and his Post Office is boycotted at present by the people of Kilmacow and district. The Post Office in there was raided by armed men recently, and the raiders were able to seize the Old Age Pension money, owing to the Post Master having cashed the cheque the night before he should have done so. I cannot say whether this action was done with the intention of facilitating the raiders or not, but [with] a man like

Williams, who I believe has no character, and who got the Post Office because he was in the I.R.A. previous to the Truce, is unsuitable from every point of view.[13]

Some astute business owners were using the turmoil for their own advantage. Keane's Drug Store in Kilkenny City advertised the miraculous healing powers of one specific cream, something they recommended everyone should carry in case they accidentally found themselves in the middle of an ambush. This was prior to the mass production of antibiotics, so a well-founded paranoia existed amongst the people, as even a relatively minor wound could become infected, resulting in death: 'An ambush in High Street might cause many casualties – wounds, cuts, broken knees, etc. ... all would be safe if *Kureacut*, the great healing ointment, was applied.'[14]

Deaths Escalate: October 1922

No amount of ointment could save the lives of Free State soldiers Thomas Brownrigg, from Dunnamaggin, and Patrick Hayes, from Kilkenny City, who were both fatally wounded in an ambush in Tipperary in the early morning of Monday, 2 October 1922. The deaths were eerily reminiscent of Joseph Bergin's death in August, who was killed in the same area while travelling the same route. Brownrigg and Hayes were in a Crossley Tender, along with ten of their comrades, and were proceeding from Clonmel to Cahir. About 4 km beyond Woodroofe, in the townland of Knockagh, the Free State group was ambushed by an anti-Treaty IRA column under the command of Paddy Dalton. Fire opened from a number of directions and the Free State soldiers attempted to speed through the ambush position, at which point the driver was shot. The vehicle came to a halt in the middle of the ferocious firing. Free State captain, Joseph Walsh, was shot dead as he alighted. The Free State soldiers rolled on the ground underneath a fence for protection but during this manoeuvre Brownrigg and Hayes were shot. There was a brief exchange of fire between the two sides but the Free State soldiers quickly surrendered. Their ammunition and rifles were seized by the anti-Treaty men, along with a pair of new boots. The uninjured soldiers were then given permission to return to Clonmel with the body of their deceased Captain, the two badly injured Kilkenny Privates, and the driver Patrick Lawlor (who survived his injuries).[15]

One of the men, 24-year-old Thomas Brownrigg from Danganmore in Dunnamaggin, was mortally wounded, having being shot in the head. He died in St Joseph's Hospital, Clonmel, some days later and his body was transferred to Windgap for his funeral. He had been a farm labourer before joining the Free

State Army. He had seven siblings and lived with his parents in Dunnamaggin. His mother, Kate Brownrigg, received the maximum allowed compensation of £100 for the death of her son.[16]

Patrick Hayes from Barrack Street, in Kilkenny City, also died in St Joseph's Hospital on 12 October 1922 as a result of the injuries he received in the ambush. He had been shot in the right lung, which later became gangrenous. His remains were brought back to Kilkenny City the following day where his funeral, with full military honours, took place. He also had been a farm labourer prior to enlisting in the Free State Army. He had three sisters and was the only son of Mary Hayes. Mary's husband, James, had died in the Boer War in South Africa prior to Patrick's birth, leaving her a widow at the age of 27 with five young children (another daughter, Bridget, died in 1901, aged 1). Mary was compelled to return to live with her parents – the Hickeys of Maudlin Street – for some time. Mary Hayes received £40 compensation for her son's death. She received a reduced amount compared to Brownrigg's mother because she was receiving a British Army pension of £1 per week on account of her husband's death over twenty years previously.[17]

During October 1922, the hierarchy of the Catholic Church in Ireland released a pastoral letter which threatened those in the anti-Treaty IRA with the denial of sacraments – effectively excommunication from the Church – if they did not 'abandon methods which they now know … are un-Catholic and immoral'.[18] The pastoral letter was signed by the Bishop of Ossory, Dr Brownrigg, and by the Coadjutor Bishop of Ossory, James Downey, who was performing most of the administrative roles in the diocese in place of the frail Brownrigg.[19] This partisan support for the Free State side by the Catholic Hierarchy angered many within the anti-Treaty IRA. Of course, the significance of this threat differed from person to person, depending on an individual's faith and beliefs. The anti-Treaty soldiers still on the run fighting the guerrilla campaign had little time to dwell on it. However, for those who were already imprisoned, they faced a difficult choice; adherence to the Republic or adherence to their God. Even for the moderately devout, the withdrawal of the sacrament of Communion, while also losing the comfort of Absolution, would no doubt have weighed heavily on their minds.

Notices also appeared in October in all national and local newspapers detailing the 'Public Safety' resolution which had been passed in Dáil Éireann. This enabled the establishment of military courts to try those who were 'using force against the National Forces'. Furthermore, anyone caught in possession of a firearm was liable to be tried through these military courts, with the maximum penalty of death. This would have severe consequences for two Kilkenny men just two months later. The anti-Treaty IRA were given a two-week amnesty – until 15 October 1922 – in which they could hand in their arms and surrender. Unsurprisingly, they were unwilling to acquiesce to this ultimatum.

At 9.30 am on Wednesday 18 October – three days after the Free State amnesty expired – a fierce gun battle broke out in Kilmanagh between a party of Free State soldiers from Urlingford and an anti-Treaty IRA ASU. The Free State soldiers were passing through the area that morning when they were ambushed by a burst of machine-gun fire from the side of the road. The Free State troops, under the command of Captain Anthony Lalor, took cover and returned fire. The battle raged on for nearly three hours. The machine gunner for the anti-Treaty men, Thomas O'Dea, was killed in the initial stages of the attack.[20] Eventually the anti-Treaty IRA withdrew. The Free State soldiers managed to capture a section of ten of the IRA party, along with two rifles and the Lewis machine gun.

The deceased anti-Treaty gunner, 24-year-old Thomas O'Dea, was a member of the 3rd Tipperary Brigade and a native of Robert Street, Mitchelstown, County Cork. Margaret Meagher, who was an officer in the Callan/Kilmanagh branch of Cumann na mBan and whose husband was 7th Battalion officer Thomas Meagher, brought the remains of O'Dea to Callan. With the help of Mary Teehan, another Cumann na mBan member, she washed and laid out the remains, before procuring a coffin. She then travelled with the remains to Mitchelstown to convey O'Dea's body to his family and inform them of the circumstances of his death.[21]

One Free State Private was also killed in the altercation. He was 22-year-old Patrick Quigley, from Liss, Tullaroan. Quigley was the youngest of the eight children of Timothy and the late Ellen Quigley (née Grace). He was killed only 7 km from his homestead. Patrick Quigley was buried in his native Tullaroan two days later, having a funeral with full military honours.[22] Local schoolchildren, army bands and members of the local Sinn Féin clubs took part in the procession. Quigley's 73-year-old father, Timothy, later received £50 compensation for the loss of his son. The fact that Timothy was over 70 years meant he received the state pension, which counted against him getting any additional compensation.[23]

A few days later, another Kilkenny family was grieving the loss of their child. However, 18-year-old Free State soldier James Burke was not killed in action. Instead, he died in a tragic accident while doing sentry duty in the town of Cashel, County Tipperary. On the evening of 22 October 1922, Burke was commencing his twelve-hour shift at a sentry outpost on the Clonmel Road, when at approximately 7.20 pm, he accidently fired his gun. The bullet passed through his body, killing him instantly. His commanding officer, Captain

Shore, later commented that Burke 'was a fearless and efficient soldier and a strict T[ee]T[otaller]'. His funeral took place in Urlingford two days later, with interment in Graine cemetery. Prior to the Civil War, Burke had been a farm labourer. He was from a family of nine children. His parents Patrick and Margaret Burke – from Loughinny, Barna, near Urlingford – received £50 compensation for their son's death.[24]

Sergeant James Dunne from Threecastles was another victim of the rudimentary training given to Free State recruits. Ironically, Dunne himself was very knowledgeable in soldiering, having survived several close encounters during his life. He was a Private in the British Army for many years and served in India with the 1st Connaught Rangers prior to 1914. He was also a member of his local IRA Company during the War of Independence, later joining the Free State Army upon its inception. On 24 October 1922, he was garrisoned with his Company at the Workhouse in Dungarvan, County Waterford. One of his subordinates, who was in the process of cleaning a gun, accidently fired the weapon, shooting Dunne in the abdomen. He lived for two days but died on the evening of 26 October. The following day, his body was brought back to Threecastles where a funeral with full military rites took place, with burial in Tulla cemetery. James Dunne was 35 years old when he died.[25]

A Gloomy Winter Continues: November 1922

Nearly a year to the day of the great Kilkenny jailbreak – when IRA prisoners burrowed their way to freedom – there was yet another cunning escape from Kilkenny jail. However, in stark contrast to the previous year, the escape was not comprehensively reported, as on this occasion it was the Free State authorities that were embarrassed by the anti-Treaty IRA, as opposed to Crown Forces the year previously. Just a few weeks before this second escape, the Free State Army had widely reported that it had foiled an attempted breakout from the jail. However, the prisoners apparently had a 'plan B', as just before midnight on 15 November 1922, twenty-five inmates escaped from a purposelessly constructed tunnel that led from one of the basement cells of A wing to uninhabited warders cottages nearby, a plan that was very similar to the breakout scheme the year before. It was a number of hours before the Free State warders in the prison realised the escape had taken place so none of the twenty-five were recaptured.[26] The prison authorities tried to play down the escape to Free State GHQ commenting that 'the men missing are not important'. As punishment, cigarettes were stopped for all other prisoners. For one of the escapees, it would have been better if he stayed in prison. Jim Hayes, brother of future Fianna Fáil politician Seán Hayes, was shot dead by Free State soldiers in County Tipperary two days after his escape.[27]

Other prisoners, such as Bob Kenny from Green's Bridge, found less dramatic ways to escape from Kilkenny jail. This story also demonstrates the personal local complexities involved in the Civil War, as Free State warders may have actually known – or even attended school with – prisoners in their charge. The acting governor of Kilkenny jail filed the following report in November 1922 regarding Kenny's escape, which also required him having to reprimand his own officer:

> Bob Kenny, Greensbridge, Kilkenny, escaped at 6.30, Sunday evening [5 November 1922], [by] getting on to No.6 Sentry Box by means of a shed, and jumped from there to [the] field outside. Sentry on No.5 Box, O'Meara, says he did not see him going. O'Meara is from Kilkenny, and knew Kenny. O'Meara is under arrest.[28]

Generally the prisoners inside Kilkenny jail were well cared for, mostly because of the work of the local Cumann na mBan members. The women had a rota, taking it in turns to visit the anti-Treaty internees to boost morale and to deliver provisions. In just one day alone, 4 November 1922, 220 parcels were delivered to Kilkenny jail. Some of these were likely sent from the prisoners' families, but the majority can be attributed to members of Cumann na mBan who used the money they collected to make hampers for the prisoners. To put the volume of parcels into context, only twenty-three regular letters were received that day, while the prisoners sent out sixty-three letters.[29] The amount of prisoners in Kilkenny jail was not publicly reported, but it can be assumed that all prisoners got at least one treat that specific day. The volume of post also meant more work for the Free State warders who were required to examine each delivery, especially the contents of the parcels.

In November 1922, Hanna Murphy, the Cumann na mBan Kilkenny Brigade O/C, described the activities of the organisation in Kilkenny City in a report to her superiors in GHQ in Dublin. It offers a different perspective on the conflict. It also indicates how little support the organisation had generally in Kilkenny City, as Murphy stated there were just 'nine active members'. She also draws attention to the sufferings of the families of the anti-Treaty men who were incarcerated:

> As the city is military [Free State] HQ, the girls are constantly watched by 'Cumann na searchers' & reports sent [back] to [the Free State] Barracks... One

girl is very good & entered the Barracks & took a plan of it. Literature is posted up on walls & gates about every week & stencilled mottos appear here & there on the walls. The literature is generally torn down but the stencil & paint brush work has not been interfered with... Dependents [of anti-Treaty IRA in prison or on the run] are been [*sic*] looked after ... not nearly all cases, some cases are very bad. Families of young children left without support.[30]

Of course the women of Cumann na mBan were far more likely to be imprisoned during the Civil War than had been the case during the War of Independence (about fifty women were imprisoned during the War of Independence versus approximately 700 during the Civil War). It was most likely the case that the Free State authorities understood their capabilities, having fought alongside the women of Cumann na mBan during the independence era and therefore knew the value of women in attempting to fight a guerrilla war. Hence, the Free State were far more likely than the British ever were to arrest and intern Cumann na mBan members. Ellen Leahy, a member of Cumann na mBan attached to the 7th Battalion, had endured many raids by Crown Forces during the Independence era as her brother, James, was 7th Battalion O/C. She considered the Free State raids worst of all:

> we always referred to the Free State Army as the 'Tans' as they gave us far more trouble here. Some of them being callers [to the house] while they were in the movement in the 1920 and 1921 period. Then the split came and some turned their 'coats' and persecuted those who had befriended them.[31]

Mary Josephine (Mary Jo) Commins (née Power) originally from Brenor, Piltown but married in Ninemilehouse, was one of the principal Cumann na mBan officers in the Kilkenny Brigade. She was Captain of her native Templeorum branch (8th Battalion). Her home was situated just inside the Tipperary border, which provided a perfect resting place for the ASUs that roamed west Kilkenny. Thus, her responsibilities increased during the Civil War as ASU men regularly stayed at her home which required her to do many practical tasks such as cooking, cleaning, sewing, washing and purchasing clothes for her anti-Treaty IRA visitors. She was present in the fields around Carrick-on-Suir during the fighting there in August 1922, rendering first aid to those who required it. She was arrested by Free State soldiers in March 1923 and imprisoned in Kilmainham Gaol in Dublin. She subsequently took part in two hunger strikes while she was incarcerated. The conditions within the jail were horrendous, with massive overcrowding in a damp, cold environment.

She was eventually released on health grounds in November 1923 after a thirty-day hunger strike. She experienced ill-health for the remainder of life, including persistent 'rheumatic attacks', which she attributed to the conditions she endured in prison, as well as the hunger-strikes. In endeavouring to pay her the highest compliment, Ned Aylward, anti-Treaty IRA Brigade O/C, said 'there were few better than her in the county' and she was, in his opinion, 'the most trustworthy "man" in the area'.[32] In later years, Mary Jo Commins was awarded a grade D military pension for her efforts, after she had appealed her initial ranking of grade E. A number of well-known combatants of the era, including Dan Breen and Bill Quirke, also praised her contribution to the cause. Mary Jo Commins died in 1980 at the age of 88.

The First Fatality in An Garda Síochána: November 1922

Henry Phelan – a native of County Laois – holds the grim title of being the very first member of An Garda Síochána (or 'The Civic Guard' as it was more commonly known then) to be killed in service. He was also the only Garda to be killed in a violent manner during the Civil War. Phelan and his fellow officers were the first members of the fledgling police force to be based in Callan, arriving at the end of October 1922. As the old RIC Barracks had been burnt down the previous July, the guards took up residence in unused buildings nearby. Less than three weeks into their new posting, during the afternoon of Tuesday, 14 November 1922, tragedy struck for Henry Phelan. He and two other officers, Garda Irwin and Garda Flood, were given permission from their superior in Callan, Sergeant Kilroy, to cycle to Mullinahone – just 10 km away across the border in Tipperary – to purchase 'a hurling ball'. While in Mullinahone they visited Mullally's shop for some drinks. Three members of the anti-Treaty IRA, two of them armed, rushed inside the premises. Before there was even time to shout 'hands-up', the man carrying the revolver fired a shot. It passed clean through Phelan's head, and he died almost instantly. Bridget Mullally, who had been serving the men, ran from the shop to get help. The IRA man with the rifle asked his companion; 'What are you after doing? Why did you fire?'. The anti-Treaty IRA demanded that the Gardaí give them any arms they had; but of course they were unarmed. Just before he left, the man who had killed Phelan said; 'You can take it from me it was an accident.' Mullally had got the help of a nurse, quickly followed by two priests and a doctor. However, Phelan had already passed away by the time they arrived. The killing of the young unarmed policeman was very unpopular; both locally and nationally. Just a few weeks later, an order was circulated from the anti-Treaty IRA leadership ordering its members not to fire on unarmed policemen. It was not until two years later, in 1924, that two of the IRA party were arrested as 'aiders and abettors' to the crime – both however were later acquitted.[33]

It was a sad end for 22-year-old Henry Phelan, whose short life was bookended by tragedy. Phelan was a posthumous child – his father, Patrick, having passed away before Henry was even born. Patrick was only 45 years old when he died unexpectedly in November 1899, leaving his wife a widow in her early 30s, with eight – and soon to be nine – children under the age of 11. Henry was born the month after his father's passing, on 24 December – a little chink of light in what must have been a very bleak household that yuletide season. Henry Phelan was a member of his local IRA Company during the War of Independence. Two days after his death, there was a High Mass offered in Callan in his honour. The coffin 'was borne through the streets of the town [of Callan] on the shoulders of comrades of the deceased'. Henry Phelan's remains were then brought home to his native Mountrath, where he was interred alongside the father he had never known and his misfortunate mother Norah, who had died from stomach cancer in 1919.[34]

As the grim winter of 1922 progressed, the sporadic guerrilla warfare continued. For the most part, anti-Treaty IRA attacks were generally focused in two main areas; in the southeast of the county, and in the west of the county in a large radius around Callan. The latter had many supporters and safe-houses in this vicinity, which included parts of nearby Tipperary. In the rural southeast of the county, the Free State Army were at a disadvantage as they had no soldiers stationed in a large area south of Thomastown. This was not an oversight by the Free State authorities, merely they did not have suitable fortified locations in these areas due to the destruction of so many RIC and military barracks throughout the previous years. This meant a large swathe of the hilly countryside – including the districts of Inistioge, The Rower, Tullogher and Graiguenamanagh – were without a permanent Free State presence.[35] Thomastown garrison was under-resourced in terms of both manpower and equipment, which was a poor reflection on Colonel-Commandant Prout's leadership. In November 1922, the Free State Commandant in Thomastown Barracks wrote an irate report decrying the resources he had at his disposal:

There is no transport in South Kilkenny to act on the information received regarding isolated districts where Irregulars [anti-Treaty IRA] resort. The Garrison in Thomastown is too small. There are only 18 men here and a garrison has to be left there to guard the Town. I would want four bicycles in Thomastown.

Intelligence Officer would want to be supplied with a civilian coat. When definite information is received, it is sometimes not worked [on] until it is too late, and sometimes it is not worked on at all. The Irregulars are around Flood Hall this evening [8 km away]. No [motor] transport available to move.[36]

State of Play: Midway Through

By the middle of November 1922 there was 738 Free State Soldiers stationed in eight locations throughout County Kilkenny. These were; Kilkenny City Barracks, Kilkenny jail, Callan, Castlecomer, Mooncoin, Mullinavat, Thomastown and Urlingford. As mentioned, the location of some of these garrisons was dictated by the availability of suitable premises, rather than by strategic choice. Kilkenny Barracks was by far the largest garrison, with 457 of the total number of soldiers based there. The number of troops based in County Kilkenny fluctuated throughout the Civil War. The Free State Army was on a near continuous recruitment drive, which of course expanded the garrisons, but soldiers based in Kilkenny were also transferred to more volatile areas of the 2nd Southern Command – such as the garrisons in Cashel, Clonmel and Waterford – as situations arose. The average age of the Free State forces in Kilkenny was 25. The oldest Free State soldier was 57-year-old John Riordan from Kilkenny City, who was stationed in the nearby barracks. The youngest Free State soldier was 14-year-old Patrick Hogan from Walkin Street in Kilkenny City, who was also based in Kilkenny Barracks. He had only enlisted in the army the previous month, October 1922, falsely stating his age as 15 years.[37] In its effort to quickly defeat the anti-Treaty IRA, the Free State authorities recruited hastily and only provided rudimentary training. The type of men recruited by the Free State irked many within the anti-Treaty IRA, as some of the recruits were former British soldiers or labourers who had not fought with the IRA during the War of Independence. From the anti-Treaty viewpoint, these men had not been willing to volunteer and fight against the Crown Forces the previous years, but were now prepared to accept payment to fight against their fellow Irishman.

Midway through the Civil War the Free State Army published a large recruiting advertisement in the *Munster Express*, whose main circulation area was the working-class city of Waterford, as well as parts of south Kilkenny. The 'conditions of service' were prominently displayed in the advertisement, including the relatively generous wage for a Free State soldier of 3/6 per day. The terms also included a dependant's allowance: wives received 4 shillings per day, which increased to 7/6 if there was a wife and three or more children.[38]

At this stage of the Civil War, attempting to calculate the precise number of active anti-Treaty IRA within the Kilkenny Brigade is much more difficult. The battalions within the county were by and large working as independent units. At the start of the Civil War, the nominal number of anti-Treaty IRA within the Kilkenny Brigade was 2,151.[39] This was the total enrolled number of members, although the majority would have been part-time soldiers or perhaps not have taken an active part. In addition, by November 1922, many of the anti-Treaty IRA had been imprisoned.

A Bleak Month: December 1922

During the evening of Friday, 1 December 1922, a party of anti-Treaty IRA entered the village of Johnstown in northwest Kilkenny. They ordered everyone off the streets and took cash from the post office. Word of the happenings in Johnstown was communicated to the Free State forces in Urlingford, 4 km away. They subsequently arrived on the outskirts of the village around midnight, at which point they were fired upon. The anti-Treaty IRA, however, quickly retreated. The Free State soldiers cautiously made their way through Johnstown village, which was deserted by this time. At the upper end of the village they saw six anti-Treaty IRA running across 'Morrissey's field'. The Free State soldiers ordered the men to halt. One of the IRA men, Captain Patrick Cormack, fired a rifle shot at the Free State troops. They then returned fire, injuring Cormack, while the rest of the anti-Treaty party escaped. Cormack had been shot in the leg and was bleeding profusely. A Free State soldier attempted to bandage the wound. The local doctor, Matthew Mitchell, was called for and treated the injured man in a house nearby. Cormack was then transferred by car to Urlingford Barracks. However, he passed away in the early hours of 2 December, before he had even arrived at the barracks. The bullet had severed the femoral artery in his right leg, which caused him to bleed to death. Cormack was a native of the parish, from the townland of Grangefertagh, just a few hundred metres from where he was shot. He was 24 years old and from a family of ten children. He was Captain of the Galmoy IRA (F Company) during the War of Independence and was a member of Johnstown Hurling Club. He was buried in the family plot in Fennor graveyard and his funeral was 'the largest ever witnessed in the district'. The family were well known in the area as Patrick's grandfather, James, had been prominent locally in the Land League movement.[40]

The Irish Free State formally came into existence on 6 December 1922, one year to the day from the signing of the Treaty. The Provisional Government was replaced by the Free State Government – which was known as the 'Executive Council' – albeit it contained the same personnel. There was extra importance attached to the historical day for the people of Kilkenny as the President of this new Executive Council – and therefore the de facto Prime Minister – was local TD William T. Cosgrave. He did not forget his constituents as he recommended and appointed two Kilkenny people to the newly created Senate. They were the Mayor of Kilkenny, Peter DeLoughry, and Ellen, Dowager Countess of Desart, who was a philanthropist and Gaelic revivalist.[41]

Anti-Treaty Forces Spring a Surprise: December 1922

Colonel-Commandant Prout's career in the Free State Army had begun in dramatic circumstances with the siege of Kilkenny City. He was widely praised for his efforts in suppressing the anti-Treaty IRA within a few days, while he received similar plaudits for his actions in Waterford and Carrick-on-Suir some weeks later. But in December 1922 the anti-Treaty IRA made an audacious counter-offensive, which embarrassed Prout, the Free State Army, and the new Executive Council.

Developments started in the town of Carrick-on-Suir, close to the southwest border of Kilkenny. On the night of 9 December 1922, Tom Barry – the well-known War of Independence Commandant from West Cork – led an ASU of about one hundred anti-Treaty IRA who swept into the town late in the evening. There was a gun battle near Westgate, where two Free State soldiers and a civilian were shot. Eventually, the approximately seventy Free State soldiers in the town surrendered. They were marched to Main Street where they were kept under armed guard. The workhouse and the Hibernian Hall, which had accommodated the two Free State garrisons, were set on fire. The anti-Treaty IRA seized 107 rifles, two Lewis machine guns, a Crossley Tender and two motor cars.[42]

On the following Thursday, 14 December, a section of this IRA column – under the overall command of Bill Quirke and Dinny Lacey of Tipperary – travelled by motor vehicle into County Kilkenny. The Kilkenny contingent of the column was led by Ned Aylward. Their aim was to capture the Free State garrisons in Callan, followed by Thomastown and Mullinavat. It would later become clear to the Free State authorities that the strategy of the anti-Treaty IRA that night had been planned for some time. It also quickly became apparent that there was disloyalty within the Free State ranks. Two Free State officers in Callan and Thomastown Barracks, namely Captain Edward (Eamonn) Somers (aged 33) and Lieutenant Martin Kerwick (aged 21), had met some of the anti-Treaty IRA leaders in the weeks previously, with the purpose of organising some kind of truce arrangement, but the Free State officers were instead persuaded to cross over to the anti-Treaty IRA side. Another Free State captain, Jimmy Kelly, who was in charge of Mooncoin Barracks, also defected. Kelly, Kerwick and Somers were from the Callan district and were members of the 7th Battalion during the War of Independence; thus they would have known many of the anti-Treaty men personally. A further reason as to why Free State soldiers decided to switch sides was because of the initiation of the death penalty. Just a few weeks previously, the Free State Government began a policy of executions, which some within the Free State Army believed was a step too far.

The capture of the three barracks in County Kilkenny on the night of 14 and 15 December was accomplished in much the same manner. It went along the following lines. First Somers requested admittance to the garrison. As the sentries knew Somers as a Free State Captain, they let him proceed. Somers was accompanied by a small party of anti-Treaty IRA men. However, these men were in disguise, as they were wearing the uniforms of the Free State Army, the outfits having been stolen from the soldiers in Carrick-on-Suir a few nights previously. Once the doors of the barracks had been open, the disguised anti-Treaty IRA and others that were hiding nearby stormed the building, without a shot being fired.[43]

The anti-Treaty IRA arrived in Callan around 6.45 pm on the evening of 14 December. Somers then went inside the garrison, which was located at the time in the Workhouse complex. Once inside he entered the soldiers' common area. He told the privates that a truce had just been agreed in the county and to hand in their weapons. Somers was aided in Callan Barracks by Lieutenant Doyle, who was also complicit in the deceit. Once all the Free State soldiers had been disarmed, the barracks was then flooded with anti-Treaty IRA men. All the soldiers were then brought to the canteen 'where Somers gave £1 for free drinks, and made a speech'. He said he 'was now sacrificing his £4 per week [wages]' and encouraged the Free State soldiers to join him. Only six Privates of the approximately forty-two soldiers in the garrison joined the defectors. Three of the six were natives of Kilkenny City, while the other three were Castlecomer men. The remainder of the disarmed Free State soldiers were let go free about 9.30 pm that night.[44]

After taking sixty rifles from Callan, the anti-Treaty IRA column proceeded to Thomastown. They entered the town at around 2.00 am and took the barracks quickly, with Somers and his party once again pretending to be Free State soldiers. The IRA also captured the Nore View Hotel where some of the Free State troops were garrisoned. The IRA column then spread out through the streets looking for Free State soldiers billeted in houses around the town. They would ask the same question once the knock on the door was answered; 'is any of our fellows staying here.' As the IRA men were wearing Free State uniforms, 'our fellows' implied Free State soldiers. In this way, all Free State troops in the town were rounded up and lodged in the Nore View Hotel. They were given the option of defecting to the anti-Treaty side, of which nine acceded. The Courthouse in Thomastown was also seized. The members of the Civic Guard who were based there were given five minutes to leave, before the building was set alight. After gathering all the weapons and destroying the telegraph system in the local post office, the anti-Treaty IRA left the town. Just before leaving, IRA leader Lieutenant Kerwick addressed the captured Free State soldiers and said; 'Good Bye now lads … go to bed now.'[45]

After acquiring all the munitions in Thomastown, the anti-Treaty men made their way to Mullinavat. They cut down trees and cut telegraph lines along the way in order to prevent any Free State reinforcements arriving quickly. Arriving in the village after 5.30 am, Somers performed his, by now, usual guise. He changed the story slightly saying his group of 'Free State' soldiers had been 'attacked by the Irregulars in Callan' and having followed them to Hugginstown had lost them. Hence they came to Mullinavat for shelter. Once Somers and his faux Free State soldiers were inside, the small garrison was quickly overrun.[46] Once again, all weapons and ammunition were transported away in four lorries. The majority of the anti-Treaty IRA column then moved south and crossed the River Suir into County Waterford.[47] Later that same day, Mullinavat garrison was evacuated by the Free State forces as they had no means of protecting themselves. Three days later, the barracks was set alight and destroyed by the local anti-Treaty IRA who were commanded by a man named 'McDonald'.[48]

Captain Somers continued to fight with the anti-Treaty IRA until he was killed four months later by Free State soldiers. On 16 April 1923, he was sheltering in the ruins of Castleblake Castle in Rosegreen, County Tipperary. The castle was surrounded and Somers and his comrade, Theo English, were shot dead while attempting to escape. Somers owned and managed a mill in Mallardstown, Callan, before his death (his family were originally from Tipperary). He was 33 years old when he died.[49]

To add insult to injury for the Kilkenny Free State authorities, in a separate incident, Martin Medlar's east-Kilkenny ASU captured the Free State outpost at Coon Barracks in the north of the county before Christmas 1922. This was another simple encounter, as the anti-Treaty men had organised ladies 'to entertain' the seven Free State soldiers inside the barracks before they surprised them, taking their uniforms and arms.[50]

In the aftermath of the anti-Treaty victories, the IRA were keen to emphasise the courteous nature in which they treated the captured Free State soldiers. This was undoubtedly a jibe at the Free State Government who, by this stage, had executed a dozen republican prisoners. The anti-Treaty publicity pamphlet, *The Republican War Bulletin*, commented after the capture of the four Kilkenny barracks; 'not a single one of these Colonials [Free State soldiers] has been maltreated, not to say murdered ... we do know what chivalry is. No one expects otherwise from an Irish army, and the people now realise which is the Irish army [i.e. anti-Treaty IRA].'[51]

Bill Quirke, who was by then O/C of the 2nd Southern Division anti-Treaty IRA, described how the capture of so many barracks was the shot in the arm the anti-Treaty IRA required at the time, giving them a much needed morale boost:

> our forces captured Carrick-on-Suir (Tom Barry O/C Operations of Southern Command was with us for this event and the first man in the gate). A week later we captured Callan, Thomastown and Mullinavat, thereby creating a very favourable atmosphere along the borders of Kilkenny and Waterford and distributing something like 200 rifles to previously unarmed IRA. Things had gone pretty badly with the [anti-Treaty] IRA in most counties but new life had come with the successful fighting of the 2nd Southern. After Mullinavat we retreated across the Suir for a much needed rest in the Nire Valley [Waterford].[52]

In the aftershock of these embarrassing debacles, the Free State authorities were searching for someone to whom they could apportion blame. The gravest offence was the disloyalty of some Free State officers, while a large haul of rifles and ammunition were now in anti-Treaty IRA hands. From the perspective of the Free State Government, the fault rested solely on the shoulders of Colonel-Commandant Prout. His Free State Army superiors had also been critical of his command for some time. Just a few months earlier, his soldiers in Clonmel were singled out as being one of the most undisciplined in the country. After Prout requested more arms in December, he received a curt response from Free State Army GHQ; 'your officers and men are letting us down at a critical moment and throwing away the fruits of months of work'.[53] It could have been worse for Prout. The Cabinet of the Free State wanted Prout removed from his command as they were 'dissatisfied' with his performance. To avoid further embarrassment, Richard Mulcahy, Minister of Defence and Commander-in-Chief of the Free State Army, ignored the instructions of his fellow cabinet colleagues, affording Prout another chance.[54] The sensational capture of the Kilkenny barracks made headlines both nationally and internationally. The cheeky ruse employed by the anti-Treaty IRA and the ease in which the barracks were captured, brought the kind of unwelcome attention the young Free State Government could do without.

Although the capture of the barracks in Kilkenny had been bloodless, the capture of the town of Carrick-on-Suir the weekend previously was not so orderly. A gunfight developed at Westgate, near the Clonmel Road, after a Free State soldier in plain clothes called on some anti-Treaty IRA men to halt. In the resultant battle, one Kilkenny native – Lieutenant James Gardiner, who was the Free State Intelligence Officer in the area – was hit by a bullet in the forehead. He lingered for some hours but passed away on Sunday, 10 December 1922. He was from Chatsworth Street in Castlecomer and was just two weeks shy of his 29th birthday. His body was brought back home to Castlecomer for his funeral. A full military guard of honour was present, led by Captain Brennan of the Free State Army in Castlecomer, which lined the route to the Protestant graveyard where Gardiner was laid to rest. A firing party from Kilkenny Barracks discharged a volley of shots in his honour.[55] Lieutenant Gardiner had spent eleven years in the British Army and came close to being killed on more than one occasion during the First World War. His mother Sarah received £60 compensation for the death of her eldest son. Sarah had already experienced much hardship, as during the First World War, her second son, Joseph, was killed.[56] Lieutenant James Gardiner received much praise from a former (unnamed) comrade, who wrote a touching tribute which included the following:

> His tenacity was remarkable. I can say without the least fear of being contradicted that once he set out to do a thing he could not rest content until it was done ... Could he not, if so willed, have surrendered, knowing the odds were against him? But no ... he preferred to fight ... His service was short; but truly it was meritorious if ever such there was.[57]

Tensions in Kilkenny Barracks

The close of 1922 did not offer any reprieve from grief. Captain Fred Lidwell, a newly qualified solicitor from Dún Laoghaire (Kingstown) in Dublin, was sent to Kilkenny Military Barracks in November 1922 to act as assistant legal officer for the Free State Army in the 2nd Southern Command. During the afternoon of 22 December he was accidentally shot in the head by a Free State soldier in the barracks. Little information was released by Free State Army GHQ at the time about the circumstances of Lidwell's death, only that it was 'purely accidental'. Cahir Davitt, the son of Land League founder Michael Davitt, was at this time Judge Advocate-General for the Free State Army, whose main responsibility was to oversee the legal framework of the numerous court-martials that were taking place. Davitt had appointed Lidwell to his position in Kilkenny. He later remarked that the tensions had been running high in the barracks; specifically between Joe Mooney – the chief Legal Officer – and the military commanders in Kilkenny Barracks. Just a few days previously, Mooney and Lidwell had been part of the legal team that oversaw the court martial of two young Kilkenny men, who were found guilty and sentenced to death. Davitt described what he had heard occurred on the ill-fated afternoon:

> Two men, John Phelan and John Murphy, had been tried some days previously by Military Court in Kilkenny, and Joe Mooney had acted as Legal Officer on the Court. They were convicted on the usual charges and sentenced to death. Mooney was much upset, and this combined with the approach of the festive season was sufficient to start him on a drinking bout. He had got into trouble of some kind and had been taken to the Guard Room. Lidwell, as his Assistant, was sent for and requested to take charge of him; and, while trying to persuade him to go to his quarters, was shot through the head by a stupid soldier who was carelessly handling his rifle.[58]

The official inquest, which was not made public at the time, describes more specifically how some jesting in the orderly room led to Lidwell's death. There were a number of people in the room, including Lidwell, who were boisterous and participating in some horseplay. Lieutenant Murphy, the assistant barrack adjutant, entered the orderly room and told everyone to clear out as it was too crowded. Those in the room thought he was joking and made no effort to leave. Murphy, who by now was losing patience with the men, called for two sentries to come in with fixed bayonets and clear out the room. One of these sentries, Private Edward Kelly, was the person who accidently fired the shot. He explained to the inquest what happened:

> He [Lieutenant Murphy] said 'Clear these men out'. I went over to the men and they paused for a while, so I shoved a round up the breech of my rifle; it's a fashion I can't get rid of [having fought in the First World War]; and I did it

mostly to frighten them more than anything else. Then the three men [Lidwell, Harney and Mooney] started to walk out of the Orderly Room ... I shoved him [Lieutenant Harney] with my rifle ... Murphy said 'that's the way to get them out'. My sleeve got caught in the knob of the orderly room door, I had my finger on the trigger and the shot went off ... I had no intention of firing the shot whatsoever.[59]

Fredrick Lidwell died in Kilkenny Military Barracks a few minutes later on 22 December 1922, aged 22 years. He had been a member of the Dublin IRA during the War of Independence. He was buried in Glasnevin Cemetery on 27 December, with full military honours.[60] Fred was the only son of Josephine Lidwell from Dún Laoghaire. The family were well known in Dublin as Fred's late father, John George Lidwell, ran a solicitors' firm in Dublin city centre. Josephine Lidwell received a total of £300 for her son's death.[61]

Executions of John Phelan and John Murphy: 29 December 1922

The Christmas season brought no armistice. On the contrary, the first Free State executions outside of Dublin and Kildare took place in Kilkenny Military Barracks on 29 December 1922. The two unfortunate individuals were 32-year-old John Phelan (sometimes spelt 'Whelan') from Thomastown and 22-year-old John Murphy from Bishopslough, Bennettsbridge. The Free State Government had begun its policy of executions the month previously. The legislation for this had been approved by the Dáil in September; in practice it was martial law in all but name.

Both men had been arrested at the same time two weeks previously, on 13 December 1922. On that day, Free State soldiers in Kilkenny received information that a party of anti-Treaty IRA was raiding a house at Blackwell, Bennettsbridge. Ten Free State soldiers proceeded to the location but the men had left by then. They suspected Murphy was involved and travelled to his mother's house in nearby Bishopslough where they found the men. After searching the house the Free State party found 'two rifles and ammunition, one revolver and two bombs [grenades]'.[62] The men were arrested on charges of theft and for possessing firearms without a licence. It is safe to assume that when Murphy and Phelan were initially arrested they could not have imagined that they would be facing a firing squad two weeks later. There were others arrested in Kilkenny that were found to have ammunition or arms, who had not been confronted with the death penalty.

The special court that charged the men was convened in-camera in Kilkenny Military Barracks, just before Christmas. Both men were found guilty and told they were sentenced to death by firing squad. The verdict, however, was not disclosed to the general public. Hence, their executions in the middle of the Christmas season were a surprise and a shock to most when the news was announced. The Free State Army GHQ issued the following brief statement to the press following their execution on Friday, 29 December 1922:

> John Phelan, Thomastown, Co Kilkenny, and John Murphy, Bishopslough, Co Kilkenny were charged with being in possession, without proper authority, of arms and ammunition, and further, with being concerned in a raid on Sheastown [aka Sheestown] House, when property to the value of £189 was taken. The accused were found guilty of both charges, and were sentenced to death. The executions were carried out today [29 December] at 8 a.m. [in Kilkenny Military Barracks].[63]

Prior to the execution, two priests, Fr Kavanagh of St John's, and Fr Martin Drea who was Chaplain to the Free State Army in Kilkenny (later parish priest of Thomastown), attended to the men. They remarked afterwards that the two condemned men 'walked steadily to the place of execution, and unflinchingly faced the firing squad'. The two priests rushed to anoint the men after they had been shot. The volleys of shots were heard all around Kilkenny City at about 8.15 am. Murphy's uncle just happened to be walking by the barracks on his way to work when the shots suddenly rang out, startling him. He did not discover until later in the day that it was in fact his relative who had met his end, just a few metres away from behind the barracks wall.[64] The two men were buried in the grounds of the military barracks.

It has only recently come to light that the Free State Army's chief legal adviser, Judge Advocate General Cahir Davitt, queried the validity of the death sentences on the Kilkenny men and actually advised against the executions. The Free State Army authorities in Kilkenny, however, were not obliged to heed his advice and proceeded with the executions anyway. Recalling the case some years later, Davitt remarked:

> When the proceedings in the case of Phelan and Murphy came to me for my advice as to confirmation [of the death sentences], I found them to be unsatisfactory. I cannot now remember what was wrong; but I know that, while technical, it was sufficient to induce me to advise against confirmation. My advice was not adopted, however; the findings and sentences were confirmed; and the sentences were carried out on December 29th.[65]

John Murphy was from a family of seven children. His father, James, had passed away in 1912, though his mother, Kate Murphy (née Maddock), was left to grieve his loss. Indicative of the complexities of Irish history, John Murphy fought with the British Army during the First World War in the Royal Field Artillery unit. After he returned to Ireland in 1919, he joined the 5th IRA Battalion, Kilkenny Brigade. He took the anti-Treaty position at the outbreak of the Civil War. He wrote a farewell letter to his mother the night before his execution, in which he said:

Dear Mother,

Just a line, the last I shall ever write you. John Phelan and myself are to be shot at 8 o'clock to-morrow morning, so this will be the last time I shall write to you. Dear mother, do not be downhearted. God is good. I am sending a brooch to you in memory of me… I am sorry I did not get the chance of meeting you all … I am dying a soldier's death. I will draw to a finish as it is dark and I can't see what I am writing. I do hope this news won't cause much trouble, so cheer up all, and keep a brave heart, you will not help me by worrying …

From your loving son,
John [66]

He signed off by stating: 'P.S. I am quite satisfied to meet my God.' Kate Murphy eventually received £112 from the Irish Government in 1934 for the loss of her son. She previously received a donation of £126 from the nationalist Irish White Cross organisation as she had been reliant on John to provide her with an income prior to his execution.[67]

John Phelan came from a milling family from Mill Street in Thomastown, and took up the profession himself from a young age, working with his brother and father at Dangan Mills. John Phelan married Bridget Kelly, also from Mill Street, in January 1915. At the time of his execution in December 1922 Bridget was aged 27. The couple had three young children; Mary aged seven, Frances aged five and Bernard aged nine months. Between 1922 and 1933, Bridget and the children survived with the help of the Kelly and Phelan families. They were also appreciative of the Irish White Cross which granted Bridget £250 and gave an allowance of £9 per month for the children. In 1933, Bridget received a modest widow's allowance from the Irish Government and £18 per child, per year, until the girls reached the age of 21 and Bernard reached the age of 18.[68]

Although both Phelan and Murphy were guilty of the crimes they were charged with, they were very unfortunate to have been arrested at that specific moment of the Civil War in Kilkenny. While both men had been active members of the 5th Kilkenny IRA Battalion during the War of Independence, neither were leading players in the anti-Treaty IRA Brigade. Their subordinate rank within the organisation was one way of warning impressionable young men of the consequences of joining the anti-Treaty forces. Moreover, the Free State leadership in the county had suffered severe embarrassments the very week Murphy and Phelan were arrested when the anti-Treaty forces captured three military barracks. Prout and his staff must have feared an increase in support for the anti-Treaty IRA in the local area after such a daring feat, especially after a number of Free State officers defected to the other side during the debacle. Considering the anger that had been brewing in GHQ over Prout's leadership of the Division, he needed to show his bosses he was capable of making tough decisions.[69] Hence, the Free State Army in Kilkenny needed to show some ruthlessness; John Murphy and John Phelan just happened to be – quite literally – in the firing line. They were the only two people made an example of in County Kilkenny during the Civil War, as they were the first and last executions in the county. Thus, the killings of Murphy and Phelan at this particular juncture of the Civil War must be considered through the local and national contexts of what was happening during that particular period.

Nearly two years after their deaths, the bodies of the two men were exhumed and returned to their families on Tuesday, 28 October 1924. The tricolour-draped coffins processed through Kilkenny City headed by St John's Brass Band, with a guard of honour provided by their former IRA comrades. An 'enormous concourse of people' met the cortège at Bennettsbridge and walked behind the two coffins to Thomastown. Civil War tensions were still prevalent. Prior to the funeral service commencing, two lorries of Free State soldiers arrived at the burial site in St Mary's old cemetery in Thomastown in order to prevent any former anti-Treaty IRA men firing shots over the graves. The Sinn Féin (anti-Treaty) TD, Michael Shelly, gave the graveside oration in which he criticised the Free State Government who he said were more interested in 'finding jobs for their 31st cousins'.[70]

CHAPTER 12

The Close of Civil War and its Aftermath (January–September 1923)

'... nine men all armed with rifles and revolvers and carrying petrol tins entered the yard. I was in bed. I saw the men pumping petrol on the outhouses and I got up and went to the bedroom window'.

– Mary Walsh, Portnascully Mill, Mooncoin

The New Year began much as the old one had closed. The attacks by the anti-Treaty IRA on infrastructure and the commandeering of supplies and money continued unabated. There was, however, a decline in the number of ambushes by anti-Treaty IRA columns. It is difficult to ascertain exactly the reason for this, and there is no documented evidence that the executions of their comrades in Kilkenny Barracks unnerved them in any way. It was more likely the Free State Army policy of arresting and interning large numbers of anti-Treaty IRA was having an effect. This was especially true when prominent members were captured.

The Slow Move Towards Ceasefire: January–February 1923

On 4 January 1923 for instance, Richard 'Dick' Brennan and Patrick Walsh – two leading members of the anti-Treaty IRA in the south of the county who had been on the run in areas around Mooncoin, Piltown and Kilmacow – were captured and interned. Later that month a large party of Free State soldiers from Mooncoin had a long-running gun battle with anti-Treaty IRA soldiers as they pursued them through fields across the Walsh Hills between Templeorum and Hugginstown. No casualties were reported and the anti-Treaty men escaped. However, it does highlight how the noose was beginning to tighten on the anti-Treaty IRA as their adversaries were now willing to proactively engage them in inhospitable parts of the countryside.[1] This was exemplified the following month when Denis 'Dinny' Lacey, who had been a thorn in the side of Colonel-Commandant Prout since the beginning of the Civil War, was killed in action in the Glen of Aherlow.[2]

On 2 February 1923, a section of Martin Medlar's east Kilkenny anti-Treaty ASU attempted to ambush a convoy of Free State soldiers in Shankill, Paulstown, close to the Carlow border. The plan backfired as the much larger than anticipated Free State forces fought back and gave chase to the anti-Treaty IRA. Some of the column stayed behind to hold up the advancing Free State soldiers and allow their comrades to escape. It was during this altercation that 18-year-old anti-Treaty IRA member Patrick Barcoe was shot and killed. He was a native of Neigham, Gowran, and also lived for a period in nearby Goresbridge. Barcoe's IRA Company Captain, Pierce Bolger, remarked that he 'was a true and fearless soldier'. Five of the ASU column were captured by the Free State forces during the fight.

It was another tragedy for the Barcoe family. Patrick Barcoe's father, also called Patrick, had accidently drowned in the River Barrow at Goresbridge in 1919. This left his mother, Mary, and four siblings – the youngest of which was 10 years old – to grieve the loss of a father, son and brother.[3]

The anti-Treaty IRA were down, but certainly not out. During February 1923, they opened fire on the building in Callan that was acting as a base for the Civic Guard. The twelve guards inside, who initially refused to surrender, eventually relented. The building was then set alight. The Civic Guard building was saved, as the police managed to remove the burning furniture before the fire took hold.[4]

During this period there was another death of an anti-Treaty IRA internee in Kilkenny jail; once again it was a Waterford native. Andrew Power, aged 24 years and from Ballygunner Castle, died on 27 January 1923 after contracting diphtheria. He had fought in the British Army during the First World War where he spent much of his time in a German prisoner-of-war camp. He subsequently joined his local IRA Company at the outbreak of the War of Independence. He was arrested in Waterford the previous August and sent to Kilkenny prison for incarceration. It was here he was taken ill and was moved to the Central Hospital where he passed away.[5]

From the early stages of the Civil War, anti-Treaty IRA prisoners could be released from Kilkenny Military Barracks and Kilkenny jail if they signed a declaration stating they would no longer take up arms against the Free State Government. Very few prisoners in Kilkenny are recorded as signing this in

1922, but this changed in early 1923. Liam Deasy, an anti-Treaty IRA officer from Cork, had been captured near Clonmel and ordered the men under his command who were imprisoned in Kilkenny jail to sign the declaration to avoid being executed. The Free State authorities allowed representatives of the anti-Treaty prisoners to move between the barracks and the jail in Kilkenny to discuss the 'Deasy peace agreement'. 'Several prisoners' in both locations approved of Deasy's motives and were released soon after signing the declaration.[6] The declaration was as follows: 'I promise that I will not use arms against the Parliament elected by the Irish people, or the Government for the time being responsible to that Parliament, and that I will not support in any way any such action. Nor will I interfere with the property or persons [possessions] of others.'[7]

'Big House' Burnings: February–March 1923

At the beginning of the Civil War, the first 'Big House' destroyed in County Kilkenny was Woodstock in Inistioge. This was set alight by anti-Treaty forces to prevent the Free State Army from reoccupying the building. Additionally, two other 'Big House' burnings took place within a week of each other at the latter end of the war, in February and March 1923.

Desart Court, Cuffesgrange

The first house destroyed was Desart Court, home of Hamilton Cuffe, 5th Earl of Desart. The house was about 10 km south of Kilkenny City in Cuffesgrange. It was a Palladian mansion built in 1733, designed by Edward Lovett Pearce, who is famous for designing the Irish Houses of Parliament on College Green in Dublin. The Earl of Desart was well known. His late brother, Captain Otway Cuffe, had been an active organiser of the Gaelic League in Kilkenny City. The reason for the destruction of the house by the anti-Treaty IRA was in reprisal for the activities of the earl's sister-in-law, Ellen Cuffe, the Dowager Countess of Desart, who had once resided at Desart Court. She had accepted W.T. Cosgrave's offer to be one of his nominations to the Free State Senate. The anti-Treaty IRA had begun a nationwide campaign of destroying the homes of Free State senators; hence the destruction of Desart Court was – as the the IRA saw it – reparation for Lady Desart accepting a seat in the Upper Chamber.

The anti-Treaty IRA entered the mansion at about 10.30 pm on Thursday, 22 February 1923. The earl at this time was in England. The only occupants of the house were two maid servants and the elderly gardener of the estate. They were ordered to take their belongings and leave the building. The anti-Treaty IRA began hacking and breaking the furniture, before piling it into the centre of the rooms. The windows were smashed to allow a draught into the building. Petrol was sprinkled around the rooms. Once all occupants had left, the building was set on fire. Most of the building was destroyed except for one wing.[8]

The furniture and artwork that were in the section of the building where the fire failed to take hold were salvaged. No doubt the earl was thankful for this small mercy. One month later, a van and a 'four-ton lorry' arrived at Desart Court to transport what remained of the furniture and artwork to Kilkenny railway station for onward delivery to England. The vehicles had only left the estate when they were stopped by armed anti-Treaty men, before they had even reached the village of Cuffesgrange. The drivers were ordered to get out of the lorry and van. Petrol was poured over the furniture and paintings and set alight. Once the fire took hold, the petrol tanks in both vehicles exploded destroying the vehicles. This time the furniture did not escape the flames. The haulage contractor from Kilkenny City who owned the lorry, Tom Walsh, had been hired by a number of aristocratic home owners in the area to transport their valuables to England.[9] This was perceived as an affront by the anti-Treaty IRA, as there was a belief that this property belonged to Irish people; in other words, the tenant farmers who had provided much of the wealth to the landed gentry for generations. Thus, they did not want to see it leaving the country. Hence, the Earl of Desart drew the short straw once again – while Tom Walsh could no longer provide the transport service.

The Earl later received £12,709 compensation from the Irish Free State to rebuild the house (although he estimated its worth to be £22,259), which was completed within five years of its destruction. However, this new house was allowed to fall into disrepair and was demolished in the 1950s after the Land Commission acquired the estate and distributed the lands.[10]

Bessborough House, Piltown

The week after the Desart Court fire another mansion in the far south of the county was destroyed. Bessborough House in Piltown, owned by Vere Brabazon Ponsonby, 9th Earl of Bessborough was built in the 1740s for the 1st Earl and was designed by Francis Bindon – the same architect responsible for Woodstock House in Inistioge. The earl had handed over the day-to-day management of the servants who ran the estate to the local parish priest in

Piltown. The earl was relatively unknown to locals in Piltown, having spent most of his forty-one years living in England. It could not be said that the Ponsonby family were not liked in the area, it was more that they were unknown. They were therefore the typical 'absentee landlords'. Since the War of Independence, Bessborough House was often used as a resting place by IRA columns. The estate also produced large quantities of food; including apples, beef, mutton, pork, eggs and wheat. Thus it was a prime base for the anti-Treaty IRA during the Civil War.[11]

The Free State Army in this area of south Kilkenny were losing patience with the anti-Treaty IRA, especially with their constant destruction of the railway system in the area. This annoyance reached a climax in the days prior to the Bessborough incident when the anti-Treaty IRA burnt down Grange railway station in Mooncoin, and attempted to ignite Fiddown railway station near Piltown. Consequently, in an unusual occurrence, it was the Free State forces in the area who decided to destroy the local 'Big house'. Thus, Bessborough House was burnt down not for any ideological reasons but purely to deprive the anti-Treaty IRA of its main base in south Kilkenny.

On the night of Thursday, 1 March 1923, thirty Free State soldiers entered the house. They were dressed in civilian clothing to disguise the fact that they from the National Army; it would therefore appear that the plan had not been sanctioned by their superiors. All those inside were told to leave. Then the windows were smashed and the house was covered in petrol, before it was set alight. The fire lit up the night sky for miles around. Very little remained of the house by the following morning. The charred ruins of Bessborough House became something of a morbid tourist attraction in the area during the following weeks, as people travelled to view the site for themselves. Luckily for him, the earl had moved much of the valuable furniture and the extensive art collection to his home in England during the course of the previous year, fearing an event like the one that transpired. Nevertheless, he estimated the total financial loss was upwards of £100,000.[12]

The Earl of Bessborough was livid following the destruction and demanded the Free State Government rebuild Bessborough House to the exact designs of the original. All fittings and furniture were also to be replaced. This was eventually acceded to by the near bankrupt Free State Government. It was perhaps the nearest admission of guilt as to the Free State Army's involvement in the destruction of the house – something that was never admitted publicly. The total cost eventually paid by the State was £51,422. This was by far the highest individual amount paid for Civil War damage in Kilkenny and would be the equivalent of over €3 million in today's money. The earl himself supervised the rebuild in Piltown. When the new Bessborough House was completed in 1929, government ministers arrived for the formal unveiling. Afterwards, the Earl of Bessborough was quoted as saying; 'I will never enter this accursed house again.'[13] He was true to his word, as he never again returned to Piltown. He sold the house to the Oblates of Mary Immaculate religious order in 1940, which they used as a seminary. Over 300 priests were trained in the house over the next thirty years. In 1971 the estate was sold to the Department of Agriculture. Kildalton College, the largest agricultural college in the country, is now centred around Bessborough House.

'Small' House Burnings: February–April 1923

So, in total, the number of 'Big Houses' destroyed in County Kilkenny during the Civil War was three – with different motives for each burning. However, political property burnings were not solely reserved for aristocratic dwellings. More typical homes were also destroyed. Both sides used the tactic, in occurrences eerily reminiscent of the Black and Tan era. The peak period for property burnings in County Kilkenny was at the tail end of the Civil War, between February and April 1923. It followed a pattern of reprisal and counter-reprisal by the anti-Treaty IRA and Free State forces.

For instance, the home of the Teehan family in Kilmanagh – known as Shipton or Sheeptown House – was burnt down on the night of 20 March 1922 by Free State soldiers. Bridget Teehan and her family were given five minutes to leave, before the house was set alight. Bridget's sons were members of the anti-Treaty IRA and her daughters were leading members of Cumann na mBan in the area. Moreover, the Teehan's home was a hub for resting IRA men on the run. Bill Quirke, O/C of the 2nd Southern Division anti-Treaty IRA, defined it thus; 'the Teehan home at Shipton might be described as a Field GHQ for a considerable period until it was eventually burned down by the very men it often sheltered'. Mary (Molly) Teehan (later Foley), daughter of Bridget, described what happened that night, prior to the burning. It was evident that Free State forces were watching the house:

> President [Éamon] De Valera called during [the] night with [Frank] Aiken, Austin Stack, Seany Dowling, Tom Derrig [and] Seany Hyde. There was no man to help them. All the local men were on the run & were it not for our help, the whole crowd could have been captured in a strange countryside. [I] got safe conduct for them [to Tipperary] & that night, scarcely had the company gone, when the house was raided & burned by armed & masked men [Free State soldiers].[14]

In retaliation for the destruction of Shipton House, the anti-Treaty IRA set fire to the dwelling house, grocery and bakery of James Walsh, a Kilkenny County Councillor and businessman residing in Templeorum, Piltown.[15] Although his premises were over 30 km from Kilmanagh, Walsh had been vocal in his denunciations of the actions of the anti-Treaty IRA, both locally and during council meetings. In October 1922 he had been taken prisoner by Richard Brennan's south Kilkenny ASU.[16] Therefore, as Walsh was very much the anti-Treaty IRAs *bête noire* in the area, they probably did not take much persuading in having to destroy his property.

Property burnings were also used by the anti-Treaty IRA as punishment for informing. Although undoubtedly upsetting, this was a less severe form of penalty compared to the War of Independence where a number of executions took place. Not everyone was safe from death however. In one case, sheds and farm machinery owned by Maria (Mary) Mackey from Granny, were destroyed in March 1923 after she was accused of giving information to Free State forces. Her cat was killed by the anti-Treaty IRA men and hung on a gate, with a message affixed to its body: 'convicted spy – beware – the same penalty will be laid out to the owners if found out giving any information. IRA.'[17]

It was usually the women of a family who suffered the brunt of the arson attacks, as the male members would often be on the run and not living at home. Mary Walsh, the mother of Jack 'Na Coille' Walsh – the south Kilkenny anti-Treaty IRA leader from Portnascully Mill, Mooncoin – was awoken by non-uniformed Free State soldiers on the morning of 4 April 1923. She described what occurred:

> nine men all armed with rifles and revolvers and carrying petrol tins entered the yard. I was in bed. I saw the men pumping petrol on the outhouses and I got up and went to the bedroom window. One of the men told me to get up at once and open the door. I refused … he drove in the window. My daughter came down and opened the door. One of the men rushed in and ordered us all out … We dressed and went out. The men then sprinkled petrol on the chairs and tables and on the children's bed. We went out into the yard and let the cattle into the field. The dwelling house was then set fire to. Bombs must be used as the walls shattered.[18]

The War against Trains

One of the most engrained memories of those who lived through the Civil War era was the near constant disruption to the railway network. From the very beginning of the Civil War, the anti-Treaty IRA leadership issued orders for the destruction of the rail infrastructure across the country. The main objective of this policy was to block the movement of Free State equipment and personnel by rail. Historian Michael Hopkinson classed this anti-Treaty IRA offensive as 'the most successful aspect' of its military policy.[19] Of course destroying the rail network also caused a great deal of upheaval to the general public. The negative public reaction was one of the main reasons the IRA had not pushed a similar strategy during the War of Independence. As the majority of public opinion was against the anti-Treaty IRA already, they had little to lose. It is impossible to underestimate the value of train transport to ordinary members of the public during this era. Although there were motor vehicles in use in Kilkenny, it was still the era of the pony-and-trap, or perhaps bicycles for those who could afford them. The train offered a lifeline. It was often used for short journeys between villages and towns in the county. Furthermore, trains were widely used to transport mail and goods around the country, along with the daily newspapers. Thus, the disruption to the railways affected the lives of Kilkenny people both directly and indirectly.

There were three main rail lines running through County Kilkenny. In the far south, the Limerick to Waterford/Rosslare train line dissected the county roughly horizontally, passing through the parishes of Piltown, Mooncoin, Kilmacow, Slieverue and Glenmore. This line was also used by people in the south of the county for travelling to Dublin via Wicklow. Another line from Waterford dissected the county in a vertical direction. This line passed through the county from Kilmacow, through to Kilkenny City. The line branched in two near Kilkenny City. One route continued northwards from the city through Ballyragget, before terminating in Portlaoise (for onward connection to Dublin). This line from Kilkenny City to Portlaoise is no longer in use. Another line went from Kilkenny City towards Carlow town, with a stop in Gowran along the way (it was also linked to Dublin). This route is most familiar to people presently, as it is now the main rail route to the capital. Furthermore, there were additional branches from these lines which linked the coalfields in and around Castlecomer to the main rail network. The people to the east of the county were serviced by the Wexford line, which passed close to the village of Goresbridge. There were also many more railway stations along the lines than currently exist today. For instance, there were stops at Piltown (Fiddown), Mooncoin (Grange), Glenmore, Kilmacow, Ballyhale, Mullinavat, Bennettsbridge, Gowran, Goresbridge and Ballyragget.

Barely a week of the Civil War went by in County Kilkenny without some report of an attack on the railways. On the less severe end of the spectrum this involved the severing of signal cables or the cutting of trees on to tracks. More serious cases involved digging up tracks, blowing up bridges, and setting fire to railway stations. In addition, trains were often held up by the anti-Treaty IRA, with passengers searched, post taken and goods commandeered. As early as July 1922, Liam Lynch – the anti-Treaty IRA Chief-of-Staff – ordered the destruction of railway lines and stations in south Kilkenny to prohibit the movement of Free State troops from Kilkenny and Waterford cities, into County Tipperary. He commented: 'a hundred bridges blown up was just as effective a blow ... as a hundred barracks blown up'.[20] For anti-Treaty members in Kilkenny, attacking the rail network in rural parts of the county offered them a way of helping the cause, with little risk of being captured or killed in the process.

To complicate matters even further, the railways in the country were in private ownership. The lines that ran through Kilkenny were mostly owned and operated by the Great Southern and Western Railway Company. The company often received threats from the anti-Treaty IRA, warning them against repairing the damage to the tracks, as it would be perceived as aiding and abetting the Provisional or Free State Government. The railway company often heeded these threats, as it was easier – and often more financially neutral – to do nothing; as even if the lines were fixed, they could quickly be destroyed again. [21]

The most frequent attacks were on the Waterford–Kilkenny line, usually in the section from Kilmacow to Thomastown. For instance, in September 1922, a goods train was stopped by a group of anti-Treaty IRA men at Lukeswell, Mullinavat. The carriages were detached, before the train was purposely derailed by travelling at full speed over tracks that had been dug up. It resulted in 'extensive damage' being caused to the locomotive.[22] Examples of other occurrences can be derived from the reports of the railway company themselves. An account about an incident at Ballyhale station on 3 October 1922 stated:

> As it [the train] leaves the station the driver sees some individuals at the lineside acting in a suspicious manner. When the train passes them, one man hurls a missile [bomb] which lands inside a full carriage. Seated with the civilian passengers are Lieuts. Foley and O'Rourke of the Free State army, who promptly dispose of the bomb through a window before it can explode.[23]

In another reported event in Glenmore on 3 November 1922, a train is held up and raided just a few kilometres outside Waterford City:

the evening Waterford–Dublin mail train is held up at a steep embankment near Glenmore station. Twelve armed men, who order passengers to remain in their seats and not look out the windows … painstakingly search the parcels. They are apparently looking for articles of clothing, expecting to find a large consignment of wearing apparel and bicycles from Waterford firms. The search lasts nearly an hour, after which some bicycles and parcels are removed and the train allowed to proceed. It reaches Westland Row, Dublin, two hours behind schedule.[24]

The Free State Army could do very little to stop these attacks, besides capturing people whom they believed were in the anti-Treaty IRA. Occasionally, they did recover some of the commandeered goods. During Christmas 1922, Free State soldiers raided the home of 9th Battalion anti-Treaty captain, Patrick Walsh, from Clogga, Mooncoin. They found nothing incriminating in the house but when they searched the haycocks outside they discovered goods that had been taken when a train was held up in nearby Rathcurby two weeks earlier.[25] Walsh was one of the officers in Dick Brennan's ASU and was eventually captured a week later.[26]

Another tactic employed by the anti-Treaty IRA in its war against the railways was the destruction of some of the more rural train stations. Bennettsbridge, Grange (Mooncoin) and Fiddown stations were all set alight, causing varying amounts of damage.[27] On 10 February 1923, some unfortunate passengers taking the 11.00 am train from Limerick to Waterford experienced two holdups and two derailments, during the one journey. The trip proceeded as usual until just outside the village of Kilsheelan in south Tipperary. The train was captured there by a party of anti-Treaty IRA and derailed. The passengers had to walk to Kilsheelan station where a motor car brought them to Carrick-on-Suir. After waiting in Carrick for some time they eventually boarded a 'special', which was a train sent from Waterford specifically to collect the stranded travellers. However, close to the village of Mooncoin, this train was once again held up. One of the passengers, who did not give his name, described in vivid detail to a journalist exactly what occurred that evening. It was an experience many civilians faced during the period:

all went well until we had arrived at about a quarter of a mile at the Waterford side of Grange station [in the townlands of Ballincur or Rathcurby, Mooncoin]. Then for the second time that day, I was to bear a further volley of shots, this time, as far as I could gather, discharged from a machine gun. As on the occasion of the earlier derailment, all passengers promptly threw themselves on the floor, and the train was brought to a standstill. At this time it was pitch dark, by the light of the train we were able to discern the arrival on the scene of some 20 armed men [anti-Treaty IRA] ... all passengers were ordered off ... The raiders apologised for the inconvenience they were causing, and in the case of one lady passenger, who was accompanied by her three children, permission was granted for the removal of her trunks from the train. An escort was then provided, and under their direction the passengers were conveyed about a quarter of a mile... where they were shown the road ... As we left the permanent way we observed some of the armed party digging holes in the railway bridge at this point, and we presumed that they were about to lay mines or bombs. On gaining the road ... the passengers proceeded in the direction of Waterford [about 6 miles away] ... When we arrived on a hill about a mile from the scene of the hold-up, we heard the engine being put under steam [acceleration], and the next we saw, on looking around, was a blazing train rapidly approaching the railway bridge ... as the train proceeded towards the bridge, we heard the noise of several loud explosions, which I took to be bombs. When the train arrived at the bridge there was a terrific detonation and from our position it appeared to us that the train had toppled over the bridge and on to the road below. Even in this position the fired train continued to burn brightly lighting up the whole countryside ... Even when we arrived at the outskirts of Waterford, shortly before seven o'clock, we could still see the lurid reflection in the sky.[28]

As can be deduced, the destruction of railway bridges sometimes afforded the anti-Treaty IRA the added bonus of blocking a main road. A 'large bridge on the road between Paulstown and Bagenalstown, at a place called Royal Oak' was blown up in the early hours of 15 December 1922, which had the net effect of completely blocking the main road from Kilkenny and Carlow.[29] Of course the Free State Government were required to compensate the rail companies, as it needed the routes to be in working order. This would amount to thousands of pounds over the course of the war. For example, they compensated the railway company £899, 8s, 8d, to rebuild the small station in Grange, Mooncoin.[30] During the Civil War there was much debate in government about nationalising the railways. The headaches caused by the war must have encouraged many of the shareholders to part with their assets as quickly as possible.

At the beginning of 1923 the government published the projected cost of running the Free State that year. The budget arithmetic made for grim reading for the ordinary citizens of the country. The cost of running the state in 1923 was projected to be £42 million (sterling). Of this, £10.8 million was to be spent on compensation for 'malicious injuries' and £10.6 million was to be spent on the Free State Army. In other words, nearly 50 per cent of the national exchequer's total budget was to be spent on the ongoing war effort. Expected income, however, was only estimated to be £26 million, leaving a large deficit.[31]

A Series of Tragic Events: March 1923

The weeks before and after St Patrick's Day 1923 witnessed a number of clashes between the opposing forces. There were also numerous fatalities, which brought misery to the doorstep of eight local families. On 8 March 1923, a convoy of Free State soldiers was ambushed near the village of Mullinavat. Three of their party were wounded in the attack. The Free State Army immediately organised a counter-offensive and reinforcements were requested from Kilkenny, Clonmel and Waterford. They planned an encircling manoeuvre with the aim of flushing out the anti-Treaty IRA who were based in the rural southeast of the county – specifically in the areas around Listerlin, Tullogher and Inistioge.[32] The following day, Friday 9 March, they began an encircling movement coming from different directions. Some of the Free State soldiers moved from Mullinavat, others from Graiguenamanagh and New Ross. Sections of Free State soldiers covered 'a 20 mile area' and they all moved in the direction of Brandon Hill – the highest point in County Kilkenny, which is located 4 km south of Graiguenamanagh. The strategy was to ensnare the anti-Treaty men in an ever-tightening cordon. Having passed through the village of Tullogher, one of these sections, led by Commandant James O'Hanrahan, came into contact with the anti-Treaty IRA column near the banks of the River Nore. A gun battle broke out which lasted a number of hours as the Free State soldiers pursued the anti-Treaty men through the unforgiving terrain. As darkness fell, the anti-Treaty IRA escaped northwards through the parish of Inistioge. There were a number of casualties on both sides, including one Free State soldier fatality, whose body was not discovered until the following morning. The anti-Treaty IRA were reported to have had six wounded.[33]

The Free State soldier killed during the altercation was Gerald Jeremiah Comerford, a native of Clogharinka, Ballyfoyle, County Kilkenny – in the parish of Muckalee. His body was found at Coolnamuck, Inistioge, having been shot a number of times during the exchange of fire. Comerford was 23 years old at the time of his death and had worked on his father's farm prior to joining the Free State Army. He had been an active member of the 3rd Battalion IRA during the War of Independence. His funeral, with full military honours, took place in Muckalee on Sunday, 11 March. He was the eldest son of Michael and Anne Comerford's fourteen children. His father was awarded £25 for the death of his son, which was later increased to £50 on appeal.[34]

Just after midnight on 10 March, a group of anti-Treaty IRA attempted to raid the home of James Buggy in Ballyouskill, which is located 8 km north of Ballyragget, near the border with County Laois. Buggy was 'a strong supporter of the Treaty and the [Free State] Government'. The anti-Treaty men were attempting to take firearms they knew were in his possession. The raiding party requested that Buggy open the door. He refused and the anti-Treaty men fired shots through the downstairs windows. Buggy then opened fire on the men from the upstairs windows. The anti-Treaty IRA returned fire but retired soon afterwards. During the initial burst of fire, Buggy shot one of the anti-Treaty party. Thomas Mealey, a 19-year-old carpenter from Coolbawn (Upper Hills), Castlecomer, was mortally wounded, having been shot through the lung. His comrades decided they had to leave him to avoid being captured themselves, but they stopped at the local priest's house in Ballyouskill to inform Fr Comerford of the badly injured man who was in the vicinity of Buggy's home. It was nearly daylight before the priest and members of the Buggy family found the body of Mealey. He had passed away sometime during the night. His body was brought by the Free State forces to Durrow Military Barracks where a brother of the deceased identified the remains. A 'largely attended' funeral was held for Thomas Mealey in Castlecomer two days later.[35] Mealey had been a member of the 3rd Battalion IRA during the War of Independence. His brother, William Mealey, was Vice O/C of the 3rd Battalion anti-Treaty IRA during the Civil War. Thomas was fourth in a family of six children and left his mother, Elizabeth, and father Thomas senior – with whom he worked as a carpenter – to grieve his loss.[36]

Kilkenny men in other parts of the country were not having good fortune during the bleak month of March 1923. On Tuesday 6 March, 18-year-old Richard Duggan of Scart, Mullinavat, was accidently shot by a comrade in Waterford Infirmary (Workhouse) where he was stationed. Duggan had been on the night shift acting as a sentry, guarding the barracks. After finishing his shift at 7.30 am, he handed in his rifle – as was the usual procedure – to Private Thomas Carbery who was responsible for cleaning the weapons. The two men stayed chatting for a few minutes. As they stood conversing, the rifle which Carbery was holding accidently went off, shooting Duggan in the neck. His wounds subsequently became infected and he died the following Sunday, 11 March, from 'septic pneumonia'. His funeral took place in his native Mullinavat. He was from a family of eight children. His parents Ellen and Patrick received £80 compensation for the death of their son.[37]

Hanna(h) Murphy née Dooley (1891–1961), Dunningstown. O/C Kilkenny Cumann na mBan Bde 1919–23; active at Hugginstown attack, Friary St, Battle of Kilkenny, Carrick-on-Suir. Said trauma of the constant military raids on her family home led to the premature deaths of her mother and 2 sisters, all dead by 1924 (courtesy of Declan Lacey).

Woodstock House, Inistioge. From August 1920 it was HQ of A Company, Auxiliaries. Interrogations – often violent – took place in the cellar. Burnt down by the anti-Treaty IRA on 2 Jul. 1922 (courtesy of Ciarán O'Riain).

Friary St, *c.*1910, view from Capuc
Friary (facing High St) where a fai
ambush on Crown forces took place
21 Feb. 1921. IRA members Thor
Dermody and Michael Henne
and civilian Thomas Dollard w
fatally wounded (courtesy of the I
Capuchin Archives, CA-PH-1-98).

Ned Aylward (1895–1976), Callan. O/C 7th Battalion ASU at the end of War
of Independence and O/C Kilkenny anti-Treaty IRA Brigade during Civil War;
elected TD May 1921. Left: Aylward, early 1921, with rifle and typical garments
of a flying column member. Right: Aylward in later life (courtesy of Jim Maher).

George O'Dwyer (1884–1948), Castlecomer. O/C Kilkenny IRA Bde and O/C 1st Kilkenny ASU during final months of the War of Independence. Highest-ranking local man present when Kilkenny military barracks was handed over to the Free State (courtesy of James Stephens Barracks Museum).

Captain Patrick Walsh, Dunnamaggin native, member of 8th Battalion and West Kilkenny ASU. Fatally wounded by Crown Forces at Knocknagress, Tullaroan, when 22-year-old Seán Quinn, Mullinahone, was also killed (courtesy of Liam O'Sullivan).

2/3 May 1922, Battle of Kilkenny. A likely staged photograph in the days following the fighting (due to the impracticalities of taking a 'live' image), it nonetheless shows what occurred during the initial assaults where Free State troops attempted to hack through the wooden gate of the anti-Treaty stronghold (Bettmann/Getty Images).

22 May 1921: women of Cumann na mBan process through Dunnamaggin village ahead of the remains of Captain Patrick Walsh, fatally wounded by Crown forces near Tullaroan (courtesy of Liam O'Sullivan).

6 May 1922: Kilkenny Military Barracks, anti-Treaty prisoners behind the church railings in the military barracks (still in existence) shake hands with their Free State jailers, just prior to their release after the Battle of Kilkenny (courtesy of Kilmainham Gaol Museum, 20PC-1A45-11).

12 June 1922: Mooncoin, 'Pact Election' rally. 1916 veteran Cathal Brugha gives a speech with Éamon de Valera seated behind. Brugha was dead just 3 weeks later, following a clash with Free State forces after the outbreak of civil war (National Library of Ireland, POOLEK 0420).

12 July 1922: wedding of Col-Comdt J.T. Prout (leader Free State forces, southeast division) to Mary Conba, St John the Evangelist (O'Loughlin Memorial) Church, Kilkenny City, with a Free State guard of honour (courtesy of Michael Cannady, private collection).

Mary-Jo Commins née Power (1892–1980), Cap Templeorum Cumann na mBan. In the Civil War her home was used by anti-Treaty IRA units. Arrested in March 1923, she went on a 30-day hunger-strike at Kilmainham Jail. Awarded years' military service pension – likely the longest duration for a woman in Kilkenny (courtesy o Laura Commins).

Above: anti-Treaty IRA prisoners John Murphy (Bennettsbridge) and John Phelan (Thomastown) were executed by a Free State firing squad at Kilkenny military barracks on 29 Dec. 1922 on charges of larceny and possessing firearms. Below: bullets can still be seen in the wall of the exercise yard in the detention centre of the barracks (photographs by author, courtesy of James Stephens Barracks Museum).

6 May 1923: Rathcurby, Mooncoin. Remnants of a train derailed and destroyed by the anti-Treaty IRA who had a policy of attacking the vitally important rail network, to frustrate the Free State (courtesy of the Irish Railway Record Society Archive).

25 April 1923: Newrath, Kilmacow. Train derailed by anti-Treaty IRA. Much of the destruction of the rail network occurred in the south of the county due to a larger number of anti-Treaty units. Rarely did a week of the Civil War pass without a rail incident (courtesy of the Irish Railway Record Society Archive).

A young wife, Kate McCormack, a native of Mountfinn in Urlingford, lost her Free State soldier husband in tragic circumstances on the night of 12 March 1923. Tipperary-born Patrick McCormack was undertaking sentry duty at the Free State garrison in Cashel Hospital, County Tipperary, when he was accidently shot by one of his comrades in the guardroom. Kate McCormack was left a widow at the age of 21, with three young children, aged three, two and three months. She was required to move back to live with her parents in Urlingford to support her family. She was remarried four years later to John Moriarty, a native of Urlingford. Her life never received a merited happy ending, as in 1934 Kate died from cancer of the womb, aged 33 years. Her three children with Patrick were taken in by their grandmother in Urlingford, Catherine Neary. Thus, the three children were orphaned before they reached the age of 14.[38]

On 13 March 1923, yet another Waterford prisoner in Kilkenny jail received fatal wounds after an altercation with a Free State prison guard. John Walsh, a native of Kilmacthomas, decided he was no longer going to give his name during the usual evening rollcall. Some of his fellow prisoners agreed to join him in the protest. The typical procedure was that the anti-Treaty IRA prisoners of 'A wing' were paraded every evening and their names checked off a list. After refusing to cooperate, Walsh was brought out to the exercise yard where he had a heated argument with the irritated Free State solider who was attempting to ascertain his name. This soldier told Walsh he would obtain his name and the names of his fellow prisoners, by whatever means necessary. Walsh took this as a loaded threat and 'rushed at' the Free State guard. Another soldier then struck Walsh with the butt of his rifle, at which point the Free State officer in charge that evening came into the exercise yard and got between the warring men. Walsh then attempted to grab the revolver from the holster of the officer who had intervened and another struggle ensued as both wrestled for the control of the gun. It was during this scuffle that the revolver went off, shooting Walsh in the abdomen. He was taken to the military hospital where he passed away the following evening, 14 March.

Walsh's family were understandably angry about the nature of his death, especially as it concerned such a trivial matter as not giving a name. They argued that because he was incarcerated in Kilkenny jail since the previous August, there were plenty of guards in the prison who knew his name. Walsh, who was 23 years old when he died, had been a member of the West Waterford ASU during the War of Independence. He was one of the six children of Maurice and Catherine Walsh. His remains were transferred to his home in the village of Kilmacthomas, County Waterford, where his large funeral took place on St Patrick's Day, 17 March 1923.[39]

On 15 March 1923, a patrol of Free State soldiers who were raiding houses in the Windgap area were ambushed by an anti-Treaty IRA column at Coolhill. A gun battle lasting more than three hours ensued. During the clash, Free State solider Michael Brown, aged 21 years, died instantly when he was caught in a volley of machine-gun fire from the anti-Treaty forces. Brown was a native of Mountrath, County Laois, just like Garda Henry Phelan who had died in Mullinahone some months previously. The coincidences do not end there. Brown, like Phelan, was also a posthumous baby, his father John Brown having passed away from pneumonia aged 35 years, five months prior to Michael's birth. This left Michael's mother, Elizabeth, to fend for seven children. She later remarried, but that marriage ended in separation. She received £50 for the loss of her son. Brown's remains were brought back to Mountrath for his funeral.[40]

A clandestine visit to a public house on the afternoon of Friday, 23 March 1923 had fatal consequences for two Kilkenny men who were Free State soldiers stationed in Palace East, County Wexford. The main purpose of this army outpost, which was about 10 km east of New Ross, was to protect the railway line nearby. At 2.00 pm, Sergeant Edward Gorman from Kilkenny City and Private Patrick Horan from Callan, decided to visit McCabe's public house at Ballagh, Palace East, about 3 km from their barracks. The men had not sought permission to leave the garrison, although they were in civilian clothes. Some local anti-Treaty IRA obviously observed the secret trip to the pub, as within a few hours the premises was surrounded. As Horan and Gorman left at about 8.00 pm that evening, they were quickly captured. A false report that Free State soldiers 'were creating a disturbance at the public house' was received by the Free State garrison in Palace East. Two other Free State soldiers, Lieutenant Thomas Jones and Private John Croke, were sent to McCabe's to investigate. They entered through the back kitchen of the premises and sat at the fire, oblivious to the fate of their now captured comrades. Soon after, the anti-Treaty IRA entered the kitchen shouting 'hands up'. Private Croke tried to fire his revolver but was shot a number of times by an anti-Treaty soldier. Lieutenant Jones was then led out of the premises where he was escorted away from the area, along with the already captured Gorman and Horan. The anti-Treaty men – which Free State intelligence reports stated were led by 'O'Rahilly from Dublin' – sent for a priest and doctor to attend to Private Croke who was now laid out on a chair in McCabe's.[41] After the Free State soldiers in the garrison at Palace East heard about what had happened, they presumed an attack on their barracks was imminent, but this never transpired.

The following morning, the garrison received grim news from a local priest. Their three comrades had been found dead in a farm outhouse in the village of Adamstown, 10 km away. Free State lorries were sent from New Ross to collect the bodies of the three men – Lieutenant Jones from Dublin, Sergeant Gorman and Private Horan from Kilkenny – who had been executed by the anti-Treaty IRA during the night. Dr Furlong, who examined the bodies of the Kilkenny men, said Gorman 'had twelve bullet marks on the body – five in the legs, five in the body, and one each behind the ears'. On examining Private Horan's body he found 'a bullet wound in the right hip, two in the lower part of the abdomen, two in the back, two in the jaws and one at the base of the skull'.[42] Although he probably did not think it at the time; the fact that Private Croke was shot in the pub was a stroke of good fortune for him. Although the bullets had passed clean through his body and lodged in the furniture behind, he recovered, and avoided being executed along with his comrades. Undoubtedly, the executions of the three Free State soldiers were in reprisal for the execution of three anti-Treaty IRA prisoners in Wexford jail the week previously.[43]

The bodies of the two Kilkenny men were returned home for their funerals. Edward Gorman was 23 years old and was a school teacher prior to enlisting in the Free State Army, which he had only joined the month previously. He was from a family of seven siblings and had fought in the First World War as a member of the Royal Irish Regiment. His large funeral took place at St Mary's Cathedral in Kilkenny City the following Tuesday, 27 March. He was buried in nearby St Rioch's cemetery. Patrick Horan was 25 years old at the time of his death and a native of Flag Lane and later Haggards Green, in Callan. He was from a family of at least five children, including a number of half-siblings as his mother was married previously. He was an office clerk before enlisting in the Free State Army at the beginning of 1923. He had also fought in the First World War where he had reached the rank of sergeant. After his funeral Mass in Callan he was buried in Kilbride cemetery.[44]

Edward Gorman's father, Patrick Gorman from Chapel Lane/Wellington Place in Kilkenny City, a well-known postman in the area, received £50 compensation for his son's death. Similarly, Patrick Horan's father, Patrick senior, also received £50 compensation.[45] In 2007, a monument was erected in Adamstown, County Wexford, in memory of the dead men.[46]

The old adage of things 'getting worse before they get better' rang true. Considering the high death toll of Kilkenny natives in March 1923, the final eight weeks saw little fighting, and few casualties.

Hope Springs Eternal: April–May 1923

As the evenings became longer in the late spring of 1923, there was growing optimism that there was indeed some light at the end of the tunnel, with hopes of a truce on the horizon. For many, the ill-fated death on 10 April 1923 of Liam Lynch, the Chief-of-Staff of the anti-Treaty IRA, at the hands of the Free State Army, brought a renewed expectation that the Civil War would soon be over. Prior to his death, Lynch was conveyed through south Kilkenny by a number of Kilkenny men on his final journey in March 1923. Lynch was met in County Carlow, close to Graiguenamanagh, by Martin McGrath of Listerlin, Tullogher – former O/C of the 6th Battalion. McGrath escorted Lynch, accompanied by two armed anti-Treaty IRA men, by motor car through south Kilkenny to Mooncoin. From here, Ted Moore and other members of the 9th Battalion brought Lynch over the Tipperary border.[47] Lynch was subsequently killed some weeks later on the Knockmealdown Mountains, which straddle the border of counties Tipperary and Waterford.

Therefore much of the national media focus in April was on south Tipperary where the principal anti-Treaty leaders were based. The Kilkenny anti-Treaty IRA Brigade was also lacking leadership as Brigade O/C Ned Aylward, resigned his position. He said he had 'an argument' with others in the leadership of the 2nd Southern Division and told them of his decision to withdraw from the fighting. As Aylward was a wanted man, he surrendered himself at Windgap and was brought to Kilkenny Military Barracks where he explained his stance. He was released having only spent one night in the barracks and played no further role in the Civil War.[48]

The tangled web that is Irish history was evident in the death of one Kilkenny native who passed away on 8 April 1923. Free State Private Thomas Davis, who was from Low Street in Thomastown, died in Clones Military Hospital, Monaghan, where he had been stationed. He was 28 years old and was ill in the barracks for over week, dying of a suspected pneumonia infection. Commandant James O'Hanrahan, who was an officer in the Free State garrison in Kilkenny Military Barracks, was informed by his colleagues in Clones that Davis's remains would be arriving in Kilkenny the following morning by train. The coffin would be draped in the tricolour, therefore implying a funeral with full military honours was required. O'Hanrahan then called James Blanchfield, a Free State Private who was a native of Thomastown, to his office and asked him who was 'Thomas Davis of Thomastown'. Blanchfield was taken aback. Thomas Davis had been employed by the Auxiliaries in Woodstock for over a year during the War of Independence. When names and addresses of suspected

IRA members were sent to Woodstock, Davis and another man, Richard Hall, were responsible for pointing out the location of the addresses on a map. When the Auxiliaries were disbanded in early 1922, Davis returned to Thomastown. However, the local IRA gave him twenty-four hours to leave the country or suffer the consequences. He subsequently departed for England via Rosslare. Unbeknown to the IRA in Thomastown, Davis evidently returned and enlisted in the Free State Army.

To compound matters further, James O'Hanrahan, the Free State officer in Kilkenny City, was one of the people captured and taken to Woodstock at the time of Ernie O'Malley's arrest. Thomas Davis had actually identified James O'Hanrahan when he was brought to Woodstock House in December 1920. O'Hanrahan had suffered a severe beating at the hands of the Auxiliaries in the cellar of Woodstock.

Unsurprisingly, O'Hanrahan was not going to allow Davis to receive a military funeral although they were now in the same army. He informed Lieutenant Connolly of Thomastown Free State Barracks that 'under no circumstances was a military funeral to be given to the remains'. When the train stopped in Kilkenny railway station on its journey to Thomastown, the coffin was stripped of the tricolour flag. The train with the remains of Davis was then allowed to proceed to Thomastown where a regular funeral service took place.[49]

There was much gloom in the Callan area on 19 April when 27-year-old Jim Egan, one of the best combatants during the War of Independence, was killed near his home in Poulacapple, County Tipperary, in a shootout with Free State forces. He had been a prominent member of the 7th Battalion. Egan's four brothers were also arrested and interned following the clash at Poulacapple.[50]

At the beginning of April, in City Hall, Kilkenny, Senator Peter DeLoughry presided over the formal establishment of a local branch of the new Cumann na nGaedheal political party.[51] The party mostly comprised of the pro-Treaty Sinn Féin TDs. The party was headed by W.T. Cosgrave who had first been elected to national office by the people of Kilkenny City as a Sinn Féin candidate in 1917. In the 1930s, Cumann na nGaedheal amalgamated with other smaller parties to become Fine Gael.

The conclusion of the Civil War in County Kilkenny was in complete contrast to the dramatic opening; in that, the war came to a slow, inevitable, cessation. During the last two months – April and May 1923 – there were few confrontations. There was the odd shot fired at Free State barracks – unsurprisingly in Callan – but very little serious altercations. Furthermore, the intentional destruction of private property and the transport network also reduced dramatically. Perhaps the clearest sign that things were beginning to return to normal was the reappearance of localised agrarian disputes which sparked off in the lead-up to summer harvest season.[52]

On 4 May 1923, James O'Keeffe, a Free State soldier from Grange, Mooncoin, succumbed to self-inflicted injuries he received three months previously. On 16 February, the unfortunate O'Keeffe had survived an ambush at Knocklofty, near Clonmel. The Free State soldiers in their Lancia car had sped through the ambush site. Some distance away they were ordered to dismount. Still full of adrenalin, O'Keeffe jumped down from the car, whereupon his rifle discharged. As his gun was pointed upwards, the bullet entered above his eye and exited out through the top of his head. He was brought to hospital where his situation looked bleak, but he miraculously survived. He was discharged and returned to Mooncoin where he was just about to start a new employment on the nearby railway. However, he began experiencing headaches at the end of April and passed away on 4 May in Kilkenny Military Hospital. He had just turned 21 years of age on 1 April. The doctors believed the manner in which his wound healed had put excessive pressure on his brain, causing swelling, which subsequently led to his death. His father, Daniel, was awarded £50 compensation.[53]

The anti-Treaty IRA Executive meeting that effectively ended the Civil War was held on 20 April 1923 at Poulacapple, Mullinahone, County Tipperary – just a few kilometres over the Kilkenny border near Callan. In attendance were Tom Barry, the veteran fighter, and Frank Aiken, the new chief-of-staff of the anti-Treaty IRA, who had replaced the recently killed Liam Lynch. The well-disguised hideout where the meeting took place was known locally as 'Kathmandu'.[54] During the meeting, it was decided to suspend 'all offensive operations [nationwide] as from noon on Monday, April 30th'. Subsequently, on 24 May 1923, Frank Aiken released a statement ordering his soldiers to dump arms; thus officially ending a melancholic era of Irish history. No fanfare greeted the end of hostilities in Kilkenny; as although the anti-Treaty IRA had been overcome, nothing had been 'won'. It was perhaps an early instance of the self-induced amnesia that many people – on both sides of the divide – used as a coping strategy, in an effort to forget painful memories.

There was, however, one celebration in the aftermath of the war. 'President Cosgrave' made his first trip to Kilkenny in nearly a year, during the weekend after hostilities officially ceased. No doubt he had one eye on the elections that were due to take place later that summer. Huge crowds turned out on The Parade to hear his speech. The visit gave a chance for a contemplative E.T. Keane of the *Kilkenny People* to reflect on events of recent years:

In less than six years this most extraordinary revolution has been wrought. When in July 1917, William T. Cosgrave was introduced to the electors of Kilkenny, the City was flooded with British military and police. On Saturday evening last [26 May 1923] when he stepped off the train ... this man, who by a miracle escaped the British firing squad [in 1916], was received by a Guard of Honour of the National Army commanded by a young Kilkennyman [Commandant James O'Hanrahan from Inistioge] ... Truly a marvellous change![55]

The Aftermath

Although the people of Ireland had now reached the long desired promised land of self-determination, the utopian society envisaged by some did not appear imminent. For the majority, little changed in their day-to-day lives. After the Civil War ended, the Free State Government was mostly concerned with rebuilding the country's infrastructure after years of being ravaged by war. They were also devoting a lot of time to determining – and rejecting – the large volume of compensation claims. In August 1923, just three months after hostilities ended, there was another election. Although anti-Treaty Sinn Féin, under the leadership of Éamon de Valera, increased its number of TDs, it made no impact as they abstained from taking their seats.

The ending of hostilities did not mean an end to deaths, unfortunately. A number of combatants died in the weeks and months following the end of the conflict. At 1.30 am on 13 June 1923, two anti-Treaty IRA prisoners, James Morrissey and Michael Dowling, both from Kilkenny City, attempted to escape from Kilkenny jail. The men had made an improvised rope by tying a number of bedsheets and blankets together. They attempted to use the 'rope' to climb down from the wall of the prison near the exercise yard. However, the sentries on duty spotted the two men and opened fire. James Morrissey was shot a number of times – including a bullet in the head – and was found lying fatally wounded at the bottom of the prison wall. Dowling was recaptured.[56]

James 'Duffer' Morrissey, from 35 Blackmill Street, was 28 years old and was a member of the anti-Treaty IRA since before the outbreak of the Civil War. He was one of the anti-Treaty party inside Kilkenny Castle during the siege of the city the previous year. He had also fought with the British Army during the First World War. The Free State authorities in the prison were severely criticised by their superiors and the media for the actions of sentries, as they opened fire on the prisoners when they posed little threat. In addition, a ceasefire had been in operation for a number of weeks; thus the actions of the Free State soldiers in the prison was perceived to be, at a minimum, heavy-handed. Unproven rumours also spread around the city that Morrissey was summarily executed by the soldiers after the escape attempt failed.[57]

Morrissey's death was all the more tragic considering that his wife of two years, Julia (née Graham from Larchfield in Kilkenny City), was expecting their second child. Their first child, Mary, was nearly two years old, having been born a month after her parents' marriage in July 1921. Julia gave birth to a son on 22 August 1923, two months after the death of his father. The child was given the Gaelic form of his father's name; Séamus. Once again, it was the ever-industrious Irish White Cross that provided financial support for the bereaved family. The White Cross, which was mostly organised by Cumann na mBan women, was the only form of support open to families of the republican dead during the 1920s. When Fianna Fáil came to power in the 1930s, they opened the military service pensions to the anti-Treaty dead, and it was in 1933 when Julia began receiving a widow's pension and an allowance for Mary (until she reached 21 years) and Séamus (until he reached 18 years).[58]

In a similar occurrence to the death of Morrissey, an anti-Treaty internee, Patrick Joseph Hanlon, was mortally wounded when shot by sentry Joseph Barry in Kilkenny jail on 3 September 1923. Hanlon, who was 16 years old, was a native of Carrick-on-Suir, County Tipperary. He had been a member of his local Na Fianna Éireann Battalion – the nationalist version of the boy scouts – since the middle of the War of Independence. Hanlon was shot by the sentry while looking out from his cell window in Kilkenny jail. He bled to death some hours later on route to The Curragh military hospital.

Very little detail of the circumstances surrounding his death were released to the print media, which implies the Free State authorities were not happy with how he came to be wounded. The inquest took place in Kildare and the jury present chastised the Free State authorities in the final verdict, stating; 'we consider the order issued with regard to [the] prisoners a disgrace'. This suggests that the sentries had been ordered to fire at prisoners if they were attempting to communicate from the jail windows. The jury also reprimanded the Free State Army for not having as witnesses the other men in Hanlon's cell who witnessed his death.[59] Similar to the death of Kilkenny native William Purcell who was killed on duty the previous year, the Free State Army reported Hanlon's age at death as 18 years. Patrick Hanlon's mother had died just two weeks before he was shot.[60] This was most certainly a traumatic few weeks for his father, Patrick senior, and his 14-year-old sister, Bertha (Elizabeth).

Most of the interned anti-Treaty IRA prisoners were released in a general amnesty just before Christmas in 1923, with the remainder released in the New Year.

The long-term impact on the health of combatants and their families is difficult to quantify. Some relatives believed the after-effects led to the early demise of their family members. For instance, Michael Burke, an anti-Treaty IRA combatant from Graigue, Windgap, died in July 1929, at the age of 34. His family believed his premature death was due to the ill-treatment he received in prison at the end of the Civil War. His cell mate in Mountjoy Prison, Matthew Connolly, recalled the treatment Burke received while on the sixth day of a hunger strike in September 1923:

> one thing will long live on in my memory ... Michael Burke was a prisoner with me in Mountjoy and was what I might describe as my pal and I remember that about this week [in September 1923] he was taken from his cell, knocked to the ground and hosed for fully twenty minutes [by the Free State wardens] ... he had been hosed several times and had to sleep with his cell practically full of water ... two members of the [Free State] military police in my presence expressed horror at the cruelty and cut the hose... the incident was practically the cause of a mutiny amongst the Army of the Free State.

> ... he was as fine a specimen of Irish manhood as one could wish to see, and in one week [after the hosing] you would think twas a mere boy you were speaking to.[61]

In another example, Norah Somers, sister of anti-Treaty IRA member Ned Somers who was killed during the Civil War, received life-limiting injuries as an indirect result of the conflict. As her brother was on the run, 18-year-old Norah was required to help in the corn mill owned by Ned. She began working full time in place of her brother. She hurt her back badly when 'lifting a four stone weight on to the weighing scales'. Her injuries became worse over time due to a 'tubercular disease of the spine', which left her 'an invalid' by her late twenties.[62]

CHAPTER 13

Civil War:
Civilian Fatalities and Analysis

'... it is believed he was shot by a National soldier,
it is not proposed to attempt his identification'

A total of four civilian fatalities were recorded as a direct result of Civil War activities in County Kilkenny. They occurred between August and December 1922.

John O'Keeffe

Towards the end of summer 1922, after the anti-Treaty IRA had been dislodged from the major towns, they reverted to a mostly guerrilla strategy. At about 4.00 pm on Tuesday, 15 August 1922, a group of Free State soldiers was travelling by lorry from Carrick-on-Suir to Waterford. Due to the destruction of the bridges in the south of the county, they took the longer route to Waterford via the village of Mullinavat. About 3 km before the village, at Rochestown, they were ambushed by a group of anti-Treaty IRA. Trees had been cut to block the road and the anti-Treaty men called on the Free State soldiers to surrender. They refused and a gunfight broke out. In the altercation, 34-year-old John O'Keeffe from Alexander Street in Waterford City was killed instantly, having been shot four times. He was not actually a member of the Free State Army. He had travelled to Carrick-on-Suir the previous day in order to enlist in the forces. Unfortunately for him, he jumped on to the ill-fated lorry in Carrick-on-Suir to get a lift home. The senior officer told him to 'get out' as civilians were not supposed to be on board. He stayed on board, and 'no more notice was taken of him'.[1] O'Keeffe was employed as a dock labourer and was mourned by his wife and six children. A fund was opened in Waterford City for the deceased man's widow and children, with the Mayor and local Catholic Bishop being the first to donate money.[2]

Patrick Griffin

A Wednesday morning walk through the streets of Kilkenny turned to disaster for one man. On 29 November 1922, Patrick Griffin, from Patrick Street, was walking to the train station to collect his delivery of *Irish Independent* newspapers. Griffin was the local agent for the City, distributing that newspaper to vendors. Having crossed over John's Bridge, he began making his way up Lower John's Street, when he saw a Crossley Tender lorry, with Free State soldiers in the back, coming down the street from the direction of the railway station. Suddenly, the lorry picked up speed. Some of the soldiers jumped from the now fast-moving vehicle. The lorry then swerved to avoid a horse-and-cart on the road and mounted the footpath. A group of teenagers jumped behind some scaffolding to avoid the lorry. It came careering towards Griffin at such a speed that he did not have time to remove himself from its path. He was hit by the lorry just outside the post office and dragged some distance back towards the bridge, before the lorry eventually came to a halt. Afterwards, the driver explained that 'the steering gear got out of action and the lorry sped off at a ferocious pace'.

Patrick Griffin, who was 47 years old, died within minutes. He left a wife, Johanna, and 12 children under the age of 23.[3] Controversially, the coroner 'decided against an inquest on the strength of representations made to him by the military'. This appeared to most people to be an evasion of responsibility on the part of the Free State Army. However, this of course, was of little consolation to Johanna and her grieving family.[4]

Patrick Martin

Attempting to assist the Free State Army had dire consequences for one civilian. On the evening of Saturday, 16 December 1922, two armed members of the anti-Treaty IRA – natives of Kilkenny City – raided the post offices in Fiddown and nearby Piltown. They also stole a large amount of alcohol earlier the same day. Both men had previously been in the Free State Army but switched to the anti-Treaty side. It was not believed they were following any specific orders but instead were acting on their own volition. They also held up a lorry driven by Edward Meade of Fiddown. Meade was on his way to a Christmas market with a consignment of turkeys. The IRA men took two of the largest turkeys and allowed the lorry to proceed.[5] Patrick Martin, who had been socialising in a local pub after a funeral that day, began talking to the two men as he recognised them from the Free State Army – Martin himself had enlisted at one point. However, when one of the IRA men was asleep on the roadside Martin seized his revolver. In the meantime, a Lancia motor car containing a number of Free State soldiers from Clonmel was travelling towards Piltown, having received a message about the disturbances in the village. Tensions were already running high that week as the Free State Army had been left shell-shocked by the anti-Treaty IRA after the latter captured the barracks in nearby Carrick-on-Suir, Callan, Thomastown and Mullinavat. As the Free State soldiers came near the village of Piltown they saw Patrick Martin waving the revolver. Believing he was one of the reported IRA men they opened fire, hitting Martin a number of times in the chest. It was only later the soldiers realised their mistake; Martin had been waving the gun it in an effort to attract their attention. Martin died quickly, leaving behind a wife and young family. He had previously been wounded in action during the First World War. Later that evening, the Free State party fired on the two anti-Treaty IRA men, badly injuring one named 'Kelly'. The other IRA man, Michael Fitzpatrick, was arrested and imprisoned in Clonmel. It was a tragic turn of events for 28-year-old Mooncoin native Paddy Martin, in what was an ill-fated attempt to do his civic duty.[6]

Edward Burke

The Burke family of Urlingford had a bleak Christmas in 1922 following the death of their 19-year-old son, Edward. On Christmas Eve Burke had been out with his friends in the village of Johnstown, just 4 km down the road. They were celebrating the festive season when his friends got into an altercation with the new Civic Guards in the area. Fighting broke out between the two groups and the guards called the military garrison for support. The scuffle continued when the Free State soldiers arrived. Burke attempted to stop one of his friends from going into the street to engage the soldiers. Just then a shot was fired by the military which resulted in Burke being hit in the head. He was brought to Urlingford for medical help but died there three hours later. Burke came from a family of eleven. His body could not be released to his family until an inquest was heard, which could not take place until the evening of 26 December, due to the break for Christmas Day. The inquest, held in Urlingford, found that Edward Burke died as a result of 'a gunshot wound which caused laceration of the brain fired by some person or persons unknown'.[7] The Free State Army in Kilkenny let it be known to GHQ that they had no intention of punishing the soldier responsible. In a report dated 27 December 1922, the following was stated; 'Edward Burke, shot during [an] attack on Civic Guard – it is believed he was shot by a National [Free State] soldier, it is not proposed to attempt his identification.'[8]

Analysis of the Civil War in County Kilkenny

For the general public throughout County Kilkenny, the disruption caused by the Civil War was far more acute than had been the case during the War of Independence. The main reason for this was the near constant destruction of bridges and railway lines, which discommoded people over a twelve-month period. This had a knock-on effect of frustrating postal and business services. Thus, even if someone never travelled by train, or journeyed long distances, their life was still affected in some way or another. As the anti-Treaty IRA had no source of income, they were required to requisition money and supplies in the areas in which they operated. Businesses and farmers were sometimes compensated by the Free State Government, but this was a long drawn-out process.

Just like the War of Independence, it was the town of Callan and its surrounding hinterlands that saw most activity, as the anti-Treaty IRA moved up and down the Kilkenny/Tipperary border. Additionally, the south and south-east of the county experienced fighting and infrastructural attacks on a far greater scale than had been the case during the War of Independence. Besides the siege on the eve of civil war, Kilkenny City escaped relatively unscathed from the fighting, although its jail saw a huge increase in the prison population as more and more anti-Treaty IRA were captured and interned as the Civil War progressed. Similarly, there were very few ambushes or large attacks in the north of the county.

Perhaps the most glaring element of this conflict was the high number of deaths. More fatalities occurred in County Kilkenny during the civil conflict than occurred during the War of Independence. Therefore, the one year Civil War claimed more lives than the two-and-a-half-year War of Independence.

The total fatalities within County Kilkenny was twenty-six. Using the same criteria, the total number of deaths in Kilkenny during the War of Independence was twenty (this figure excludes deaths in Mullinahone, County Tipperary). It is possible that there were anti-Treaty IRA deaths that were never recorded. That is to say, there was no death certificate, no military report, no compensation claim, or no newspaper article documenting the death(s). Of the twenty-six fatalities in County Kilkenny, thirteen were anti-Treaty IRA (50 per cent), nine were Free State soldiers (35 per cent) and four were civilians (15 per cent). Although the anti-Treaty IRA were the highest grouping killed, the figures do not explain the full story. Seven of the thirteen anti-Treaty IRA deaths occurred in either Kilkenny Barracks or in the jail. This included two official executions, while the remainder died from illness or were shot by Free State wardens.[9] Hence, Free State soldiers were far more likely to be killed in clashes on the front line against the anti-Treaty IRA than the other way around. Five out of nine Free State deaths occurred in this way. Just four out of the thirteen anti-Treaty IRA deaths occurred on the front line. Of the twenty-six fatalities within County Kilkenny, fourteen were Kilkenny natives, while the remainder were from the counties of Waterford, Tipperary, Wexford, Laois, Cork and Dublin.

Aside from those who died within the boundaries of County Kilkenny, an additional fifteen Kilkenny men died serving in the Free State Army or anti-Treaty IRA in other counties. Therefore, more Kilkenny natives died outside the county than within during the conflict. Two were killed in Dublin in the first two days of the Civil War, one died in Monaghan, while the remainder were killed in other areas or outposts of the 2nd Southern Command of the Free Army – namely south Tipperary, Waterford and south Wexford. Thus, the total number of Kilkenny natives who died as a result of the Civil War – both inside and outside the county – was twenty-nine. At the time of writing, no definitive research exists about the total number of fatalities nationally during the Civil War, so a comparison with the rest of Ireland cannot be determined accurately.

Another disturbing statistic was the amount of self-inflicted or 'friendly-fire' fatalities, which amounted to nine (encompassing those who died in Kilkenny and Kilkenny natives who died outside the county in incidents of this kind). All but one of these deaths were Free State soldiers. This highlights the inexperience and lack of proper training provided within the Free State Army.

Of the Free State soldiers who lost their lives, the majority classified their occupation prior to joining the army as 'labourer'. As labouring was usually low paid, with unreliable days of employment, it is fair to assume that many of the rank-and-file joined the Free State Army for financial reasons rather than a sense of patriotic duty. Even in death, a person's class could denote how much coverage their demise merited in the local media. The Free State soldiers and civilians from more 'respectable' families usually received greater coverage after their deaths, while their funeral services were also reported. Those who were killed and from more humble backgrounds – usually farm labourers – received much less coverage in the local press.

Four of the thirteen anti-Treaty IRA fatalities (31 per cent) were attributed to Free State sentries shooting prisoners inside Kilkenny jail. Four civilians were killed during the Civil War in County Kilkenny, the same amount as the War of Independence. In contrast to the earlier conflict, no females were killed as a direct result of the violence during the Civil War, while nobody was recorded as having been executed as an informer.

Table 8. Fatalities in County Kilkenny as a direct result of the Civil War

Date of Death	Name	Age at Death	Category	Location where wounds received or place of death	Native Place	Details
28 June 1922	John Moran	23	Free State	Kilkenny Military Barracks	Moneenroe	Shot accidentally by a comrade when getting out of bed in Kilkenny Military Barracks.
20 July 1922	Michael Costello	25	Free State	Ferrybank	Dundrum, Co. Tipperary	Shot during the attack on Waterford City. Died in a temporary field hospital near Ferrybank.
30 July 1922	Samuel Oakes	21	Anti-Treaty	Kilkenny City	Waterbarrack, Kilkenny City	Shot dead by Free State soldiers during a search of Dowling's pub, Blackmill Street, Kilkenny City. He was unarmed. He was sent by his brother, Bill (who was Company Captain), to deliver ammunition to members of an ASU.

Date of Death	Name	Age at Death	Category	Location where wounds received or place of death	Native Place	Details
2 Aug. 1922	Patrick Murphy	22	Free State	Piltown	Enniscorthy, Co. Wexford	Shot dead near Piltown during an attack on an outpost of anti-Treaty IRA troops near Carrick-on-Suir.
14 Aug. 1922	Edward Maher	26	Free State	Urlingford	Gortnahoe, Co. Tipperary	Died in Urlingford Barracks having been accidently shot by one of his comrades while alighting from a car during a search of a house at nearby Baunmore.
15 Aug. 1922	John O'Keeffe	34	Civilian	Mullinavat	Waterford City	Killed during an anti-Treaty IRA ambush near Rochestown, Mullinavat, while travelling with a party of Free State soldiers.
19 Aug. 1922	John J Edwards	22	Anti-Treaty	Kilkenny Jail	Waterford City	Shot by a Free State sentry in Kilkenny Jail while he was talking to someone on the street outside the prison.

Date of Death	Name	Age at Death	Category	Location where wounds received or place of death	Native Place	Details
21 Aug. 1922	Frank Byrne	21	Anti-Treaty	Castlecomer	Crettyard, Co. Laois	Shot accidentally by a comrade who was fixing a gun in Crutt, while they were resting on a haystack.
18 Oct. 1922	Patrick Quigley	22	Free State	Kilmanagh	Liss, Tullaroan	Killed during an ambush on Free State soldiers by an anti-Treaty IRA ASU near Kilmanagh.
18 Oct. 1922	Thomas O'Dea	24	Anti-Treaty	Kilmanagh	Mitchelstown, Co. Cork	Killed during an ambush on Free State soldiers near Kilmanagh. O'Dea was reported to be manning the anti-Treaty machine gun when he was shot dead by Free State soldiers during a long-running gun battle.
29 Nov. 1922	Patrick Griffin	47	Civilian	Kilkenny City	Patrick Street, Kilkenny City	Accidentally knocked down by a Free State Crossley Tender lorry that careered down John's Street and onto the footpath.

Date of Death	Name	Age at Death	Category	Location where wounds received or place of death	Native Place	Details
2 Dec. 1922	Patrick Cormack	24	Anti-Treaty	Johnstown	Grangefertagh, Johnstown	A patrol of Free State soldiers opened fire on a group of anti-Treaty IRA running across Morrissey's field in Johnstown village. Cormack was shot in the leg and died some hours later.
16 Dec. 1922	Patrick Martin	28	Civilian	Piltown	Mooncoin	Shot by Free State soldiers who thought he was trying to fire a revolver at them. He had taken the gun from an anti-Treaty IRA man and wanted to hand it in to the authorities.
22 Dec. 1922	Fred Lidwell	22	Free State	Kilkenny Military Barracks	Dublin	Accidentally shot in the head by a Free State soldier in Kilkenny Military Barracks who was trying to clear out a crowded room.

Date of Death	Name	Age at Death	Category	Location where wounds received or place of death	Native Place	Details
24 Dec. 1922	Edward Burke	19	Civilian	Johnstown	Urlingford	Died after being shot by Free State soldiers on Christmas Eve after an altercation broke out between Burke, his friends and the Civic Guard. Free State soldiers were called, some of whom shot Burke outside a pub.
29 Dec. 1922	John Phelan	32	Anti-Treaty	Kilkenny Military Barracks	Thomastown	Arrested on 13 December 1922 for larceny and possessing firearms.
	John Murphy	22	Anti-Treaty	Kilkenny Military Barracks	Bishopslough, Bennettsbridge	Sentenced to death by a Free State military court. Execution carried out at 8.15 am on Friday, 29 December 1922, at Kilkenny Military Barracks.
27 Jan. 1923	Andrew Power	24	Anti-Treaty	Kilkenny City	Ballygunner, Co. Waterford	Arrested in Waterford in August 1922 because of anti-Treaty IRA activities. Sent to Kilkenny Jail where he contracted diphtheria. Died from the disease having been sent to Kilkenny Central Hospital.

Date of Death	Name	Age at Death	Category	Location where wounds received or place of death	Native Place	Details
2 Feb. 1923	Patrick Barcoe	18	Anti-Treaty	Paulstown	Neigham, Gowran. Also; Annalack, Goresbridge	A member of Martin Medlar's east Kilkenny ASU, Barcoe was shot dead in an altercation with Free State forces near Shankill. He was covering the retreat of his column when he was fatally wounded.
9 Mar. 1923	Gerald Comerford	23	Free State	Inistioge	Clogharinka, Ballyfoyle	Shot dead while taking part in a Free State offensive to capture an anti-Treaty IRA column.
10 Mar. 1923	Thomas Mealey	19	Anti-Treaty	Ballyragget	Coolbawn, Castlecomer	Part of an anti-Treaty IRA group who attempted to raid the home of the Buggy family. The family shot at the intruders, killing Mealey.

Date of Death	Name	Age at Death	Category	Location where wounds received or place of death	Native Place	Details
14 Mar. 1923	John Walsh	23	Anti-Treaty	Kilkenny Jail	Kilmacthoma, Co. Waterford	Died from wounds received in Kilkenny Jail after he was shot by a Free State soldier/ prison warden.
15 Mar. 1923	Michael Brown	21	Free State	Windgap	Mountrath, Co. Laois	The anti-Treaty IRA ambushed a party of Free State soldiers who were searching houses in the Windgap area. Brown was killed during an initial burst of machine-gun fire.
4 May 1923	James O'Keeffe	21	Free State	Tipperary	Mooncoin	Accidentally shot himself on 16 February 1923 when dismounting from a Lancia car. Wounds seemed to be healing but he died at Kilkenny Military Barracks two months later.

Date of Death	Name	Age at Death	Category	Location where wounds received or place of death	Native Place	Details
13 June 1923	James Morrissey	28	Anti-Treaty	Kilkenny Jail	Kilkenny City	Shot by a Free State soldier/sentry while trying to escape from Kilkenny Jail. The shooting caused much controversy as Morrissey was well known in the City, while a ceasefire was also in operation.
4 Sept. 1923	Patrick Hanlon	16	Anti-Treaty	Kilkenny Jail	Carrick-on-Suir, Co. Tipperary	Shot by a Free State soldier/sentry at Kilkenny Jail as he looked out from a window. Died the following day while in transit to a military hospital in Kildare.

Total: 26

Table 9. Fatalities of Kilkenny natives *outside* the county as a result of the Civil War

Date of Death	Name	Age at Death	Category	County where wounds received/ place of death	Native Place in Kilkenny	Details
29 June 1922	James Walsh	22	Free State	Dublin	Killaloe, Callan	Killed in Dublin during the storming of the anti-Treaty garrison lodged in the Four Courts.
01 July 1922	Daniel Brennan	18	Free State	Dublin	Kilkenny City	Shot dead when sniping from the Ballast Office towards the anti-Treaty IRA garrison on O'Connell Street in Dublin city centre.
16 Aug. 1922	Joseph Bergin	21	Free State	Tipperary	Skehana, Castlecomer	Killed on the very day of his 21st birthday in Woodroofe, near Clonmel, having been ambushed by an anti-Treaty IRA column.
21 Aug. 1922	Richard Cantwell	22	Free State	Tipperary	Clough, Castlecomer	Died after being shot in an anti-Treaty IRA ambush at Redmondstown, Co. Tipperary.

Date of Death	Name	Age at Death	Category	County where wounds received/ place of death	Native Place in Kilkenny	Details
30 Sept. 1922	William Purcell	16	Free State	Tipperary	Kellymount, Paulstown	Shot accidentally in the stomach by a comrade in Templemore Free State Barracks.
08 Oct. 1922	Thomas Brownrigg	24	Free State	Tipperary	Danganmore, Dunnamaggin	Both men died from bullet wounds received in an ambush near Woodroofe, Co. Tipperary, on 2 October 1922.
12 Oct. 1922	Patrick Hayes	20 (approx.)	Free State	Tipperary	Barrack Street, Kilkenny City	
22 Oct. 1922	James Burke	18	Free State	Tipperary	Barna, Urlingford	Accidentally shot himself while on sentry duty in the town of Cashel.
26 Oct. 1922	James Dunne	35	Free State	Waterford	Threecastles	Shot accidentally by a Free State comrade in Dungarvan Military Barracks, which was situated in the local workhouse.
10 Dec. 1922	James Gardiner	28	Free State	Tipperary	Castlecomer	Shot in the head at Westgate, Carrick-on-Suir, during an anti-Treaty takeover of the town.

Date of Death	Name	Age at Death	Category	County where wounds received/ place of death	Native Place in Kilkenny	Details
24 Mar. 1923	Edward Gorman	23	Free State	Wexford	Kilkenny City	Both men were executed in Adamstown, Co. Wexford, by the anti-Treaty IRA, after they had been abducted from a pub the previous night in nearby Palace East. Their executions were in reprisal for Free State executions in Wexford Jail.
	Patrick Horan	25	Free State	Wexford	Flag Lane, Callan	
11 Mar. 1923	Richard Duggan	18	Free State	Waterford	Scart, Mullinavat	Accidentally shot by a comrade he was in conversation with in Waterford City on 6 March 1923, passing away some days later from sepsis.
8 Apr. 1923	Thomas Davis	28	Free State	Monaghan	Low Street, Thomastown	Died in Clones, Co. Monaghan, from a suspected pneumonia infection. Prior to enlisting in the Free State Army he was employed by the Auxiliaries in Woodstock

Date of Death	Name	Age at Death	Category	County where wounds received/ place of death	Native Place in Kilkenny	Details
						House to help with their searches. For this reason he was a denied a military funeral in Thomastown.
16 Apr. 1923	Edward Somers	33	Anti-Treaty	Tipperary	Mallardstown, Callan	Captain Ned Somers was a Free State officer until he defected to the anti-Treaty side in December 1922. He was shot dead by Free State soldiers near Rosegreen, Co. Tipperary, when he attempted to escape from the ruins of a castle he was resting in, which had become surrounded.

Total: 15

Note: Regarding Civil War fatalities; the scope of the listings is all those who died as a result of the Civil War, from June 1922 to September 1923. Note some deaths mentioned in the main text are not included in the listing. For instance, although Laois native Garda Henry Phelan – the first member of An Garda Síochána to be killed in action – was based in Callan, he met his end in Co. Tipperary, thus, he is not included in the figures. Similarly, the husband of Kate McCormack (Patrick) is also not included. Although Kate was a native of Urlingford, Patrick was born in Co. Tipperary and was accidentally shot in Cashel in Tipperary in March 1923, so does not meet the criteria here. Michael Walsh (from Paulstown) who died on 29 Nov. 1923 from injuries inflicted accidentally by a comrade in Waterford City is also not included as it is outside the scope. Similarly, anti-Treaty IRA leader Jim Egan was killed in Co. Tipperary in April 1923.

CHAPTER 14

Everyday Life in County Kilkenny in Times of Trouble (1919–1923)

*There is a virgin page in the book of life before us today, and what story
1919 will see written on that page no man can in the least foretell ...
The one thing absolutely beyond doubt is that the New Year will mark
one of the most momentous ... of periods in human happenings.[1]*

– *Kilkenny Journal* Editorial January 1919

Although focus on the revolutionary era has generally centred on
the political and military spheres, to gain a more comprehensive
understanding of the period it is important to recognise the experiences of the
general population in County Kilkenny. It is difficult to believe anyone escaped
the conflict completely unscathed in some form or other. This chapter will look
at the lives of the non-combatants to attempt to understand their experience
of these defining years.

1919

During the month of the 'official' beginning of the War of Independence in
January 1919, County Kilkenny was still experiencing the euphoria of the
general election just a few weeks previously when two Sinn Féin candidates
were elected to represent the two Kilkenny constituencies. Large meetings were
held on The Parade in Kilkenny City to celebrate the victory of the candidates.[2]

The air of confidence continued into May 1919, when William T.
Cosgrave, the recently elected TD for North Kilkenny and 'true-souled
patriot',[3] received the Freedom of Kilkenny City in front of a large crowd.[4]
When four members of the Thomastown Sinn Féin club were arrested for
collecting money for the republican cause before Sunday Mass, large crowds
turned out to protest at the local RIC station. During the ensuing court case,

a baton charge was launched by the RIC against the crowds, which caused widespread anger locally.[5] The direct result of this action was an increase in support for Sinn Féin in terms of the membership in Thomastown and subscriptions to the Dáil Loan Fund.[6]

Labour strife affected many parts of Ireland during 1919 and Kilkenny was no exception, although strikes were not as pronounced as in other parts of the country.[7] The ITGWU was the largest union in the county with an estimated 4,200 members.[8] In March, the pro-labour *Kilkenny Journal* newspaper reported that the largest labour demonstration 'in the past 30 years' assembled on The Parade in the City. The protest, which included 'Corporation employees, Printers and Transport Union workers', gathered in support of the clerical workers of Mr Statham & Co motor dealers, who would not recognise the Clerical Workers Union.[9] The clerical workers in Statham's had gone on strike in solidarity with the mechanics, who were employed by the same company. The class tensions in the City surfaced again as the *Kilkenny People* published 'scab' advertisements by Statham's looking for replacement workers. The strike eventually ended in April. In May 1919, the employees of the Kilkenny Woodworkers Factory also followed suit when they went on strike, demanding higher wages.[10] Some of the criminal offences that occurred during the year were also attributed to strikes, including the burning of sixty tons of hay in Loughbrack, which was blamed on the Agricultural Labourers strike.[11]

According to the local Catholic clergy, the military were making a nuisance of themselves in an unusual way during the summer months of 1919. 'In all the city churches' attention was drawn to the 'degrading practice of mixed bathing [men and women]' in the local river, with the chief culprits being the 'contemptible snobs' of the 'Army of Occupation [British soldiers]'.[12]

The year 1919 also saw something of a transport revolution in Kilkenny when James Joseph (J.J.) Kavanagh founded one of Ireland's first private bus companies in Urlingford. He established a route by motorised 'omnibus' – meaning 'a bus for everyone' – from Urlingford to Kilkenny City, passing through the village of Freshford as well as other townlands. Prior to the bus route, locals in this area may have only made the 29-km journey from Urlingford to the City once or twice a year – with walking, cycling or pony-and-trap being the only means of transport. Now daily excursions to the City could be contemplated with relative ease. Similar services were founded in Callan (Tom Nolan's omnibus) and Castlecomer (Hoyne's).[13]

Attention of the general public also turned to matters non-political during the summer months of 1919, following the horrific death of an 11-year-old girl named Bridie O'Brien from Kilkenny City. What at first seemed like a death from natural causes was soon upgraded to a murder investigation following an autopsy which suggested she died from 'shock and injuries due to [sexual] violation'.[14] The attack on the girl had occurred in the home of a neighbour of the family, who had invited Bridie in to play. A 66-year-old male was found guilty and imprisoned for her manslaughter, with the court case making for grim headlines both locally and nationally.[15]

Highlighting the lack of up-to-date police intelligence, in September 1919 the Kilkenny RIC once again arrested those they considered to be the chief protagonists in Sinn Féin circles, namely James Nowlan, President of the GAA, and E.T. Keane, editor of the *Kilkenny People* newspaper. For the second time in two years the *Kilkenny People* was shut down, with its printing press confiscated.[16] The charges against the men were for the unauthorised possession of firearms, with both stating that they had them for legitimate purposes. Underlining their lack of militant credentials, both men recognised the court and Nowlan actually called on a British Military Corporal acquaintance as a witness.[17] The fact they recognised the court was a good result for the County Inspector who stated in November that these two men were now the 'object of public ridicule' and 'fallen angels', for going against the principles they had preached.[18] In reality Nowlan and Keane had no direct involvement in the IRA at the time.

1920

Amateur dramatics did not escape the upheaval. A production of the play *The Parnellite* by the Kilkenny City branch of the Gaelic League, scheduled for Saint Patrick's night 1920, was prohibited. The orders were signed by Major General Strickland who stated that the holding of the play would give 'rise to grave disorder'.[19] The military gained possession of the Empire Theatre before the stated time of the performance. Subsequently, a baton charge was ordered and shots were fired to disperse the crowd, resulting in a number of people being injured in the 'rush and trampled on'.[20]

A large Feis was held in St James's Park in Kilkenny City in June 1920 where the Lord Mayor of Cork, Terence MacSwiney, made a speech in front of an estimated crowd of 10,000 people. His speech revolved around the Irish language and his ambition that it would become 'the spoken language of the entire country'.[21] When he died just four months later – from one of the longest hunger strikes ever recorded at the time – there were memorial Masses held in many Kilkenny churches. The local newspapers dedicated entire front pages to his life and encased all the headings and columns in black lines to express mourning.[22] Even in the early stages of his hunger strike, Thomastown District Council suspended its monthly meeting in support of MacSwiney and passed a resolution condemning 'the barbarous treatment meted out to our distinguished fellow countryman'.[23]

The Archbishop of Adelaide, Dr Robert Spence, was presented with the Freedom of Kilkenny City in August 1920. Although from Cork, he had spent six years as Prior of the Dominican Black Abbey in the City. In a provocative acceptance speech, he declared that 'Ireland had found her soul in 1916.' In reference to the turmoil and hunger strikes that were going on at the time, he referred to Lloyd George as the 'little Welsh Prime Minister' and, using Australian slang, accused him of having 'gone completely off his nut'.[24] The Catholic Church in Australia was dominated by Irish natives and the Bishop of Perth, Patrick Clune, would go on to act as an intermediary between the Irish and British governments in late 1920.

The attitude of the local Catholic Church hierarchy in Kilkenny was very different however. In particular the views of the 85-year-old Catholic Bishop of Ossory, Rev. Abraham Brownrigg (1837–1928), who was strongly opposed to the IRA and the Sinn Féin movement in general. Bishop Brownrigg, who had been Bishop of Ossory since 1884, supported enlistment in the British Army at the beginning of the First World War,[25] and during the 1918 general election campaign he wrote an open letter to the national newspapers declaring his support for 'constitutionalism' and endorsing the Irish Parliamentary Party candidate in Kilkenny (this fervent support of the IPP by a leading clergyman was unusual during the 1918 General Election as most chose to remain neutral, in public at least).[26] In a strongly worded letter read at Masses on Christmas Day 1920, Bishop Brownrigg gave thanks for 'the forbearance under provocation which the people of this city [Kilkenny] and, indeed of the diocese generally, have shown'. He left little doubt as to his opinion of events enveloping the country; 'let us pray also for the cruel men, who direct their present regime of death and destruction on our county, asking God to open their eyes to the wrong they do our people'.[27] The 'cruel men' he referred to were of course the IRA, although it is ironic that the language he used was very similar to that used to describe the Crown Forces by the Republican side.

Similar to Ireland generally, there were many stories of the distress and damage caused by raids by the Crown Forces. One of the more unusual searches was in the largest secondary school in the county, St Kieran's College in Kilkenny City, which also functioned as a seminary. The 'sleeping rooms and private apartments' of the students and priests were 'thoroughly searched', although it was unclear what was the motivation behind the search.[28]

John O'Carroll, an engineer in Thomastown District Council, suffered an immense upheaval in December 1920, when the house he and his family were renting was 'commandeered by Major General Strickland [British Military Governor in Kilkenny] for the use of a policeman's wife'. O'Carroll was subsequently arrested for protesting against this and detained for over a month in Auxiliary headquarters. He was also used as a hostage on their patrols. O'Carroll's wife and two children, aged three and six months, had to live with her parents in another village. A year later O'Carroll was still between homes as he could not secure his previous home or afford an increase in rent.[29]

Lawless Law Enforcers: 1920–1

The arrival of Auxiliaries, Black and Tans, and soldiers from military regiments in Kilkenny during the summer of 1920 was intended to benefit the people of the county with the hope of restoring law and order. County Inspector Whyte had high hopes for the new recruits: 'An Auxiliary force of 100 men formed a post at Inistioge. It is hoped good will come from them. In any case it will give Independent and loyal people a chance of freedom.'[30]

The opposite of what CI Whyte had hoped actually occurred. In one of the earliest histories of this period, an infamous event that happened in Kilkenny was recounted. In Frank Pakenham's *Peace by Ordeal*, originally published in 1935, he stated the following: 'But they [the Auxiliaries] did not always operate in uniform, and sometimes, as when they visited Kilkenny post office, they blacked their faces and put on masks and afterwards called Heaven to witness the sneaking vileness of Sinn Féin.'[31] Pakenham was referring to an incident that occurred on 11 September 1920, when a number of Auxiliaries dressed to resemble IRA Volunteers, stole eleven bags of mail at gunpoint from the Kilkenny Post Office yard. They beat Thomas Bourke the driver of the motor car who was transporting the mail.[32] The mail was brought to Auxiliary headquarters in Woodstock, Inistioge, where an unknown quantity of money was taken from the letters.[33] The identity of the perpetrators only became public knowledge after the Commander of the Auxiliaries in Ireland, Brigadier-General Frank Crozier, reported the matter after his resignation from the force in February 1921.[34] The Auxiliaries had only arrived in County Kilkenny a few weeks before the robbery.

What was even more unusual about the incident was the fact that the main instigator was a 30-year-old army Major named Ewen Cameron Bruce. He was from Gloucestershire in England and was surreptitiously dismissed after the Kilkenny raid 'for striking a civilian'.[35] There was a strange follow-up however, which made headlines both locally and nationally. On 10 October 1920 Major Bruce, along with his 20-year-old nephew Auxiliary cadet Alan Thomas Bruce, committed another larceny. Their target on that occasion was the home of the creamery manager in the village of Kells, approximately 16 km south of Kilkenny City.[36] On their way to Kells in a rented car they collected two soldiers, Lieutenant Cooper and Sergeant Blake of the Devonshire Regiment, in Thomastown. The creamery manager, John Power, in the subsequent court case said he was awoken at 2.00 am with shouts of; 'Come down and open the door immediately. We are the Black and Tans.' When he opened the door, he was ordered to put out the lights, presumably as not to identify their faces but also to conceal Major Bruce's distinctive characteristic; a missing arm which he had lost in 1917 during the First World War. The keys of the safe were demanded and £75 was stolen.[37] After the event Bruce quickly left Ireland and returned to his home in Cheltenham. However, he was arrested there on 21 October and sent back to Waterford where he faced trial. He received a one-year prison sentence. Bruce never admitted guilt and appealed the verdict on a number of occasions. He accused creamery manager Power of embezzling money from the creamery, while he also suggested that the Auxiliaries were scapegoating him as he had information on the infamous post raid in September 1920.[38] Bruce's nephew received a three-month prison sentence, while the two soldiers who accompanied them were not charged as they did not enter the premises.[39] The Kells Creamery incident was discussed in the House of Commons, with the supposed 'cover-up' being the main talking point. Belfast IPP MP Joe Devlin challenged the Chief Secretary for Ireland, Sir Hamar Greenwood, on the matter. An intelligence officer based in Kilkenny military barracks had ordered the local press not to report on the evidence given at the initial trial. Greenwood defended the press censorship, stating it was the correct procedure at the time.[40] Interestingly, Auxiliary chief, General Crozier, later asserted that the untoward events committed by Bruce in County Kilkenny benefited the county in the long run as there was more discipline enforced on the Auxiliaries in the county than had been the case elsewhere. He stated: 'Only in Kilkenny under Captain Webb [A Coy Commander] did sanity and honour appear to hold sway … because the commander was sound and the men had been taught a lesson over Bruce and the post office robbery.'[41]

Members of the British Crown Forces were again on trial a few months later, this time as a result of a looting spree on the night of 27 February 1921. Five Black and Tans, who 'had drink taken', captured three local men at gunpoint and held them as hostages. They used the local knowledge of the men to point out certain homes on King's Street in Kilkenny City (now Kieran's Street). They subsequently went to one of the men's boarding houses and stole money from his landlady.[42]

There were problems also within the confines of their barracks. In April 1921 a Black and Tan constable who was in charge of the canteen absconded with £100, although he was arrested the following day while trying to board a ferry to Holyhead.[43]

In a separate incident in February 1921, a hostage was taken from Woodstock on a late-night patrol by Auxiliaries. They travelled around the Goresbridge area. One of the Auxiliaries, John Grant Cooney, was taunting the hostage along the journey. The hostage said the following occurred: 'we had been travelling about an hour-and-half when I was fired at, the bullet striking me in the mouth and came out over my left ear ... I do not know what happened after that'. The hostage survived his injuries. Cooney had replaced the spent cartridge with a fresh one to conceal his actions but he was reported by one of his comrades. Cooney was brought to court in May 1921 for the injuries he caused but was found not guilty.[44]

Martial Law for Kilkenny Inhabitants: 1921

If the inhabitants of Kilkenny were hoping the New Year of 1921 would bring them some respite from the fighting, they were very much mistaken. The six-month period from January 1921 to the Truce on 11 July 1921 was the most tumultuous of the War of Independence in the county. Tragedies also struck in ways unrelated to the fighting.

When martial law was announced on 30 December 1920, everyday life for the inhabitants was affected in a myriad of ways, ranging in scale from the irritating to the traumatic. Curfews were implemented in many towns and districts. Military raids became even more commonplace throughout the county. In Kilkenny City, residents were required to list the names of all inhabitants within their home on the front door,[45] while simply owning something as innocuous as a prayer book written in the Irish language could cause undesired attention.[46]

The weekly excursion to Sunday Mass could be interrupted, as occurred in Piltown, where the entire congregation 'including women', were searched upon leaving.[47] Many roads and bridges in the county became impassable due to constant trenching by the IRA to impede the progress of the Crown Forces. Law-abiding business people were caught in an unenviable position.

If they offered their services to members of the Crown Forces they received threatening letters from the local IRA and if they did not serve the Forces they were liable to unwanted attention from them.[48] In some instances, there was nothing businesses could do to protect themselves, such as a number of public houses in Kilmanagh, where Black and Tans arrived and drank 'till they were satisfied' before turning their 'attention to the tills which they emptied'.[49] The local magistrates, under the British administration, heard numerous cases and complaints relating to the behaviour of the Crown Forces. Kilkenny magistrate P.D. O'Sullivan complained to Dublin Castle about the 'behaviour of the soldiers in Kilmaganny',[50] while also criticising the 'conduct of DI White [sic] at Freshford police station'.[51]

Love Blossoms through Adversity: February 1921

In the midst of this troubled period, it was still possible for the sparks of romance to be ignited. In early January 1921, two members of the East Waterford IRA Brigade were badly wounded in a disastrous ambush near Tramore. The wounded men, Mick Wyley and Nicholas Whittle, travelled between safe houses, but by February it was deemed too unsafe to keep them in County Waterford. Wyley had worked in Carrigeen Creamery near Mooncoin and had many IRA contacts in the area. It was decided to smuggle the two injured IRA men across the River Suir by cot – a fishing boat particular to that area of Ireland – under the cover of darkness to the parish of Mooncoin in County Kilkenny, which was on the other side of the river. Thomas Brennan, a lieutenant in the Waterford IRA, accompanied them on their journey. The recuperating IRA men were accommodated at Portnascully Mills at the home of Mary Walsh and her son, Jack 'na Coille', who was O/C of the 9th Kilkenny Battalion. Jack's sister Lena took extended 'sick leave' from her job as a nurse in the South Infirmary in Cork to care for the two patients. Brennan stayed a number of days in the mill to allow his comrades settle in. During this time, he struck up a friendship with Lena. Over the coming months he made frequent visits to the mill, ostensibly to check on the patients, but also to see Lena. Their friendship blossomed into romance and they were married after the troubles – revealing that there were times of happiness in the midst of adversity.[52]

A Family Tragedy: March 1921

The afternoon of Good Friday, 25 March 1921, was a catastrophic day for the Fahy family – consisting of married couple John and Bridget and their

7-year-old daughter Bridie – who resided at Upper Patrick Street in Kilkenny City. At around 2.00 pm an explosion was heard from inside the Fahy household. A neighbour, Michael Foley, ran across the street and entered the smoke-filled house. He found 38-year-old Bridget Fahy lying in the hallway. He then found her daughter Bridie lying on the floor in the kitchen. He carried both outside to the street. He stated in the inquiry held afterwards that; 'in my opinion the child was then [already] dead'. Another neighbour, Margaret Shiels, bandaged a large wound on Bridget Fahy's head, but she too succumbed to her injuries the following day. The husband and father of the deceased, John Fahy, had only stepped outside his home a few minutes earlier in order to get 'a £1 note changed at Kenny's public house' with the aim of getting a present for Bridie, whose birthday was the previous day.[53] As the public house did not have sufficient change he went to Cleere's shop from where he heard the explosion. He ran home and called a doctor, but it was to no avail.[54]

It took the RIC a number of hours to arrive. Owing to the troubled times, the RIC would usually only venture outdoors when a large contingent of men was available. Similarly, it is understandable that many would assume that any explosion was related in some way to the military conflict. When the RIC investigated the house they 'found nothing at all to indicate the cause of the explosion'. However, 'all the bricks in the fireplace had been blown out' while the kettle was also broken into a number of pieces. It later became apparent that 'the coal dust, or some foreign matter in the coal' had caused the explosion. John Fahy stated he bought the coal locally at 'Murphys' and that it was imported 'English coal', which was sometimes cheaper to purchase because of the lower quality. It was discovered that the force of the explosion had caused the metal implements surrounding the fireplace to shatter into pieces much like shrapnel. A piece of the kettle had pierced the heart of young Bridie, killing her almost instantly. Her mother, Bridget, similarly succumbed to bleeding from her injuries caused by pieces of metal propelled by the explosion.[55] Discovering the cause of the tragedy was of little consolation to John Fahy, who interred his wife and child together in St Patrick's cemetery on Easter Sunday.

Sport, Farming and Entertainment Discommoded: Spring 1921

The playing of GAA matches was severely curtailed during the period. All matches were banned under martial law between January and July 1921. However, disruption occurred over a number of years due to the political climate. The significant consequence was that the club hurling and football championships were not completed between 1920 and 1922.[56]

In April 1921, Glenmore, Glenpipe and Mullinavat creameries, along with satellite creameries, were compulsorily closed down by the RIC. County Inspector Whyte believed – mistakenly – that the closing of the creameries would have an 'excellent effect' as it would 'affect very much the farmers who are the backbone of the IRA'.[57] This was not an accurate reflection of the situation. As historian Peter Hart noted in his study of IRA members, 'it was farmers, and large farmers in particular, who held aloof from the struggle or at best were only fair-weather republicans'.[58] In Kilkenny, a substantial number of middling to small farmers sons' were members of the IRA. However, the strong farmers were, for the most part, not active IRA members.[59] The decision to close the creameries had important implications for the primarily agricultural economy of the southeast area of the county. The Chief Secretary, Sir Hamar Greenwood, had to defend the closures in the House of Commons. He highlighted his ignorance of the situation by comparing the area to Bansha in County Tipperary, around 80 km away, where a constable had been killed 'prior to the closing of the creamery'.[60] It is difficult to understand the logic behind the closures in this specific area as no ambushes or fatalities had taken place up to that point there. The same action was taken with Tullaroan and Kilmanagh creameries following the execution of two informers by the IRA in that area in May 1921.[61] In any case, the creamery closures would have little effect on the activities of the IRA battalions, and no direct effect on the Kilkenny ASUs who were active at the time. In hindsight, it was the lesser of two evils, as many creameries in other parts of Ireland were burned down by Crown Forces. Luckily for local farmers, none of Kilkenny's thirty-six creameries suffered the same fate.

In another event in April 1921, a community hall in Kilkenny City, which was owned by the Catholic Diocese of Ossory, was destroyed under orders of the military. The hall had been used as the principal position for a sniping attack by the IRA on a nearby RIC barracks and this was the pretext given for its destruction.[62]

A Motor Accident: June 1921

On 13 June 1921, Thomas Meade, aged 56 from Upper Patrick Street in Kilkenny City, died in a fairly rare occurrence for the time. He received fatal injuries in a motor car incident during a period when horses and bicycles were still by far the most common type of transport. He was crossing the main junction at the end of The Parade in Kilkenny City and did not see or hear the oncoming Ford motor vehicle proceeding from the direction of the Clubhouse Hotel. The car was driven by Pat McDonnell, who had been hired to drive Italian tourist and businessman, Luigi Carbella, who was from Milan. Carbella had travelled to Kilkenny with the hope of purchasing some hunting hounds. Thomas Meade stepped out from behind a number of jarvey cars situated in front of the Bank of Ireland at the corner of The Parade/Patrick Street junction and was knocked down. The driver and his passenger placed Meade into the motor car and drove him to the local hospital.[63] However, Meade unfortunately died two hours later as a result of a fractured skull. He was originally from Galway and left a widow, a daughter aged 24, a son aged 21, and two stepdaughters.[64] The inquiry held the following day found that 'Patrick McDonnell was not to blame for the accident; but that Mr Thomas Mead[e] lost his head when shouted at, and made the accident unavoidable.'[65] There was also a recommendation that 'the present stand for jarvey [taxi] cars, namely in front of the Bank of Ireland, is dangerous for traffic' and that 'another place be found for them to stand'.[66]

Violence against Women during the Revolutionary Years

No war has taken place without violence being wrought on females. However, this aspect of a conflict is often the least likely to be studied, as evidence is usually quite rare, while it is often regarded as a taboo subject. This also applied to the Irish revolutionary era. Historian Marie Coleman has grouped violence experienced by women during the revolutionary years into four distinct categories – physical, psychological, gendered and sexual.[67]

Regarding physical assaults, the most obvious example was the previously mentioned death of 36-year-old Margaret Ryan, who was fatally wounded by a member of the Crown Forces in a drive-by shooting as an RIC funeral passed her business premises in Callan. Ryan was one of the rare female fatalities of political violence in Ireland.

In June 1921, the 3rd Battalion IRA in Castlecomer discussed the possibility of executing Florrie Dreaper who informed on the ill-fated Coolbawn ambush which lead to the deaths of two IRA members, but the majority of the IRA officers were not in favour of executing her, burning down her house instead in reprisal.

Although not prevalent, the most reported type of violence used against women in Kilkenny was forced haircutting, also known as 'hair-shorning'. It was a punishment used by the IRA and the Crown Forces, both of which thought it a lenient penalty for a 'crime'. The principal targets of Crown Force attacks were women who aided and abetted the IRA in its activities – usually members of Cumann na mBan. Similarly, women who consorted with members of the British Military often came to the attention of the IRA. This type of assault is classified as gendered and physical, as it only applied to women, while there was the physical act of holding a women down and cutting her hair. In consequence, women often suffered psychologically as they were now 'marked' and felt like pariahs in their local communities with their short hair. Other types of psychological punishment included boycotting. In Mullinavat, wives of the RIC constables in the village were subjected to a 'vigorous boycott'. They were shunned by their local community which impacted their day-to-day tasks, such as buying food. Those in the village who did not participate in the boycott were also targeted. Property and belongings of William Kelly were maliciously destroyed after he gave the Sergeant's wife a lift to Kilmacow in his pony-and-trap.[68]

After the Truce was declared, those who had helped the Crown Forces were still shunned. Bridie Morris, from Thomastown, was employed by the Auxiliaries in Woodstock as a female searcher. She journeyed with the Auxiliaries on their excursions throughout County Kilkenny, along with the neighbouring counties of Wexford and Waterford. She usually travelled by private motor car driven by an ununiformed officer. Some months after the Truce was declared, she lost her job in Woodstock as her services were no longer required. She was warned by the IRA in Thomastown to leave the area within twenty-four hours or face the consequences. Morris heeded the warning and departed for England.[69]

Women whose hair was cut often received very little sympathy. John Curran, a miner from Castlecomer, brought a case to a Kilkenny court requesting compensation for the forced haircutting of his daughter, Mary, and his niece, Julia Tobin, on 25 May 1921. The girls were accused by the local IRA of 'keeping company with Black and Tans'. On the night in question, at around 11.00 pm, 19-year-old Mary was sitting at the fireplace of her home with her two brothers and sister when a knock was heard at their door. There were twelve armed men outside who told Mary's parents they 'wanted her for a moment'. They took her down the road where she was joined by her cousin Julia, who had been required to get out of bed to go with the men. Both women were then blindfolded and brought 'a considerable distance' through fields. At a location that was unknown to them, they were informed of the charge and the penalty. Both women rejected the accusation. Mary stated that 'the Black and Tans used to go to the mines with explosives and some of them spoke [to her]' but that she 'never kept company with any of them'. However, the women had already been found guilty and their hair was cut. Both women were brought back to their homes at around 1.00 am.

If the ordeal of having their hair forcibly cut was not traumatic enough, the experience of the courtroom was certainly not going to lessen their anxiety. The interactions between the judge, barrister and victims were an example of the prevailing opinions and views about women in Ireland at the time. Even the journalist who reported on the trial – which was held five months after the event – felt obliged to define how each of the women looked, at one stage describing Julia Tobin as; 'an attractive looking girl of 20 years'. The following were some of the other exchanges:

> Judge: What sort of a head of hair had you got?
> Barrister Mooney: Was it to your shoulders or to your waist?
> Mary Curran: It was to my waist.
> Judge: Is it 'bobbed' now? Let us see it [at this point Mary removed her hat].
> Barrister Mooney: Is it [your hair] not as nice now as it was before?
> Julia Tobin: No
> Barrister Mooney: You would prefer it long?
> Julia Tobin: I would of course
> Judge: A good many prefer it 'bobbed' (laughter)
> Barrister Mooney: That is the New York fashion, but New York is not Castlecomer (laughter)[70]

Although the women were reported to have taken the questions in good humour, they were most likely not as calm on the night of the haircutting. The judge said that he did not regard the episode as humorous and granted each of the women £25 in compensation.

In terms of sexual violence, no evidence exists of it being used as a weapon by combatants during the revolutionary era in Kilkenny. The only documented mention of sexual violence in the BMH Witness Statements was in relation to a non-political assault, in which a man was charged with an 'attack on a girl'.[71] Marie Coleman's conclusion regarding the War of Independence was that 'sexual violence took place but was rare' and she also contends that violence towards women 'was limited in nature and scope, especially by contemporary European standards'.[72] It is of course correct to mention, that even if women were sexually attacked, the vast majority would never report it due to the associated social stigma. Thus, whether rare or more common, it is unlikely the true scale of sexual attacks will ever be fully revealed.

The Truce (July 1921–June 1922)

The establishment of the Truce in July 1921 came as a relief to the general populace who had been starved of entertainment, fairs and sporting events during the troubled period – especially since the imposition of martial law seven months earlier. Although the local county club championships did not go ahead owing to the backlog, the Kilkenny football and hurling county teams competed in their respective championships. The Kilkenny senior hurling team reached the Leinster Final on 11 September 1921, held in Croke Park. Although they were beaten by Dublin, the Kilkenny team and officials had the pleasure of meeting the famed War of Independence leader Michael Collins, who also threw in the sliotar to start the match.[73]

The Kilkenny Agriculture Show which took place on 22 September 1921 was the largest on record, in terms of both the number of entries to the show and the attendance. The event was held in St James's Park just outside Kilkenny City, with local Sinn Féin TD, W.T. Cosgrave, officially opening the event.[74]

A large Feis was organised for Kilkenny City on Sunday, 9 October 1921, with special trains provided to transport the large crowds from Dublin, Carlow and Waterford. The star attraction – as advertised throughout the local and national newspapers – was that Michael Collins, the War of Independence leader regarded by many as having 'won the war', had accepted an invitation to open the event.[75] The appearance of Collins at a public event just a few months previously would have been unimaginable. He had been an enigma. The chance to see what he looked like – and how he sounded – was a draw for many. Sadly, the crowds were to be disappointed. It is unclear if, or when, Collins cancelled his appearance. He did have some very good reasons not to show up. The day before he was due to appear at the Kilkenny Feis, he became engaged to Kitty Kiernan, with some celebrating doubtlessly ensuing. Just three days later he was due at 10 Downing Street to begin the Treaty negotiations.[76] He left for London on the day he was due to appear at the Kilkenny Feis.

The reprieve in the political hostilities was of little consolation to 30-year-old Bridget Smitheram (née Guilfoyle), who had already suffered great tragedy in her life. In April 1917, her husband William was killed in action during the First World War. She suffered yet more heartbreak in October 1921 when their 7-year-old son, Frederick Smitheram, was killed when playing with his friends on the Fair Green in Kilkenny City. Frederick had been swinging on 'heavy iron railings' surrounding a cattle weighing machine when a portion of the railing came loose and pinned him to the ground causing him to become unconscious, before he sadly passed away. Subsequently, Bridget tried to claim compensation from the Corporation for the death of her son but her claim was rejected as they indicated that the fault of the accident did not lie with them.[77]

The Truce allowed families to publicly remember the dead without fear of interference. On the one-year anniversary of the Friary Street ambush, a Mass was held for the repose of the souls of IRA members Thomas Hennessy and Michael Dermody who died in the fracas. The Mass was held in the Capuchin Friary, just a few metres from where the men were shot. The civilian victim, Thomas Dollard, was not mentioned. This was not unusual for the time as combatants were usually remembered separately, and more [publicly], than civilian casualties. Some of Hennessy and Dermody's former comrades, now in possession of the military barracks in Kilkenny, marched to the church service to honour the two men.[78] In a similar event, over 2,000 people attended a memorial Mass in Dunnamaggin to mark the one-year anniversary of the death of Patrick Walsh, 'who died so that Ireland might live'. Over 600 IRA men mustered in nearby Baurscoob and marched to the graveyard. After saying the rosary and prayers, three volleys of shots were fired over his grave. It was a far cry from the previous year when vast numbers of Crown Forces had been present at the funeral.[79] The dead of the recent War of Independence quickly became revered, with their graves becoming makeshift shrines. One correspondent to a local newspaper explained how he travelled around Kilkenny visiting the different graveyards to pay his respects to recently deceased 'brave sons of Erin'. He was very impressed with the way Nicholas Mullins's grave was kept in Thomastown, but was critical that the final resting place of Seán Hartley in Glenmore was not given equal treatment.[80]

Great excitement swept the county on the evening of Saturday, 25 March 1922, when it was learned that Michael Collins would be travelling through the county by train on his way to Waterford City for a pro-Treaty rally. Locals lined the railway route throughout the countryside, with large crowds congregating in Kilkenny and Thomastown stations to cheer on the famous visitor as he passed through. In an occurrence that was surely more than coincidental, the signalling system between Ballyhale and Mullinavat stations was cut. The driver had to stop the train in Ballyhale and wait for over an hour until the signal line was fixed. This gave the locals an opportunity to get a closer view of Collins and shake his hand through the window of the saloon carriage.[81]

The More Things Change, the More they Stay the Same

Although Ireland was experiencing sweeping changes relating to its civic and political governance, some deeply ingrained moral attitudes showed no signs of altering. The country remained a very hostile place for unmarried mothers and their children. As single pregnant women often found themselves ostracised by their families and communities, they usually had no alternative in Kilkenny but to seek shelter in the local union workhouse hospital, or 'County Home' as they became known at this time. These were multifunctional healthcare providers that were financed through local rates. For this reason, Kilkenny County Council had oversight of the management of these hospitals. In May 1922, after an unmarried woman from the Freshford district gave birth to an 'illegitimate child' in the County Home, it was decided by the County Council to establish a committee 'to inquire into this and other cases that may arise'. Local Councillor and Farmers' Party representative, Denis J. Gorey, said the Council 'should lose no time in deciding on the most effective means to put down this evil [illegitimate children]'.[82] Gorey was far from the only person in Kilkenny to hold these opinions at this time. There existed a view, held by many, that ratepayers money should not be used to pay for 'fallen women' who had become pregnant. It was agreed by all in attendance at the Council meeting – including the chairman Mayor Peter DeLoughry – to establish a committee to deal with the issue of illegitimate children in the county.

There was a similar but sad event in Thomastown the following month. An unmarried young 'servant girl' residing at the home of her employer, Joseph O'Keeffe, in the townland of Columbkille, was charged with the alleged concealment of a birth. She was unaware she was pregnant and gave birth in her bedroom to a baby boy, who passed away soon after being born. The day in question, 11 June 1922, was 'pattern Sunday' which was a religious celebration locally for the feast day of Saint Columbkille. The young women wrapped the remains of the baby in a piece of cloth and put it in a soapbox. She buried the box in the old graveyard in Columbkille. Later that afternoon, at the pattern day ceremonies in the graveyard, she told a friend about what had happened and where the box was buried. Stories began circulating around the parish and two weeks afterwards the body of the infant was discovered by a member of Thomastown IRA who was investigating the rumours. The mother of the deceased baby was arrested on charges of the concealment of a birth and the secret disposal of a body. Two doctors carried out a post-mortem at Thomastown Workhouse, but their findings were conflicting. Dr O'Connor found that 'the baby was dead when born' but Dr Mitchell believed 'the baby was born alive or partially alive'. The young girl was later reprieved however, as the coroner was 'unable to determine whether the child had been born alive' due to 'the absence of skilled attention at birth'.[83]

In neither of these two cases was the other party mentioned publicly – that is to say the fathers of the children. The 'blame' appears to have fallen solely on the shoulders of the women.

Civil War: A Return to Turmoil (June 1922– May 1923)

On the eve of the outbreak of Civil War, 26 June 1922, Thomas Tyrrell, a farmer from Cloughpook, Muckalee, met a sad end. He had been suffering from mental health issues, which had resulted in him causing some trouble in the district. The previous day he had attacked some locals by throwing stones at them. As a result of this, his house was surrounded by the Civic Guard who were attempting to arrest him as he was deemed to be 'a lunatic'. Upon seeing the police, Tyrrell charged from his house 'with a stick in his hand' and ignored calls to halt. A shot was fired by one of the policemen hitting Tyrrell in the chest. He died shortly afterwards. The inquest returned the verdict that Tyrrell died 'as a result of a bullet wound accidently received' and that 'there were no persons to blame for the occurrence'.[84]

During the summer of 1922, although the country was in the grips of Civil War, many in Kilkenny were more engrossed in the sensationalist divorce trial of a local couple than anything on the political scene. Evadne Bell, of Kilcreene House on the outskirts of Kilkenny City, sought to divorce her husband of over twelve years, Isaac Bell, who was well known locally as the Master of the Kilkenny foxhounds. Evadne – who was an All-Ireland winning croquet player – accused her husband of 'alleged misconduct with a person unknown'. Her husband had originally asked for a divorce the previous August as he wanted to marry someone else but Evadne rejected the idea as she did not want to 'break up their home', which included their 8-year-old daughter Diana Maud. In February 1922, a court ordered the 'restitution of conjugal rights' which 'had not been complied with' on Isaac's part. Eventually, Evadne petitioned for divorce and at the subsequent trial, two employees of a London hotel gave evidence stating that Isaac had stayed in the hotel with 'a lady who was not his wife'. In July 1922, the divorce was granted, with 42-year-old Isaac found guilty of alleged misconduct. Evadne – who was aged 37 at the time of the divorce – said they had lived 'a quiet life' but her husband 'was a difficult man to manage, and she was never entirely happy'.[85]

At the beginning of the Civil War, the Bank of Ireland in Graiguenamanagh was raided by people claiming to be members of the anti-Treaty IRA. They stole over £3,700 in notes. However, £3,043 of this was cancelled tender. Some months later, Catherine Murphy of Mary Street in New Ross, County

Wexford, was arrested having attempted to tender £100 of the cancelled cash in the National Bank on College Green in Dublin. During a search at the Murphy's house in New Ross, it was discovered that some of the cash stolen in Graiguenamanagh was 'undergoing a chemical process' in an attempt to remove the 'cancelled' stamp from the notes. Her husband, Patrick, who was a local publican, had fled but was eventually caught in December 1922. Murphy said he was instructed to send his wife to Dublin by members of the anti-Treaty IRA in an attempt to lodge the cancelled tender in the bank. Catherine Murphy, who had been imprisoned in Mountjoy for a number of weeks, was released on bail as she had 'a number of small children' including a recently born baby.[86]

The tumultuous summer of 1922, which saw commencement of civil strife, was even more tragic for the Walsh family of Smithstown, near Thomastown. Their 2-year-old child had a horrendous death when he fell into a pot of boiling water. This type of incident was sadly all too common throughout Ireland, as open fires, with large cooking pots, were a necessity.[87]

Possibly the only people in Kilkenny that were happy about the outbreak of the Civil War were the students of St Kieran's College. As there had been so much upheaval in Kilkenny and the surrounding counties over the summer months of 1922 – and the fact that many students travelled long distances to board at the school – the college authorities decided at the last minute to extend the summer holidays by nearly two weeks. Hence, the school did not reopen until Tuesday, 12 September 1922. For these students, every cloud certainly had a silver lining.[88]

A Close Call, the Near Loss of an Iconic Artist: September 1922

The events of the Civil War in Kilkenny nearly cost the Irish art world one of its greatest exponents. A young boy living in Callan, Tony O'Malley (1913–2003), who would later achieve renown as an artist of note, came close to ending his life as a 9-year-old boy during the period. The accident was as a direct result of the 'Big Bridge' in Callan having been blown up by retreating anti-Treaty IRA in July 1922. The bridge had not been fixed by September as O'Malley returned to school, although makeshift planks had been placed across the badly damaged structure to allow people to cross – if they were brave enough to do so. O'Malley was told by his mother under no circumstances was he to attempt to cross the Big Bridge on his way to school. Instead he was to use the small crossing at the Friary, which the friars had permitted the general public to use. Of course, like most young boys, O'Malley ignored his mother's advice as the thrill of crossing the planks with his schoolmates seemed more appealing. In later life he described the episode himself:

> Myself and three or four others, nothing would do us but to go across the planks. I slipped in the middle of the bloody planks, fell into the river and broke my arm. An old man on the bridge smoking a pipe came in and rescued me. He took me up and pulled me out and we all went to school together. This will tell you what the terror of authority was at the time. I was drenched, with my arm limp [broke], and I stood in the schoolroom above and it had to be explained to the Christian Brother what had happened to me … I was taken up to Dr Phelan and he bandaged me up and sent me home. I had to go back by the Friary. Then there was great wailing from my mother about doing the wrong thing and going across on the plank – recriminations and character assaults.[89]

Everyday Life Affected in Numerous Ways: September–December 1922

The hurling and gaelic football championships – both at local and inter-county levels – continued to be delayed because of the Civil War. The friendly games that did take place were played with much difficultly. A motor car containing 'members of [the] Kilkenny County Hurling Team' was pursued by a large number of Free State soldiers travelling on lorries from Urlingford. The military had presumed the men were a party of the anti-Treaty IRA. The hurlers were eventually allowed to continue on their journey.[90] Driving motor cars during the Civil War was a risky business. Firstly, the roads were often blocked or trenched, while bridges were regularly destroyed. In addition, from the anti-Treaty point of view, the sound of an engine usually meant Free State soldiers were nearby. Likewise, young men travelling by motor-car rang alarm bells for the Free State soldiers. Those civilians who owned cars were required to regularly renew their permit. Driving long journeys required an additional permit from the Free State authorities.

Another casualty of the tumult was the Piltown Agricultural Show, known colloquially at the time as 'the Piltown Show'. It was due to be held on Thursday, 21 September 1922, but had to be cancelled for one of the only times in its near 100-year history owing to the 'disturbed conditions prevailing' in the country.[91]

Although the country was in the throes of Civil War, Kilkenny City Corporation continued to meet regularly to carry out its usual business. In a special meeting of the Corporation held in November 1922 – during the thick of civil war – the council approved one of its most ambitious plans yet – an electric lighting scheme for Kilkenny City. The council believed Kilkenny was lagging behind similar sized towns in the country and so approved the project for 'the public lighting of the city by electricity'. Prior to this, the majority of the City would have been in darkness at night – with the exception of some gas lamps on the main thoroughfares, while some private businesses often illuminated the area in front of their shops. The electricity was to be generated using water power, with a hydro station at Greensbridge.[92]

Although families and neighbours were often divided politically, human decency was still evident during the Civil War. The home of anti-Treaty IRA Captain Patrick Walsh in Clogga, Mooncoin was constantly raided by Free State soldiers, and at one stage it was happening twice weekly. Walsh was therefore obliged to go on the run. However, in his absence, the Doherty family who lived next door and who were 'ardent Free Staters', helped Pat's new wife and elderly father with the farm.[93] In another occurrence, Peter DeLoughry, the Mayor of Kilkenny and Free State Senator, wrote a letter to a judge pleading for clemency for Martin Medlar from Paulstown, who was facing a possible death sentence for his anti-Treaty IRA activities.[94]

The *Kilkenny People* was worried about the health of women during this time, and it was not in relation to the continuing Civil War. The newspaper printed advice from doctors in England who decried the 'enormous increase of cigarette smoking among women'. It went on to say that smoking amongst the female population: 'is in many instances, passing beyond a pleasure and becoming a vice. The absorption of nicotine produces a condition of nervous distress, and women's delicate nervous organism was certainly never intended to endure large doses of this poison.'[95]

The Strikes Return, and an Entrepreneurial Enterprise: January–February 1923

At the beginning of the New Year in January 1923, there was an unwelcome strike in Kilkenny. The newspaper printers in the three printing offices – *Kilkenny People, Kilkenny Moderator* and the *Kilkenny Journal* – went on strike as their weekly wages had been cut by five shillings. The printing process was quite a skilful practice at the time, especially amongst typesetters, who had to place the individual metal type letters in columns with the words reading backwards. When printed, the sentences would read the usual left to right. The *Kilkenny People* left no ambiguity as to who they believed was to blame for the ever-increasing cost of producing newspapers; 'the outrageously high price charged for gas in Kilkenny by the so-called Kilkenny Gas Company, which, like the Holy Roman Empire, that was said to be neither holy, roman, nor an Empire – is neither Kilkenny, Gas, nor a Company'. It was 'the first time in over 100 years' that no newspaper was published in County Kilkenny.[96] The strike continued until the end of February 1923. To some, it was likely to have been a reprieve from the ever-constant gloomy news.

The newly formed Civic Guard put the kibosh on one Urlingford farmer's fledgling enterprise in February 1923. When the police entered the property of 54-year-old William Paddle, a farmer from The Islands in Urlingford, they found him in the process of 'attending to a [distillery] still which was in full working order'. They also found a petrol tin full of 'mountain dew'; which was the colloquial name for poitín. All the illicit alcohol was seized by the Civic Guard. In the subsequent court case in Johnstown, Paddle admitted to the offence but said he 'had got nothing for his barley that year' and that he 'thought it was no harm'. The judge fined him £100, but reduced it to £10 because of his hardened circumstances.[97]

More Haircutting, and the GAA Ban: March–April 1923

Women who 'stepped out' with the 'wrong' men were still liable to have their hair forcibly cut. Although hair-shorning was most associated with the combatants of the War of Independence, it was still in existence during the Civil War. Armed men took away a 'young girl named Kirwan' from her home in Jerpoint, near Thomastown, early on a Monday morning, 19 March 1923. They brought her 'four miles outside the town and "bobbed" her hair'. The party of – presumably – anti-Treaty IRA men told her it 'was done as punishment for her association with a member of the National [Free State] army'.[98] It is more difficult to ascertain if anti-Treaty women in Kilkenny suffered the same fate at the hands of the Free State Army – as was reported nationally – as the local media were all pro-Treaty, and were therefore much less likely to report such events.

In April 1923, as the Civil War was coming to its bitter conclusion, the GAA held their annual congress in Dublin. The most notable matter discussed at the conference was a motion by the Cork County Board to lift the ban that prohibited soccer and rugby players from being GAA members. The removal of the ban was supported by GAA President Dan McCarthy, who had replaced James Nowlan from Kilkenny who retired two years earlier. However, in an illustration of how sport and politics inevitably mix, General Eoin O'Duffy of the Free State Army strongly voiced his opinion against the lifting of the ban. He was acting in his capacity as secretary of the Ulster GAA Council, but emphasised how the Free State Army and the Civic Guard had 'unanimously decided that they would not play rugby or soccer and they did not want the rule changed'. He declared that the removal of the ban would be 'an outrage on the living and dead'. The motion was heavily defeated by fifty votes against, to twelve in favour, while 'the result was received with applause'.[99] In welcome news, the Kilkenny senior hurlers went on to win the 1922 Championship final by defeating Tipperary. The match was held in September 1923, just four months after the official ending of the Civil War. Almost half a century would pass until Kilkenny next beat their near neighbours in a championship final.

Non-Political Tragedy in South Kilkenny: April 1923

A harrowing event occurred in Mullinavat in April 1923. William Holden, who was one-and-a-half years old, died as a result of burns he received in the family home in Rochestown, Mullinavat. On the evening of Saturday 21 April, his mother, Mary Holden, had to go on an errand to get materials for a Confirmation outfit for her eldest son. She left William and two other siblings in the family home in the care of their older brother, Patrick, aged eight. Mary's husband, John, was still at his employment at a nearby farm. When Mary returned she discovered that William had been badly burnt. He passed away two days later as a result of his injuries. Patrick Holden told his mother that their neighbour, 64-year-old Patrick Aylward, had come into the house, lifted Willie from his bed and put him on the fire grate over the open fire. Aylward was described as 'returned American', having lived nearly forty years in the United States. Since his return he had been in dispute with the Holden family. Aylward said the quarrel had started as a result of some of the Holden children chasing his sow, while he also believed they dirtied his spring well. The morning of the incident he also became angry about their goats entering his yard.

At the inquest there was some mild (and insensitive) humour between the coroner and the jury as to whether they should take the usual oath, which was sworn in 'the name of his majesty the King', or replace it with 'Saorstát Éireann'. The latter option was eventually agreed, as they 'had that [other] gentleman long enough'. Aylward strongly refuted all allegations against him. He went on to state; 'there is no man in his senses who would take a child like that and put it in the fire. There is no man would do it'. There was an attempt to swear in 8-year-old Patrick Holden but as he did not attend school he could not read the oath. The coroner allowed his evidence to be heard unsworn. Patrick Holden repeated his version of what happened. After all evidence had been heard, the jury returned an open verdict stating that the child died of 'shock and toxaemia' as a result of burns, 'but that there was no sufficient evidence to show how the child came to get into the fire'.[100]

That was not the end of the story however. A few weeks later, Patrick Aylward was arrested on a charge of murder. In the subsequent court case in Dublin, 8-year-old Patrick Holden, and his 5-year-old brother Michael, both testified against Aylward. Patrick stated:

> Paddy Aylward came and knocked [on the door] … I opened it and he came in and said 'what do you mean letting the goats in the haggard'. He then broke a mug … He fell up along the bed and took the child and put it across the fire … I tried to take my brother Willie off the fire … he [Aylward] would not let me.

Five-year-old Michael Holden was the last witness called. He said that he saw Patrick Aylward burning William on the fire. Michael also said; 'Paddy tried to take the child off the fire but Pat Aylward rose a stick at him.' He also heard Aylward say; 'Don't let them goats into my haggard anymore.'[101] Another medical witness described Patrick Aylward as 'mentally abnormal'. The jury returned a verdict of guilty and Patrick Aylward was sentenced to death by hanging. However, his sentence was later commuted to penal servitude for life.[102]

Aylward was to have further good fortune. In 1932, the country was gripped by scenes of unparalleled religious fervour on account of the Eucharistic Congress being held in Dublin that year. Clemency and forgiveness were the order of the day. Patrick Aylward was one of a batch of prisoners who were released on compassionate grounds. He returned to his home in Rochestown, Mullinavat, where he passed away of a stroke in 1935, aged 76 years.[103]

Family Sufferings in Revolutionary-Era Kilkenny

The suffering and anxiety of the parents of Cumann na mBan and IRA Volunteers through the revolutionary years is often overlooked. They endured physical punishment, such as the father and brother of Hugginstown IRA member Ned Halloran, who were beaten and shot by Crown Forces.[104]

People also suffered psychologically, as in many cases they had very little knowledge of their sons' and daughters' activities and often could not understand their reasons for participating in such dangerous work. In turn, they did not know on any given day if their children were going to return home safely or not. On the morning of the funeral of IRA volunteer Nicholas Mullins in Thomastown, his mother, Anne is quoted as saying that she would 'sacrifice three more of her sons, if necessary, for the sake of Ireland's freedom'.[105] There were undoubtedly other parents who were not as resolute and tough as Anne in the face of such unbearable tragedy.

Ellen Cassin, the mother of an IRA member from Glenmore, eloquently and simply describes the worry and anxiety she experienced during this period. It perhaps best illustrates, in an unassuming way, the anguish endured by so many Kilkenny families:

> I was always worrying about Jimmy – as I was always afraid that these activities would lead to some trouble. The real trouble did not come until the Black and Tans came … During that bad time there were days and nights when I envied the cows and horses and chickens and other animals that have none of the worries that were a burden to myself.[106]

CHAPTER 15

Conclusion: County Kilkenny Was Not So Slack

'... in those days, every night was Cumann na mBan'

– Maisie O'Kelly (née Stallard),
Kilkenny City Cumann na mBan

To return to the initial question posed: 'was Kilkenny slack' when it came to commitment to the military campaign during the War of Independence? The answer is almost certainly no. Neither was it on a par with the likes of Tipperary or Cork in terms of its contribution to the political and military conflicts, but this was not for the want of trying. In terms of the Civil War, the charge of slackness can surely not be levelled against the Free State forces and the anti-Treaty IRA in Kilkenny. Even prior to the official commencement of hostilities the county saw fighting. During the conflict both Free State and anti-Treaty IRA soldiers displayed many acts of courage, commitment and selflessness.

In the years after the Civil War, some of those who fought with the anti-Treaty IRA felt the need in later life to explain their actions. One anti-Treaty IRA Captain from Mooncoin, Patrick Walsh, reflecting on the conflict remarked; 'we all believed we were doing the right thing [for the country] at the time.'[1] Many who fought with the anti-Treaty IRA found it difficult to find employment during the 1920s as prospective employers often took an unfavourable view of their actions during the Civil War. Subsequently, many of those on the anti-Treaty side were obliged to emigrate to England or the United States to find work.

What was apparent while examining the revolutionary era was that life for Kilkenny residents was affected in so many ways. Just focusing on the military elements could never fully paint a picture of the experiences of all inhabitants of revolutionary period Kilkenny. Many people carried scars from those years – psychological, physical and emotional – so it has become clearer that it was not just the combatants who were directly affected.

The women of Cumann na mBan also sacrificed much. Perhaps Maisie Stallard, who was Cumann na mBan Brigade President from 1922, put it most succinctly. During the process of applying for her military service pension, she was asked for specific dates relating to her different Cumann na mBan activities. As her duties had consumed her life, she wrote to them some days later having thought about it, stating; 'you had better leave it out [the date], as in those days, every night was Cumann na mBan'.[2]

Military Service Pensions

The vast mountain of sorrow and anger that is the Military Service Pensions Collection is breathtaking in its scope, but heartbreaking in its detail. Veterans of the revolutionary era were required to plead their case to justify receiving a military pension from the Irish Government. Many of those who applied were suffering financial hardship during the economic stagnation of the country in the decades after independence. On a national scale, approximately 82,000 people (both men and women) applied for a pension or compensation, but only 15,700 of those were successful.[3] In other words, 66,300, or 81 per cent of the people who applied had their applications rejected. The complex bureaucratic process involved in applying for a pension has been an unintended boon for historians, as a huge volume of paperwork was generated.

Applicants were denied a pension if they did not meet the criteria for 'active service'. After analysing many of the applications made by Kilkenny natives, the overriding element for an applicant to receive a pension was if they had taken part in an attack or ambush. In other words, firing a gun – at least once – in the general direction of the enemy usually meant a pension was approved. A range of activities were generally deemed not sufficient to merit a pension, much to the annoyance of applicants. Activities typically omitted from active service included: raids for arms, electioneering duties, censoring mails, collecting subscriptions for the Dáil Loan, delivering dispatches, scouting, trenching roads, cutting communication lines and parading/drilling. It was therefore much more difficult for women to have their applications sanctioned. They could have spent years feeding and nursing IRA men, raising funds, delivering dispatches, buying and mending clothes, but still have their applications rejected. To be granted a pension, women usually had to prove that they transported or concealed weapons/ammunition (even on just one occasion), carried out intelligence work, or were present when an ambush or attack was taking place. One of the most active women in the Kilkenny Cumann na mBan Brigade,

Mary Teehan of Shipton House, was angry when her application was initially rejected. Aged in her early twenties, she was Captain of the Kilmanagh/Callan Cumann na mBan Battalion throughout the revolutionary era and spent most of the Civil War working full-time for the cause. Frustrated with the outcome of her application, she wrote to the Pensions Board in 1942 asserting the role played by women during the period: 'We stood in the gap and had no guns to defend us. The men aught be proud of themselves. [But] I wonder where, or how long would the IRA last, if they weren't fed & cleaned & encouraged by the women.'[4] If a person was lucky enough to be approved for a pension, they were often unhappy to be ranked the lowest and most common grade; E. Approved applicants were frequently riled when the Pensions Board excluded years of their contribution to the cause, as their activities were not considered 'active service'. Indeed, it is difficult to find any person in Kilkenny who was entirely satisfied with their pension claim.[5]

One positive element of the MSPC was that it demonstrated how Civil War animosities were often put to one side. During the 1930s, each IRA and Cumann na mBan Battalion O/C, and all Company Captains, were required to compile a list of volunteers under their command in 1921 (War of Independence) and 1922 (Civil War). As can be expected, after the split, many were on opposing sides when it came to the Civil War. What is somewhat unexpected was that Captains and O/Cs appear to have been very fair-minded when listing everyone under their command, no matter if they were on opposing sides in later years. For instance, William Oakes was Captain of A Company 1st IRA Battalion during the War of Independence and the Civil War, which was mostly made up of men from Kilkenny City. In 1935, he compiled listings of all men under his command during both conflicts. He also recorded the men who joined the Free State Army during the Civil War, in other words his adversaries during the Civil War.[6] Thus, he was not going to deny these men the option of claiming pensions for their War of Independence service. Furthermore, Oakes had more reasons than most to dislike the Free State Army. His unarmed brother, Samuel Oakes, was shot dead by a Free State soldier in July 1922. So the pension records reveal a large measure of decency and integrity on the part of the former IRA members.

In a similar way, James Lalor – the former vice-O/C of the Kilkenny Brigade – acted as coordinator for veterans from the Kilkenny Brigade who were applying for pensions.[7] He helped establish a committee at which the applicants met and discussed their claims. He also obtained the relevant references for the claimants. Lalor's records show that he too was impartial, making no distinction between those that remained in the IRA during the

Civil War, joined the Free State Army, or finished their service at the time of the Truce. Of course, as the application process dragged on, there was often gossip and bitterness espoused by the applicants about who did or did not receive a pension. However, this hostility was usually not based on Civil War animosities, but instead on what they perceived to be the merits or demerits of certain individuals' service to the cause.

Besides Aylward and Treacy who were ranked Grade B, other members of the Kilkenny IRA Brigade were ranked Grade C under the 1934 Pensions Act. These included; Martin Mulhall (from Danville/Kilkenny City, O/C of 1st Kilkenny Battalion 1920–1923), Ned Halley (from Callan, 7th Battalion vice-O/C and O/C 1921–1923), Thomas Meagher (from Callan, Quartermaster anti-Treaty IRA Brigade), Patrick Egan (Callan, Captain B Company, 7th Battalion), Thomas Kenny (from Callan, Quartermaster anti-Treaty IRA Brigade for part of the Civil War), Patrick Talbot (from Urlingford, 2nd IRA Battalion O/C), Martin McGrath (from Tullogher, 6th Battalion O/C and anti-Treaty IRA Brigade Quartermaster) and Seán Byrne (from Kilkenny City and later Galway; Adjutant of the Kilkenny IRA Brigade 1921–1923). By the early 1940s, 1,404 individuals from the Kilkenny Brigade had applied for a military service pension, the majority being rejected.[8]

Even more challenging were the applications concerning compensation for the loss of a relative who was killed. Attempting to put a monetary value on the life of a deceased child or spouse was always going to be an unattainable figure. The relatively meagre compensation paid out by the fledgling Free State often added insult to injury. From a modern perspective, the way the compensation was calculated for a deceased relative – especially with the 1924 Pensions Act – was not particularly rational or fair. Firstly, a dependency on the deceased person had to be established. The projected earnings or wages the deceased received prior to death were also evaluated. Obviously, farm labourers – which represented the most common occupation of Kilkenny deaths in the Free State Army during the Civil War – were the lowest earners, with their families in turn receiving some of the lowest compensation. Thus, the poorest in society often received the least amount of money. There were some exceptions, which were usually as a result of an appeal with political pressure being applied.

Writing to the Pensions Board assessors in the 1930s, Hanna Murphy, Kilkenny Cumann na mBan Brigade O/C (who was awarded a Grade D pension), pleaded for compassion for the women who had served under her command regarding their pension claims: 'I hope your board will see their way & do something for the poor girls who risked their lives & gave all to help Ireland. I assure you they done a man's part in places.' One anti-Treaty IRA column leader, Martin Medlar, left no doubt as to his opinion of the importance of Cumann na mBan. Referring to the industrious Margaret Prendergast (née Walsh) of Paulstown Company, he said; 'I would put women of her record on a par with members [/the men] of the Flying Column.'

One theme that emerged repeatedly from the Kilkenny combatants throughout the revolutionary period was a fundamental belief in the justness and nobility of the cause. They were prepared to sacrifice, and did sacrifice much for their beliefs, but they were not one-dimensional – nor were their opponents. Evidence of that can be gleaned from the case of Ned Aylward, the leader of the 7th Battalion ASU and anti-Treaty IRA Brigade O/C in the Civil War. During the Truce, he actually became friendly with the British Commander of the Crown Forces in Callan through a shared passion for fowling. Two men, who had recently been aiming guns at each other, were now side by side, with birds their mutual target. The British officer even offered Aylward a commission in the British Army in Australia, an offer that was firmly rejected. They stayed in contact until their respective deaths in the 1970s.[9] Irish history will never be short of contradictions.

What was achieved as a result of the War of Independence and Civil War is something that is still being debated, and will be for a considerable time to come. An overarching theme that developed once the long sought freedom was achieved was a general sense of unhappiness and disappointment, with the contention; 'this is not the Ireland we fought for', becoming a common refrain. As the Free State, and later the Republic, came into existence, many of the aspirations and dreams of the 'Independence generation' did not turn out as expected. In some cases, the optimism of their youth withered to cynicism in their latter years. It could be argued that the type of Ireland many were fighting for was not achieved until after most of the Independence generation had died. Perhaps now, in twenty-first century Ireland, we are finally reaping the fruits of their labour.

Life Ever After:
Protagonists After the Revolution

Thomas Treacy

Thomas Treacy was Captain of the Kilkenny Irish Volunteers, and later Commandant of the Kilkenny IRA Brigade, from 1914 to 1920 inclusive. Treacy lived his whole life in the City and never strayed too far from his native Maudlin Street, residing most of his life at Dean Street. He was born in December 1885, the son of John, a former RIC policeman, and Kate Treacy. He married Elizabeth O'Regan on 6 September 1915 in St John's Church, Kilkenny City and the couple went on to have eight children. They did not have an easy start to their married life as Thomas lost his job in the probate office after he was arrested in the weeks after Easter 1916.

Treacy was in charge on the night of the first successful RIC Barracks capture in Leinster, which occured in Hugginstown in March 1920. He spent much time on the run and went on hunger strike in prison in May 1920. After his arrest in November 1920 he was sent to Ballykinlar internment camp, County Down, where he was elected camp O/C. He was absent for the bleakest period of the War of Independence in the first six months of 1921 and was only released from his confinement with the signing of the Treaty in December 1921. He was awarded a Grade B military service pension, the joint highest grade awarded in the County Kilkenny Brigade area (the other Grade B rank was awarded to Ned Aylward). Treacy was employed by Kilkenny County Council for most of his working life. For a period he was in charge of the registration of births, deaths and marriages in the district. He sometimes rectified mistakes in the birth and death registers of his IRA comrades, at one stage fixing errors in his own birth record.[1] He was appointed Secretary of the Kilkenny County Board of Health in 1922. He was instrumental in organising meetings in the 1940s and 1950s about compiling detailed witness statements for the Bureau of Military History, making sure the information in his Brigade area was complete and accurate.[2] He died on 14 April 1975, at the age of 89. Elizabeth died in June 1987, aged 93. They were buried in Foulkstown cemetery near Kilkenny City.[3]

Peter DeLoughry

Peter DeLoughry was the public face and most dominant presence of revolutionary era Kilkenny. DeLoughry married Winnie Murphy in 1911 and the couple went on to have six children. The DeLoughrys welcomed Seán MacDiarmada to their home in November 1915, just six months before his execution. DeLoughry was transporting and providing weapons for the local Irish Volunteer Company during Easter week – although Kilkenny did not take an active part, for which DeLoughry received some criticism afterwards. As a member of the local corporation he was the voice of Sinn Féin in Kilkenny. He became more famous nationally after it became known that he made the key that led to the escape of Éamon de Valera from Lincoln Prison in 1919. During the War of Independence, his home life and business suffered as the family were constantly raided by Crown Forces. He did not play an active role in the military side of the War of Independence, although surprisingly he was elected Brigade O/C. His appointment lasted less than three weeks as he was arrested in December 1920 (his pre-eminent position in the Sinn Féin movement being the likely reason for his selection). He later became a strong pro-Treaty voice in Kilkenny. He served six consecutive terms as Mayor of Kilkenny, while he was also appointed to the first Senate of the Irish Free State. In later life he became a Cumann na nGaedheal TD.

Before de Valera had escaped from Lincoln prison in 1919, DeLoughry made him promise to return his handiwork (the prison key he had made) some time in the future. Harry Boland had the key in his possession and after he was killed in 1922, the family were not too inclined to part with it. Having met de Valera in the Dáil Éireann restaurant in 1929, DeLoughry once again demanded the key to be returned to him. De Valera obviously put Civil War animosities aside, as he obtained the key from the Boland family and handed it to DeLoughry in Leinster House, ten years after his escape. Much had changed in the intervening years since the two men were in prison together. DeLoughry did not have much time to admire his creation as, in 1931, he began suffering from kidney failure. He died at his sister Lil's home in Richmond Avenue, Milltown, Dublin, on 23 October 1931, aged 49 years.[4]

Father Patrick H. Delahunty

Fr P.H. Delahunty became famous locally in the lead-up to the War of Independence for his denunciations of the British authorities and was known as 'the rebel priest'. He had completed his training in St Kieran's College seminary in 1905. He was arrested at the end of 1920 for the possession of 'seditious literature' (Volunteer magazines etc.) and sentenced to two years in prison. He gained international attention during the Truce when he was one of the escapees from Kilkenny jail. After taking the anti-Treaty IRA position in the Civil War – which included him administrating to the spiritual needs of the anti-Treaty forces in Dublin – he fell out of favour with the hierarchy of the Catholic Church in Ossory. He was forced to return to live with his mother in Curraghmartin, Carrigeen, Mooncoin, as he was barred from performing his priestly duties in the diocese. She died in 1924 but Fr Pat was unable to participate at her funeral Mass in Carrigeen Church due to his suspension. In 1927 he moved to Kansas in America, as the bishop there agreed to allow him to practise. He was chaplain of a Kansas prison for many years, but never spoke about his own imprisonment or his involvement in the Irish revolution. On a number of occasions he accompanied inmates on death row to their execution by electric chair. He died in Kansas on 4 April 1955 at the age of 75 and was buried at St Mary's College, Leavenworth, Kansas. A High Mass was held in Carrigeen, Mooncoin, two weeks after his death, with twenty-three priests in attendance. In 1957, a new street in Kilkenny City – Delahunty Terrace – was named in his honour. The street is aptly located near the scene of the great Kilkenny jailbreak.[5]

John Thomas Prout

Tipperary native John T. Prout was the leader of the Free State forces in the 2nd Southern Command – which included Kilkenny, south Tipperary, Waterford and part of Wexford – during the Civil War. He was given the rank Colonel-Commandant. No doubt his experience as a captain in the US Army's 69th Regiment during the First World War was key to his promotion. His reputation grew quickly, especially after he dislodged the anti-Treaty IRA in the Battle of Kilkenny City without the loss of life. The other battles, including Waterford City, Carrick-on-Suir and Clonmel, were also successful, though the amount of resources and time it took to defeat the anti-Treaty forces was criticised. His troops also launched the attacks on the Knockmealdown Mountains which killed Dinny Lacey and later Liam Lynch, both leading members of the anti-Treaty IRA.

However, his division was regularly singled out by GHQ for its lack of discipline and his reputation was in tatters after a number of his officers defected to the anti-Treaty IRA in December 1922 which resulted in the capture of three barracks.[6] On the other hand, anti-Treaty IRA members in Kilkenny were not subjected to extra-judicial executions, which had been the case in other parts of the country (although two official executions did take place in the county during the Civil War).

His personal life was also eventful. He was the only child of farm labourer Maurice Prout and his wife Mary, from Gurtussa, Dundrum, County Tipperary. Having emigrated to New York in 1904 and married his first wife Catherine there in 1907. He joined the 'fighting' 69th Infantry Regiment of the US Army in 1908, rising to the rank of Captain. John and Catherine's son John T. Prout junior ('Jack') was born on 12 May 1910. Prout and John junior travelled to Ireland in 1919 after his father Maurice's death. Prout joined the 3rd Tipperary IRA Brigade during the War of Independence. In July 1922, between the Battle of Kilkenny City and the Battle of Waterford, Prout married his second wife in St John's Church, Kilkenny (his first wife having died by this time). She was Mary Conba, a school teacher from Kilmallock, County Limerick, who was seventeen years younger than him (he was aged 42 years and she was 25). In 1927, having been demobbed from the Free State Army in 1924, Prout returned to the United States. Jack also returned to America and joined the US Army just before his 18th birthday in March 1928. While living in New York, Prout Snr worked as a salesman for a telegraph company. In 1940, Prout was working as a technical adviser in Los Angeles on the Hollywood film *The Fighting 69th*, based on his regiment during the First World War. He died on 27 April 1969, in Windham County, Vermont, aged 88 years. Jack (John junior), who had been called a 'brat' during the Battle of Kilkenny by the opposing forces and whose life was also threatened in letters, subsequently lived a long life. He died on 23 May 1988 in El Paso, Texas, aged 78.[7]

Ned Aylward

Ned Aylward, from Riversfield, Callan, rose to prominence as O/C of the West Kilkenny ASU in the latter stages of the War of Independence. Just prior to the Truce he was appointed O/C of the 7th Battalion by Ernie O'Malley. As a TD he rejected the Treaty and when the Civil War broke out, he reformed his ASU and went back on the run. He became Kilkenny anti-Treaty IRA Brigade O/C at the commencement of Civil War. Even though he joined the IRA 'within a week of ordination' to the priesthood (although he never took vows), he was arguably the most tenacious member, of the most aggressive battalion, and certainly participated in the most attacks. He was present at most of the major altercations in the area during the War of Independence, including the attack on Hugginstown and Drangan RIC Barracks, the Ninemilehouse Ambush, the shoot-out at Garryricken House, and the takeover of Kilmanagh village, amongst many other engagements. During the Civil War he was present at the fighting in Carrick-on-Suir, while he also led his party of men in the cunning takeover of three Free State barracks in December 1922. He was never captured by his enemies but did spend much time on the run between 1920 and 1923.

After the Civil War he moved to Chicago, Illinois, where he married Nuala Moriarty from Kerry, on 1 June 1932. They returned to Ireland and set up home in Christendom, Ferrybank, in the far south of the county, just a few kilometres from Waterford City. Ned Aylward became a sales manager in the nearby Clover Meats factory in 1935, where he remained until retirement. The couple had four sons and one daughter. Aylward received numerous requests for references from men and women of the 7th Battalion, and the Kilkenny Brigade generally, regarding their military pension applications. Aylward himself received a Grade B pension, echoing the rank of the previous Kilkenny Brigade O/C, Thomas Treacy. Ned Aylward died of pancreatic cancer on 24 February 1976 at the Rosario Nursing Home, Ferrybank. He was 80 years old. When she died, Nuala was one of the last people in the country still receiving a military service pension (spouse's pension). She passed away on 21 January 2004, aged 96, eighty-five years after her husband came to prominence.[8]

Endnotes

INTRODUCTION

1 Ernie O'Malley, *On Another Man's Wound* (Dublin, 2013), p. 279.
2 *Irish Press*, 19 December 1936. *Kilkenny People*, 26 December 1936.
3 Michael Hopkinson, *The Irish War of Independence* (Dublin, 2004), p. 123.
4 Of the nine Battalions in the Kilkenny Brigade, there is at least one witness statement for eight of the Battalions. The omission is the 9th Battalion based in the far south of the county, although this was somewhat supplemented by historian Jim Maher who recorded interviews with two of its members in the 1960s. However, voices of Kilkenny women are lacking from the BMHWS.
5 Donal Cadogan, *About Kilkenny* (Kilkenny, 2015), pp. 108–16.
6 Mike Cronin, Mark Duncan and Paul Rouse, *The GAA – A People's History* (Cork, 2009), p. 37.
7 Paul Rouse, *Sport and Ireland – A History* (Oxford, 2015), pp. 199–200. Rouse also wrote Cahill's entry in the *Dictionary of Irish Biography*.

CHAPTER 1

1 W.E. Vaughan and A.J. Fitzpatrick (eds), *Irish Historical Statistics, Population 1821–1971* (Dublin, 1978), pp. 4, 31, 66. The population of County Kilkenny in 1841 was 202,420 persons.
2 Niall Brannigan and John Kirwan, *Kilkenny Families in the Great War* (Thomastown, 2012), p. xii.
3 William Walsh, *Kilkenny: The Struggle for Land 1850–1882* (Kilkenny, 2008), p. 21.
4 Jonny Geber, 'Burying the Famine dead: Kilkenny Union Workhouse' in *Atlas of the Great Irish Famine*, ed. John Crowley *et al.* (Cork, 2012), pp. 341–3 and *The Irish Times*, 20 May 2010. Kilkenny Union Workhouse was opened in 1842 with a capacity to hold 1,300 inmates. From 1921 to 1942 the building was known as the Kilkenny Central Hospital. The mass Famine grave was discovered in 2006 during preliminary works for the MacDonagh Junction Shopping Centre. The remains discovered were buried between the years 1847–1851. Sixty per cent were aged less than 18 years. The bones were reinterred in an outside section of the new shopping centre in 2010.
5 Walsh, *Kilkenny: The Struggle for Land* (Kilkenny, 2008), pp. 48, 95.
6 Local Government Board, *Return of Owners of Land of One Acre And Upwards* (Dublin, 1878), p. 42.
7 Local Government Board, *Return of Owners of Land* (Dublin, 1878), pp. 35, 36, 39–41.

8   Registry of Deeds, Kings Inns, Dublin 1, *Kilkenny 1910–1914*, Index Volume 1139. Sometimes land transfers were not given transaction details (left blank), which usually implied the transfer to the Land Commission i.e. the same as folio number transfers. Also note; many folio numbers (usually individual fields) could be transferred to one specific farmer. Thus, one farm transfer may have generated numerous land transactions.

9   Erhard Rumpf and Anthony C. Hepburn, *Nationalism and Socialism in Twentieth-Century Ireland* (Liverpool, 1977), p. 54.

10   Walsh, *Kilkenny: The Struggle for Land* (Kilkenny, 2008), p. 110.

11   John Borgonovo, John Crowley, Mike Murphy and Donal Ó Drisceoil (eds), *Atlas of the Irish Revolution* (Cork, 2017), p. 535. Only Antrim, Down and Dublin had a lower proportion of small farms than Kilkenny.

12   NA CO 904/99, January 1916.

13   Borgonovo *et al.*, *Atlas of the Irish Revolution* (Cork, 2017), p. 556.

14   Louise Walsh, *The Role of Piltown and Clogga Creameries: 1930s–1980s*, unpublished BA Thesis, Mary Immaculate College, Limerick (2011). The Avonmore Creamery records are housed in the Kilkenny Archives in St Kieran's College, Kilkenny. Satellite branches were also important. The flourishing Piltown Creamery had sub-branches in Mullinbeg in the north of the parish, another in Clogga in neighbouring Mooncoin parish, and the third sub-branch in Ballinura near Carrick-on-Suir, demonstrating the widespread impact of creameries even in the most rural places.

15   Walsh, *Kilkenny, The Struggle for Land* (Kilkenny, 2008), pp. 295, 299, 380.

16   Michael O'Dwyer, *The History of Cricket in County Kilkenny – The Forgotten Game* (Kilkenny, 2006). This publication contains a detailed history of the many cricket clubs in County Kilkenny. Cricket was probably the most played sport throughout Ireland at this time. Its popularity in Kilkenny peaked in 1896 when there were fifty teams.

17   Mike Cronin, Mark Duncan and Paul Rouse, *The GAA – A People's History* (Cork, 2009), p. 37. The game was played on 15 February 1885, just three months after the GAA was formed, under rules devised by Maurice Davin (first president of the GAA) from nearby Carrick-on-Suir. The Canal End in Croke Park is named in his honour today.

18   During this era, local club teams represented the county in the All-Ireland series. 1893: Kilkenny, represented by the Confederates (Kilkenny City), lost to Cork. 1895: Kilkenny, represented by Tullaroan, lost to Tipperary. 1897: Kilkenny, represented by Tullaroan, lost to Limerick. 1898: Kilkenny, represented by Threecastles, lost to Tipperary.

19   Cronin *et al.*, *The GAA – A People's History* (Cork, 2009), p. 43.

20   James J. Comerford, *My Kilkenny I.R.A. Days, 1916–22* (Kilkenny,1978), p. 180.

21   E.G. Ravenstein, 'On the Celtic Languages of the British Isles: A Statistical Survey', in *Journal of the Statistical Society of London*, vol. 42, no. 3, (London, 1879), p. 583. See also; *Census of Population 1926, VIII Irish Language* (CSO statistics – historical trend of Irish language since 1851).

22   Máirín Nic Eoin, 'Irish Language and Literature in County Kilkenny in the Nineteenth Century' in *Kilkenny: History and Society*, ed. William Nolan and Kevin Whelan (Dublin,1990), pp. 465–7.

23   *Kilkenny People*, 13 August 1910.

24   Comerford, *My Kilkenny I.R.A. Days* (Kilkenny, 1978), p. 906.

25   Patrick Maume, 'Standish James O'Grady' in *Dictionary of Irish Biography*, eds James
      McGuire and James Quinn (Cambridge, 2009). F.J. Bigger, Douglas Hyde and J.J. O' Kelly
      ('Sceilg') were other notable figures who visited Kilkenny during this period.

26   'Aut Even' is an anglicised form of the Irish; 'áit aoibhinn' meaning 'beautiful place'. The
      Kilkenny Theatre closed in 1962. At the time of writing, the Zuni restaurant is located
      in the former theatre building. 'Carnegie Libraries' were being built all over the world
      in this era as a result of the philanthropic efforts of Andrew Carnegie, the richest man
      in the world. He had a fund which provided money for the construction of library
      buildings.

27   Helen Andrews, 'Ellen Odette Cuffe – Countess of Desart' in *Dictionary of Irish Biography*,
      eds McGuire and Quinn (Cambridge, 2009). The Countess of Desart is sometimes referred
      to as 'Lady Desart'. She also believed she was the first Jewish person to receive the Freedom
      of any city in the world. The Countess went on to become a Free State Senator (and
      Ireland's first Jewish member of Parliament), while in later life she financed the evacuation
      of Jewish children from Nazi Germany. A footbridge over the River Nore in Kilkenny City
      was named in her honour in 2014.

28   Liam O'Bolguidhir, 'The Early Years of the Gaelic League in Kilkenny 1897–1903' in
      Kilkenny Through the Centuries; Chapters in the history of an Irish City, eds John Bradley
      and Michael O'Dwyer (Naas, 2009), p. 462.

29   Rev. Gerard Rice CC, *St Kieran's College Record 1965* (Kilkenny, 1965).

30   UCDA P150/478 (Éamon de Valera Papers). Information sent to Éamon de Valera from
      the President of St Kieran's College. The accounts were written in 1955 for a school
      publication.

31   Minutes of the Gaelic League, Kilkenny Branch. Rothe House, Kilkenny City.

32   Shane Kenna, *16 Lives, Thomas MacDonagh* (Dublin, 2014), pp. 40, 44. 'West-British' was a
      derogatory term used during this era to denote those who were supportive of England and
      its customs.

33   Edd Winfield Parks and Aileen Wells Parks, *Thomas MacDonagh; The Man, The Patriot,
      The Writer* (Athens, Georgia, 1967), p. 8.

34   Muriel McAuley, *In the Shade of Slievenamon; The Flying Column West Kilkenny*, book
      launch and speech, MacDonagh Junction, Kilkenny City, 4 June 2015. Unusual as it was
      for a Tipperary man to be evoked in Kilkenny, MacDonagh was idolised as a 'local' hero in
      subsequent decades.The local railway station was named after him in 1966, while in recent
      years, the adjacent shopping centre was also named in his honour.

35   In 1901 only thirteen people between the ages of 10 and 18 in the Castlecomer District
      could speak Irish. In 1911, this had grown to 209, a sixteenfold increase. It was probably a
      similar story of a teacher introducing Irish to the classroom in the Thomastown District.
      In 1901 there were sixteen teenagers who could speak Irish, but this increased to 110 in
      1911.

36   Census Office of Ireland, *Census of Ireland, 1911 – Province of Leinster – County Kilkenny*
      (Athlone, 1912), pp. 126–7. Overall, there was a net reduction of 8.5 per cent in the number
      of Irish speakers in County Kilkenny, decreasing from 3,568 (1901) to 3,264 (1911). It can
      be inferred that if the Gaelic League had not been established, this reduction would have
      been drastically more. The largest decrease of Irish speakers occurred in those aged 60
      or over; from 1,493 (1901) to 602 (1911) persons, which was a decrease of nearly 60 per

cent. The largest increase was in the 10 to 18 age category, increasing from 273 (1901) to 1,280 (1911).

37   Roy F. Foster, *Modern Ireland, 1600–1972* (London, 1989), p. 19.

38   Much of their wealth stemmed from their right to charge excise on all wine imported into Ireland.

39   *Freeman's Journal*, 2 May 1904.

40   *Cork Examiner*, 2 May 1904.

41   Ibid.

42   *Anglo-Celt*, 18 April 1899.

43   *Cork Examiner*, 14 April 1904.

44   Ibid.

45   Jim Walsh, *James Nowlan, The Alderman and the GAA in his Time* (Kilkenny, 2013), pp. 26, 56–7.

46   *Cork Examiner*, 23 April 1904. Daly eventually received the Freedom of the City in November 1904.

47   *Kilkenny People*, 9 April 1904.

48   BMH WS 699 (Josephine Clarke née Stallard).

49   Michael Connolly, *Kilkenny People – A Review of the Century* (Kilkenny, 1992), p.18. *Kilkenny People*, 6 August 1904.

50   Census Office, *Census of Ireland, 1911 … County Kilkenny* (Athlone, 1912), pp. 105, 121. Note; children under 9 years of age are excluded from literacy statistics.

51   The official name for the newspaper known as 'The Kilkenny Moderator' was *The Kilkenny Moderator and Leinster Advertiser*. At the end of 1919 its name changed to just *The Moderator*. To avoid confusion, it will be referred to as the *Kilkenny Moderator* throughout. The company closed in 1925. The *Kilkenny Journal* was founded as *Finn's Leinster Journal* in 1766, later becoming the *Leinster Journal*, before being renamed the *Kilkenny Journal* in 1830. It ceased production in 1965. Other newspapers from surrounding counties published information relating to Kilkenny, mostly notably *The Munster Express* based in Waterford City which had a weekly section on south Kilkenny.

52   BMH WS 1,093 (Thomas Treacy).

53   BMH WS 1,032 (James Lalor). Upton would have canvassed on behalf of Cosgrave in North Kilkenny, but as Cosgrave was set to be returned unopposed, Upton's services were required in nearby County Laois.

54   *Waterford News & Star*, 6 December 2016 (by Pat McEvoy, sourced from articles by Dr Anthony Keating). A large gathering was held on 29 January 1922 in honour of Upton, prior to his departure (see *Kilkenny Moderator*, 4 February 1922).

55   Brannigan and Kirwan, *Kilkenny Families in the Great War* (Thomastown, 2012), pp. xii, xv. The total number of Kilkenny recruits was initially believed to be around 2,900, but this has recently been revised upwards to 3,129 (*Kilkenny People*, 13 August 2015). First World War Victoria Cross recipients included; William Burke from Cuffesgrange (Royal Irish Regiment) who was awarded the VC 'for holding six Germans and rescuing a wounded Officer'. Also, Frederick William Hall (5th Canadian Battalion), born in Kilkenny, but living in Canada, was awarded the VC posthumously for attending to a wounded man in Ypres.

56   Brannigan and Kirwan, *Kilkenny Families in the Great War* (Thomastown, 2012), pp. x,xii, xiv.

57   *The Irish Times*, 28 March 2016.

58   Comerford, *My Kilkenny I.R.A. Days* (Kilkenny,1978), p. 45.

59   Tom Burnell and the Kilkenny Great War Memorial Committee, *The Kilkenny War Dead* (Kilkenny, 2014). Updated figures; *Kilkenny People*, 13 August 2015.

60   NA CO 904/101, October 1916.

61   Connolly, *Kilkenny People – A Review of the Century* (Kilkenny, 1992), p. 26.

62   *Kilkenny Journal*, 22 May 1915. He flew from Fishguard in North Wales, landing in County Wexford, one hour and forty minutes later. Denys Corbett Wilson became a lieutenant in the Royal Flying Corps (RFC) during the First World War, and was killed in an aircraft accident, aged 33 years, while performing reconnaissance in May 1915.

63   After the 1848 rebellion, Stephens escaped first to Urlingford. As he began to distrust his supporters in the safe house there, he then walked to Carrick-on-Suir where he met with his associates John O'Mahony and Michael Doheny, and they all subsequently went by foot to Dungarvan, County Waterford, via the Comeragh Mountains and Mount Melleray. Stephens then traipsed around Cork and Kerry for at least two months, and tried to avoid being arrested, which was helped greatly by *The Kilkenny Moderator* which reported that he had died. He then escaped to France. He became fluent in the French language, becoming so proficient that he translated Charles Dickens's novel *Martin Chuzzlewit* into French, to provide some income. He secretly returned to Ireland in 1856, and began what he called his '3,000-mile walk' around Ireland, gathering support for what would become the IRB. He was exiled from Ireland for a period of twenty-five years, returning in 1891. He settled in Blackrock, County Dublin.

64   NAI C.S.O. ICR/14.

65   Desmond McCabe, 'Joseph Denieffe' in *Dictionary of Irish Biography*, eds McGuire and Quinn (Cambridge, 2009). *Kilkenny People*, 15 July 1922 – Article by John Devoy.

66   Walsh, *James Nowlan* (Kilkenny, 2013), p. 7.

67   Declan Dunne, *Peter's Key, Peter DeLoughry and the Fight for Irish Independence* (Cork, 2012), pp. 17–18, 23.

68   BMH WS 1032 (James Lalor).

69   Dunne, *Peter's Key* (Cork, 2012), pp. 34–5. The ideology of Sinn Féin was to emphasise the idea of self-reliance, i.e. 'Ourselves' here living in Ireland have everything we could possibly need for a happy life, such as music, song, dance, industry, history/mythology, sport, culture, manufacturing, crafts, food production etc.

70   NA CO 904/82, June 1910.

71   BMH WS 513 (Thomas Furlong).

72   Dunne, *Peter's Key* (Cork, 2012), p. 44.

73   Comerford, *My Kilkenny I.R.A. Days* (Kilkenny,1978), p. 76.

74   BMH WS 1614 (Timothy Hennessy), and *Kilkenny People*, 14 March 1914.

75   NA CO 904/92, May 1914.

76   NA CO 904/120/4, Crime Branch.

77   *Sunday Independent*, 13 October 1912. Prominent Kilkenny attendees included the Earl of Desart, Mr Prior-Wandesforde (Castlecomer) and Mr Ponsonby (Piltown).

78   *Kilkenny People*, 30 April 1910. Mary Kettle (née Sheehy) was the daughter of an MP. She was somewhat of a muse of James Joyce whom she met at university. She was a sister of Hanna Sheehy-Skeffington, and sister-in-law of Francis Sheehy-Skeffington. Mary's

husband, Tom Kettle, was a Home Rule MP, Professor of Economics in UCD, and a poet. Both Mary and her sister Hanna were widowed in 1916 as Hanna's husband was executed during the Rising, while Mary's husband was killed during the Battle of the Somme. Mary had one child, Betty, with Kettle, and she later became a Dublin City Councillor.

79 *Irish Independent*, 28 May 1913.

80 *Kilkenny People*, 14 June 1913.

81 *Kilkenny People*, 14 June and 25 March 1911.

82 BMH WS 513 (Thomas Furlong).

83 BMH WS 1614 (Timothy Hennessy).

84 BMH WS 590 (Thomas Treacy).

85 Where the Dunnes Stores car park is located currently, near John's Bridge in Kilkenny City centre. In October 1914, John Redmond addressed a British Army recruitment meeting in Kilkenny City, where over 5,000 spectators turned out to greet him.

86 BMH WS 590 (Thomas Treacy).

87 Diarmaid Ferriter, *A Nation and Not a Rabble, The Irish Revolution 1913–1923* (London, 2015), pp. 143–4.

88 The term 'Sinn Feiner' became an umbrella term to denote anyone with advanced nationalist views and not just members of Sinn Féin or the Irish Volunteers. Hence the 1916 Rebellion was incorrectly called 'the Sinn Féin Rebellion'.

89 NLI, MS 10549 (3), Col. Maurice Moore Papers, letter to National Volunteer HQ from Major James H. Connellan, dated 4 September 1914.

90 NLI, MS 10549 (3), Moore Papers, letter to Robert Barton (HQ) from Major Joyce, dated 5 September 1914.

91 NLI, MS 10549 (3), Moore Papers, letter from R.H. Prior-Wandesforde, dated 19 August 1914.

92 NLI, MS 10549 (3), Moore Papers, National Volunteers Survey – Callan, 25 March 1915.

93 NLI, MS 10549 (3), Moore Papers, National Volunteers Survey – Inistioge, 17 February 1915.

94 NLI, MS 10549 (3), Moore Papers, National Volunteers Survey, 15, 17, 27 February and 6 March 1915 respectively.

95 NA CO 904/95 and 97. 'Rabble' was derogatory terminology which usually referred to troublemakers, or 'disorderly youths'.

96 NA CO 904/99, January 1916.

97 BMH WS 590 (Thomas Treacy).

98 BMH WS 1,032 (James Lalor).

CHAPTER 2

1 BMH WS 258 (Mrs McDowell (Maeve Cavanagh) – Courier Easter Week 1916.

2 BMH WS 699 (Dr Josephine Clarke, née Stallard).

3 MA MSPC/34/SP/60441 – Mary (Maisie) O'Kelly (1891–1984). The establishment of Cumann na mBan in Kilkenny was relatively late compared to other counties.

4 MA MSPC/34/SP/60441 – Mary (Maisie) O'Kelly. Maisie also guided Liam Mellows through Kilkenny during the week prior to Easter, on his way to lead the County Galway

Volunteers in rebellion. Mellows escaped to America after the Rebellion disguised in a nun's veil. He was executed by the Free State Government during the Civil War.

5   NA CO 904/99, Report for January 1916 (dated February 1916).

6   NA CO 904/99, Report for March 1916 (dated April 1916).

7   Comerford, *My Kilkenny I.R.A. Days* (Kilkenny, 1978), pp. 69, 71. In 1918, one Volunteer described Banba Hall/Kilkenny Volunteer HQ as follows; '[it] was a storage warehouse – and looked to be very much neglected. The building had several lofts and all its windows were boarded up. However, it was dry and somewhat warm inside. The place looked very forlorn … Its very lonesomeness and abandoned appearance made it a good place for such meetings'. The Volunteers used to practise shooting with a .22 rifle in the loft of the building.

8   BMH WS 590 (Thomas Treacy).

9   BMH WS 1,093 (Thomas Treacy) – note; his second statement.

10   NA CO 904/99, February 1916.

11   BMH WS 590 (Thomas Treacy).

12   BMH WS 699 (Dr Josephine Clarke née Stallard) – Appendix A: Letter from Tom Stallard.

13   BMH WS 1,032 (James Lalor).

14   BMH WS 590 (Thomas Treacy).

15   BMH WS 685 (Mrs Bulmer Hobson née Claire 'Gregan').

16   MSPC/34/60559 – Kitty O'Doherty.

17   BMH WS 355 (Mrs Kitty O'Doherty).

18   BMH WS 1,032 (James Lalor).

19   BMH WS 590 (Thomas Treacy).

20   Ibid.

21   BMH WS 1006 (Martin Kealy).

22   BMH WS 1,101 (Martin Cassidy).

23   *Kilkenny People*, 29 April 1916.

24   BMH WS 541 (Dr Nancy Wyse-Power). Nancy Wyse-Power was the daughter of Jennie Wyse-Power who was a feminist, politician and founding member of both Inghinidhe na hÉireann and Cumann na mBan. Jennie's vegetarian restaurant on Henry Street in Dublin was the location where most of the seven leaders of the 1916 Proclamation signed the original document. After her trip to Kilkenny, Nancy returned to Dublin where she was part of the GPO garrison during Easter Week.

25   BMH WS 699 (Dr Josephine Clarke née Stallard). When Clarke gave her statement DeLoughry was deceased, consequently it is understandable that she would defend her friend's response to the Rising.

26   In the aftermath of the Rising in Dublin, Josephine Clarke aided her future brother-in-law Ted O'Kelly in escaping from Jervis Street Hospital. With the help of O'Kelly's aunt, Sister Assisium who was employed at the hospital, they smuggled him out by dressing him in priests' clothing. Ted O'Kelly subsequently recuperated in the Stallard family home in Danville House near Kilkenny City, and was nursed by Maisie (Mary) Stallard – whom he would later marry. O'Kelly was visited in the Stallard home by his friend and Irish Volunteer Liam Clarke, whom Josephine Stallard later married. Thus, the turmoil of revolution appears to have had some advantages! Ted O'Kelly was later killed in the

London Blitz in 1940. His friend Liam Clarke was also badly wounded in the fighting during Easter Week.

27   BMH WS 258 (Mrs McDowell aka Maeve Cavanagh).

28   BMH WS 1,032 (James Lalor).

29   *Irish Independent*, 29 May 1916.

30   Lorcan Collins, *1916: The Rising Handbook* (Dublin, 2016), p. 66.

31   BMH WS 1,271 (Patrick Dunphy).

32   BMH WS 590 (Thomas Treacy).

33   BMH WS 1,101 (Martin Cassidy). In addition, Thomas Neary, 1st IRA Battalion, hid weapons in the roof of the Church of Ireland Bishop's Palace in Kilkenny City (see; BMH WS 1,208 – Daniel J. Stapleton).

34   *Kilkenny People*, 29 April 1916.

35   Walsh, *James Nowlan* (Kilkenny, 2013), p. 85.

36   *Kilkenny People*, 11 March 2016, Centenary Supplement. The tax was to be imposed on all entertainment and sporting events, not just the GAA. However, Nowlan obviously won the argument that the GAA was an amateur organisation, as the GAA was later exempted.

37   BMH WS 590 (Thomas Treacy).

38   NA CO 904/99, April 1916, dated May 1916.

39   *Irish Independent*, 3 June 1916.

40   *Kilkenny People*, 20 May 1916.

41   *Kilkenny People*, 3 June 1916.

42   BMH WS 1,093 (Thomas Treacy).

43   *Kilkenny People*, 20 May 1916.

44   Comerford, *My Kilkenny I.R.A. Days* (Kilkenny, 1978), p. 894.

45   GRO, Index Reference (John Kealy): July–September 1916, Kilkenny, Volume: 3, Page: 293. 'Heart Disease Probably' was somewhat of a generic term used mainly in cases where the exact cause of death was not fully known.

46   BMH WS 1,006 (Martin Kealy).

47   BMH WS 590 (Thomas Treacy).

48   NA CO 904/99, April 1916, dated May 1916.

49   *Kilkenny People*, 29 April 1916.

50   NA HO/45/10810/312350 (the commission report is also widely available online).

51   The men stayed in lodgings owned by Dr James White at 19 High Street, Kilkenny City. Dr White was the physician to St Kieran's College from 1884 to 1925 (see; UCDA P150/478 – Éamon de Valera Papers).

52   *Kilkenny People*, 11 March 2016, Centenary Supplement.

53   *The Irish Times*, 7 April 1966. Article by his son Owen Sheehy-Skeffington.

54   The Bowen-Colthurst's family seat was Blarney Castle.

55   Patrick Maume, 'Francis Sheehy-Skeffington' in *Dictionary of Irish Biography*, eds McGuire and Quinn (Cambridge, 2009).

56   *The Irish Times*, 30 March 2015. The German ship, the *Aud*, was captured by the British Navy, with the ship subsequently being scuttled by its captain with the contents sinking to the bottom of Cork Harbour. Crotty also raised money to erect a cross in Limburg in memory of the Irish prisoners of war who died there.

57 NAI, 'Patrick Bealin', 1901 Census: Loan (Loon), Castlecomer, Kilkenny. 1911 Census: Kilkenny Street, Castlecomer, Kilkenny. GRO, Index Reference; Patrick Baylon, Birth: April–June (11 May 1890), Castlecomer, Volume 3, p. 381.

58 *Kilkenny People*, 18 March 2016.

59 source.southdublinlibraries.ie/bitstream/10599/11507/5/Fragment1916.pdf, accessed February 2018.

60 *Kilkenny People*, 29 April 2016.

61 *The Banba Review,* January 1963.

62 Ibid.

63 MA MSPC/34/SP/805, Richard Healy.

64 *Munster Express*, 6 December 2016, Christmas Supplement.

65 MA, MSPC/34/SP/43602, John O'Shea.

66 Ibid.

67 MA MSPC/34/SP/41963, John O'Shea.

68 *Kilkenny People*, 4 November 2016.

69 GRO, Index Reference; William Phelan Birth 12 February 1889: January–March, Kilkenny, Volume 3, p. 413.

70 This Rebellion took place near Ballingarry, County Tipperary and is sometimes referred to as the 'cabbage patch rebellion' as it was solely focused around one house. As 1848 is considered the 'year of rebellions' around Europe, this is sometimes seen as Ireland's contribution to the revolutionary year. Kilkenny man James Stephens acted as aide-de-camp for Smith-O'Brien, and a statue of the latter now graces O'Connell Street in Dublin.

71 GRO, Index References; Thomas Phelan Death: 30 October 1897, Kilkenny, Volume 3, p. 295. Margaret Phelan Death: 22 July 1899, Kilkenny, Volume 3, p. 296. Thomas Phelan and Margaret Kirwan Marriage: 1867, Kilkenny, Volume 13, p. 401.

72 NAI, 1911 Census. District: St Canice's Street: Troysgate (part of).

73 MA, MSPC/34/49639 and MSPC/34/SP/51244, William Phelan.

74 https://familysearch.org/ark:/61903/1:1:Q2WT-C3S5, accessed 11 January 2017. *Australia Cemetery Inscriptions 1802–2005*, William O'Brien Phelan, died 05 December 1971.

75 Charles Townshend, *Easter 1916, The Irish Rebellion* (London, 2015), pp. 184, 200.

76 Brannigan and Kirwan, *Kilkenny Families in the Great War* (Thomastown, 2012), p. 33.

77 *Kilkenny People*, 18 March 2016, Centenary Supplement – article by Jim Maher.

78 Lawrence William White, 'Father Albert Bibby' in *Dictionary of Irish Biography*, eds McGuire and Quinn (Cambridge, 2016).

79 *Kilkenny People*, 18 March 2016.

80 *Kilkenny People*, 21 October 2016.

81 Las Fallon (curator), 'Dublin Fire Brigade and the 1916 Rising' Exhibition (Dublin City Hall, 2016).

82 *Kilkenny People*, 21 October 2016.

83 NA WO35/69/1/10. Wounded List from Sinn Féin Rebellion.

84 NAI PLIC/1/2846. Patrick T. Kelly and Mrs M. Kelly.

85 NAI PLIC/1/2955, Reverend James R. McCaffrey.

86 NAI PLIC/1/2784 and 2849 and 3916 and 3929 and 5018.

87 NAI PLIC/1/5634, Richard Woodlock.

88   NAI PLIC/1/1979, Lawrence Dowdall. Dowdall's home at The Grange was maliciously
      burned down during the War of Independence on 27 April 1921 (see NA CO 904/115,
      April 1921).
89   NAI PLIC/1/4199, Glenmore Cooperative Dairy Society (James O'Donovan).
90   NAI PLIC/1/6301 (Tullaroan) and   6314 (Callan) and 6324 (Windgap) and 6348
      (Bennettsbridge).

CHAPTER 3

1   James Lydon, *The Making of Ireland: From Ancient Times to the Present* (Abingdon, 2012),
      p. 343.
2   Michael Laffan, *The Resurrection of Ireland: The Sinn Féin Party* (Cambridge, 1999), p. 94.
      Local events, such as the bestowing of the Freedom of Kilkenny City on Count Plunkett
      (father of the 1916 leader, Joseph, recently elected in North Roscommon constituency) in
      March 1917 helped to ratchet-up the patriotic fervour.
3   *Kilkenny People*, 30 December 2016. Article by his nephew, Noel Delahunty.
4   Jim Maher, *The Flying Column – West Kilkenny, 1916–1921* (Dublin, 1987), p. 1.
5   NA CO 904/99, June 1916.
6   Maher, *The Flying Column – West Kilkenny* (Dublin, 1987), p. 2.
      During the following year, 1917, a large Sinn Féin conference elected the following as Sinn
      Féin club presidents; Seán Gibbons President of the North Kilkenny Executive, E.T. Keane,
      editor of the *Kilkenny People*, was elected President of the Kilkenny City Executive, while
      Fr Delahunty was elected President of the South Executive.
7   BMH WS 1,093 (Thomas Treacy).
8   BMH WS 1614 (Timothy Hennessy) and BMH WS 699 (Josephine Clarke née Stallard).
      The INAVDF was created after the amalgamation of two competing groups collecting
      funds; namely the Irish National Aid Association and the Irish Volunteers Dependent
      Fund.
9   Dunne, *Peter's Key* (Cork, 2012), pp. 83–5.
10   *Kilkenny People*, 16 June 1917.
11   BMH WS 1,032 (James Lalor).
12   Ibid.
13   Jim Maher, *In the Shade of Slievenamon, The Flying Column West Kilkenny, 1916–1921*
      (Dublin, 2015), p. 29.
14   O'Brien was a close friend and confidant of IPP leader John Redmond. In a rare show of
      public emotion, Redmond is said to have broken down in grief at his funeral.
15   Michael Laffan, *Judging W.T. Cosgrave* (Dublin, 2014), pp. 57–8.
16   *Freeman's Journal*, 7 August 1917.
17   Anthony J. Jordon, *W.T. Cosgrave 1880–1965* (Dublin, 2006), p. 39.
18   *Kilkenny People*, 26 December 2014 – Professor Michael Laffan.
19   Stephen Collins, *The Cosgrave Legacy* (Dublin, 1996), pp. 14–15.
20   As far back as 1900 Keane had been in conflict with the authorities regarding his staunch
      support of Home Rule and his negative comments about the reception afforded to Queen
      Victoria in Dublin. He was also prosecuted in 1909 for promoting an agrarian assembly

liable to cause disaffection. The censorship of his newspaper after the 1916 Rebellion had also made national headlines.

21 *Cork Examiner*, 20 July 1917.

22 BMH WS 384 (J.J. O' Kelly, aka 'Sceilg').

23 Magennis was born in Maudlin Street in Kilkenny City in 1870. He was conferred with the Freedom of Kilkenny City in 1952 and died in 1953. The surname was later gaelicised to 'McGuinness', which is how later generations of the family spelt it. Magennis was a grand-uncle to the more recent Fianna Fáil TD John McGuinness.

24 *Sunday Independent*, 29 July 1917.

25 *The Irish Times*, 11 August 1917.

26 BMH WS 1,093 (Thomas Treacy).

27 *Ulster Herald*, 18 August 1917.

28 Collins, *The Cosgrave Legacy* (Dublin, 1996), p. 15.

29 *Irish Independent*, 15 August 1917, *Cork Examiner*, 15 August 1917.

30 *Ulster Herald*, 18 August 1917.

31 BMH WS 1,093 (Thomas Treacy).

32 MA MSPC/34/50645 (Thomas Treacy).

33 BMH WS 1,006 (Martin Kealy), WS 1,101 (Martin Cassidy), WS 1,586 (James Holohan).

34 BMH WS 1,614 (Timothy Hennessy).

35 BMH WS 1,093 (Thomas Treacy).

36 Comerford, *My Kilkenny I.R.A. Days* (Kilkenny, 1978), p. 100.

37 BMH WS 966 (John Walsh). *Kilkenny People*, 4 May 1918. BMH WS 980 (Edward Aylward).

38 *Irish Independent*, 12 June 1918.

39 Comerford, *My Kilkenny I.R.A. Days* (Kilkenny, 1978), pp. 93–5, 110–11.

40 BMH WS 1,006 (Martin Kealy).

41 MA MSPC/34/SP/15748 (Simon O'Leary).

42 *Cork Examiner*, 31 July 1918.

43 BMH WS 1,609 (Michael O'Carroll).

44 NA WO 35/94/55, Breach of DRR, Letter from J. Meylon, dated 16 October 1918.

45 Richard Sinnott, *Irish Voters Decide: Voting Behaviour in Elections and Referendums Since 1918.* (Manchester, 1995), p. 25.

46 BMH WS 690 (Mrs James O'Mara – M.A. O'Mara). A Limerick native, James O'Mara (1873–1948) was independently wealthy due to the family bacon processing business. He spent twenty years living in London and when he was elected to the House of Commons in 1901 he was the youngest member along with Winston Churchill. He introduced the Bill in the House of Commons that made Saint Patrick's Day a bank holiday in Ireland for the first time in 1903. O'Mara was the chief organiser for the 'bond drive' (raising of funds) in America during the War of Independence.

47 Maher, *The Flying Column West Kilkenny* (Dublin, 1987), p. 4.

48 Dunne, *Peter's Key* (Cork, 2012), p. 78.

49 *Kilkenny Moderator*, 1 January 1919.

50 BMH WS 1,032 (James Lalor).

51 Caitriona Foley, *The Last Irish Plague, the Great Flu Epidemic in Ireland 1918–19* (Dublin, 2011), p. 14

52 Foley, *The Last Irish Plague* (Dublin, 2011), pp. 19–21.
53 *Kilkenny People*, 2 November 1918.
54 BMH WS 1,093 (Thomas Treacy).
55 Private Papers, Kathleen Long-Walsh, Clogga, Mooncoin, Co Kilkenny. Letter from Sr Bernard (Callan) to Kattie Long (née Kirwan), Vinesgrove, Dunnamaggin.

CHAPTER 4

1 Seán O'Casey, *The Shadow of a Gunman*, (1923, 1998:39). Kathleen Ní Houlihan was the name given to the female personification of Ireland (sometimes referred to as the 'Sean-Bhean Bhocht'). Made most famous by W.B. Yeats.
2 Hopkinson, *The Irish War of Independence* (Dublin, 2004), p. 123.
3 The Mullinahone Company transferred officially to the 7th Kilkenny Battalion from the Tipperary Brigade in June 1920. The nearest town to Mullinahone was Callan and it was deemed more logical (see BMH WS 1,243 (Thomas O'Carroll)).
4 Military Archives, MSPC/RO/163A. Also, MSPC/34/660 (Hannah Murphy).
5 BMH WS 1,093 (Thomas Treacy).
6 BMH WS 1,601 (Garrett Brennan). O'Dwyer was voted Kilkenny Brigade O/C in the middle of January 1921, meaning the Brigade was without a leader for over a month during a crucial period.
7 MA MSPC/RO/154-163A.
8 Towards the end of the War of Independence, the RIC County Inspector estimated membership of the IRA to be 2,370, which was reasonably accurate (see, NA CO 904/116, July 1921).
9 Peter Hart, *The I.R.A. & Its Enemies, Violence and Community in Cork 1916-1923* (Oxford, 1999), p. 163.
10 BMH WS 1,093 (Thomas Treacy), BMH WS 1,208 (Daniel J. Stapleton).
11 Joost Augusteijn, *From Public Defiance to Guerrilla Warfare: The Experience of Ordinary Volunteers in the Irish War of Independence, 1916-1921* (Dublin, 1996), p. 175.
12 NAI 1911 Census: Peter DeLoughry, James Lalor, Ned Comerford and BMH WS 1,093 (Thomas Treacy)
13 MA MSPC/CMB/153-162 – membership at the time of the Truce. Many Companies were only officially established in the final months of the war in 1921.
14 NA CO 904/116, July 1921. Women with an active role in the organisation did not escape the scrutiny of Crown Forces. Under a section on 'IRA Personal', a British Intelligence report from May 1921 stated that: 'Mrs Luc[e]y of Callan is the leading local spirit of the Cumann na mBan.' See, BMH WS 883 (John M. MacCarthy) Appendix N – Copy of *Weekly Intelligence Summary* dated 17 May 1921.
15 MSPC/CMB/153 (Hanna Murphy letter – 15 August 1938).
16 The Tithe War (1830–1836) was ignited by protests against the paying of tithes – a form of agrarian-based taxes – which were utilised for the upkeep of the Established (Anglican) Church. The unyielding attitude of many of the local Church of Ireland clergy in County Kilkenny and their refusal to lower the rates in many cases, escalated the situation.

17 Noreen Higgins-McHugh, 'The 1830s Tithe Riots' in *Riotous Assemblies, Rebels, Riots &*
    Revolts in Ireland, eds William Sheehan and Maura Cronin (Cork, 2011), pp. 80–90.

18 Maher, *In the Shade of Slievenamon* (Dublin, 2015), p. 271.

19 Fin Dwyer, 'Secret Societies, Communism & Coal; Life in Castlecomer Colliery Part 1'.
    Irish History Podcast (2015), https://itunes.apple.com/ie/podcast/irish-history-podcast/
    id363368392, accessed 31 March 2017.

20 Samuel Clarke, *Social Origins of the Irish Land War* (Princeton, 2014), p. 212.

21 A.D. Harvey, 'Who Were the Auxiliaries?', *The Historical Journal*, 35, no. 3 (1992), pp.
    665–9.

22 *Kilkenny People*, 4 January 1919.

23 *Kilkenny Moderator*, 25 January 1919.

24 Dunne, *Peter's Key* (Cork, 2012), pp. 158–67.

25 *Kilkenny Moderator*, 23 March 1919 and *Irish Independent*, 24 March 1919.

26 BMH WS 1,093 (Thomas Treacy).

27 *Kilkenny Moderator*, 21 February 1920.

28 Laffan, *The Resurrection of Ireland* (Cambridge, 1999), p. 311.

29 Rouse, *Sport and Ireland* (Oxford, 2015), p. 114.

30 *Kilkenny Moderator*, 15 February 1919.

31 *Irish Independent*, 24 February 1919. *Cork Examiner*, 26 February 1919.

32 BMH WS 1,335 (James Leahy).

33 *Kilkenny Moderator*, 1 February 1919.

34 *Kilkenny Moderator*, 1 March 1919.

35 Now James Stephens Barracks.

36 BMH WS 1,032 (James Lalor).

37 Comerford, *My Kilkenny I.R.A. Days* (Kilkenny, 1978), p. 766. See also; BMH WS 1,271
    (Patrick Dunphy).

38 *Sunday Independent*, 28 September 1919. *Kilkenny People*, 4 October 1919.

39 UCDA P133/12 (James Lalor Papers). Statement by John Kinsella, Patrick Street, Kilkenny
    City.

40 BMH WS 1,093 (Thomas Treacy).

41 MA MSPC/34/50645 (Thomas Treacy). BMH WS 1,335 (James Leahy).

42 BMH WS 1,601 (Garrett Brennan).

43 *Cork Examiner*, 3 March 1920.

44 BMH WS 1,614 (Timothy Hennessy).

45 BMH WS 1,093 (Thomas Treacy). The moon cycle for 1920 can be sourced here; www.
    fullmoon.info/en/fullmoon-calendar/1920.html, accessed 25 September 2017.

46 BMH WS 1,093 (Thomas Treacy).

47 MA MSPC/34/50645 (Thomas Treacy).

48 BMH WS 1,032 (James Lalor).

49 BMH WS 1,335 (James Leahy).

50 *Munster Express*, 12 June 1920 and *Kilkenny Moderator*, 13 March 1920.

51 BMH WS 1,614 (Timothy Hennessy).

52 *Cork Examiner*, 11 March 1920.

53 *Kilkenny Moderator*, 12 June 1920.

54 *Kilkenny People*, 13 March 1920.

55   Michael John Buggy (1857–1935) was the principal solicitor used by numerous Kilkenny councils for decades. He died at sea while returning from a holiday in New York. He left an estate valued at £46,805. *Kilkenny People*, May 1935.

56   *Kilkenny Moderator* and *Munster Express*, 12 June 1920.

57   *Kilkenny People*, 23 April 1921.

58   BMH WS 1,705 (Nicholas Carroll) and BMH WS 1,032 (James Lalor).

59   *Kilkenny Moderator*, 5 June 1920.

60   *Kilkenny People*, 28 August 1920.

61   NA CO 904/112, June 1920.

62   BMH WS 1,705 (Nicholas Carroll).

63   These dates were chosen for burnings throughout the country by IRA GHQ. While Easter was already symbolic as a result of the Rising four years previously, by choosing Holy Days to carry out attacks it insured many members of the IRA would be free from work obligations on those dates – which aimed to protect them from suspicious employers etc.

64   BMH WS; 1,642, 1,335, 1,618, 1,609, 1,006, 1,271, 1,601, 1,614, 1,586. *Irish Independent*, 10 February 1921, *Kilkenny Journal*, 10 November 1920. County Kilkenny had about thirty-eight RIC Barracks in 1911.

65   BMH WS 1,609 (Michael O'Carroll).

66   *Cork Examiner*, 23 July 1920.

67   MA MSPC/34/SP/35524, James Walsh (Mooncoin) and BMH WS 1,614 (Timothy Hennessy), BMH WS 1,335 (James Leahy), BMH WS 966 (John Walsh).

68   Chief Secretary of Ireland Registered Papers, November 1920 – 'Callan and Thomastown courthouses commandeered by military'. CSORP/CR/331/1920/19298.

69   *Kilkenny Journal*, 10 April 1920 – This was to impede the collection of local taxes, the funds of which would have been sent to the British Local Government Board.

70   MA CP/03/15 – Collins Papers. Martin Cassidy was one of the IRA party who decided not to interfere with the office on the night in question. Sq ee; BMH WS 1,101 (Martin Cassidy).

71   *Kilkenny Moderator*, 19 June 1920, *Kilkenny People*, 16 July 1921. Also, Stoneyford Courthouse and RIC Barracks were found to be worth £1,200.

72   *Kilkenny Journal*, 16 July 1921.

73   NA CO 904/111 March 1920.

74   NA CO 904/112 August 1920.

75   Ibid., Also; Jim Maher, *The Flying Column West Kilkenny, 1916–1921* (Dublin, 1987), pp. 12–13.

76   BMH WS 1,454 (James Leahy).

77   *www.theauxiliaries.com/men-alphabetical/men-k/kirkwood/kirkwood.html*, accessed 20 May 2017.

78   MA MSPC/24/SP/5679 and BMH WS 1,360 (Colonel James Delaney).

79   BMH WS 1,609 (Michael O'Carroll). Michael O'Carroll, a member of the 5th IRA Battalion, travelled to Dublin and met Collins in Vaughan's Hotel. The price paid was £9 each for nine rifles, and £12 for a 'Peter the Painter' automatic pistol.

80   BMH WS 1,335 (James Leahy).

81   Comerford, *My Kilkenny I.R.A. Days* (Kilkenny, 1978), p. 166.

82   MA Con.Ran/130 (John Murphy) and Con.Ran/69 (William Bolger). Murphy had fought
      in the First World War and was aged 25 at the time of the mutiny, while Bolger was aged 23
      and had enlisted the previous year. Murphy Army No: 7143527, Bolger Army No: 7144515.
      During the 1930s they both applied to the Irish Free State for a military pension which was
      offered to participants of the India Mutiny, but because they had not officially been court-
      marshalled in India – while they also had not been imprisoned for the required twelve
      months – their claim was rejected.

83   BMH WS 1,609 (Michael O' Carroll).

84   BMH WS 1,335 (James Leahy).

85   BMH WS 1,642 (Ned Halley).

86   *Kilkenny Moderator*, 11 September 1920.

87   MA MSPC/24/SP11874 (James Blanchfield).

88   BMH WS 966 (John Walsh).

89   NA CO 904/113, November 1920 and BMH WS 1,609 (Michael O'Carroll).

90   BMH WS 966 (John Walsh).

91   MA MSPC/24/SP/13532 (James O'Hanrahan).

92   *Kilkenny People*, 20 April 1921.

93   NA WO 35/136, Court Martial Case Registers, Patrick Lanigan and Edward Naddy.

94   *Kilkenny People*, 28 January 1922 and BMH WS 966 (John Walsh).

95   Joseph McKenna, *Guerrilla Warfare in the Irish War of Independence, 1919–1921* (Jefferson,
      2011), p. 155.

96   NA WO 35/124, Civilian Courts Martial, Patrick Funcheon, 7 November 1920.

97   MA MSPC/34/SP/39315. This event occurred in March 1921. Beck was later refused a
      military pension, as he did not have the defined 'active service'.

98   Thomas J. Whyte, *The Story of Woodstock in Inistioge* (Dublin, 2007), p. 303.

99   BMH WS 1,032 (James Lalor).

100   MA MSPC/34/SP/60441 – Mary (Maisie) O'Kelly (née Mary Stallard).

101   UCDA P133/10 (James Lalor Papers). Edward Holland pension application No: 19897. 1st
      Battalion O/C, Timothy Hennessy, selected Holland to accompany O'Malley (see; BMH
      WS 1,614).

102   *Kilkenny People*, 26 December 1936.

103   O'Malley, *On Another Man's Wound* (Dublin, 2013), pp. 281–3.

104   *Kilkenny People*, 26 December 1936. Margaret Hanrahan lived for another three years,
      passing away on 2 June 1923, aged 83 years.

105   NA CO 904/113, December 1920.

106   NA WO 35/75 – 'Arrests at Cappagh'.

107   O'Malley, *On Another Man's Wound* (Dublin, 2013), pp. 284–5.

108   NA WO 35/208/120 and WO 35/135 – Courts Martial of Civilians (including Case files) –
      Edward Holland

109   Dunne, *Peter's Key* (Cork, 2012), p. 200.

110   BMH WS 1,601 (Garrett Brennan). Because of DeLoughry's prestige in the community,
      and the fact that he was not to the forefront of the military campaign, he was released six
      weeks later in January 1921.

111   BMH WS 980 (Edward J. Aylward), BMH WS 1,335 (James Leahy), *Kilkenny Moderator*,
      25 December 1920. Death Index; GRO, (Thomas Walsh): April–June 1921, Callan, vol. 4,
      p. 315. Walsh was unmarried.

112 *Kilkenny Journal*, 24 December 1920, *Irish Independent*, 24 December 1920.
113 *Cork Examiner*, 18 April 1921.
114 *The Times*, 22 December 1920.

CHAPTER 5

1 *Irish Independent*, 5 January 1921. Martial Law was declared at the end of December 1920, and came into effect in the second week of January 1921.
2 BMH WS 1,335 (James Leahy).
3 BMH WS 1,601 (Garrett Brennan).
4 Comerford, *My Kilkenny I.R.A. Days* (Kilkenny, 1978), pp. 529–30.
5 BMH WS 1,601 (Garrett Brennan).
6 NA WO 35/147A/53 – Inquiry in Lieu of Inquest; Michael Cassidy – 3rd Witness: Elizabeth Olive Campion.
7 Comerford, *My Kilkenny IRA Days* (Kilkenny, 1978), pp. 530–2. *Irish Independent*, 6 January 1921.
8 NA WO 35/147A/53 – Inquiry in Lieu of Inquest; Michael Cassidy – 1st Witness: John Cassidy.
9 *The Police Gazette, Hue-And-Cry*, 12 April 1921.
10 NA WO 35/147A/53 – Inquiry in Lieu of Inquest; Michael Cassidy – 5th Witness: Captain Sinclair.
11 *Irish Independent*, 15 February 1921.
12 BMH WS 1,496 (John Hynes), BMH WS 1,335 (James Leahy).
13 The military barracks in Kilkenny is now known as 'James Stephens Barracks'. Kilkenny Jail/Gaol was located on Gaol Road but no longer exists. A housing estate is built on the location.
14 BMH WS 1,614 (Timothy Hennessy).
15 *Irish Independent*, 22 February 1921 and *Kilkenny People*, 26 February 1921.
16 NA WO 35/151 – Inquiry in Lieu of Inquest; Thomas Hennessy and Thomas Dollard – 4th, 5th, 6th, 7th Witnesses.
17 BMH WS 1,614 (Timothy Hennessy). Also see; MSPC/1D351 (Michael Dermody). John Dermody received £75 from the Free State Government for the loss of his son.
18 Maher, *In the Shade of Slievenamon* (Dublin, 2015), pp. 146–7. John Fitzgerald, *Kilkenny, a Blast from the Past* (Cork, 2005), pp. 325–8.
19 Maher, *In the Shade of Slievenamon* (Dublin, 2015), pp. 156–63.
20 BMH WS 1335 (James Leahy).
21 NA WO 35/157B/22 – 'Court of Enquiry into the Affray at Garryricken House …', 1st, 3rd Witnesses.
22 BMH WS 1335 (James Leahy).
23 *The Police Gazette, Hue-And-Cry*, 12 April 1921.
24 *Kilkenny People*, 19 March 1921.
25 Maher, *In the Shade of Slievenamon* (Dublin, 2015), p. 171.
26 NA WO 35/157B/22 – 'Court of Enquiry into the Affray at Garryricken House …', Findings.
27 BMH WS 1,335 (James Leahy) p. 29.

28   BMH WS 980 (Edward J. Aylward).

29   *Kilkenny People*, 16 July 1921 and 22 October 1921.

30   John Borgonovo *et al.*, *Atlas of the Irish Revolution* (Cork, 2017), p. 350. Also; *Kilkenny People*, 7 May 1921.

31   BMH WS 1,335 (James Leahy).

32   *Cork Examiner*, 12 April 1921.

33   NA HO 144/22334 – 'Special advances to widows of members of Royal Irish Constabulary murdered on duty'. The largest pay-out was to the widow of DI Lea-Wilson, who was assassinated in Wexford on the orders of Michael Collins. She was awarded £17,000.

34   BMH WS 1,101 (Martin Cassidy) and BMH WS 980 (Edward J. Aylward). Another attempt was made to kill Whyte with a bomb at his home, but he also avoided injury on that occasion.

35   Maher, *In the Shade of Slievenamon* (Dublin, 2015), p. 290. Jack Donovan was the unfortunate boy who shot Brett. The funeral that passed through Callan on 25 August 1921 was one of the 'biggest ever seen in the area'.

36   MA MSPC/34/18092 (Nano Meagher). Mangolds were a type of root vegetable (similar to sugar beet) which were usually grown by farmers to feed livestock during the winter months.

37   BMH WS 1,335 (James Leahy).

38   NAI DELG 14/9. Minutes of Thomastown RDC Meeting, 8 August 1921.

39   BMH WS 151 (James Ryan).

40   MA MSPC/34/SP/62536 and 24/1P2 (William Aylward). BMH WS 1618 (Michael Connolly). William Aylward (1901–1977) spent the remainder of his life in Melbourne, Australia. John Kearns was Captain of the Knockmoylan Company IRA but later moved to Nicholastown, Mooncoin. Mullinavat Barracks had been attacked in January and April 1921. Separately, on other occasions, shots were fired and grenades were thrown at the barracks.

41   BMH WS 1,642 (Ned Halley).

42   BMH WS 1,705 (Nicholas Carroll).

43   BMH WS 980 (Edward J. Aylward).

44   NA CO 904/115, April 1921.

45   BMH WS 980 (Edward J. Aylward).

46   BMH WS 1,642 (Ned Halley).

47   *Irish Independent*, 25 May 1921.

48   *Kilkenny People*, 21 May 1921, *Irish Independent*, 16 May 1921, *Cork Examiner*, 24 June 1921.

49   Maher, *In the Shade of Slievenamon* (Dublin, 2015), pp. 220–5. Also see; MA MSPC/1D101 (John Quinn).

50   Hansard House of Commons Debates, 23 June 1921, '*Military Operations*'. Mr Denis Henry in response to question of Mr James Kiley (vol: 143 cc: 1518-20).

51   Maher, *In the Shade of Slievenamon* (Dublin, 2015), pp. 235–6.

52   *Kilkenny Journal* and *Kilkenny People*, 28 May 1921.

53   BMH WS 980 (Edward J. Aylward).

54   *Cork Examiner*, 18 May 1921, *Kilkenny People*, 21 May 1921. GRO, Death Index (Martin Dermody): October–December 1921, Kilkenny, Volume:3 Page: 299 (note; Dermody's age is incorrectly stated as 45).

55 NA WO 35/162 – Register of Cases (45566/202), dated 29 May 1921.

56 *Kilkenny Moderator*, 21 May 1921.

57 UCDA P7/A/19(2), Mulcahy Papers, Mulcahy to Brigade Commandant Kilkenny, 1 June 1921. In later life, Mulcahy became leader of Fine Gael.

58 NA CO 904/115, June 1921.

59 BMH WS 966 (John Walsh).

60 *www.theauxiliaries.com/men-alphabetical/men-f/french/french.html*, accessed 1 May 2017. Kirke lived to the age of 71, passing away in 1963.

61 *Nenagh News*, 18 June 1921. *Kilkenny People*, 18 June 1921. *Kilkenny Journal*, 28 January 1922.

62 *Kilkenny Moderator*, 28 January 1922.

63 A number of Crown Force soldiers were injured during the Uskerty Wood ambush on 2 May 1921. A convey of military lorries – which were required to personally deliver pensions to former RIC and British soldiers in the area due to the IRA's policy of raiding mail – were ambushed 4 km southeast of Castlecomer. The failed Bagnelstown RIC Barracks attack was scheduled for the night of 16 April 1921 (see; BMH WS 1,601).

64 BMH WS 1,601 (Garrett Brennan). Michael Fleming was formerly in the RIC. His brother had been the Battalion O/C up until 1920 when he was replaced by O'Dwyer.

65 Tom Lyng, *Castlecomer Connections* (Kilkenny, 1984), pp. 162–3. BMH WS 1,601 (Garrett Brennan).

66 BMH WS 1,601 (Garrett Brennan). Brennan had joined the Irish Volunteers on the night of their formation in Dublin in 1913. He was a student in UCD where his lecturers included Eoin MacNeill and Thomas MacDonagh. In later life, Brennan became Deputy-Commissioner of An Garda Síochána.

67 BMH WS 1,102 (James Brennan).

68 Lyng, *Castlecomer Connections* (Kilkenny, 1984), pp. 163–5.

69 The location of the Coolbawn memorial is roughly the position where Nicholas Mullins died. Seán Hartley died behind the ditch on the opposite side of the road from the monument.

70 BMH WS 1,360 (Colonel James Delaney). *Irish Independent*, 20 June 1921.

71 NA WO 35/155A/17 – Inquiry in Lieu of Inquest; Nicholas Mullins – 3rd, 4th Evidence.

72 MA MSPC/1D218 (Seán Hartley). MSPC/1D222 (Nicholas Mullins) – applications by Annie (mother) and Kathleen Mullins (sister). Eventually Annie Mullins, Nicholas's mother, received £100 for the loss of her son from the Free State Government. She also received a military pension of £180 per year in 1953 but died in 1955, aged 91. Seán's father, Edward Hartley, received £50 for his son's death, although initially he asked for £3,000.

73 NAI DELG 14/9. Minutes of Thomastown PLU Meeting, June 1921. Proposed and seconded by Councillors McDonald and Moore.

74 NLI, MS 22,116, J.J. O'Connell Papers. 'Activities in Glenmore …', Statement by Mrs Ellen Cassin.

75 UCDA, P133-1, James Lalor Papers. Doyle was released from prison in January 1922.

76 Comerford, *My Kilkenny IRA Days* (Kilkenny, 1978), p. 707.

77 Comerford, *My Kilkenny IRA Days* (Kilkenny, 1978), pp. 761–5.

78   NA CO 904/116, July 1921. Dreaper's house was burned down on the night of 7 July 1921 by '30' IRA men. For compensation claim, see; NAI FIN/COMP/2/10/154. The sisters also received money from the British Government in a scheme initiated to help loyalist supporters who were targeted during the troubles. Also; Lyng, *Castlecomer Connections* (Kilkenny, 1984), p. 167.

79   *Cork Examiner*, 20 June 1921.

80   NA WO 35/146A/27 – Inquiry in Lieu of Inquest; Albert Lawrence Bradford – 1st and 2nd Evidence (Bradford was originally from Essex in England).

81   NA CO 904/115, June 1921.

82   Interview notes; Jim Maher in conversation with Jack 'Na Cuille' Walsh (1968), O/C 9th Kilkenny Battalion.

83   *Irish Independent*, 21 June 1921and *Kilkenny People*, 12 November 1921.

84   NA CO 904/115, June 1921 – occurred 26 June 1921.

85   *Cork Examiner*, 13 July 1921. Maher, *In the Shade of Slievenamon* (Dublin, 2015), pp. 245, 250.

CHAPTER 6

1   *Cork Examiner*, 28 December 1920.

2   NA WO 35/158 – First Inquiry 24 December 1920 (Margaret Ryan) – 2nd Witness, Josephine Delaney.

3   NA WO 35/158 – First Inquiry 24 December 1920 – 1st Witness; Michael Ryan.

4   *Kilkenny Journal*, 29 December 1920.

5   General Register Office. Index Reference: Margaret Ryan, October–December 1920, Callan, Volume:4, Page: 276

6   Maher, *The Flying Column*, (Dublin, 1987), p. 61.

7   NA CO 904/113, December 1920.

8   NLI, MS 49,810/12, Laurence Ginnell Papers 1913–1923. *Statement of Atrocities on Women in Ireland, made and signed by Mrs. Hanna Sheehy-Skeffington.*

9   NA WO 35/158 – Inquiry in lieu of Inquest – Margaret Ryan, '3rd Witness'.

10   NA WO 35/158 – Inquiry in lieu of Inquest – Margaret Ryan, Letter from Captain Gordon 'A' Coy.

11   NA WO 35/158 – Letter from 'HQ 6th Division Cork' to 'GHQ Parkgate Dublin' – 24 April 1921.

12   NA WO 35/158 – 3rd Inquiry – Victoria Barracks 4 May 1921.

13   *Kilkenny People*, 1 January 1921.

14   *Freeman's Journal*, 22 February 1921.

15   NA WO 35/151 – Inquiry in Lieu of Inquest; Thomas Hennessy and Thomas Dollard – 4th Witness (Hawthorn).

16   *Kilkenny People*, 26 February 1921.

17   Maher, *In the Shade of Slievenamon* (Dublin, 2015), pp. 301–2.

18   *The Irish Times*, 28 February 1921.

19   NA WO 35/151 – Inquiry in Lieu of Inquest; Thomas Hennessy and Thomas Dollard – Finding No 6.

20 NA WO 35/18/151B – Inquiry in Lieu of Inquest; James Hoban – 2nd, 3rd Witnesses: Michael/Anastasia Hoban.
21 *Cork Examiner*, 28 April 1921.
22 *Kilkenny People*, 30 April 1921.
23 NA CO 904/115, April 1921.
24 NA WO 35/157A/65 – Inquiry in Lieu of Inquest; Thomas Phelan – 1st–5th Evidence.
25 NAI, 1901/1911 Census. District: Ballyragget, Barony: Fassadinin, Townland: Oldtown. Thomas Phelan was born in Oldtown on 4 June 1902. His father John Phelan died in Oldtown on 1 August 1902 (see; GRO, Death Index Reference: John Phelan, July–September 1902, Castlecomer, Volume: 3, Page: 277).
26 GRO, Index Reference: Thomas Phelan, April–June 1921, Castlecomer, Volume: 3, Page: 297.
27 NA CO 904/113, October 1921; NA CO 904/114, May 1921; NA CO 904/115, June 1921.
28 Augusteijn, *From Public Defiance to Guerrilla Warfare* (Dublin, 1996), p. 15.
29 BMH WS 966 (John Walsh).
30 BMH WS 1,642 (Edward Halley).
31 Hart, *The I.R.A. & Its Enemies* (Oxford, 1999), p. 229.
32 McKenna, *Guerrilla Warfare in the Irish War of Independence* (Jefferson, 2011), p. 155.
33 BMH WS 980 (Edward J. Aylward).
34 Maher, *In the Shade of Slievenamon* (Dublin, 2015), p. 66.
35 MA MSPC/24/SP/13532 (James O'Hanrahan). O'Hanrahan did not have much opportunity to fight either way, as he was arrested in his cousin's house in Inistioge at the same time as Ernie O'Malley.
36 BMH WS 1,601 (Garrett Brennan).
37 MA CP/03/15 – Collins Papers.
38 BMH WS 1,208 (Daniel J. Stapleton). The three explosive compounds Stapleton created – usually at Joe Sweeney's old farmhouse in Dunningstown – were known as follows; 1. Warflour (nitric and sulphuric acid, powdered resin, wheaten flour and potassium chlorate) 2. Irish Cheddar (informal title for cheddite; it was scarce due to the difficulty in obtaining the ingredients; potassium chlorite, nitrobenzene and castor/paraffin oil). 3. Paxo (potassium chlorate and paraffin wax).
39 Eunan O'Halpin, 'Counting Terror, Bloody Sunday and the Dead of the Irish Revolution' in *Terror in Ireland 1916–1923*, ed. David Fitzpatrick (Dublin, 2012), p. 152.
40 O'Halpin, 'Counting Terror' in *Terror in Ireland 1916–1923*, ed. David Fitzpatrick (Dublin, 2012), p. 152. The other county with twenty deaths was Donegal.
41 Augusteijn, *From Public Defiance to Guerrilla Warfare* (Dublin, 1996), p. 180.

CHAPTER 7

1 *Irish Independent*, 1 June 1920.
2 BMH WS 1,093 (Thomas Treacy). It has not been possible to discern the exact number of Republican Police in Kilkenny, as no listing appears to have existed.
3 BMH WS 1,093 (Thomas Treacy).
4 Maher, *In the Shade of Slievenamon* (Dublin, 2015), pp. 104–5

5   Hopkinson, *The Irish War of Independence* (Dublin, 2004), p. 44.
6   BMH WS 1,093 (Thomas Treacy).
7   The house and land are now a well-known hotel and golf course.
8   BMH WS 980 (Edward J. Aylward).
9   *Kilkenny Moderator*, 5 June 1920.
10 *Kilkenny Journal*, 5 June 1920.
11 BMH WS 1,271 (Patrick Dunphy).
12 BMH WS 1,006 (Martin Kealy).
13 *Kilkenny Moderator*, 5 June 1920.
14 BMH WS 1,271 (Patrick Dunphy).
15 *Kilkenny Journal*, 12 June 1920.
16 UCDA, P133–4, James Lalor Papers. Letter from Mícheál Ó Coileáin (Michael Collins) to James Lalor. Dated: 20 February 1920.
17 UCDA, P133–4, James Lalor Papers. Letter from Mícheál Ó Coileáin (Michael Collins) to James Lalor. Dated: 15 March 1920. In another letter he asks specifically about the town of Ballyragget (23 March 1920).
18 UCDA, P133–4, James Lalor Papers. Letter from Fleming to Lalor. Dated: 22 December 1922.
19 PR was introduced by the British Government primarily to provide representation for minority groupings; most specifically to benefit southern Unionists.
20 Marie Coleman, *The Irish Revolution, 1916–1923* (London, 2013), p. 61.
21 *Irish Independent*, 17 January 1920.
22 NA CO 904/111, January 1920.
23 NA CO 904/113, October 1920.
24 Borgonovo *et al.*, (eds), *Atlas of the Irish Revolution* (Cork, 2017), p. 585.
25 *Kilkenny Moderator*, 24 January 1920. DeLoughry was first elected to public office as an Urban Councillor in January 1911. He later became a TD and Free State Senator, a position he held until his death in 1931.
26 UCD Archives, P133–4, James Lalor Papers. Letter from Minister for Local Government to James Lalor, 30 March 1920.
27 *Kilkenny Journal*, 5 May 1920.
28 *Kilkenny Moderator*, 3 January 1920.
29 Dunne, *Peter's Key* (Cork, 2012), p. 182.
30 *Freeman's Journal*, 23 October 1919.
31 *Kilkenny People*, 5 June 1920.
32 *Kilkenny Moderator*, 12 June 1920.
33 Comerford, *My Kilkenny I.R.A. Days* (Kilkenny, 1978), pp. 198–9.
34 *Kilkenny Journal*, 12 June 1920. *Munster Express*, 12 June 1920. *Freeman's Journal*, 10 June 1920.
35 *Irish Independent*, 14 June 1920 and *Kilkenny People*, 12 June 1920. For the Kilkenny County Council seats; Ballyragget Electoral District returned four out of four seats to Sinn Féin; Thomastown Electoral District also returned four out of four seats to Sinn Féin; Piltown Electoral District returned five out of five seats to Sinn Féin; Kilkenny (City) Electoral District returned three seats to Sinn Féin, two to Labour and one to an Independent. As outlined, the vast majority of District Councillors were returned for Sinn Féin and Labour affiliated

candidates. One seat in the Knocktopher area was won by Richard Holohan, representing the 'Farmers [Union] Board', while the Freshford area also returned an Independent. Labour's biggest success of the District Elections was in Thomastown, where they won three seats compared to Sinn Féin's two. This success was as a result of an agreement between the parties which saw three Sinn Féin candidates withdraw prior to election day.

36   *Kilkenny People*, 12 June 1920.

37   NA CO 904/112, June 1920.

38   *Kilkenny People*, 19 June 1920.

39   NAI DELG 14/1–15.

40   NAI DELG 14/2 and DELG 14/14.

41   BMH WS 980 (Edward J. Aylward).

42   *Kilkenny Journal*, 25 June 1921.

43   Dáil Éireann Debates Vol: F No: 20. Kevin O'Higgins, 'Debate on Reports, Department of Local Government', 11 March 1921.

44   NAI DELG 14/1. 'RE: Callan Union', Letter to Dáil LGB from J. Henderson, 13 October 1921.

45   NAI DELG 14/1. Letter to the Clerk Callan Union from Dáil LGB, 20 September 1921.

46   NA CO 904/113, November 1920.

47   NAI DELG 14/11. Minutes of Urlingford PLU Meeting, 15 January 1921.

48   NAI DELG 14/11. Minutes of Urlingford PLU Meeting, 12 February 1921. *Freeman's Journal*, 10 June 1920.

49   NAI DELG 14/5. Letter from Minister of Local Government to Denis O'Carroll, 9 September 1920. Also, see letter from O'Carroll to Cosgrave, dated 2 September 1920, for biographical information. Some years earlier, O'Carroll had written books about local history.

50   NAI DELG 14/5. Minutes of Castlecomer Board of Guardians, 3 November 1920.

51   NA WO 35/122/26 – Civilians Tried by Courts Martial – 'James Butler and three others' – copy of letter confiscated by Crown Forces in Castlecomer, sent from Dáil LGB and dated 14 December 1920.

52   *Kilkenny Moderator*, 13 November 1920.

53   NAI DELG 14/9. Minutes of Thomastown Board of Guardians, 13 November 1920.

54   NA WO 35/122/26 – Civilians Tried by Courts Martial – James Butler, John Lacey, Patrick Mulhall, Thomas Conroy – Witnesses 1, 2 and 3 present at Board meeting.

55   NAI DELG 14/4. Letter from Kevin O'Higgins to Chief of Inspection, 8 April 1921. Kevin O'Higgins was later a member of the Cumann na nGaedheal party (subsequently Fine Gael) and was assassinated by the IRA in 1927.

56   NAI DELG 14/4. Minutes of a joint meeting of Castlecomer Board of Guardians and Rural District Council held on 18 July 1921 and 22 July 1921.

57   NAI DELG 14/4. Minutes of Castlecomer Rural District Council held on 5 December 1921.

58   NAI DELG 14/13. Minutes of Waterford Rural District Meeting, 30 October 1920.

59   NAI DELG 14/13. Minutes of Waterford Rural District Council No 2 (Co Kilkenny), 25 September 1920. Inhabitants of Belfast, and other Ulster towns, would go on to suffer further violence in early 1922 during the Truce period.

60   NA CO 904/115, May 1921.

61   *Kilkenny Journal*, 20 October 1920.

62   Marilyn Silverman and P.H. Gulliver, *In the Valley of the Nore* (Dublin, 1986), p. 187.

63   NA CO 904/153. Breaches of the Truce in Kilkenny. 'Found posted at Ballyragget', 25 September 1921.

64   NAI DELG 14/15. Letter from Minister of Local Government to R.H. Smithwick, 10 November 1921.

65   NAI DELG 14/9. Letter from Clerk of Thomastown Union to Minister of Local Government, 13 June 1921.

66   NAI DELG 14/9. Minutes of Thomastown PLU Meeting, 17 December 1920.

67   NAI DELG 14/9. Minutes of Thomastown PLU Meeting, 5 February 1921.

68   BMH WS 1,413 (Tadhg Kennedy) – Appendices A–F, 'Commission of Inquiry into Local Government'. The Thomastown Workhouse/Hospital is now known as 'St Columba's'.

69   NAI DELG 14/13. Minutes of Waterford Rural District Meeting, 25 June 1921.

70   *Kilkenny People*, 27 July 1912. The council did not take the letter seriously with one member recommending that Walsh should be put 'into a bath [to cool down]'. Women could be voted onto the Board of Guardians at this time but it was an all-male board in Kilkenny.

CHAPTER 8

1   *The Irish Times*, 21 October 1921. Question asked to the Chief Secretary of Ireland by Colonel Gretton MP.

2   *Kilkenny Moderator*, 16 and 23 July 1921.

3   *Kilkenny Moderator*, 16 July 1921.

4   Ibid.

5   NA CO 904/116, September 1921.

6   *Kilkenny People*, 24 December 1921 (Christmas Supplement).

7   NA CO 904/116, August 1921. *Evening Herald*, 29 August 1921. *Freeman's Journal*, 30 August 1921.

8   *Kilkenny Journal*, 3 September 1921. The nun, Sister Margaret, had been staying at the home of her cousins, the Gaffneys, in Cuffesgrange.

9   NA CO 904/116, July and August 1921.

10   NA CO 904/116, September 1921. In addition to local disputes, farm prices across all farming sectors – including cattle, pigs and sheep – continued to decline throughout 1921. Milk prices also decreased, with Kilkenny farmers receiving 9 pence per gallon of milk by October 1921. This amount was less than Wexford prices which were 12 pence (1 shilling) per gallon, but compared favourably to farmers in Roscommon and Armagh who received 7 pence and 5 pence per gallon respectively (see *The Irish Times*, 13 October 1921).

11   *Kilkenny Journal*, 17 December 1921. Women were not included in the unemployment figures at this time.

12   *Kilkenny People*, 5 and 12 November 1921. *Freeman's Journal*, 22 September 1921.

13   *Kilkenny People*, 26 November 1921.

14   *Belfast News*, 26 September 1921.

15   NA CO 904/153, Breaches of the Truce in Kilkenny, September 1921. Also *Kilkenny People*, 1 July 1922.

16 *Kilkenny People*, 8 October 1921.

17 *Kilkenny People*, 17 December 1921.

18 NA CO 904/116, September 1921.

19 *Kilkenny People*, 12 November 1921.

20 NA CO 904/153, Breaches of the Truce in Kilkenny.

21 www.greyhound-data.com, accessed July 2017.

22 *Cork Examiner*, 14 November 1921.

23 *Kilkenny Journal*, 26 November 1921.

24 BMH WS 1,006 (Martin Kealy).

25 BMH WS 1,373 (Edward Balfe). It is unknown if any of these photographs still exist.

26 Bill Kelly, 'The tunnel out of Kilkenny jail' in *IRA Jailbreaks 1918–1921* (Cork, 2010), pp. 285–6.

27 Kelly, 'The tunnel out of Kilkenny jail' in *IRA Jailbreaks* (Cork, 2010), pp. 288–9.

28 BMH WS 1,006 (Martin Kealy).

29 Kelly, 'The tunnel out of Kilkenny jail' in *IRA Jailbreaks* (Cork, 2010), p. 290.

30 BMH WS 1,373 (Edward Balfe).

31 *Evening Herald*, 18 November 1921. The prisoners first travelled by ship to Waterford from Cork and then by train from Waterford to Kilkenny.

32 BMH WS 1,135 (William McNamara).

33 *Freeman's Journal*, 22 November 1921.

34 BMH WS 1,373 (Edward Balfe).

35 Maher, *In the Shade of Slievenamon* (Dublin, 2015), p. 258. Among the escapees were Edward Punch and Timothy Murphy who, just a few months previously had been sentenced to death following the fatalities of a number of RIC who were killed in an ambush in Limerick. The men were granted a reprieve during the Truce.

36 BMH WS 1,135 (William McNamara), BMH WS 859 (Laurence Condon). *Kilkenny People*, 3 December 1921.

37 Maher, *In the Shade of Slievenamon* (Dublin, 2015), pp 260–61. Just two months previously, Donoghue and Power had lined out for Kilkenny against Dublin in the Leinster Hurling Final in Croke Park and both got to meet Michael Collins before the game.

38 Kelly, 'The tunnel out of Kilkenny jail' in *IRA Jailbreaks* (Cork, 2010), pp. 292–3.

39 William Murphy, *Political Imprisonment and the Irish, 1912–1921* (Oxford, 2014), p. 234.

40 *Kilkenny People*, 26 November 1921.

41 Maher, *In the Shade of Slievenamon* (Dublin, 2015), pp. 261–2.

42 BMH WS 1,373 (Edward Balfe).

43 Kelly, 'The tunnel out of Kilkenny jail' in *IRA Jailbreaks* (Cork, 2010), pp 292-3. In later life, one of her brothers, Patrick Teehan, became a Fianna Fáil TD and Senator.

44 BMH WS 404 (Mrs McWhinney AKA Linda Kearns) and WS 859 (Laurence Condon).

45 *Kilkenny Moderator*, 26 November 1921.

46 *The New York Times*, 23 November 1921. Examples from the Australian press include: *The Daily News* and *The Maitland Daily Mercury*, 24 November 1921; *Advocate*, 25 November 1921; and *Western Mail*, 1 December 1921.

47 *Kilkenny People*, 3 December 1921.

48 Murphy, *Political Imprisonment and the Irish* (Oxford, 2014), p. 235.

49 BMH WS 1,404 (Thomas Dargan). Hansard House of Commons Debates, 16 March 1922, 'Kilkenny Prison Officers', Sir Hamar Greenwood in response to a question from Thomas Griffiths, vol: 151 cc: 2389-90W.

50 *Kilkenny Moderator*, 3 December 1921.

51 NA CO 904/153, Breaches of the Truce in Kilkenny, December 1921 (DI Moynihan RIC).

52 *Cork Examiner* and *Belfast Newsletter*, 3 December 1921.

53 MA MSPC/24/SP11874 (James Blanchfield). *Kilkenny People*, 17 December 1921. GRO, Death Index (Michael Byrne): October–December 1921, New Ross, Volume: 4, Page: 391. DOD; 10 December 1921.

54 *Kilkenny Journal*, 17 December 1921.

55 *Kilkenny People*, 17 and 24 December 1921.

56 *Kilkenny People*, 17 and 24 December 1921.

57 *Irish Independent*, 10 December 1921.

58 *Kilkenny Journal*, 17 December 1921. Bishop Brownrigg was celebrating his 37th year as Bishop of Ossory that month also.

59 *Kilkenny People*, 10 December 1921.

60 *Kilkenny Journal*, 10 December 1921.

61 *Kilkenny People*, 10 December 1921.

62 R.F. Foster, *Vivid Faces: The Revolutionary Generation in Ireland 1890–1923* (London, 2015), p. 272.

63 *Kilkenny Moderator*, 10 December 1921. The Northern Ireland parliament was opened by King George V in June 1921. The prime minister of Northern Ireland at the time the Treaty was signed was Sir James Craig. The mention of a 'new boundary' was a reference to the establishment of a 'Boundary Commission', which was an element in the Treaty which was expected, by some, to grant large parts of Counties Tyrone and Fermanagh to the Irish Free State, along with the cities of Derry and Newry.

64 *Kilkenny Journal*, 31 December 1921.

65 *Cork Examiner*, 3 January 1922.

66 *Kilkenny Journal*, 7 January 1922. *Freeman's Journal*, 2 January 1922.

67 *Cork Examiner*, 9 December 1921.

68 All four had gained their seats unopposed in the uncontested election of June 1921. James O'Mara, who previously held the South Kilkenny seat, did not run in 1921. Aylward was O/C of the 7th Battalion ASU at the time of the election. See BMH WS 980 (Edward J. Aylward).

69 Dáil Éireann Debates, 6 January 1922, Vol: T No: 14. Deputy Eamonn Aylward, 'Debate on the Treaty'.

70 Dáil Éireann Debates, 6 January 1922, Vol: T No: 14. Deputy Gearóid O'Sullivan, 'Debate on the Treaty'.

71 *Freeman's Journal*, 26 January 1922. *Kilkenny People*, 28 January and 8 April 1922. Watters was kidnapped again in April 1922, with the same aim and a similar outcome when his abductors brought him home after a few days. Tinnypark House is now a private nursing home. Watters died in 1928 at the age of 76.

72 Hansard House of Commons Debates, 16 February 1922, 'Disturbances', Winston Churchill in response to a question from Lieut-Colonel Croft, Vol: 150 cc: 1185-9.

73   *Kilkenny Journal*, 11 February 1922. *Kilkenny Moderator*, 11 and 18 February 1922. The pit reopened in early April 1922.

74   *Evening Herald*, 10 February 1922. *Kilkenny People*, 1 July 1922.

75   *Kilkenny People*, 3 and 31 December 1921.

76   *Kilkenny People*, 31 December 1921. A subvention for the hospital was to be taken from the wages of the miners. This arrangement ran into trouble in less than a year, with Kilkenny Council insisting the hospital close as the owners and miners were not keeping to 'their part of the agreement' in contributing 50 per cent (*Kilkenny People*, 7 October 1922).

77   Comerford, *My Kilkenny I.R.A. Days* (Kilkenny, 1978), p. 885.

78   Ibid., p. 892. Comerford later became a judge in New York.

79   *Kilkenny Moderator*, 11 February 1922. The barracks was initially handed over to the higher ranking Captain Fulham, representing the Provisional Government, who subsequently handed over possession to O'Dwyer.

80   *Freeman's Journal*, 20 March 1922. There was another ceremony the following month in which Archdeacon Doyle blessed the tricolour flag which was handed over by Free State Commandant, Patrick O'Daly (see *Kilkenny Journal*, 29 April 1922).

81   *Kilkenny Journal*, 18 March 1922. *The Soldier's Song* had become popular as a marching song during the 1914–18 era when the Volunteers were at their peak. Peadar Kearney wrote the lyrics for the song in 1907 and it was adopted as the National Anthem of the Irish Free State in 1926.

82   *The Irish Times*, 13 March 1922. *Kilkenny People*, 11 March 1922. The RIC in Castlecomer and Ballyragget began evacuations on 3 March 1922.

83   *Evening Herald*, 25 February 1922 and *Kilkenny Moderator*, 4 March 1922. John's Street RIC Barracks was located close to the entrance of Kilkenny College, currently the Kilkenny County Council offices (County Hall).

84   MA MSPC/34/SP/60441 – Mary (Maisie) O'Kelly (née Stallard).

85   *Evening Herald*, 1 April 1922, and *Kilkenny Moderator*, 8 April 1922.

86   *Kilkenny People*, 25 March 1922. For instance, a number of anti-Treaty IRA raided the business premises of Mayor Peter DeLoughry and stole a motor car. DeLoughry, who was a mechanic by profession amongst other things, had been repairing the car for the new Free State Army. The motor car of RIC CI Whyte had been stolen some weeks previously (see *Kilkenny Moderator*, 11 March 1922).

CHAPTER 9

1   Republican oath adopted in 1919: 'I, [Name], do solemnly swear (or affirm) that I do not and shall not yield a voluntary support to any pretended Government, authority or power within Ireland hostile and inimical thereto, and I do further swear (or affirm) that to the best of my knowledge and ability I will support and defend the Irish Republic and the Government of the Irish Republic, which is Dáil Éireann, against all enemies, foreign and domestic, and I will bear true faith and allegiance to the same, and that I take this obligation freely without any mental reservation or purpose of evasion, so help me, God.'

2   The Oath was in Article 4 of the Treaty. Collins had also received IRB approval for the oath the weekend before the Treaty was signed. The Treaty oath was: 'I [name] do

solemnly swear true faith and allegiance to the Constitution of the Irish Free State as by law established and that I will be faithful to H.M. King George V., his heirs and successors by law, in virtue of the common citizenship of Ireland with Great Britain and her adherence to and membership of the group of nations forming the British Commonwealth of Nations.'

3   Technically the Free State did not come into existence until 6 December 1922, one year after the Treaty was signed and six months into the Civil War. However, the term 'Free State Army' was often used by the newspapers from the beginning of the Civil War.

4   The National Army would later become known as the Defence Forces/Óglaigh na hÉireann. They trace their lineage to the founding of the Irish Volunteers in 1913, later renamed the 'Irish Republican Army' (IRA). Hence, there were four name changes. The uniform of the army in modern times is very similar to that of the original Irish Volunteers uniform, including the buttons engraved with the initials 'IV'. Furthermore, all defence force personnel wear the Irish Defence Forces Cap Badge, with the initials FF or 'Fianna Fáil' (meaning 'soldiers/warriors of Ireland').

5   Ferriter, *A Nation and Not a Rabble* (London, 2015), p. 255.

6   MA MSPC/RO/157. Although three out of the four 3rd IRA Battalion staff took the pro-Treaty position, there were company captains who took the anti-Treaty position. However, some companies actually became defunct in the area by the commencement of the Civil War. Additionally, it is possible that a small number of people joined the anti-Treaty IRA in 1922 who had not been members during the War of Independence but these extra men would be immaterial in skewing the figures.

7   MA MSPC/RO/161 (7th Battalion) and MSPC/RO/163 (9th Battalion).

8   MA MSPC/34/SP/60441 – Mary (Maisie) O'Kelly. Also; MSPC/CMB/153 (Hanna Murphy letters).

9   Cal McCarthy, *Cumann na mBan and the Irish Revolution* (Cork, 2014), p. 204.

10   *Kilkenny People*, 22 April and 2 December 1922.

11   Michael Hopkinson, *Green against Green: The Irish Civil War* (Dublin, 2004), pp. 66–8.

12   Comerford, *My Kilkenny I.R.A. Days* (Kilkenny, 1978), pp. 908–10.

13   John T. Prout married his Irish wife Catherine in New York in 1907. Their son John T. Prout junior – who was born on 12 May 1910 – went with his father to Ireland in 1919. John T. Prout (senior) died on 27 April 1969, in Windham County, Vermont, aged 88 years (see; 1910/30/40 Census of the United States and Burial Records, Familysearch.org, accessed September 2017).

14   *Cork Examiner*, 15 May 1922.

15   *Kilkenny Moderator*, 29 April 1922. Free State forces moved into Woodstock House on 22 April 1922, with the garrison expanding to thirty-five soldiers by 28 April. They were under the command of Captain Lacy.

16   The anti-Treaty IRA Executive had put new emphasis on the Belfast Boycott in light of the increased tensions in the north of the island which had resulted in a Catholic pogrom.

17   *Cork Examiner*, 1 May 1922.

18   *Kilkenny Journal*, 6 May 1922 – quoted from the distributed proclamation.

19   *Kilkenny Journal*, 6 May 1922.

20 Lucey, who was the county agricultural instructor, was renting the residence. The house had recently been purchased by publican John Cleere. He later sought £150 for the damage caused; see *Kilkenny People*, 27 May 1922.

21 *Kilkenny Journal*, 6 May 1922.

22 *Kilkenny Moderator*, 6 May 1922.

23 *Irish Independent*, 5 May 1922.

24 Brennan joined the British Army in 1904 (Lancashire Regiment). He was disciplined on a number of occasions. He had a traumatic First World War, having spent nearly the entire period – from August 1914 until November 1918 – as a prisoner-of-war in Germany. In addition, his 1-year-old son, George, died less than a year previously in July 1921. Brennan was living in Archer Street in Kilkenny City at the time of his death. See; Brannigan and Kirwan, *Kilkenny Families in the Great War* (Thomastown, 2012), p. 33. Also GRO, Death Index (Joseph Brennan): April–June 1922, Kilkenny, Volume: 3, Page: 312 (his death was officially certified as a 'suicide on 2 May by drowning in the River Nore at Kilkenny while suffering from temporary insanity … the same was caused by disease contracted while on active service').

25 *Kilkenny Journal* and *Kilkenny People*, 6 May 1922.

26 *Kilkenny Moderator*, 6 May 1922 and NAI FIN/COMP/2/10/92 (Arthur J. Wilsdon).

27 MA MSPC/34/56911 (Ellen Gibbs née Cahill). Ellen Gibbs lived most of her life at Ahenure, near Callan. She died at the Avondale Nursing Home in Callan on 30 January 1993, at the age of 95.

28 *Kilkenny Moderator* and *Kilkenny Journal*, 6 May 1922.

29 *Kilkenny Journal*, 6 May 1922.

30 *Cork Examiner*, 3 May 1922.

31 *Kilkenny Journal*, 6 May 1922.

32 *Kilkenny Moderator*, 6 May 1922. Also, MA MSPC/24/SP/320 (Michael Loughman)

33 *Ulster Herald*, 6 May 1922.

34 *Irish Independent*, 4 May 1922.

35 *Kilkenny Journal*, 6 May 1922.

36 *Kilkenny Journal*, 13 May 1922. The following is the list of the fifteen anti-Treaty IRA arrested in Kilkenny Castle: Thomas 'Nipper' Nowlan, Maudlin St; James Wall, Lord Edward St; James 'Legger' Mara, Patrick St; James 'Duffer' Morrissey, Abbey Street; Edward Geoghegan, Patrick Street; David Dowling, Maudlin St (all from Kilkenny City); Patrick Walsh, Ballykeeffe, Kilmanagh; Richard 'Dick' Brennan O/C, Edward Dunphy, John Foskin and Patrick Walsh (Clogga), all from Mooncoin; John Walsh and Michael Hallahan from Kilmacow; Michael Phelan, Dunmore, Ballyfoyle; Dan O'Neill, Blanchfields Park, Clifden, Clara.

37 *Kilkenny Journal*, 6 May 1922.

38 *Kilkenny People*, 6 May 1922.

39 NAI FIN/COMP/2/10/37 (James George Anson on behalf of the Earl of Ossory).

40 *Kilkenny Moderator*, 6 May 1922.

41 *Kilkenny People*, 6 May 1922.

42 *Kilkenny People* and *Kilkenny Moderator*, 6 May 1922, and *Freeman's Journal*, 4 May 1922. The Pro-Treaty *Kilkenny People* newspaper only listed the Free State Army wounded. Most of these had a Dublin address: Private (Pte) John Burke, Rathfarnham; Pte Con

Reilly, Gardiner Street; Pte Lee Daly, Mary Lane; Pte JJ Kavanagh, Bride Street; Pte Michael O'Neill, 17 Robert Street; Pte Patrick Keogh, James Street; Pte Tom Morris, 14 Charlemont Mall; Pte Dan Conroy, Two-Mile-Borris, Tipperary; Pte John Martin, Pte Thomas Young, Sergeant Fennelly and James Kennedy (address not stated). Four anti-Treaty IRA were believed to have injuries also, (including O/C Dick Brennan) along with the two civilians.

43   The delegation included Liam Lynch and Liam Mellows on the anti-Treaty IRA side and Eoin O'Duffy on the Free State side. Within a few months they were arch-enemies. Lynch and Mellows later died during the Civil War.

44   *Irish Independent*, 5 May 1922. The anti-Treaty IRA remained in situ at Thomastown RIC Station and cooperated with the pro-Treaty side for a number of weeks until the outbreak of civil war.

45   *Irish Independent*, 5 May 1922, and *Kilkenny Moderator*, 6 May 1922, and *Kilkenny People*, 13 May 1922.

46   MA MSPC/34/8596 (William Quirke).

47   Ibid. Some of the more badly wounded were brought to Callan Hospital.

48   BMH WS 1,763 (Daniel Breen) and MA MSPC/34/8596 (William Quirke).

49   *Irish Independent* and *Kilkenny People*, 6 May 1922. *Cork Examiner*, 8 May 1922.

50   *Irish Independent*, 6 May 1922.

51   *Cork Examiner*, 12 May 1922.

52   *Freeman's Journal*, 6 May 1922.

53   *Irish Independent*, 8 May 1922. John (Jack) Prout Jnr was not attacked in Ireland, and returned with his father to America in 1927, where he joined the United States Army. He died on 23 May 1988 in El Paso, Texas, aged 78.

54   *Ulster Herald*, 6 May 1922. Incorrect newspaper and Dáil Éireann reports at the time had estimated twenty fatalities. The fact that no civilians were killed increased sympathy for the anti-Treaty IRA who were seen as the underdogs and who fought gallantly against a superiorly armed force.

55   Michael Gallagher, 'The Pact General Election of 1922', *Irish Historical Studies* 21, no. 84 (1981), pp. 404–21. There was no polling for the election the previous year as Sinn Féin won its 124 seats unopposed. The pact arrangement – agreed less than three weeks after the Battle of Kilkenny on 20 May 1922 – caused much annoyance within the British Government as it was considered to be too generous to the anti-Treaty faction who would most likely have been widely defeated if they had to compete against pro-Treaty candidates.

56   *Irish Independent*, 6 June 1922.

57   *Nationalist and Leinster Times*, 1 April 1922.

58   As the register was not updated beforehand, women under 30 could not vote. Before the Pact was agreed, four candidates had been selected to represent the pro-Treaty side. The two additional candidates were Kilkenny County Council Chairman Seán Gibbons and Councillor Edward O'Gorman. As only two pro-Treaty candidates were required after the pact, these had to make way for the better known Cosgrave and O'Sullivan. In addition, prior to the agreement, the anti-Treaty candidates had planned to run under a new party with the title; 'Cumann na Poblachta'.

59   *Kilkenny Moderator*, 10 June 1922. Denis John Gorey (1874–1940) went on to join Cumann na nGaedheal, later the Fine Gael party.

60　*Freeman's Journal* and *Irish Independent*, 15 June 1922. In his speech, Aylward also echoed Stack's words, saying that 'the time was inopportune' for the farmers and labourers to contest the election.

61　*Kilkenny People*, 17 June 1922. The pro-Treaty candidates had spent the previous days canvassing in Urlingford and Freshford.

62　*Kilkenny Journal*, 10 June 1922.

63　*Kilkenny Journal*, 24 June 1922. The quota was 6,246. Voter turnout in the Carlow–Kilkenny constituency was 61 per cent, fractionally below the national average. Voters appeared to have no issue with the practicalities of the PR system, as only 525 votes out of 31,227 were non-transferable. The national average of votes for pro-Treaty candidates was 78 per cent. Gorey's Farmers' Party won a respectable seven seats, and would go on to win fifteen seats in an election the following year.

CHAPTER 10

1　The IRA's 2nd Southern Division included Kilkenny, South Tipperary and Limerick.

2　MA MSPC/2D464. James Walsh died on 29 June 1922. He was a veteran of the First World War. The newspapers incorrectly reported that a 'George Walsh' from Kilkenny had died. His father, Patrick, later received compensation of £50 for the death of his son.

3　*Kilkenny People*, 5 and 8 July 1922.

4　*Kilkenny People*, 5 July 1922. Bibby had been in the Four Courts during the previous days, administering to Rory O'Connor and his men fighting there. He was captured when they surrendered, but was quickly released as a man of the cloth. He then made his way to the Gresham Hotel to help those fighting there. The destruction of the Four Courts also led to the ruin of the Irish Public Records Office (PRO) which was based there – an event which haunts Irish historians to the present day.

5　*Kilkenny Moderator*, 1 July 1922.

6　*Kilkenny People*, 1 July 1922.

7　Ibid. – inquest into Moran's death.

8　*Kilkenny People*, 5 and 8 July 1922. The only person left in the Barracks after the evacuation was a prisoner called 'Neary' who had been arrested by the anti-Treaty forces for stealing.

9　Woodstock Heritage Museum (WHM), Inistioge; William Rogers to Major E.J. Hamilton. Letter dated 29 June 1922. The Tighe family had been mostly based in England in the years prior to the outbreak of the Troubles. Lady Louisa Tighe, who died in 1900, was very popular in the area and had lived in the house for seventy-five years. The estate was inherited by her nephew, Edward, who was murdered in England in 1917. His wife Viola owned the house and grounds in the era 1920–1922. Woodstock House and Gardens is now a public park maintained by Kilkenny County Council. The house was never rebuilt, with just a few walls remaining.

10　*The Irish Times*, 27 January 1999.

11　WHM, Inistioge; Rogers to Hamilton. Letter dated 2 July 1922.

12　WHM, Inistioge; Rogers to Hamilton. Letter dated 18 July 1922.

13　*Kilkenny Journal*, 2 September 1922 and NAI FIN/COMP/2/10/299 (Viola Tighe). The library was conservatively valued at £955. Nearly £2,000 was the estimated amount of the late Captain Tighe's clothes (he had been murdered in a robbery in England some years earlier). This was discounted as the garments only had 'sentimental' value, while it was also said he had a 'mania for hoarding clothes'.

14   BMH WS 1,763 (Daniel Breen). Lacey was killed in February of the following year (1923) near the Glen of Aherlow, in a fight between Free State forces, under the command of Prout.

15   *Kilkenny People*, 8 July 1922, *Irish Independent*, 12 July 1922 and *Freeman's Journal*, 14 July 1922. The three inside the barracks reported as injured were; Privates Roche and Loughman (New St, Kilkenny City), and Captain Edward Holland.

16   BMH WS 1,763 (Daniel Breen).

17   *Freeman's Journal*, 13 July 1922, and *Evening Herald*, 14 July 1922.

18   The special war edition of the *Kilkenny People* began publication on Wednesday, 5 July 1922. The newspaper referred to the outbreak of the Civil War as 'Ireland's Crown of Sorrow' (*Kilkenny People*, 1 July 1922).

19   *Kilkenny Journal*, 15 July 1922.

20   *Kilkenny People* and *Ulster Herald*, 22 July 1922.

21   *Kilkenny People*, 29 July 1922. Also, MSPC/34/660 (Hannah Murphy), MSPC/34/1271 (Eamon MacCluskey).

22   WHM, Inistioge; William Rogers to Major E.J. Hamilton. Letter dated 18 July 1922.

23   *Kilkenny People* and *Freeman's Journal*, 22 July 1922.

24   *Irish Independent*, 20 July 1922.

25   *Cork Examiner*, 21 July 1922 and *Sunday Independent*, 23 July 1922.

26   MA MSPC/2D33 and *Irish Independent*, 25 July 1922. Costello died on 20 July – the day after he was shot – in a field hospital that had been set up in south Kilkenny during the battle. His mother, Helena, later received a total of £150 compensation for the loss of her son. Like the majority of parents who lost a child in the Civil War, the small amount was not acceptable for the death of her loved one. Writing in 1924, Helena requested additional compensation as the family were suffering financially due to Michael's death, as he had been the main provider. She appealed to the Government; 'especially for those who have suffered in the melancholy civil strife of 1922, will [you] award me a substantial compensation. I respectfully submit that a grant of £300 … is neither unreasonable nor extravagant for the loss of a dear and dutiful son'.

27   MA MSPC/DP2130 (Samuel Oakes).

28   MA MSPC/DP2130 (Samuel Oakes). In 1932 the Oakes family received £85 compensation from the Government for the loss of their son.

29   *Kilkenny Moderator* and *Kilkenny People*, 5 August 1922. *Freeman's Journal*, 1 August 1922. The coroner stated that 'a portion of his skull had been blown away'. Media reports at the time incorrectly stated his age as 17 years old but he was born on 8 February 1901. Some eleven men in and around the public house were arrested, including the sons of Maria Dowling.

30   BMH WS 1,763 (Daniel Breen).

31   *Kilkenny Journal*, 5 August 1922 (taken from *The Freeman's Journal*).

32   *Kilkenny Journal*, 5 August 1922.

33   BMH WS 1,763 (Daniel Breen).

34   *Freeman's Journal*, 4 August 1922. Also, MSPC/34/660 (Hannah Murphy).

35   MA MSPC/34/8596 (William Quirke).

36 *Kilkenny Journal*, 12 August 1922. The Free State position was based on a farm owned by the O'Donnell family. Tinvane House was owned by the Bowles family.

37 MA MSPC/2D263. Murphy's comrade, Michael Ryan, carried him on a stretcher to a nearby ambulance, but he had already died on arrival. Patrick's mother, Mary Murphy, received £30 for her son's death. The local curate in Enniscorthy, Fr Cummins, who was asked to help in filling out Mary's forms for compensation, was not very sympathetic, writing on the form; 'this woman is stupid & forgetful & it is very hard to fill in above [form] but I have done my best. I have filled up many forms re above deceased [Patrick Murphy] & I hope this is the last as the process of getting details required is a very slow one indeed'. Captain Balfe was the former O/C of the North Wexford IRA Brigade during the War of Independence, while he was also one of the escapees of Kilkenny jail the previous November. For death of animals see compensation claims; NAI FIN/COMP/2/10.

38 MA MSPC/34/8596 (William Quirke).

39 UCDA P133/11 (James Lalor Papers). Military Service Pension statement of Michael Walsh (No: 16724).

40 *Kilkenny People*, 2 September 1922. Taken from the captured diary of the anti-Treaty Intelligence Officer in Carrick. The writer moved with the anti-Treaty forces to Clonmel. He was equally unimpressed with that town: 'I hope they [the Free State Army] will blow Clonmel to atoms. It will be a small loss, for the people – with few exceptions – are hostile. They sneer at us passing in and out of the barrack.'

41 *Kilkenny People*, 12 August 1922.

42 BMH WS 1,763 (Daniel Breen).

43 MA MSPC/CL718. Also, MSPC/2D280. Maher's family, who ran a public house in Gortnahoe, received £100 compensation for his loss.

44 BMH WS 1,763 (Daniel Breen). *Kilkenny People*, 26 August 1922.

45 MA MSPC/2D11. Bergin was christened William Joachim, but was known as 'Joseph'. His death did not deter his older brother Michael from joining the Free State Army the following month, September 1922. Indeed, it may have inspired him to join in memory of his deceased brother. In 1953, at the age of 80, Annie Brennan eventually began receiving a military pension as a result of her son's death (£180 per annum). She died on 21 February 1959, 37 years after her son Joseph.

46 GRO, Birth Index (William Joachim Bergin): July–September 1901, Castlecomer, Volume: 3, Page: 339. DOB; 16 August 1901, Mother; Anne Bergin née Kelly, father; William Bergin (from Skehana).

47 *Kilkenny Journal*, 26 August 1922 and *Kilkenny People*, 2 September 1922. John J. Edwards's large funeral took place in the Cathedral of the Most Holy Trinity in Waterford City on 21 and 22 August 1922. Some of his prison companions were given parole to attend the funeral.

48 MA CW/OPS/10/05 – Intelligence Report, Waterford, 27 December 1922.

49 BMH WS 1,763 (Daniel Breen).

50 He would have been 23 years old on 28 September. Michael Cantwell was originally only offered £30 compensation but he appealed to W.T. Cosgrave to intervene, which later resulted in an additional £70.

51   MA MSPC/DP2440 (Frank Byrne). After much correspondence, Frank's mother, Elizabeth, eventually received a military pension in respect of her son's death, in 1960 (£180 per annum). However, she died in 1963 at the age of 90.

52   *Kilkenny Moderator*, 19 August 1922.

53   *Kilkenny People*, 19 August 1922. Ryan often submitted poetry to the local press.

54   *Kilkenny People, Kilkenny Journal, Kilkenny Moderator*, 26 August 1922.

55   *Kilkenny Journal*, 2 September 1922.

56   *Kilkenny Moderator* and *Kilkenny People*, 2 September 1922.

57   *Irish Independent*, 30 August 1922. The businesses in Callan also closed down from 11.00am – 1.00pm on the day of Collins's funeral.

58   *Kilkenny People*, 2 September 1922.

CHAPTER 11

1   MA MSPC/34/23666 (Martin McGrath).

2   UCDA P133/11 and 12 (James Lalor Papers). Mulhall was from Danville near Kilkenny City.

3   MA CW/OPS/10/05 – Free State Intelligence Report, 10 October 1922.

4   MA MSPC/34/SP/15748 (Simon O'Leary) and MSPC/34/SP/38728 (Martin Bates).

5   MA CW/P/14/01, Waterford prison register. Count of all entries where the address is Kilkenny. The overall total was likely to be more, as by the end of the year the addresses of the prisoners were not recorded, only their names.

6   MA CW/OPS/10/05 – Carrick-on-Suir Daily Intelligence Report, 30 October 1922.

7   MA CW/OPS/10/05 – Intelligence Report, Mooncoin, 21 December 1922.

8   *Kilkenny People*, 30 September 1922. The fact they did not have firearms was a decision reached by the government to discourage attacks on the new force by the anti-Treaty IRA. Shooting an unarmed police officer was generally considered to be cowardly. Other areas of Kilkenny received their new recruits the following month, which included; Callan, Thomastown, Castlecomer and Graiguenamanagh (Castlecomer received its detachment on 20 October, Callan on 28 October and Thomastown on 29 October 1922). They had to make do with old buildings or parts of buildings, as the RIC barracks had been destroyed previously.

9   MA MSPC/F320, 2D136, and 1032B (William Purcell). Also; GRO, Death Index (William Purcell senior): October–December 1918, Kilkenny, Volume: 3 Page: 375. Birth Index (William Purcell junior): January–March 1906 (4 March 1906), Kilkenny, Vol 3, p,390. Death Index (William Purcell junior): October–December 1922, Thurles, Vol 3, p.337. Annie received £65 compensation for the loss of her son. She had originally been offered just £40 – as publicans were considered to be slightly better off than average – but this was increased to £65 after she appealed to W.T. Cosgrave. Two years later, frustrated at the slow nature of the process, Annie wrote to the compensation board stating; 'Now I hope this will be my last letter that I will have to write. Its only god that knows what I have suffered for the last 2 years & 2 months for the loss of my poor boy.'

10   *Kilkenny People*, 7 October 1922. The attempted arson of Gowran Park grandstand was on the night of 27 September 1922, the same night McCalmont's petrol store was stolen at

Mount Juliet in Thomastown. It is most likely some of this petrol was used in the attempt to burn the grandstand.

11   NAI FIN/COMP/2/10 (Kilkenny Files). Oxo Limited (FIN/COMP/2/10/58), Francis Bailey (FIN/COMP/2/10/128) and Arthur Curran (FIN/COMP/2/10/30). The most frequent claims related to the stealing or destruction of goods that were transported by rail. Over forty of the claims related to the 'commandeering' of motor vehicles (cars, lorries, motor bikes) usually by the anti-Treaty IRA, although the Free State Army was not adverse to requisitioning transport when the need arose. Over fifteen claims were related to the destruction or loss of property (broken windows etc.) as a result of the Battle of Kilkenny in May 1922.

12   *Kilkenny Journal*, 21 October 1922, *Kilkenny People* and *Munster Express*, 4 November 1922.

13   MA CW/OPS/10/05 – Intelligence Report, Waterford, 27 December 1922.

14   *Kilkenny People*, 7 October 1922. Alexander Fleming did not discover the antibiotic substance penicillin until later in the 1920s.

15   BMH WS 1,763 (Daniel Breen). Captain Joseph Walsh was a native of Mullinahone, Co Tipperary. He had been a teacher in Callan some years previously. The driver of the tender who was shot in the arm, Patrick Lawlor, was also from Kilkenny.

16   MA MSPC/2D322, and *Cork Examiner*, 10 October 1922. Thomas Brownrigg was attached to the 47th Battalion of the National Army. Kate Brownrigg had originally requested £1,000 but instead received the maximum permitted, £100. Thomas's father, Michael, was a farm labourer but had been 'invalided' for over a year prior to his son's death, and was unable to work.

17   MA MSPC/2D486. NAI, 1901 Census. District: Kilkenny No 2 Urban, Maudlin Street. No public birth record or death record exists for Patrick Hayes, so it is difficult to ascertain his precise age. He had only joined the Free State Army on 28 July 1922.

18   NLI, Michael Logue, *Pastoral Letter of His Eminence Cardinal Logue, the Archbishops and Bishops of Ireland: To the Priests and People of Ireland* (Dublin, 1922).

19   Brownrigg unexpectedly outlived Downey by one year. Downey died aged 53 in 1927, with Brownrigg passing away the following year aged 91.

20   MA CW/OPS/10/05 – Intelligence Report, Urlingford, 20 October 1922.

21   MA MSPC/34/46259 (Margaret Meagher née Peggy O'Keeffe). MSPC/2RB84 (Thomas O'Dea). MSPC/34/44960 (Mary Teehan-Foley).

22   *Kilkenny Journal*, 21 October 1922, *Freeman's Journal*, 20 October 1922, *Kilkenny People*, 28 October 1922. The same group of anti-Treaty soldiers had been involved in a gunfight with Free State troops in Callan two days prior to the Kilmanagh fight.

23   MA MSPC/2D220. Patrick Quigley was employed as a farm labourer prior to joining the National Army. Timothy Quigley was initially offered £30 compensation, which was increased to £50 on appeal.

24   MA MSPC/2D281. MA CW/OPS/10/05 – Intelligence Report, Cashel, 23 October 1922. James Burke was nearly 19 years old, as he was born on 2 December 1903.

25   *Kilkenny People* and *Munster Express*, 4 November 1922. GRO, Birth Index (James Dunne): July–September 1887, Kilkenny, Volume: 3, Page: 401. Brannigan and Kirwan, *Kilkenny Families in the Great War* (Thomastown, 2012), p. 135. James Dunne was born in Threecastles on 18 June 1887. He was the son of Richard and Mary Dunne (née McEvoy).

Two of his brothers, Paddy and Richard, also fought in the First World War. The Dunne brothers also joined the Free State Army and the Civic Guard in 1922.

26 *Freeman's Journal*, 10 October 1922. *Evening Herald*, 16 November 1922. Also, MA MSPC/ 34/SP/57476 (Alice Cantwell née Luttrell). The prisoners once again escaped from A Wing.

27 MA CW/OPS/10/05 – Daily Reports, [Kilkenny] Jail, 17 November 1922.

28 MA CW/OPS/10/05 – Daily Reports, [Kilkenny] Jail, 7 Nov. 1922.

29 MA CW/OPS/10/05 – Daily Reports, [Kilkenny] Jail, 6 November 1922. Although the day in question was exceptional in terms of the volume of parcels, hamper deliveries arrived constantly for the internees.

30 MA CW/CAPT/Lot 34 (Captured Documents). Cumann na mBan papers taken at a raid on the Baby Club, Werburgh Street, Dublin on 7 February 1923. Kilkenny Brigade report dated 8 November 1922. Hanna Murphy did not sign the document for security reasons. However, she had very distinctive handwriting which left no doubt as to the author.

31 MA MSPC/34/57287 (Ellen Leahy).

32 MA MSPC/34/4873. Mary Josephine Commins (1892–1980) was awarded a 'grade D' military pension, which was equal to the grading of the O/C of Kilkenny Cumann na mBan Brigade.

33 *Kilkenny Journal*, 18 November 1922. Colm Wallace, *The Fallen, Gardaí Killed in Service, 1922–49* (Dublin, 2017), pp. 21–5. The two men arrested in 1924 were James Daly, from Coolagh near Callan and Philip Leahy, from Poulacapple near Mullinahone. In 1997, a plaque was unveiled at Mullinahone Garda station in memory of Garda Phelan.

34 GRO, Death Index (Patrick Phelan): October–December 1899, Mountmellick, Vol.3, p.330, and (Norah Phelan): April–June 1919, Mountmellick, Vol.3, p.406. Birth Index (Henry Phelan): January–March 1900, Mountmellick, Vol. 3, p.399. Patrick Phelan died on 4 November 1899, with his cause of death stated as 'diarrhoea'. The Phelan family were from Rushin, Mountrath, in Queen's County (as County Laois was known then). Patrick's wife (and Henry's mother) was Norah Phelan (née Austin), who were married on 28 January 1885 in Castletown.

35 The Free State Army was, however, garrisoned in New Ross, County Wexford, and Borris, County Carlow, and sometimes patrolled the areas around Graiguenamanagh.

36 MA CW/OPS/10/05 – Intelligence Report, Thomastown, 12 November 1922.

37 MA Irish Army Census Collection 1922. Summation of the number of soldiers based in the eight garrisons on the night of 12/13 November 1922. Average, lowest and maximum ages calculated from the list of 738 soldiers. Also; GRO, Birth Index (Patrick Hogan): April–June 1908 (19 April), Kilkenny, Vol. 3 p.391. Note; James Coady (based in Kilkenny Barracks and from John's Street, Cashel), was incorrectly recorded as 58 years, he was actually aged 28.

38 *Munster Express*, 27 January 1923.

39 MA MSPC/RO/154.

40 *Kilkenny People*, 9 December 1922 (Inquest Report). NAI, 1911 Census. District: Glashane, Townland: Grangefertagh. In 1911, Patrick's mother, Johanna, stated on the census that her husband (also called Patrick) had left the family home and she was unaware if, or when, he would return home. The family's name is sometimes recorded as 'McCormack'. At the time of his death, Cormack's address was stated as; Steepleview, Johnstown.

41 *Kilkenny People*, 9 December 1922. Ellen Cuffe (Countess of Desart) also became the first Jewish person to hold a seat in an Irish government. Edward Mansfield, who was a native of Mullinahone near Callan, was also elected as a senator, with support from the Labour Party. He was an active member of the Irish National Teachers Organisation (INTO) and an Irish language enthusiast. However, he resigned after only a few days in protest over the Free State Government's reprisal executions.

42 Hopkinson, *Green against Green* (Dublin, 2004), p. 209. *Munster Express,* 16 December 1922. It was believed that Barry, who 'was a law on to himself', decided to capture Carrick-on-Suir without any direction from his superiors in the anti-Treaty IRA.

43 UCDA P7/B/64, Mulcahy Papers. BMH WS 1,763 (Daniel Breen).

44 MA CW/OPS/10/05 – Intelligence Report, Carrick-on-Suir, 15 December 1922

45 *Kilkenny Journal*, 23 December 1922. UCDA P7/B/64, Mulcahy Papers.

46 MA CW/OPS/10/05 – Daily Intelligence Report, Mullinavat, 19 December 1922.

47 Hopkinson, *Green against Green* (Dublin, 2004), p. 209.

48 MA CW/OPS/10/05 – Daily Intelligence Report, Mullinavat, 19 December 1922.

49 MA MSPC/DP5756 (Edward Somers). One of Edward Somers's brothers', Patrick, was in the Free State Army during the Civil War.

50 MA MSPC/34/SP/15748 (Simon O'Leary)

51 *Belfast Newsletter*, 22 December 1922. The newspaper reprinted segments of *The Republican War Bulletin*.

52 MA MSPC/34/8596 (William Quirke).

53 UCDA P7/B/64, Mulcahy Papers. Hopkinson, *Green against Green* (Dublin, 2004), p. 209.

54 BMH WS 939 (Ernest Blythe), p. 180.

55 *Kilkenny People*, 16 December 1922.

56 MA MSPC/2D376. Tom Burnell *et al., The Kilkenny War Dead* (Kilkenny, 2014), p. 124. Joseph was 18 years old at the time of his death in August 1914.

57 *Kilkenny People*, 7 April 1923. Tribute by 'J. P'.

58 BMH WS 1,751 (Cahir Davitt). Davitt personally went to inform Lidwell's mother of her son's death but on arriving in Dún Laoghaire discovered she had departed to the countryside for the holiday season. He subsequently telegrammed her the bad news.

59 MA MSPC/2D90. Inquest, Witness 10, Edward Kelly.

60 *Kilkenny People*, 30 December 1922, *Irish Independent*, 28 December 1922. Volunteer Edward Kelly was a member of 'G Company'. The inquest discovered that he was mostly deaf and should not have been accepted into the Free State Army. Lidwell died at 2.30 pm on the afternoon of 22 December.

61 MA MSPC/2D90 and MSPC/577/12. This was the highest amount of compensation paid for a Free State Army fatality within County Kilkenny during the Civil War. The family had been in financial difficulty as their father died with debts. Fred Lidwell had three sisters; Mabel, Shelia and Doreen. His father died in 1919. Fred Lidwell's salary in the Free State Army was £400 per annum.

62 MA CW/OPS/10/05 – Intelligence Report, Kilkenny, 14 December 1922. Murphy's brother was also arrested during the raid.

63 *Freeman's Journal*, 30 December 1922.

64 *Munster Express*, 6 January 1923.

65 BMH WS 1,751 (Cahir Davitt).

66 Martin O'Dwyer, *Seventy Seven of Mine Said Ireland* (Cashel, 2006), p. 138. Extract from *Eire* newspaper. Also, Brannigan and Kirwan, *Kilkenny Families in the Great War* (Thomastown, 2012), p. 386.

67 MA MSPC/DP8258 (John Murphy) and *Munster Express*, 6 January 1923. John Murphy was son of James Murphy (aged 61 at the time of John's birth in 1900) and Kate Murphy (aged 29 at the time of John's birth). Kate died aged 69 in 1938 from heart failure (see indexes for specific years; GRO, Thomastown District). John Murphy's death also caused issues about the ownership of a house and six acres of land. At the age of 7, John was left the property in trust, following the death of his uncle Patrick. He never took official ownership of the property when he reached the age of 21, which were the terms of the will, most likely because his mother was managing the land to help raise her young family, three of whom were younger than John.

68 MA MSPC/DP1927 (John Phelan). Bridget was mostly supported by her father, James Kelly, who was a carpenter, during the period between 1922 and 1933. She received an annual widow's allowance of £67,10s in 1933. She never remarried and died in 1966, forty-three years after her husband.

69 Hopkinson, *Green against Green* (Dublin, 2004), pp. 209–10.

70 *Kilkenny People*, 1 November 1924. The bodies of three men who were executed in Wexford jail in March 1923 and buried in Kilkenny Military Barracks (then Free State HQ of the southeast region), namely; James Parle, John Creane and Patrick Hogan – were also exhumed and returned to their respective families.

CHAPTER 12

1   *Irish Independent*, 5 January 1923, *Munster Express*, 3 February 1923.

2   *Kilkenny People*, 21 February 1923.

3   MA MSPC/DP660 (Patrick Barcoe) and *Nationalist and Leinster Times*, 10 February 1923. Mary Barcoe died in March 1930, aged 61. The family were in dire financial straits after the death of Patrick and his father, and received 'about £100 from the Irish White Cross'.

4   *Belfast Newsletter*, 28 February 1923, *Kilkenny People*, 3 March 1923

5   GRO, Death Index (Andrew Power): January–March 1923, Kilkenny, Vol. 3 p. 299. Also; *Munster Express*, 3 February 1923.

6   *Cork Examiner*, 27 February 1923. There are records of at least twenty prisoners signing during 1922–23. See; MA CW/P/02/02/11. Also, there are sporadic references relating to signing the declaration in MA CW/OPS/10/05, Intelligence Reports, Kilkenny jail and Waterford Command.

7   *Kilkenny People*, 21 February 1923.

8   *Kilkenny People*, 3 March 1923.

9   *Leinster Express*, 31 March 1923.

10 NAI FIN/COMP/2/10/104 (Earl of Desart). He received additional compensation for the loss of his artwork and furniture. Also see; Whyte, *The Story of Woodstock in Inistioge* (Dublin, 2007), p. 306. The original Desart Court was where James Hoban, architect of the White House in Washington DC, received some of his early training.

11 *Kilkenny People*, 3 March 1923.

12   *Kilkenny People*, 3 March 1923. The earl purchased Stansted House, West Sussex in 1924, which became the family's main home.

13   NAI FIN/COMP/2/10/44 (Max Bollam on behalf of the Earl of Bessborough). Also see; Whyte, *The Story of Woodstock in Inistioge* (Dublin, 2007), p. 306. The 9th Earl of Bessborough became the Governor General of Canada (the King's representative there) in the 1930s. The Department of Agriculture paid £250,000 (Irish pounds) for Bessborough estate in 1971.

14   MA MSPC/34/44960 (Mary Teehan-Foley) and *Kilkenny People*, 24 March 1923. De Valera had previously visited the house in August 1922. One of Bridget Teehan's sons, Richard Teehan, was at the time of the burning incarcerated in Kilkenny jail. In addition, Shipton House was used by Cumann na mBan women from Kilkenny City who needed to deliver dispatches and ammunition to the west Kilkenny battalions; they often deposited it at Teehan's for onward delivery (see; MSPC/34/60441 – Mary O'Kelly). Also; NAI FIN/COMP/2/10/324 (Bridget Teehan). The owner of the house, J.J. Long of Limerick, received £2,865 in compensation from the Free State government, while the Teehan family received £2,569, on appeal, for loss of belongings.

15   *Cork Examiner* and *Kilkenny People*, 6 April 1923. Walsh received £4,173 in compensation.

16   MA CW/OPS/10/05 – wireless message to FS GHQ, 6 November 1922. Walsh's van was also taken in Mooncoin in December 1922 by a party of anti-Treaty IRA under the command of Patrick Walsh, Clogga (see Carrick-on-Suir Daily Intelligence Report, 13 December 1922).

17   NAI FIN/COMP/2/10/282 (Maria Mackey). She was awarded £60 by the Free State Government although she had requested £118.

18   NAI FIN/COMP/2/10/317 (Mary Walsh). Mary Walsh later received £1,387 from the Free State Government in compensation, although some within the Free State Army tried to block the claim.

19   Hopkinson, *Green against Green* (Dublin, 2004), p.198

20   Hopkinson, *Green against Green* (Dublin, 2004), pp. 198–9.

21   The train companies in Ireland had been through several turbulent years. The disruption caused by the First World War, followed immediately by the War of Independence, put a massive dent in their profits.

22   *Kilkenny People*, 23 September 1922

23   Bernard Share, *In Time of Civil War; The Conflict on the Irish Railways 1922–23* (Cork, 2006), p. 63

24   Share, *In Time of Civil War* (Cork, 2006), p. 75. A similar incident to this occurred at Ballyhale in November 1922 (see *Kilkenny People*, 2 December 1922).

25   MA CW/OPS/10/05 – Intelligence Report, Waterford, 15 December 1922. Also; Share, *In Time of Civil War* (Cork, 2006), p. 92. The raid took place on 29 December 1922 and the train was held up on 14 December 1922.

26   MA CW/OPS/10/05 – Intelligence Report, Mooncoin, 21 December 1922. The Intelligence Officer correctly names most of the other members of the ASU, even including their family nicknames to distinguish them; 'the principle [sic] members of his column are, Edward Walsh (brother), Patrick [/James] Walsh ("Risteen" [later known as "Swithin Walsh's"]), Martin Walsh (Gaymos) ... Two Lawler's (Clogga School), Patrick FitzGerald, Barrabehy, Tom Morahan, Clonmore, Michael Foskin, Riverquarter, [?] Shea, Clogga, about 17 years

of age; a great destructor. Edward Walsh Gortrush, J. Connor. Lawler and James Walsh escaped from Waterford Jail. There will be no peace in the district until every member of the above crowd is firmly held' (note; some misspelling has been rectified).

27   *Kilkenny People*, 21 February 1923. *Kilkenny People*, 3 March 1923.

28   *Munster Express,* 17 February 1923.

29   MA CW/OPS/10/05 – Intelligence Report, Kilkenny, 16 December 1922.

30   Share, *In Time of Civil War* (Cork, 2006), p. 142.

31   *Kilkenny People,* 31 March 1923.

32   *Freeman's Journal,* 9 March 1923.

33   *Kilkenny People,* 17 March 1923.

34   MA MSPC/3D9. Kathleen Comerford, Gerald's older sister, later applied for dependants allowance in respect of the death of her brother. The referees' response to this application was a good example of the petty local hostilities that existed at the time in relation to who received what in compensation. There were obviously rumours circulating locally as to how much the Comerford family had received. One referee, Garrett Brennan, stated the he had heard that Gerald's mother received £70 compensation for her son's death, with his father also claiming the same amount two years later. Another referee, James Conway, stated that both parents had claimed an allowance individually for their son's death. Both of these rumours were entirely untrue.

35   MA MSPC/DP/3064 (Thomas Meally/Mealey). A few variations of his surname are used in reports; the spelling as written on his gravestone is the one used here. Mealey's mother, Elizabeth, received £30 for the loss of her son from the Irish Government in 1933.

36   Comerford, *My Kilkenny IRA Days* (Kilkenny, 1978), p. 657. *Freeman's Journal*, 17 March 1923.

37   MA MSPC/3D232, and *Munster Express*, 24 March 1923.

38   MA MSPC/3D151. Patrick McCormack and Kate Neary were married in November 1919, just three months after Kate's 18th birthday. Patrick was aged 23 at the time of his death. William Doran suffered post-traumatic stress after the accidental shooting and had to be hospitalised. Kate married John Moriarty from Urlingford in 1926.

39   *Kilkenny People*, 24 March 1923. 'Walsh's Place', a housing development in Kilmacthomas was later named in his honour.

40   MA MSPC/3D4 and 33/APB/14. GRO, Death Index (John Brown): January–March 1901, Mountmellick, Vol. 3, p. 408. Birth Index (Michael Brown): July–September 1901, Mountmellick, Vol. 3 p. 394. Michael Brown had been a member of the IRA during the War of Independence. He was a mechanic prior to joining the Free State Army. When she married for the second time, Elizabeth Brown was known as Eliza Breen (or Brun).

41   MA MSPC/3D133 (Gorman).

42   *The Free Press*, 31 March 1923 (Wexford newspaper). Another Free State soldier, Private Keane, had gone to the pub with the Kilkenny men but luckily for him had left an hour before his comrades.

43   Three Wexford natives – James Parle, John Creane and Patrick Hogan – were executed on 12 March 1923. Coincidentally their bodies were interred in Kilkenny Military Barracks, then the Free State HQ for the region. The bodies of the three Wexford men were returned to their families in October 1924 (see, *Kilkenny People*, 1 November 1924).

44   *Kilkenny People*, 31 March 1923.

45 MA MSPC/3D133 (Gorman) and MSPC/3D32 (Horan).

46 *Irish Independent*, 23 August 2007.

47 MA MSPC/34/23666 (Martin McGrath).

48 MA MSPC/34/3739 (Edward J Aylward). Also; *Cork Examiner*, 27 February 1923.

49 MA MSPC/24/SP11874 (James Blanchfield). Blanchfield had attended school with Davis in Thomastown.

50 *Kilkenny People*, 28 April 1923.

51 *Kilkenny People*, 14 April 1923. The meeting was held on 8 April 1923.

52 *Kilkenny People*, 19 May 1923.

53 MA MSPC/4D26 (James O'Keeffe). He was a farm labourer before enlisting in the Free State Army. His funeral took place in Mooncoin on 6 May 1923, where he was buried in the nearby cemetery.

54 BMH WS 1,763 (Daniel Breen). Maher, *The Flying Column – West Kilkenny, 1916–1921* (Dublin, 2015), p. 318.

55 *Kilkenny People*, 2 June 1923.

56 *Irish Independent*, 14 June 1923.

57 *Kilkenny People*, 16 June 1923.

58 MA MSPC/DP/8041 (James Morrissey). Julia received £6 per month from the Irish White Cross until 1932, at which point this was reduced to £3 per month. From 1933 she received £67, 10s, 0d, per annum, and £18 for each of her children. Her widow's pension was increased to £250 per annum in 1953. Julia Morrissey died in January 1973.

59 MA MSPC/3D25 and MSPC/3MSRB24 (Patrick J Hanlon).

60 *Irish Independent*, 8 September 1923. MA MSPC/3D25.

61 MSPC/DP1103 (Michael Burke) – quoted from two separate letters Connolly wrote. Burke spent most of the revolutionary era as a member of the IRA in County Galway where he was employed as a mechanic. He was arrested near Tuam in 1923 and died in England. His father, Michael Burke senior, applied for compensation from the Irish Government after his son's death, but his application was rejected.

62 MA MSPC/DP5756 (Edward Somers). In 1934, Norah received an annual pension of £112 as she was deemed to be partially dependent on her brother at the time of his death.

CHAPTER 13

1 *Munster Express*, 19 August 1922. Report from the inquest held afterwards. The ambush took place at the bottom of Rochestown Hill, close to where the well-known Poulanassy waterfall is located.

2 *Freeman's Journal*, 17 August 1922, and *Munster Express*, 26 August 1922. O'Keeffe had fought during the First World War. He was buried at St Otteran's Cemetery in Waterford City.

3 *Kilkenny Journal*, 2 December 1922. Griffin was born in Patrick's Street in February 1875. After the accident, his body was removed to the Central Hospital in Kilkenny. He was waked at his residence in Patrick's Street. The funeral mass and burial was held in the nearby church.

4 DE Debates, 14 December 1922, vol. 2 no. 6. 'Questions; Kilkenny man's death. Question of Inquest'. Domhnall O'Muirgheasa, question to Richard Mulcahy.

5   Meade passed away of natural causes just one month later (see *Munster Express*, 20 January 1923).

6   MA CW/OPS/10/05 – Intelligence Report, Carrick-on-Suir, 17 December 1922. Also see; *Kilkenny Journal* and *Munster Express*, 23 December 1922. GRO, Death Index (Patrick Martin): January–March 1923, Carrick-on-Suir, vol. 4, p. 298. The military report about the incident accused Martin of 'fraternising with the two looters' during the day. Martin had been in the Free State Army in Carrick-on-Suir but deserted.

7   *Freeman's Journal*, 2 January 1923. Also; GRO, Death Index (Edward Burke d. 24/12/1922): October–December 1922, Urlingford, vol. 3, p. 374.

8   MA CW/OPS/10/05 – Intelligence Report, Urlingford, 27 December 1922.

9   The scope of the Civil War deaths encompasses the period from the commencement of the Civil War (28 June 1922) up to September 1923. This included two political prisoners who were shot in Kilkenny jail in the months after the war officially ended. Garda Henry Phelan's death is excluded, as he was not originally from Kilkenny and although he was based in Callan, he was shot in Mullinahone. Civilian fatalities and Free State soldier deaths were usually documented in some form or other. On occasion, Free State soldiers who were killed in ambushes away from their designated barracks sometimes had no death certificate. They appear to have fallen between two stools, as the military believed it was the responsibility of the hospital where their bodies were brought to register the death, while the hospitals believed the military was responsible. The grieving families also believed it was up to the military to register such deaths.

CHAPTER 14

1   *Kilkenny Journal*, 4 January 1919. The unbridled positivity was because the First World War had finished two months earlier.

2   *Irish Independent*, 7 January 1919.

3   *Kilkenny Journal*, 15 March 1919.

4   *Irish Independent*, 27 May 1919.

5   *Freeman's Journal*, 11 June 1919. *Kilkenny Journal*, 5 July 1919.

6   Maher, *In the Shade of Slievenamon* (Dublin, 2015), pp. 58–9.

7   Arthur Mitchell, *Revolutionary Government in Ireland: Dáil Éireann, 1919–22* (Dublin, 1995), p. 44

8   NA CO 904/110, September 1919.

9   *Kilkenny Journal*, 29 March 1919.

10 *Kilkenny Journal*, 14 May 1919.

11 NA CO 904/110, Nov 1919.

12 *Kilkenny Journal*, 27 August 1919.

13 *Kilkenny People*, 16 July 1921.

14 *Kilkenny Journal*, 14 May 1919.

15 *Cork Examiner*, 24 July 1919.

16 *Cork Examiner*, 13 August 1919.

17 *Freeman's Journal*, 9 October 1919.

18 NA CO 904/110, November 1919.

19   *Kilkenny People*, 20 March 1920.

20   *Irish Independent*, 19 March 1920.

21   *Kilkenny Journal*, 30 June 1920, *Kilkenny Moderator*, 3 July 1920. NA CO 904/112, June 1920.

22   *Kilkenny Journal*, 30 October 1920.

23   NAI DELG 14/10. Minutes of Thomastown District Council Meeting, 27 August 1920.

24   *Irish Independent*, 20 August 1920.

25   C.J. Woods, 'Abraham Brownrigg' in *Dictionary of Irish Biography*, eds McGuire and Quinn (Cambridge, 2009). Brownrigg's counterpart, the Anglican Church of Ireland Bishop of Ossory, Rev. John Godfrey FitzMaurice Day, was equally unsupportive of the Sinn Féin movement. During his consecration service in St Canice's Cathedral in November 1920, he remarked that his congregation were living in 'times of great difficulty' and hoped the faithful would be 'true to their God in this dark hour of their country's history' (*Kilkenny Moderator*, 6 November 1920).

26   *Freeman's Journal*, 28 November 1918.

27   *Kilkenny People*, 1 January 1921.

28   *Irish Independent*, 12 October 1920.

29   NAI DELG 14/15. Letter from John O'Carroll to W.T. Cosgrave, 19 December 1921.

30   NA CO 904/112, August 1920.

31   Frank Pakenham Earl of Longford, *Peace by Ordeal: The Negotiation of the Anglo-Irish Treaty 1921* (London, 1992), p. 54.

32   *Sunday Independent*, 12 September 1920. *Kilkenny Journal*, 16 July 1921.

33   The person responsible for the crime, Major Ewen Cameron Bruce, rumoured it was between £700 and £1100.

34   Hansard House of Commons Debates, 2 June 1921, '*General Crozier*'. Sir Hamar Greenwood in response to a question from Mr Frank Briant MP. vol. 142, cc 1214–8

35   *www.theauxiliaries.com/men-alphabetical/men-b/bruce/bruce.html,* accessed July 2017.

36   BMH WS 1,614 (Timothy Hennessy).

37   *Irish Independent*, 23 December 1920.

38   D.M. Leeson, *The Black and Tans* (Oxford, 2012), pp. 121–4.

39   Major Bruce died four years later from pneumonia, while his nephew died in an airplane accident in 1929. See; *Cheltenham Chronicle,* 2 November 1929.

40   Hansard House of Commons Debates, 18 November 1920, 'Larceny Charge Kilkenny'. Sir Hamar Greenwood in response to a question from Mr Joe Devlin MP. vol.134 cc 2063–4.

41   Leeson, *The Black and Tans* (Oxford, 2012), p. 256.

42   *Freeman's Journal*, 24 March 1921. *Irish Independent*, 24 March 1921.

43   NA CO 904/115, April 1921.

44   *Kilkenny Moderator*, 21 May 1921.

45   Dunne, *Peter's Key* (Cork, 2012), p. 205.

46   NLI, MS 22,116, J.J. O'Connell Papers. 'Typescript Statement concerning activities in Glenmore, Co Kilkenny during the War of Independence and the Civil War'. Statement by Michael Heffernan.

47   *Cork Examiner,* 11 May 1921.

48   NA CO 904/115, April 1921. NA CO 904/112, July and August 1920.

49   *Kilkenny Journal*, 2 October 1920.

50   CSORP, January 1921, CSORP/CR/331/21661. 'Kilmaganny PS, falling through of licensing sessions, behaviour of soldiers'.

51   CSORP, CR/331/22128 January 1921. 'Conduct of D.I. White at Freshford police station'.

52   BMH WS 1,104 (Thomas Brennan) and BMH WS 1,105 (Nicholas Whittle). Mick Wyley and Nicholas Whittle were shot a number of times during the Tramore Ambush but survived. Two other IRA men, Michael McGrath and Tom O'Brien, were killed in the same altercation. James 'Jim Pak' FitzPatrick of Moonveen, Carrigeen, Mooncoin, transported the men in his cot, making two separate trips. Carrigeen is the most southerly part of County Kilkenny and the diocese of Ossory. Ted Moore of Rathcurby, 9th Battalion Q/M, organised night watches at the mill in case of raids. The men could only exercise outdoors for a brief period each night. Whittle stayed there for six weeks before being sent to England for his safety. Wyley stayed a number of months at Portnascully. The Walsh's took the anti-Treaty side in the Civil War and the mill was subsequently burnt down by Free State troops in April 1923.

53   *Munster Express*, 2 April 1921.

54   NA WO 35/150/2 – Inquiry in lieu of Inquest, Bridget and Bridie Fahy – Witnesses 1, 2 and 3.

55   NA WO 35/150/2 – Inquiry, Bridget and Bridie Fahy – Findings.

56   Dermot Kavanagh, *A History, Kilkenny Senior Hurling County Finals 1887–2003* (Kilkenny, 2004), p. 103.

57   NA CO 904/115, May 1921.

58   Hart, *The I.R.A. & Its Enemies* (Oxford, 1999), p. 143.

59   BMH WS 1,093 (Thomas Treacy), BMH WS 980 (Edward J. Aylward), BMH WS 1,335 (James Leahy).

60   Hansard House of Commons Debates, 1 June 1921, '*Military Operations*'. Sir Hamar Greenwood in response to a question from Lieutenant-Commander Kenworthy MP. vol. 142 cc. 1042–5.

61   *Kilkenny People*, 25 June 1921.

62   *Cork Examiner*, 20 April 1921.

63   The accident occurred in the middle of the large junction in front of the Bank of Ireland, which is now the *Left Bank* pub. Jarvey cars (horse-driven taxis of the time) were *in situ* in front of the bank, just yards from the accident. Pat McDonnell was employed as a driver with Lewis and Sons, John's Street, who owned and rented out the motor car.

64   *Kilkenny People*, 18 June 1921.

65   NA WO 35/155A/51, Inquiry in Lieu of Inquest – Thomas Meade – 'Finding No 4'.

66   NA WO 35/155A/51, Inquiry – Thomas Meade – 'Finding'.

67   Marie Coleman, 'Violence Against Women During the Irish War of Independence, 1919–21' in *Years of Turbulence, The Irish Revolution and Its Aftermath*, eds Diarmaid Ferriter and Susannah Riordan (Dublin, 2015), p. 139.

68   *Kilkenny Moderator*, 13 November 1920. Also see: NA CO 904/115, April 1921 (example of another forced haircutting; 'two cases of outrages against women by the cutting of their hair'). Boycotting is usually termed 'insider violence', as it was psychological violence by a community towards another member of that community.

69   MA MSPC/24/SP11874 (James Blanchfield).

70   *Kilkenny People*, 15 October 1921.

71   BMH WS 1,271 (Patrick Dunphy).

72   Coleman, 'Violence Against Women …' in *Years of Turbulence*, eds Ferriter and Riordan (Dublin, 2015), p. 154.

73   *Irish Independent*, 12 September 1921. Kilkenny had beaten Wexford in the Leinster semi-final on 14 August 1921.

74   *Freeman's Journal*, 23 September 1921.

75   *Nationalist and Leinster Times*, 8 October 1921. His attendance at the event was advertised up to the day before the beginning of the Feis.

76   James Mackay, *Michael Collins: A Life* (Edinburgh, 1996), pp. 215–16.

77   *Kilkenny Moderator*, 22 October 1921. Brannigan and Kirwan, *Kilkenny Families in the Great War* (Thomastown, 2012), p. 48. Bridget married John Neary in 1919. A cattle weighing scales was referred to as an 'ouncil' at this time.

78   *Kilkenny Moderator*, 25 February 1922.

79   *Kilkenny Journal*, 20 May 1922.

80   *Kilkenny Journal*, 1 October 1921.

81   *Irish Independent*, 27 March 1922.

82   *Kilkenny People*, 13 May 1922. Meeting of the County Council's 'Board of Health'.

83   *Kilkenny People* and *Kilkenny Moderator*, 1 July 1922. The mother of the deceased baby boy was Bridget Whelan. She had been employed by the O'Keeffe's for about five years. Her employers, Mr and Mrs O'Keeffe, paid her solicitor's fees and provided £50 for a security bail bond. Whelan told her friend Lily Jordan about the baby's remains she had buried but the conversation was overheard by Margaret Murphy whose family presumably informed the authorities. In a similar incident the following November, a baby's body, 'aged about 14 days', was found in a ditch near Graiguenamanagh (see, *Kilkenny People*, 2 December 1922).

84   *Kilkenny People*, 1 July 1922.

85   *Freeman's Journal*, 25 February 1922, *Kilkenny Moderator*, 1 July 1922, *Irish Independent*, 18 July 1922. The couple had two other children besides Diana, but they did not survive infancy. Evadne Kane married Isaac Bell in Kildare on 10 October 1909.

86   *Kilkenny People*, 29 July 1922, *Cork Examiner*, 23 November 1922, *Freeman's Journal*, 8 December 1922, *Kilkenny Journal*, 23 December 1922.

87   *Kilkenny Moderator*, 2 September 1922.

88   *Freeman's Journal*, 6 September 1922.

89   Tony O'Malley, 'Inscape – Life and Landscape in Callan and County Kilkenny' in *Kilkenny: History and Society*, eds William Nolan and Kevin Whelan (Dublin, 1990), p. 619.

90   MA CW/OPS/10/05 – Urlingford Intelligence Report, 27 October 1922.

91   *Kilkenny People*, 9 September 1922.

92   *Kilkenny Journal* and *Kilkenny People*, 18 November 1922.

93   Author in conversation with Mary Quilty (née Walsh), Clogga, Mooncoin, Co Kilkenny (August 2017). She directly quoted her father, Captain Patrick Walsh (1893–1958), who fought in the 9th Battalion during the War of Independence and Civil War.

94   Dunne, *Peter's Key* (Cork, 2012), p. 236.

95   *Kilkenny People*, 9 September 1922. The article originally appeared in *The Times*.

96   *Kilkenny People*, 21 February 1923. *Evening Herald*, 5 January 1923.

97   *Freeman's Journal*, 17 March 1923.

98   *Kilkenny People*, 24 March 1923.

99   *Kilkenny People*, 7 April 1923. The ban would not be lifted until 1971.

100 *Kilkenny People*, 28 April 1923 and 26 May 1923.

101 *Freeman's Journal*, 27 November 1923.

102 *Belfast Newsletter*, 28 December 1923.

103 *Munster Express*, 6 December 1935. GRO, Death Index (Patrick Aylward): October–December 1935, Thomastown, vol. 4 p. 394.

104 BMH WS 1,705 (Nicholas Carroll). They survived their wounds but Ned's brother, Seán, died the following year aged 29 as result of complications from tuberculosis (see *Kilkenny Journal*, 24 June 1922). Also, MSPC/34/660 (Hannah Murphy). Cumann na mBan O/C Hanna Murphy blamed the constant raids on her family home by the Crown Forces for the premature deaths of her two sisters and mother in 1924.

105 *Kilkenny Journal*, 1 October 1921.

106 NLI, MS 22,116, J.J. O'Connell Papers. 'Activities in Glenmore …', Statement by Mrs Ellen Cassin.

CHAPTER 15

1   Author in conversation with Mary Quilty (née Walsh), Clogga, Mooncoin, Co Kilkenny (August 2017).

2   MA MSPC/34/SP/60441 – Mary (Maisie) O'Kelly.

3   Diarmaid Ferriter, 'Always in danger of finding myself with nothing at all' in *Years of Turbulence* …, eds Ferriter and Riordan (Dublin, 2015), p. 201. This figure includes the total of all the military pension Acts.

4   MA MSPC/34/44960 (Mary Teehan-Foley). Letter dated 28 March 1942. She was eventually awarded a grade 'E' pension with 3.25 years of service. In support of her claim, Senator Bill Quirke, a former officer in the anti-Treaty IRA, stated; 'in my opinion it is an understatement of the actual facts as I know them'.

5   One exception to the general discontent was the response of Ellen Leahy from Poulacapple, a member of the 7th Battalion Cumann na mBan. She was awarded a Grade E pension in 1942, with over two-year's active service attributed to her. She subsequently wrote to the Pensions Board stating; 'I wish to thank you most sincerely for your kindness in respect of my application for [a] service pension. I am entirely satisfied with [the] findings of [the] Board on my behalf. I always did on every occasion in the troubled period everything required of me and I feel that I have been treated well by all.' See; MA MSPC/34/57287 (Ellen Leahy).

6   MSPC/RO/155 (A Company listings).

7   UCDA P133/10 to 25 (James Lalor Papers).

8   UCDA, P133-9 and 10 (James Lalor Papers).

9   Maher, *In the Shade of Slievenamon* (Dublin, 2015), p. 280. For information on Margaret Prendergast; MA MSPC/34/SP/54377 (Margaret Prendergast).

EPILOGUE

1   GRO, Birth Index (Thomas William Treacy): January–March 1886, Kilkenny, vol. 3, p. 438 (his name had incorrectly been entered as 'Michael'). See also Seán Quinn, killed in Knocknagress. The couple's children were John (Seán), Una, Patrick, Thomas Joseph (Tomás), Philip, Philomena (Ena), Canice and Gertie. Thanks to Orla Murphy (Tom Treacy's granddaughter) for additional information.

2   UCDA, P133-8 (James Lalor Papers). Letter from Treacy to James Lalor dated 7 October 1950, in relation to a meeting about compiling a history of the 1916 rebellion in Kilkenny. Meeting was to be held in Kilkenny Theatre, Patrick Street.

3   MA MSPC/34/50645 (Thomas Treacy).

4   Dunne, *Peter's Key* (Cork, 2012), pp. 40, 260–2.

5   *Munster Express*, 15 and 22 April 1955. Maher, *The Flying Column West Kilkenny*, 1916–1921 (Dublin, 2015), pp. 262–3.

6   Hopkinson, *Green against Green* (Dublin, 2004), pp. 209–10.

7   MA MSPC/24/1763 (John Thomas Prout). Also; 1910/30/40 Census of the United States, and Burial Records, *Familysearch.org*, accessed September 2017.

8   MA MSPC/34/3739 (Edward J. Aylward). Maher, *In the Shade of Slievenamon* (Dublin, 2015), pp. 99 and 280. Another IRA widow, Kitty Meagher, wife of Thomas Meagher of Callan's 7th Battalion, died in 2011 in her 99th year (see; *The Irish Times*, 11 February 2011). Thomas Meagher's first wife, Margaret (née Peggy O'Keeffe), died in Kilkenny Fever Hospital on 9 December 1938 (see MA MSPC/34/46259 – Margaret Meagher).

Bibliography

Primary Sources

Archival Sources

Military Archives, Cathal Brugha Barracks, Dublin 6.
Bureau of Military History, Military Service Pensions Collections, Civil War Captured Documents, Collins Papers, Irish Army Census Collection (1922), Civil War Operations and Intelligence Reports Collection.

General Register Office, Werburgh Street, Dublin 2.
Births, Deaths and Marriages

National Archives of Ireland, Bishop Street, Dublin 8.
Chief Secretary's Office Registered Papers (CSORP), 1919–1921, Dáil Éireann Department of Local Government 1920–1922 (DELG), Fenian Suspects (1861–1871).

National Library of Ireland, Kildare Street, Dublin 2.
J.J. (Ginger) O'Connell Papers, Col. Maurice Moore Papers, Lawrence Photographic Collection, Poole Collection.

The National Archives of the United Kingdom, Kew.
War Office: Ireland (WO 35).
Ireland: Dublin Castle Records (CO 904).

Registry of Deeds, King's Inn, Henrietta Street, Dublin 1.
County Kilkenny Indexes 1906–1925 (Numbers: 1204, 1263 and 1139).

Rothe House, Kilkenny City.
Minute Books of the Gaelic League in Kilkenny City (1900–1902).

UCD Archives, Belfield, Dublin 4.
James Lalor Papers, Éamon De Valera Papers, Richard Mulcahy Papers, W.T. Cosgrave Papers.

UCD Special Collections, Belfield, Dublin 4.

Newspapers/Periodicals

Anglo-Celt
Advocate (Australia)
Belfast Newsletter
Cheltenham Chronicle
Cork Examiner
Freeman's Journal
Irish Independent
Irish Press
The Irish Times
Kilkenny Journal
Kilkenny Moderator
Kilkenny People
Leinster Express
Meath Chronicle
Munster Express
Nationalist and Leinster Times
Nenagh News
Skibbereen Eagle
Sunday Independent
The Daily News (Australia)
The Free Press
The Maitland Daily Mercury (Australia)
The Kerryman
The New York Times
The Police Gazette, Hue-And-Cry
The Times
Ulster Herald
Waterford News and Star
Western Mail (Australia)

Public Events

Speech given by Muriel McAuley (granddaughter of Thomas MacDonagh). Book launch *In the Shade of Slievenamon, The Flying Column West Kilkenny* by Jim Maher. Took place at MacDonagh Junction, Kilkenny City, 4 June 2015.

Secondary Sources

Books and Journals

Augusteijn, Joost. *From Public Defiance to Guerrilla Warfare: The Experience of Ordinary Volunteers in the Irish War of Independence, 1916–1921*. Dublin, 1996.
Augusteijn, Joost (ed.). *The Irish Revolution, 1913–1923*. London, 2002.

Borgonovo, John, John Crowley, Mike Murphy and Donal Ó Drisceoil (eds), *Atlas of the Irish Revolution*. Cork, 2017.

Bradley, John and Michael O'Dwyer (eds). *Kilkenny Through the Centuries; Chapters in the history of an Irish City*. Naas, 2009.

Brannigan, Niall and John Kirwan. *Kilkenny Families in the Great War*. Thomastown, 2012.

Burnell, Tom and the Kilkenny Great War Memorial Committee. *The Kilkenny War Dead*. Kilkenny, 2014.

Cadogan, Donal. *About Kilkenny*. Kilkenny, 2015.

Cadogan, Donal. *99 Lives - Kilkenny Connections*. Kilkenny, 2017.

Clarke, Samuel. *Social Origins of the Irish Land War*. Princeton, 2014.

Coleman, Marie. *The Irish Revolution, 1916–1923*. London, 2013.

Collins, Lorcan. *1916: The Rising Handbook*. Dublin, 2016.

Collins, Stephen. *The Cosgrave Legacy*. Dublin, 1996.

Comerford, James J. *My Kilkenny I.R.A. Days, 1916–22*. Kilkenny, 1978.

Connolly, Michael. *Kilkenny People – A Review of the Century*. Kilkenny, 1992.

Cronin, Mike, Mark Duncan and Paul Rouse. *The GAA – A People's History*. Cork, 2009.

Crowley, John, William J. Smyth and Mike Murphy. *Atlas of the Great Irish Famine*. Cork, 2012.

Dunne, Declan. *Peter's Key, Peter DeLoughry and the Fight for Irish Independence*. Cork, 2012.

Ferriter, Diarmaid. *A Nation and Not a Rabble, The Irish Revolution 1913–1923*. London, 2015.

Ferriter, Diarmaid. *The Transformation of Ireland 1900–2000*. London, 2004.

Ferriter, Diarmaid and Susannah Riordan (eds). *Years of Turbulence, The Irish Revolution and Its Aftermath*. Dublin, 2015.

Fitzgerald, John. *Callan, In the Rare Old Times*. Callan, 2003.

Fitzgerald, John. *Kilkenny ... Blast from the Past*. Cork, 2005.

Fitzpatrick, David. *Politics and Irish life, 1913–1921, Provincial Experience of War and Revolution*. Dublin, 1977.

Foley, Caitriona. *The Last Irish Plague, the Great Flu Epidemic in Ireland 1918–19*. Dublin, 2011.

Foster, Roy F. *Modern Ireland, 1600–1972*. London, 1989.

Foster, Roy F. *Vivid Faces: The Revolutionary Generation in Ireland, 1890–1923*. London, 2014.

Garvin, Tom. *1922: The Birth of Democracy*. Dublin, 1996.

Grenham, John. *Tracing Your Irish Ancestors, 4th Edition*. Dublin, 2012.

Hart, Peter. *The I.R.A. & Its Enemies, Violence and Community in Cork 1916–1923*. Oxford, 1999.

Harvey, A.D. 'Who Were the Auxiliaries?'. *The Historical Journal* 35, no. 3 (1992), pp. 665-9.

Higgins-McHugh, Noreen. 'The 1830s Tithe Riots'. *Riotous Assemblies, Rebels, Riots & Revolts in Ireland*, edited by William Sheehan and Maura Cronin, pp. 80–95. Cork, 2011.

Hopkinson, Michael. *Green against Green: The Irish Civil War*. Dublin, 2004.

Hopkinson, Michael. *The Irish War of Independence*. Dublin, 2004.

Hughes, Brian. *Defying the IRA?*. Liverpool, 2016.

Jordon, Anthony J. *W.T. Cosgrave 1880-1965*. Dublin, 2006.

Kavanagh, Dermot. *A History, Kilkenny Senior Hurling County Finals 1887-2003*. Kilkenny, 2004.

Kelly, Bill. 'The tunnel out of Kilkenny jail'. In *IRA Jailbreaks 1918-1921*. Cork, 2010.

Kenna, Shane. *16 Lives, Thomas MacDonagh*. Dublin, 2014.

Kennedy, Joseph (ed.). *Callan 800, 1207-2007; History and Heritage*. Dublin, 2007.

King, Carla (ed.). *Famine, Land and Culture in Ireland*. Dublin, 2000.

Laffan, Michael. *Judging W.T. Cosgrave*. Dublin, 2014.

Laffan, Michael. *The Resurrection of Ireland: The Sinn Féin Party*. Cambridge, 1999.

Lane, Pádraig G. 'Papers: The IRB, Labour and Parnell: The Kilkenny Factor'. In *Old Kilkenny Review 2008* (No 60), edited by Ann Murtagh. Kilkenny, 2008.

Leeson, D.M. *The Black and Tans*. Oxford, 2012.

Local Government Board. *Return of Owners of Land of One Acre And Upwards*. Dublin, 1878.

Lyng, Tom. *Castlecomer Connections*. Kilkenny, 1984.

Mackay, James. *Michael Collins: A Life*. Edinburgh, 1996.

Maher, Jim. *In the Shade of Slievenamon, The Flying Column West Kilkenny, 1916-1921*. Dublin, 2015.

Maher, Jim. *The Flying Column - West Kilkenny 1916-1921*. Dublin, 1987.

McCarthy, Cal. *Cumann na mBan and the Irish Revolution*. Cork, 2014.

McCoole, Sinéad. *No Ordinary Women; Irish Female Activists in the Revolutionary Years 1900-1923*. Dublin, 2015.

McGuire, James, and James Quinn (eds). *Dictionary of Irish Biography*. Cambridge, 2009.

McKenna, Joseph. *Guerrilla Warfare in the Irish War of Independence, 1919-1921*. Jefferson, 2011.

Mitchell, Arthur. *Revolutionary Government in Ireland: Dáil Éireann, 1919-22*. Dublin, 1995.

Murphy, William. *Political Imprisonment and the Irish, 1912-1921*. Oxford, 2014.

Nolan, William and Kevin Whelan (eds). *Kilkenny: History and Society*. Dublin, 1990.

O'Casey, Seán. *The Shadow of a Gunman*. Dublin, 1923.

O'Dwyer Martin. *Seventy Seven of Mine Said Ireland*. Cashel, 2006.

O'Dwyer, Michael. *The History of Cricket in County Kilkenny - The Forgotten Game*. Kilkenny, 2006.

Ó'Faoláin, Seán. *The Irish*. London, 1947.

O'Halpin Eunan, 'Counting Terror, Bloody Sunday and the Dead of the Irish Revolution'. In *Terror in Ireland 1916-1923*, edited by David Fitzpatrick, pp. 141-157. Dublin, 2012.

O'Malley, Ernie. *On Another Man's Wound*. Dublin, 2013.

O'Malley, Ernie. *The Singing Flame*. Dublin, 2012.

Pakenham, Frank Earl of Longford. *Peace by Ordeal: The Negotiation of the Anglo-Irish Treaty 1921*. London, 1992.

Pašeta, Senia. *Irish Nationalist Women 1900–1918*. Cambridge, 2013.

Ravenstein, EG. 'On the Celtic Languages of the British Isles: A Statistical Survey' in *Journal of the Statistical Society of London*, vol. 42, no. 3. London, 1879.

Regan, John M. *Myth and the Irish State, Historical Problems and Other Essays*. Dublin, 2013

Rice, Rev. Gerard CC. *St Kieran's College Record 1965*. Kilkenny, 1965.

Rouse, Paul. *Sport and Ireland*. Oxford, 2015.

Royal Institute of the Architects of Ireland (RIAI). *An Introduction to the Architectural Heritage of County Kilkenny*. Dublin, 2015.

Rumpf, Erhard and Anthony C Hepburn. *Nationalism and Socialism in Twentieth-Century Ireland*. Liverpool, 1977.

Share, Bernard. *In Time of Civil War; The conflict on the Irish railways 1922–23*. Cork, 2006.

Silverman, Marilyn and P.H. Gulliver. *In the Valley of the Nore*. Dublin, 1986.

Townshend, Charles. *Easter 1916, The Irish Rebellion*. London, 2015.

Townshend, Charles. *The Republic, The Fight for Irish Independence 1918–1923*. London, 2013.

Tynan, Pat. *Kilkenny, History & Guide*. Dublin, 2006.

Vaughan, WE and AJ Fitzpatrick (editors). *Irish Historical Statistics, Population 1821–1971*. Dublin, 1978.

Wallace, Colm. *The Fallen, Gardaí Killed in Service, 1922–49*. Dublin, 2017.

Walsh, Jim. *James Nowlan, The Alderman and the GAA in his Time*. Kilkenny, 2013.

Walsh, Louise. *The Role of Piltown and Clogga Creameries: 1930s–1980s*, unpublished BA Thesis, Mary Immaculate College. Limerick, 2011.

Walsh, Maurice. *Bitter Freedom: Ireland in a Revolutionary World 1918–1923*. London, 2015.

Walsh, William. *Kilkenny: The Struggle for Land 1850–1882*. Kilkenny, 2008.

Ward, Margaret. *Unmanageable Revolutionaries – Woman and Irish Nationalism*. London, 1995.

Whelehan, Niall. 'The Irish Revolution, 1912–23'. In *The Oxford Handbook of Modern Irish History*, (ed.) Alvin Jackson. Oxford, 2014.

Whyte, Thomas J. *The Story of Woodstock in Inistioge*. Dublin, 2007.

Winfield, Parks Edd and Aileen Wells Parks. *Thomas MacDonagh; The Man, The Patriot, The Writer*. Athens, Georgia, 1967.

Websites

www.irishgenealogy.ie
www.irishhistorypodcast.ie
www.familysearch.org
www.bureauofmilitaryhistory.ie
www.militaryarchives.ie
hansard.millbanksystems.com (House of Commons Debates)
oireachtasdebates.oireachtas.ie (Dáil Éireann Debates)

discovery.nationalarchives.gov.uk
www.theauxiliaries.com
www.census.nationalarchives.ie
centenaries.nationalarchives.ie
www.fullmoon.info/en/fullmoon-calendar/1920

Acknowledgements

Many people, in various ways, have contributed to the completion of this publication. Firstly, I want to express my gratitude to the publisher. Conor Graham, Fiona Dunne, Myles McCionnaith, Dermott Barrett and everyone at Merrion Press/Irish Academic Press have been greatly supportive of this project from the beginning. I want to particularly thank them for taking a punt on an unknown author, especially one who wanted to write about localised history. Although local histories will not make any publishers rich, they nonetheless contribute to the historiography of Ireland. Reading through this publisher's canon of books will attest to the huge array of publications that cover many different strands of the Irish story. This back catalogue, I believe, will stand the test of time and become even more valuable in the years to come.

I want to thank my former lecturer and supervisor Professor Diarmaid Ferriter for agreeing to write the foreword to this publication, and for his very kind words. The greatest compliment I can give is to say he was one of the fairest teachers I ever had; always balanced and willing to listen to everyone's opinion in class in an open and non-judgemental environment.

I would like to thank the staff of the numerous archives and repositories I frequented over the past few years. Particularly to the staff of UCD Archives, National Library of Ireland, National Archives of Ireland, General Register Office Research Centre, Registry of Deeds King's Inns, Rothe House and Woodstock Heritage Museum. I would especially like to mention the staff and facilities of the Military Archives at their beautiful new Reading Room in Rathmines. Kilkenny City is also blessed with a museum in James Stephens Military Barracks, where Captain Larry Scallan and his team are devoted to historical research. People are rightly proud of our Defence Forces; their military precision now extends to their preservation of the vast historical collections of the early years of the Irish State, which are free and accessible to all.

To my proof readers, I owe you an enormous debt. I want to give a special word of thanks to my cousin Shelly 'da Mish' Long. She gave up much of her free time to read the draft manuscript and must have been very annoyed by the end with my shoddy spelling and grammar but she never complained and was always supportive, while also making good suggestions. If she ever decides to change from her job in chemistry, a career as an editor certainly beckons. Likewise, my mother, Kathleen Long, was forced to endure many drafts. Much appreciated. I can only imagine the weariness of reading so much on this one topic but they never failed to be attentive and articulate in their responses.

Writing these acknowledgements allows for a certain amount of reflection, especially on those who influenced me over the years and helped me get to his point. The people of Kilkenny owe a great deal of gratitude to historian Jim Maher – whom I reference in this publication – for his foresight in recording and amassing interviews of local War of Independence veterans from the 1960s onwards. His work should be read by anyone with even a passing interest in this period. I also think back to my history teacher in Mooncoin Vocational School (now Coláiste Cois Siúire), John Kennedy from Kilmacow. It was easy to learn from a teacher who was so obviously passionate about the subject.

I was also reminded of my family members who are no longer around, especially my late uncle Richard Walsh, and also my late aunts Peggy Kearns and Sr Josephine Walsh, whom I enjoyed many a political and hurling debate with (sometimes bordering on arguments!). I like to think that those discussions about current topical events, along with the tracing of family histories, made me a better analyser when it came to Irish history.

If I don't mention my uncle (and godfather) Tom Walsh of Clogga, I will probably be disowned! I also want to thank my always supportive aunty Nora Walsh, Ballyhale; aunt Teresa Conlon in Leeds; my uncles Michael and Nicky Walsh; and also my uncles Michael, John-joe and Pat Long (this includes their respective spouses). I will not mention all my thirty plus first cousins and endless amount of new cousins, or I will probably need a separate publication and appendix! Suffice to say, I am grateful for the support you have always given.

I want to thank everyone in my former AIB family, especially those in the 'ex-and-current-AIB-staff-Culture-Club'. I want to particularly express my gratitude to my two Deirdres, Kelleher and Murphy/Scullion. They were supportive from the beginning, especially in the early days when I was deciding to leap back into full-time academia. Their encouragement in pursuing my love of history and sacrificing 'a good pensionable job' was what was required at the time.

An array of friends have helped me get to this point and I am always appreciative of their continued friendship; Orles Murphy - soon to be Mrs Stephen Delaney of Galmoy – cous Niamh 'da Cull' Culleton, Leanne 'Lee' Long, Edel Walsh from the one and only Boolyglass, Richard 'the Father' Hogan, Cormac 'Corms' Everard, Ian D'Arcy (Athlone), and everyone at the 1916 Rebellion Walking Tour in Dublin. I also want to give a shout out to my godchildren, Ian and Kathy Long.

I want to thank Ian Curran from An Sean Phobal, County Waterford. We discussed and talked about anything *but* 'boring history'. This was often called for and I much appreciate his friendship and continuous distraction! I am especially grateful to my fellow history nerd, Shane Browne from Waterford City. It is great to have someone to bounce ideas off and I hope to return the favour as he completes/sails-through his PhD. I would also like to thank Adam Ryan (yet another Waterford person, there's a deep irony here) for looking at some historical maths calculations for me, arithmetic never being my forte. Thanks to everyone who has helped source, or given permission to use images in this publication. Special thanks to John Kirwan (Kilkenny Archives), Ciarán O'Riain at 'Historic Kilkenny' Facebook, Michael Cannady (Society of Irish Revolutionary History and Militaria), Historic Callan, Aoife Torpey (Kilmainham Gaol Museum), Liam O'Sullivan (Historic Kells), Ruairí O'Donnell (1916 Rebellion Walking Tour), Ciarán Cooney (Irish Railway Record Society Archive), OPW Kilkenny Castle, David Grant (theauxiliaries. com), Larry Scallan (James Stephens Barracks), Brian Kirby (Capuchin Archives), Orla Murphy (for the Tom Treacy portrait), Ned Power of Brenor in Piltown and Laura Commins (for the Mary-Jo Commins photograph), and Declan Lacey (for Hanna Dooley/Murphy photograph).

To my parents, the extremely generous Paul Walsh, and the irrepressible Kathleen Long, I owe enormous gratitude. I don't think Paul ever said the word 'no' to any of his children in his life, while Kathleen is very much a free spirit. This made for a lovely environment to grow up in and allowed us to pursue whatever we chose ourselves to do in life. In addition, I want to thank my sisters Clare and Louise for always being encouraging, harsh and humorous when the occasion required it (this thanks extends to their respective other halves, Eoin 'da Crow' Crowley and Thomas 'TP' Power). For this support, and everything else, I am forever thankful.

Finally I have dedicated this book to my late grandmothers, Nanny Alice Walsh (née Henebery), from Clogga (originally from her beloved Ballybrazil), Mooncoin, and Granny Kitty Long (née O'Shea) from Tobernabrone, Piltown, but originally from Ahenny, in her (lamentably) beloved Tipperary. They were born either end of the revolutionary era. For these young ears, hearing my Nanny talking about the Civil War – including a story of how she found post strewn across the road on her way home from school after a train had been derailed – was like stepping into a time machine. I was also enthralled with stories of my father's uncles who fought with the IRA during the Irish War of Independence and Civil War. To highlight how much of a rounded upbringing I received, my Granny Long regaled me with stories of how she actually made blue shirts for the Blueshirts in the 1930s! It has helped me see things from many different perspectives, which in turn has contributed to helping me write an account of this era from as unbiased a viewpoint as humanly possible. Both women set the seeds of a love of history in the mind of a young boy, which is now bearing some fruit. For this and a whole lot more, I am eternally grateful.

Eoin Swithin Walsh, July 2018

Abbreviations

ASU	Active Service Unit. Also known as a 'Flying Column'. A mobile attacking unit that employed guerrilla tactics
BMH WS	Bureau of Military History Witness Statements. Statements given by participants of the Irish revolutionary period. Stored in the Military Archives
CI	County Inspector. Refers to the highest-ranking RIC police officer in a county
CSORP	Chief Secretary of Ireland Registered Papers. Records of the Chief Secretary's Office which was located in Dublin Castle. Papers are now preserved in the National Archives of Ireland
DE	Dáil Éireann
DELG	Dáil Éireann Department of Local Government
DI	District Inspector. Refers to the highest-ranking RIC police officer in a district
GAA	Gaelic Athletic Association
GHQ	General Headquarters. Usually refers to IRA headquarters based in Dublin
GRO	General Register Office. Irish births, deaths and marriages civil registration
INAVDF	Irish National Aid and Volunteers Dependents Fund. Established nationally in the aftermath of the 1916 Rising to aid families affected by the Rebellion (it was the amalgamation of two competing groups; the Irish National Aid Association and the Volunteers Dependent Fund)

IRA   Irish Republican Army. Usually referred to as the 'Irish Volunteers' before August 1919. During the Civil War the name became associated with the anti-Treaty side.

IRB   Irish Republican Brotherhood. Clandestine oath bound organisation that had the overall aim of establishing an Irish Republic

ITGWU   Irish Transport and General Workers Union

LGB   Local Government Board. Responsible for local government functions, including local councils, throughout Ireland.

MA   Military Archives. Cathal Brugha Barracks, Rathmines, Dublin 6

MP   Minister of Parliament. Refers to members of the British House of Commons

MSPC   Military Service Pensions Collection. Files relating to the application of pensions for military service e.g. IRA, Free State Army, Cumann na mBan. Located in the Military Archives of Ireland

NA   National Archives of the United Kingdom

NAI   National Archives of Ireland

NLI   National Library of Ireland

O/C   Officer Commanding. Commandant of a Brigade or Battalion

PR   Proportional Representation. Voting system used in Ireland since the local elections of 1920 utilising the single transferable vote.

RIC   Royal Irish Constabulary. The police force in Ireland (outside Dublin) prior to the establishment of the Irish Free State

TD   Teachta Dála. A member of Dáil Éireann

UCDA   University College Dublin Archives

UCDSC   University College Dublin Special Collections

WHM   Woodstock Heritage Museum. Inistioge, County Kilkenny

Index